4 Week Loan

This book is due for return on or before the last date shown below

15·4·13		

Acknowledgements

Many people have helped to finally bring this book to publication. I should like in particular to thank Chris Hammond, former Director of BAAF, for first suggesting the idea to me many years ago; Felicity Collier, currently Chief Executive, for pressing me to make the idea a reality; and Shaila Shah, Head of Communications for guiding me through that process with infinite patience – the book would never have been published without her constant encouragement and determination.

I must also thank all the contributors – an edited book depends on the hard work of many individuals who have to put up with the inevitable delays and the many requests for changes from the editor. There are too many for me to thank all individually, but I owe a larger debt to some who have influenced my thinking on overseas adoption over the past fifteen years: Rene Hoksbergen, who has taught me so much about the good and dark sides of adoption and become an old and trusted friend; Gunilla Andersson and Kerstin Sterky who convinced me of the important role of NGOs in mediation and encouraged my attendance at EurAdopt meetings; Gill Haworth, Jan Way and many others who have worked with me in NICA and BABICA; Mike Brennan of the DoH who has done so much to improve the structure of services in the UK; Chantal Saclier who opened my eyes to the wider implications of moving children from their birth countries; and Hans van Loon, whose *Report on Intercountry Adoption* for the Hague Conference helped me to appreciate the importance of international agreements on ICA and who has honoured me by writing the Foreword to this anthology.

Thanks also to Kathy Mason, who has shared teaching, research and writing on adoption with me for the past ten years and who read and commented on many of the chapters, while working on her PhD on intercountry adoption.

Finally, a big thank you to my wife and children for living with this book over the past few years – and especially to my son, Alexander, who translated two of the chapters from Spanish and so opened up a new perspective, which would otherwise have been missed.

*This book is dedicated to **Barbara Kahan**,*
Children's Officer for Oxfordshire County Council, 1970 to 1990,
who first introduced me to
the world of child care and adoption
and who died on 6 August 2000.

Note about the Editor

Peter Selman is Senior Lecturer in the Department of Sociology and Social Policy at the University of Newcastle upon Tyne and Chair of the Network for Intercountry Adoption (NICA). He is author of *Society and Fertility* [1979] and *Family Planning* [1988] and has published many articles and chapters on teenage pregnancy and various aspects of adoption, including contested adoptions and the permanent placement of children with special needs as well as intercountry adoption. He is currently a member of the BAAF Board of Trustees and the BAAF Research Group.

Intercountry Adoption
Developments, trends and perspectives

Edited by
Peter Selman

British
Agencies
for **A**doption
and **F**ostering

Published by
British Agencies for Adoption & Fostering
(BAAF)
Skyline House
200 Union Street
London SE1 0LX

Charity registration 275689

© Peter Selman 2000

British Library Cataloguing in Publication Data
A catalogue record for this book is available
from the British Library

ISBN 1 873868 84 7

Project management by Shaila Shah, Head of
Communications, BAAF
Photographs on cover by John Birdsall
Photography
Designed by Andrew Haig & Associates
Typeset by Avon Dataset Ltd, Bidford on Avon
Printed by Russell Press Ltd. (TU),
Nottingham

Contents

Foreword

Hans van Loon
Secretary General of the Hague Conference on Private
International Law

'*C'est un monde!*' (It's a world in itself!)

I remember well this comment by my predecessor, Georges Droz, after he had read my report, drawn up in preparation for the negotiations in the years 1990–1993 which led to the *Hague Convention of 29 May 1993 on Protection of Children and Co-operation in Respect of Intercountry Adoption*. It was a poignant characterisation of what is also the topic of this book: few international phenomena are so multifaceted, complex and pervasively interesting as the adoption of children originating from a foreign culture across borders.

This book provides an in-depth insight into many aspects of the world of intercountry adoption: its history, the ethical dilemmas, the outcomes of intercountry adoption, the situation in the UK which is very much in flux, the experiences of receiving countries other than the UK and of countries of origin, and very importantly, the personal experiences of birth mothers, adoptive parents, and the children themselves.

This publication comes at a moment when the UK is about to become a Party to the 1993 Hague Convention, whose background and implementation is the subject of the contribution by my colleague and friend, William Duncan. It is most encouraging to see how the *UN Convention on the Rights of the Child* (which deals with intercountry adoption in its Article 21) and the 1993 Hague Convention, by setting principles, by providing standards and safeguards, and by creating a network of co-operating institutions, have offered new ways of looking at intercountry adoption.

In a perfect world, without the gross inequalities of living conditions which still reign on this planet at the beginning of the new Millennium, wide scale intercountry adoption would not exist. Since our world is not perfect, however, there will continue to be large numbers of children in need of a family in the years ahead. One need only remind oneself of the devastating effect of the AIDS epidemic in Africa leaving large numbers of children without parents. Of course, the international community should in the first place intensify its efforts to improve living conditions in the countries of origin of adopted children so that they may find a home there, but we should do what we can alongside these efforts to make intercountry adoption available for children without such a home, thus giving them the opportunity to 'grow up in a family environment, in an atmosphere of happiness, love and understanding'. One may hope that ratification by the UK of the 1993 Hague Convention will facilitate adoptions that are well prepared, and flawless as to the procedures followed, so as to have a maximum of success.

In order to make this perspective a reality, insight into the complexity of intercountry adoption, and care informed by that insight, are critical. The papers collected together in this book will provide the reader with a detailed map of this fascinating world. Of course, much of the background for this book comes from the situation in the UK, and the book may have appeared differently had the situation, for example, in France, the USA, India or Colombia been taken as a starting point. Throughout the book, however, the reader is indeed also reminded of other ways of looking at intercountry adoption. Hence its great value to all who are interested in the world of intercountry adoption.

Introduction

Peter Selman

My first personal acquaintance with intercountry adoption came in 1967, as a young and inexperienced social worker in Oxfordshire Children's Department. I was sent to do welfare supervision for the adoption of a child by a couple living in a remote house in the south of the county. It was their third adoption and each child had come from a different country. The wife had married, knowing that she would never be able to have children and she and her husband had decided before their marriage that they would try to have a family that would have been impossible if they had had their own children, by taking abandoned children from countries of the Third World.

I had just read David Kirk's book, *Shared Fate* (Kirk, 1964), and was struck by how – in contrast to many of the domestic adoptions I was involved in – this was a striking example of his 'acknowledgement of difference'. The house was full of reminders of the children's birth countries and the older children talked with enthusiasm and openness about their backgrounds and were full of plans to provide a new series of pictures and mementoes for their new sibling. The adoption went through successfully but I have no knowledge of what has happened since. My feelings from this warm and loving family were that the children would do well and have a unique perspective on the world they faced as they grew up. Intercountry adoption was very rare in England in those days and I suspect that most child care officers of that period would have been as ignorant as I was about what had been happening in mainland Europe and the United States since the Korean and Vietnam Wars. They would have been equally unaware that our own country was still sending orphaned and destitute children to outposts of the British Empire: the final boatload of 90 children left Southampton for Australia in 1967 (Bean and Melville, 1989).

Intercountry adoption did not feature in my life for the next twenty years despite a continuing involvement with adoption as a practising social worker and later a member of a case committee of a voluntary society in the North of England. But in 1986 I attended my first London conference on adoption, organised by what was then ABAFA (the Association of British Adoption and Fostering Agencies – the precursor of BAAF). The theme was intercountry adoption and it was a revelation for me and an experience that aroused an interest in the ethical and policy issues which has remained with me ever since. Two things stand out in my memory. One was listening to an impassioned speech, highly critical of intercountry adoption, by Damien Ngabonziza (1988) of ISS (International Social Service); the second was an intervention by a consular representative from El Salvador asking the UK to end the hypocrisy of being self-righteous about intercountry adoption while doing nothing about the steady stream of unofficial adoptions from her country – the message was either stop them or get a structure, including an authorised agency, which would allow regulated adoptions, which her country would prefer.

By then I was teaching social policy to trainee social workers and I determined to find out more about how overseas adoption was handled in different countries and why it was relatively rare – and apparently unregulated in the UK. The influx of children from Romania (DCI, 1991) coincided with a major international conference, under the title *Adoption – an old idea in a new era,* organised in Edinburgh by BAAF in September 1991, for which I had a workshop proposal accepted. The day on intercountry adoption involved plenary papers (all published in *Adoption & Fostering,* 14:4, 1991) by John Triseliotis, Ruth McRoy, John Small, Damien Ngabonziza and Gunilla Andersson, who contributes a chapter on the Swedish experience later in this book. Gunilla and I were the only participants running workshops on intercountry adoption (Andersson, 1991b; Selman, 1991b) and at these I was privileged to meet other researchers from mainland Europe, including Monica Dalen and Barbro Saetersdal from Norway, who have contributed a chapter on their most recent research. But the memory that remains strongest in my mind was the hostility shown by many British delegates towards the Scandinavians for their support of transracial and intercountry adoption, culminating in a petition being circulated which called on the government to end adoption from abroad. Gunilla and I put on an additional joint lunchtime session to encourage discussion of the issues, which was well attended but revealed an alarming amount of ignorance and prejudice about ICA amongst professional social workers.

There have been two subsequent BAAF AGM seminars looking at intercountry adoption. At the first, in November 1992, I presented a paper on ICA services in Europe, which was later developed in two articles in *Adoption & Fostering* (Selman, 1993; Selman and White, 1994). The key-note speaker was Hans van Loon, Permanent Secretary at the Hague Conference, who talked about the *Convention on Protection of Children and Co-operation in respect of Intercountry Adoption*, which was to be finalised in May of the following year. I recall even then his pessimism about the UK's prospects of ratifying the Convention in the near future. The second seminar, in November 1996, was addressed by a wide range of speakers including Kerstin Sterky, Michael Rutter, Cherry Harnott and Sue Jardine, all of whom are contributors to this collection. Ratification was still a distant prospect, but the inclusion of papers on the DoH funded study of Romanian adoptions and on the development of services in a local authority showed that the importance of ICA in the UK was gradually being recognised.

By the mid 1990s, the importance of finding structures for ICA was clear. The International Bar Association published research on the experience of British couples adopting from abroad (IBA, 1991) and in 1993, Margaret Bennett from the IBA founded BABICA (the British Advisory Board for Intercountry Adoption) in an attempt to encourage informed discussion about ICA by all parties involved. I became a member early in 1994 and later (from 1997) followed Margaret as Chair. Meetings were attended by representatives of a wide range of organisations, including AFAA, CICA, Childlink, ISS and local authorities. Felicity Collier has been a regular attender since becoming Director of BAAF and Michael Brennan from the Department of Health has also attended meetings by invitation, whenever possible. Both have continued to meet with this wide range of interested bodies since 1998, when it was decided to change the name of the group to NICA (Network for Intercountry Adoption).

Several current members are amongst the contributors to this book.

The other influence on my thinking about intercountry adoption has arisen from my growing contacts with academics and practitioners in Europe. Twelve years ago I attended a day conference in Antwerp on the health needs of children adopted from abroad. There I met Rene Hoksbergen from the Netherlands, who subsequently became a close friend and introduced me to the complexities of intercountry adoption, not least through his own work (e.g. Hoksbergen, 1986 and 1987). At the same conference I met Ingrid Stappaerts from Belgium who ran *Interadoptie,* one of the many Belgian adoption agencies. Some years later, in 1996, Ingrid invited me to attend a meeting of EurAdopt, the organisation for European adoption agencies, at their biennial meeting which was held in Antwerp that year. This afforded me the opportunity to meet many of those involved in intercountry adoption in Europe and to appreciate the gains for all the agencies in meeting to discuss issues of common interest. I have been able to attend the open days at subsequent meetings in Florence (1998) and Vasa (2000). Kerstin Sterky from Sweden contributes a chapter about the work of EurAdopt in this collection and I owe much to the information provided by EurAdopt members for my own writing on intercountry adoption (Selman, 1991b, 1993, 1998). More recently I was invited to a conference in Oslo organised by Barbro Satersdal and Monica Dalen (Ryvgold *et al*, 1999) which was attended by academics and practitioners from a wide range of countries, some of whom kindly agree to contribute chapters for the book (Duinkerken, Carli, Gailey, Irhammar and Telfer).

I hope this brief biographical reminiscence will help the reader to understand the focus of this collection and my attempts to bring together a range of people active in ICA in the UK, alongside representatives of other countries, Although I have tried to include a wide range of opinions on intercountry adoption and to include perspectives from several other countries, the book remains a personal anthology and there are inevitably other views and other countries which would ideally have been represented if there had been no constraints of time and space. The book has a particular relevance today as new legislation passed in 1999 will enable the UK to ratify the Hague Convention and offers the prospect that we can finally begin to build an appropriate structure for overseas adoption.

I hope that the chapters which follow will stimulate discussion about how best we can do this.

Intercountry adoption in the UK in the new millennium

On 13 January 1999, Mark Oaten MP introduced a Private Members Bill to amend legislation relating to intercountry adoption in the UK and provide for UK ratification of the Convention. The Bill received its third reading on 23 April 1999 and became law in July 1999. The Adoption (Intercountry Aspects) Act 1999 is now in the process of implementation, with consultation on proposed regulations starting at the end of 2000 (see Brennan, Chapter 10).

The UK is expected to ratify the Convention during 2001. Yet we still have no agency – public or private – linking to similar organisations in the States of origin and divisions over intercountry adoption remain, if not so hostile as at Edinburgh nine years ago. For me one of the saddest features of these divisions has been antagonism between social workers and adoptive parents, as it is clear that any successful policy on ICA must involve both groups, even if some tensions inevitably continue. For this reason the contributions to the book by adoptive parents are particularly welcome.

These developments are occurring at a time when the number of inter-country adoptions worldwide is greater than ever before and seems likely to rise further, while concerns about abuses and irregularities continue (DCI, 1999). In November 2000, the Hague Conference is re-convening to review progress over the last seven years and William Duncan, First Secretary at the Permanent Bureau, outlines some of the key issues in his chapter. But alongside the negative reports, there is an accumulation of research – including an important follow-up study of Romanian adop-tions in the UK (Rutter *et al*, Chapter 6) – demonstrating the overall success of intercountry adoption, but also the persisting problems for a minority of children, particularly those with long periods of non-family care prior to adoption. All this points to the urgent need for strengthening intercountry adoption services in the UK to ensure that prospective parents are fully supported in adopting children from abroad who are genuinely in need of a permanent home and ensuring that thereafter post-adoption services are available to such families and that these can meet the needs expressed by adoptive parents and adoptees themselves (see chapters by Shead, Jardine, Samwell Smith and von Melen in section V).

An outline of the book

The aim of this collection is to provide background information and stimulation to discussion in this country as we move to ratify the Hague Convention and in the important years ahead when we shall be implementing the planned changes in our services for international adoption. The contributors are drawn from a wide range of backgrounds and include academics responsible for large-scale research into intercountry adoption, practitioners from the UK and Europe, and those involved directly in overseas adoption as adoptive parents or persons themselves adopted from abroad. In the following paragraphs I shall give an overview of the structure of the book, leaving more detailed comments to my introduction to each section and my conclusion mapping the way forward for the UK.

Section I is intended to provide a wider context by reviewing the development of ICA throughout the world, looking at the changing patterns of adoption, the demographic history of intercountry adoption and outlining the background to the Hague Convention of 1993, as well as considering some of the ethical issues in intercountry adoption as they affect the international community and the UK.

Section II looks at research into outcomes of intercountry adoption for persons adopted from abroad, with contributions from researchers in the UK, the Netherlands, Sweden and Norway, looking at the progress of adopted children at various stages in their life cycle.

Section III looks at the current situation in the UK with special emphasis on existing support systems and examples of good practice, a review which will identify a number of gaps in existing provision. Contributors range from the Department of Health to a local authority, parents' groups and voluntary bodies.

Section IV looks at policy and practice in other countries, both those such as Sweden and the Netherlands with long-established traditions of provision by government and other agencies and also countries such as the USA, where there are many private agencies and individual attorneys arranging intercountry adoption, and Australia which has developed services more recently. Two chapters from India provide the perspective of a State of origin still struggling with the development of services for both domestic and international adoption.

Section V brings together personal experiences of all members of the adoption triangle. An Argentinean psychologist talks about her work with Norwegian families who have adopted abused children from Latin America. The absent voice of the birth relatives is highlighted in a chapter from Argentina about mothers whose children have been taken from them. An adoptive parent tells us of the experience of adopting from China. Two young adults adopted from overseas in the 1970s reflect on their experience of growing up in the UK and the section ends with extracts from a book (von Melen, 1998) by a Swedish adoptee who talked with eighteen young adults adopted from abroad.

Most of the chapters on other countries have appendices with tables outlining trends in ICA in recent years and indicating those States of origin from which most children have been received. Contact points for these countries, and for organisations involved in ICA in the UK, are available in an appendix at the end of the book. A list of States that have ratified or acceded to the 1993 Hague Convention is also provided

The aim has been to raise a wide range of issues about policy and practice in intercountry adoption, informed wherever possible by research and a consideration of the experience of other countries with a longer and more extensive experience of overseas adoption. The main focus is on the responsibilities of receiving countries in ensuring that intercountry adoption is carried out in the best interests of the child at a time when the UK is planning to ratify the Hague Convention. I hope that those reading the chapters will come to appreciate the complexity of the issues involved but also to realise the great opportunity we have to build on a long tradition of domestic adoption in this country and the emerging good practice in intercountry adoption in our multiracial society.

References

Andersson G (1991a) 'To feel or not to feel Swedish?' *Adoption & Fostering*, 15:4, pp 69–74.

Andersson G (1991b) *Intercountry Adoptions in Sweden – The experience of 25 years and 32,000 placements*, Paper presented at BAAF international conference on adoption, Edinburgh University, 16–19 September 1991.

Bean P and Melville J (1969) *Lost Children of the Empire*, London: Unwin Hyman.

Defence for Children International (1991) *ROMANIA: the adoption of Romanian children by foreigners*, Geneva: DCI/ISS.

Defence for Children International (1999) *Children's Rights in International Adoption*, Geneva: DCI/ISS.

Hoksbergen R A C (ed) (1986) *Adoption in Worldwide Perspective: A review of programs, policies and legislation in 14 countries*, Lisse: Swets en Zeitlinger.

Hoksbergen R A C (1987) *Adopted Children at Home and at School*, Lisse: Swets en Zeitlinger.

International Bar Association (1991) *The Intercountry Adoption Process in the UK from the Adoptive Parents' Perspective.* London: IBA section on general practice.

Kirk H D (1963) *Shared Fate: A theory and method of adoptive relationships*, Port Angeles: Ben-Simon Publications.

McRoy R (1991) 'Significance of ethnic and racial identity in intercountry adoption within the United States', *Adoption & Fostering*, 15:4, pp 53–60.

Ngabonziza D (1988) 'Intercountry adoption: In whose best interest?', *Adoption & Fostering*, 12:1, pp 35–40.

Ngabonziza D (1991) 'Moral and political issues facing relinquishing countries', *Adoption & Fostering*, 15:4, pp 75–80.

Ryvgold A, Dalen M and Sætersdal B (1999) *Mine – Yours – Ours and Theirs?*, Oslo: University of Oslo.

Selman P (1991a) 'Intercountry Adoption: What can Britain learn from the experience of other European countries?', in Room G (ed), *Towards a European Welfare State*, 1991.

Selman P (1991b) *Romania & Beyond: Policy dilemmas in intercountry adoption in Britain*, Paper presented at BAAF international conference on adoption, Edinburgh University, 16–19 September 1991.

Selman P (1993) 'Services for intercountry adoption in the UK: Some lessons from Europe', *Adoption & Fostering*, 17:3, pp 14–19, 1993.

Selman P (1998) 'Intercountry adoption in Europe after the Hague Convention', in Sykes R and Alcock P (eds) *Developments in European Social Policy: Convergence and diversity*, London: Policy Press.

Selman P (1999) 'The Demography of Intercountry Adoption', in Ryvgold A, Dalen M and Sætersdal B (eds) *Mine – Yours – Ours and Theirs?*, Oslo: University of Oslo.

Selman P and White J (1994) 'The role of "accredited bodies" in intercountry adoption', *Adoption & Fostering*, 18:2, pp 7–13 [Reprinted in Hill M and Shaw M (eds) *Signposts in Adoption*, London: BAAF, 1998].

Small J (1991) 'Ethnic and racial identity in adoption within the United Kingdom', *Adoption & Fostering*, 15:4, pp 61–68.

Triseliotis J (1991) 'A brief overview of the research evidence', *Adoption & Fostering*, 15:4, pp 46–52.

Von Melen A (1998) *Strength to Survive and Courage to Live: 18 adoptees on adoption*, Stockholm: NIA.

Section I
The development of overseas adoption

The chapters in this section are intended to provide some context for later parts of the book by looking at the scale of intercountry adoption and its growth over the last fifty years and considering some of the key legal, ethical and sociological issues that have influenced this development.

Peter Selman looks at the demographic history of intercountry adoption and suggests that we are now entering an unanticipated period of expansion which makes many previous statements about the extent of ICA worldwide seem very dated. China and Russia have replaced South Korea as the major providers of children and the USA emerges even more clearly as the country receiving most children from abroad. The chapter also considers differences in the level of intercountry adoption in relation to population size amongst both receiving States and States of origin and shows that the extent of ICA in the latter is not clearly associated with levels of poverty or fertility.

William Duncan looks at the gradual recognition that intercountry adoption is a global issue and the development of attempts to impose some sort of international control. He looks at the background to the Hague Convention of 29 May 1993 on Protection of Children and Co-operation in Respect of Intercountry Adoption, linking this to the earlier UN Convention on the Rights of the Child, and outlines its main principles. Duncan also reflects on the process of implementation in a world where one of the main participants – Russia – has only recently signed the Convention and many others, including China, have yet to do so, while the receiving State which takes the most children – the USA – has yet to ratify. He also discusses some "operational" issues which have emerged since 1993 and which will be reviewed at a Special Commission in November 2000. These include issues about payments required by the governments of some sending countries and the problems of adoptees' access to information about their backgrounds.

Chantal Saclier looks at the world of ICA from the perspective of an international organisation – International Social Service (ISS) – concerned with the protection of children. She argues that it is no easy task to ensure that ICA is only carried out in the best interests of the child and points to the critical reports of the frenzy of adoption from Romania. She argues that intercountry adoption should only be considered as a last resort, where children would otherwise spend their lives in an institution, and that major efforts are needed to reduce the extent of abandonment and to find family-based alternatives in the States of origin. Looked at in this way, no amount of positive research on outcomes can justify waves of adoption driven by the needs of rich childless couples prepared to ignore all attempts at regulation.

Following this, **Derek Kirton** examines some of the ethical issues arising from intercountry adoption, with special reference to the debates in the UK, where ethnicity issues have had a high profile in both intercountry and domestic adoption. He argues that an ethical policy for ICA in the UK is not just about improving regulation and professional practice, but also requires attention to underpinning values and wider contexts. This would require a move from a "liberal individualist" approach to a more collective approach which better reflects Britain as a multiracial society and recognises a wider responsibility for children's welfare in sending countries.

In the final chapter of this section, **Rene Hoksbergen** reflects on changes in motivation for adoption over three generations from the perspective of a country, the Netherlands, where domestic adoption (other than step-parent adoptions) has become very rare. He shows how adopters in mainland Europe have become progressively more open in their attitudes but also recently more realistic about the problems of intercountry adoption. In doing so, Hoksbergen draws on a wide range of research in Europe and the USA, including the Dutch longitudinal study by Verhulst, which is explored in detail in the next section. A central dilemma has been that findings on the problems of older institutionalised children who have been adopted from overseas have led to a reluctance to adopt the very children who are arguably in greatest need of adoption within the framework outlined by Saclier and Kirton.

1 The demographic history of intercountry adoption

Peter Selman

Peter Selman is Senior Lecturer in Social Policy at the University of Newcastle upon Tyne and Chair of the Network for Intercountry Adoption (NICA – formerly BABICA). He is also a member of the Board of Trustees of the British Agencies for Adoption & Fostering (BAAF).

Introduction

The aim of this chapter is to give a clearer account of the growth of intercountry adoption (ICA) over the past 30 years, using available national statistics from receiving states. I shall argue that the scale of ICA is greater than is usually acknowledged and could potentially grow in the first decades of this new century, making international controls (see Duncan, Chapter 2 and Saclier, Chapter 3) even more important. I shall end by looking at some of the social and demographic characteristics of sending and receiving countries.

The early history of ICA has been described in many publications (e.g. Altstein and Simon, 1991; Selman, 1998; van Loon, 1990). Altstein and Simon (1991) note that intercountry adoption 'began primarily as a North American philanthropic response to the devastation of Europe in World War II that resulted in thousands of orphaned children'. European states were the main source of children to North America until the late 1970s (Selman, 1998) when adoptions from Korea became increasingly important in numbers, accounting for over half of all ICAs in America by the 1970s. The history in individual countries is developed in more detail in other chapters. In particular, Hoksbergen (Chapter 5) and Andersson (Chapter 19) offer an interpretation in terms of "generations" and Gailey (Chapter 17) provides a trenchant account of the history of ICA in the USA.

Child migrants from the United Kingdom

Many of the issues raised by postwar intercountry adoption were around before and alongside the growth of formal or legal adoption over national boundaries. This is particularly true for the UK with the long sad tale of child migrants (Bean and Melville, 1989; see also Hoksbergen, Chapter 5), which continues to be a major issue both in the UK and "receiving states" such as Australia and New Zealand. Estimates of the number of children involved vary, but over a period of a hundred years Britain sent at least as many children to Canada, Australia, New Zealand and other parts of the British Empire as South Korea has sent for ICA over the last fifty years.

The particular shame of that episode lies in the fact that most of the children were not placed in families and many were subsequently subjected to exploitation and abuse. But the placements were arranged by reputable childcare agencies and at the time were seen to be in the best interests of the child. Commenting on this, the House of Commons Health Committee Report (1998) concluded that 'child migration was a bad and, in human terms, a costly mistake' and urged 'extreme caution' when considering applications for intercountry adoption.

Towards a demography of intercountry adoption

While ICA was a phenomenon involving only a small number of children from relatively few countries, the possibility (or necessity) of a demographic approach was largely ignored. Today it is a phenomenon involving over 30,000 children a year moving between over a hundred countries. Just as domestic adoption has been shown to affect a large proportion of people in countries such as the USA (see Hoksbergen, Chapter 5), so most countries today have been affected by intercountry adoption, whether as States of origin, receiving States or as both (Selman, 1998; van Loon, 1990).

If we are to understand this phenomenon, it is important not only to be able to give an accurate picture of the number of ICAs taking place and of changes in that number over time, but also to identify those countries most involved. If we are to make comparisons between such countries, we also need to develop standardised measures of intercountry adoption as is routinely done for births, deaths and other demographic events (Selman, 1999). Adoptions involve three members of the so-called adoption "triangle" so that adoptions can be measured against either birth or adoptive parents. In intercountry adoption this means that we have two potential sources of data – the receiving State and the State of origin.

Problems of availability and accuracy of data on intercountry adoption

Unlike basic demographic data, there is no single volume giving numbers or rates of intercountry adoption for all countries – or for sub-sets – although there are some one-off attempts to aggregate numbers (Kane, 1993; UNICEF, 1999) using data from a selection of receiving countries.

Current statistics on intercountry adoption in receiving States

The availability and quality of data on international adoption vary greatly between receiving States. In 1990, Kane (1993) approached government offices in 21 such countries, but was able to obtain comprehensive data from only 12. Such problems continue ten years later, despite the stress in the Hague Convention on the importance of gathering data systematically.

In England and Wales, published statistics on adoption give a break-down by age and gender and whether the child was born inside or outside marriage, but do not distinguish intercountry from domestic adoptions, or transracial adoptions or relative adoptions within either group. Court records would in any case not record adoptions from designated countries and there are no published statistics derived from immigration records. The Department of Health provides, on request, the number of applications (home studies) received each year, but does not know how many actual adoptions take place (see Brennan, Chapter 10). It is estimated that, in addition, over a hundred children are being brought into the UK each year without entry clearance. Surveys (e.g. BAAF, 1991) can contribute to estimates, as can secondary analyses of immigration and other data such as that done in a special exercise for the Adoption Law Review (Department of Health, 1992). But there is no substitute

17

for an accurate series of published data.

In contrast, in the USA routine statistics are available annually for intercountry adoptions. The US Department of State, Office of Children's Issues, publishes statistics on the number of immigrant visas issued in each fiscal year to "orphans" coming to the US. The US Immigration and Naturalization Service (INS) has figures for the number of children actually entering the country on such visas. US statistics are easily accessed on the Internet (http://travel.state.gov/orphan_numbers.html).

In Scandinavia and the Netherlands, domestic non-relative adoptions are now very rare and only intercountry adoption statistics are published annually. In the Netherlands, detailed statistics on children adopted from overseas are provided by the Ministry of Justice. In Sweden, there are annual figures from their National Board (NIA) on international adoptions by state of origin. In Norway, the Governmental Office for Youth and Adoption provides information from 1979 on the annual number of children mediated by the three licensed organisations. Summary statistics for these three countries can be found in appendices at the end of the chapters by Duinkerken, Andersson and Saetersal & Dalen in this volume. The only serial data on several countries of which I am aware are those collected by EurAdopt (see Sterky, Chapter 21).

Statistics for States of origin
Published data from States of origin are more difficult to find, though some attempts were made to make informed estimates of the number of children being adopted from Romania (DCI, 1991) and routine statistics are available for some countries: e.g. through the Central Adoption Resource Agency in India (Damodaran and Mehta, Chapter 15; Apparao, 1997) or the Ministry of Health and Social Affairs in Korea (Sarri et al, 1998). Kane (1993) cites official statistics from Colombia. Because of the difficulties involved in obtaining comparative data from a range of States of origin, I have made use of data from selected receiving States to estimate the relative levels of intercountry adoption in States of origin (Selman, 1999) following earlier work by Pilotti (1990) and Kane (1993).

The growth of intercountry adoption since 1970

Considering the amount of heat generated by debates on international adoption, it is perhaps surprising that so little attention has been paid to the scale of the phenomenon. By far the best picture of intercountry adoption worldwide in the 1980s is that provided by Kane (1993). Using data from 14 countries, she calculates the minimum number of ICAs between 1980 and 1989 at just over 162,000 – an average of more than 16,000 a year. Noting that she was unable to get statistics for ICA in the UK, Israel, Ireland and Austria, and that statistics for Canada and Germany were incomplete, she concludes that there is a shortfall of 5–10 per cent and estimates the actual total for the decade as lying between 170,000 and 180,000 – an average of 17–18,000 per annum. Estimates for the early 1990s (Duncan, 1993) give 15,000 to 20,000 as the world total.

More recently, UNICEF (1999, p. 3) has made an estimate of the number of adoptions in seven major receiving States in the period 1993–1997, showing a sharp rise in numbers over this period from 16,027 to 23,199, so that by 1997 the total for these seven countries is 4–5,000 higher than the world average estimated by Kane for the 1980s.

In Table 1.1, I have built on these two exercises by extending and updating the UNICEF calculation to include the other seven countries used by Kane plus the UK, Ireland, Iceland and Cyprus. A more detailed description of numbers and trends since 1995 is provided in Appendix 1.

Table 1.1 shows that the USA is the largest recipient of children for adoption, but Canada, France and Italy also receive substantial numbers of children and many of the smaller European countries receive numbers which are relatively greater in proportion to their population. My estimates for the total number of ICAs in the 1990s, using the 14 countries covered in Kane's analysis, show a substantial increase in overseas adoption – from 19,000 in 1988 to over 30,000 by 1997–9. If we allow for an underestimate of numbers to Belgium, Canada, Spain and Germany and the absence of data on Luxembourg, Austria and Israel, it is clear that by the end of the decade the global number of intercountry adoptions must have risen to more than 32,000 a year and that the incidence seems to be rising in most receiving States.

Table 1.1

Major receiving States: number of adoptions 1980–1998

Country	Mean[1] annual adoptions 1980–1989	1988	Mean annual adoptions 1993–1997	1998 or latest year
United States	7,761	9,120	10,070	16,396**
France	1,850	2,441	3,216	3,777
Italy	1,117	2,078	2,047	2,019*
Canada	181[2]	232[2]	1,934	1,799*
Sweden	1,579	1,074	906	928
Switzerland	616	492	761	733*
Netherlands	1,153	577	640	825
Sub-total[3]	**14,257**	**16,014**	**19,573**	**26,477**
Germany	947[4]	875[4]	1,642	1,819
Norway	464	566	531	643
Denmark	582	523	510	624
Australia	509	516	247	245
Belgium[5]	605	662	183[5]	254[5]
Finland	80	78	134	181
Spain	94	93	NA	61[5]
Sub-total[6]	**17,538**	**19,327**	**22,820**	**30,304**
UK	–	–	180	258
Ireland	–	–	46	120
Iceland	–	–	11[5]	15[5]
Cyprus	–	–	NA	12[5]
Total	**[17,538]**	**[19,327]**	**[23,057]**	**30,709[7]**

Notes

[1] Mean is based on years for which Kane (1993) presents data: 9–10 years except Australia (1983–89), Canada (1985–89), Finland (1986–89), Germany and Spain (1988–89), where figure listed is mean for the years in brackets.

[2] Canadian figures for 1985–89 are for Quebec only (Kane, 1993).

[3] Sub-total for 7 countries used by UNICEF (1999).

[4] German figures for 1988–9 are estimates based on 4 northern lander (administrative areas) (Kane, 1993).

[5] Figures for 1993–8 are for "EurAdopt" adoptions only.

[6] Sub-total for 14 countries used by Kane (1993).

[7] Total for 18 countries, including 4 not used by Kane.

* 1997 figures   ** 1999 figures.

This gives a very different picture from Altstein's prediction, made in the aftermath of the Romanian influx, which he saw as temporary, that '... as a long-term world-wide phenomenon whereby nonwhite children from poor nations are transferred to families in rich, white nations ICA appears to be declining' (Altstein and Simon, 1991).

Fluctuations in levels of intercountry adoption over the past 30 years

Kane's estimate of 16,000 adoptions a year is the average number of adoptions from 1980 to 1989, but her detailed figures reveal fluctuations over the period with a peak in 1986 for total adoptions. Table 1.2 gives a picture of such fluctuations in numbers over a longer period, from 1970 to 1998, utilising four countries with good time series data. This confirms a peak in ICAs in the mid-1960s followed by a significant decline and then a sharp rise to a new peak in the late 1990s. For the individual countries the trajectories are very different with the USA trebling numbers between 1980 and 1998, while Sweden and the Netherlands have figures falling sharply from 1980 to 1995. However, all four countries show an increase in the number of adoptions from 1995 to 1998, a trend confirmed in most of the other countries in Table 1.1.

Table 1.2
Annual number of intercountry adoptions: USA, Sweden, Netherlands and Norway: selected years 1970–1998

Country	1970	1975	1980	1985	1990	1995	1998
USA	2,409	5,633	5,139	9,285	7,093	9,679	15,774
Sweden	1,150	1,517	1,704	1,560	965	895	928
Netherlands	192	1,018	1,594	1,138	830	661	825
Norway	115	397	384	507	500	488	643
Total	3,866	8,563	8,821	12,490	9,388	11,723	18,170

In many countries, there was a sharp rise in numbers of international adoptions in 1990–91 following the Romanian crisis. In the USA alone the total number of intercountry adoptions rose by nearly 2,000 between 1990 and 1991. This increase was entirely due to adoptions from

21

Romania. However, a year later the total had fallen from over 9,000 to under 6,500 as Romanian adoptions fell back to their previous level of about 100 a year.

Which countries send most children?

Altstein and Simon (1991) chart the pattern of adoption from abroad by US parents from 1948 to 1987. In the early years, the main sending countries were European (Carstens and Julia, 1995; Selman, 1998) but from the mid-1950s the main source is Korea, accounting for between 22 and 62 per cent of such adoptions in any one year. Kane (1993) identified Korea, Colombia and India as the major sending countries in the 1980s, confirming the picture given earlier by Pilotti (1990) using data from the USA, Sweden and Norway.

For a short period in the early 1990s, Romania became the largest single source of children for international adoption, although the total number of children adopted in the months following the fall of Ceausescu remains uncertain. The DCI report (1991) lists a total of 22 countries receiving over 4,000 children from Romania in the period from August 1990 to February 1991 and figures as high as 10,000 are suggested for the period March 1990 to June 1991, when a moratorium on ICA was declared (Selman, 1998).

However, by 1995, China and Russia had emerged as the main sources of children both for the USA and many other countries (Selman, 1999). Korea continues to be an important source of children but the annual number has fallen sharply and was overtaken by Vietnam in 1998. Table 1.3 gives Kane's figures for 1980–89 alongside data from the USA, France, the Netherlands, Sweden and Norway for 1995 and 1998.

Kane's top 15 countries accounted for about 80 per cent of all adoptions to the 14 sending countries in her analysis. In 1998, adoptions from the 15 sending countries listed accounted for 85 per cent of all adoptions to the five countries listed above. Data from other receiving countries would improve the picture by making the list less dependent on US figures. Inclusion of Denmark would not change the 1998 order, but the addition of Italy would have increased numbers from Brazil, Romania and Russia, and the addition of Spain the numbers from Colombia (UNICEF, 1999).

Table 1.3

Major sources of ICAs: 1980-89, 1995 and 1998 [Adoptions to selected Western countries]

Country	Mean annual adoptions 1980–89*	Country	No. of adoptions 1995**	Country	No. of adoptions 1998**
Korea	6,123	China	2,450	Russia	4,763
India	1,532	Korea	2,008	China	4,621
Colombia	1,484	Russia	1,998	Vietnam	2,240
Brazil	753	Vietnam	1,462	Korea	2,183
Sri Lanka	682	Colombia	1,102	Guatemala	1,087
Chile	524	India	641	Colombia	1,023
Philippines	517	Guatemala	539	India	747
Guatemala	224	Brazil	501	Romania	658
Peru	221	Romania	470	Ethiopia	356
El Salvador	218	Paraguay	351	Brazil	325
Mexico	160	Philippines	321	Bulgaria	319
Haiti	153	Ethiopia	266	Cambodia	302
Poland	148	Bulgaria	220	Haiti	238
Honduras	110	Thailand	132	Philippines	237
Thailand	86	Chile	131	Thailand	197

Notes
* Kane (1993) – adoptions to 13 receiving countries.
** Adoptions to USA, France, Sweden, Norway and Netherlands.

Table 1.3 shows clearly how much change there has been in the sources of children in the past decade, with six of Kane's top 15 countries – Sri Lanka, Peru, El Salvador, Mexico, Poland and Honduras – no longer featuring in the lists for 1995 and 1998. By 1998, Russia and China dominate the ICA field largely due to US adoptions, but over the period 1995 to 1998 Russian adoptions also increased sharply in France and Sweden, and Chinese adoptions in Sweden and the Netherlands. Only Paraguay experienced a sharp fall in the number of adoptions, so that the increases clearly reflect an overall rise in ICA rather than changes in the countries from which children are coming.

There are a number of different reasons for a reduction in numbers of ICAs from states of origin, which suggest that there are likely to be further changes in rank ordering in the years ahead. Examples include:

- Crisis countries where the social/economic situation has transformed, e.g. Greece and Germany which were major sending countries after World War II, but are now receiving children.
- Countries which have moved to domestic adoption, e.g. Sri Lanka. Korea and India both have policies leading in this direction, which have already significantly reduced levels of intercountry adoption.
- Suspension of adoption by either side, e.g. Romania and Paraguay. In future years we may see sharp falls in the number of children from Vietnam and Guatemala due to their governments' responses to reports of trafficking.

Standardised period measures for intercountry adoption

If we wish to compare the levels of intercountry adoption in either sending or receiving States, it is essential to develop some form of standardisation as would be routine for any other demographic event – births, deaths, marriages, divorce, etc – but is rarely found in the adoption literature. The simplest standardisation is to relate adoptions to total population – a Crude (Intercountry) Adoption Rate. This has been used to make comparisons between receiving States (Selman, 1989 and 1999; Pilotti, 1990) and shows Sweden as having a much higher rate than the USA (Table 1.4). Such a rate can also be calculated for States of origin, but could be misleading in making comparisons between States with different age structures.

I have followed an earlier analysis (Selman, 1999) in choosing 100,000 as the base for these rates (rather than 1,000 population as in Crude Birth and Death Rates) because of the low level of adoptions compared with births and deaths. In that analysis, rates were calculated for five receiving states for the years 1987 to 1995 and ranged from 11.9 per 100,000 for Norway to 1.9 for Finland. The USA, despite the large numbers of ICAs, had a rate of only 3.3. Table 1.4 shows trends in crude adoption rates for these five countries over a period of 15 years.

Table 1.4
Crude intercountry adoption rates: Sweden, Netherlands, Norway, USA and Finland, selected years: 1980–1998

Country	1980	1985	1990	1995	1998
Sweden	22.7	18.8	11.2	10.3	10.4
Netherlands	11.9	8.3	5.5	4.3	5.3
Norway	9.6	12.4	11.9	11.3	14.6
USA	2.2	4.1	2.8	3.8	5.7
Finland	–	0.2	2.0	2.0	3.5

Standardisation against live births

An alternative is to relate the adoptions to the number of births (Selman, 1989 and 1999; Andersson, 1986; Kane, 1993). I have called this an adoption ratio (Selman, 1998), defining this as the number of adoptions

Table 1.5
Intercountry adoptions per 1,000 live births – 1998 and 1989: selected receiving States

Country	No. of adoptions 1997*/1998	No. of births 1998	Adoptions per 1,000 births 1997*/1998	Adoptions** per 1,000 births 1989 [Kane]
Norway	643	57	11.2	11.0
Sweden	624	86	10.8	9.4
Denmark	928	63	9.9	8.5
Switzerland	733*	80	9.2*	6.2
France	· 3,777	713	5.3	3.0
Canada	1,799*	344	5.2*	2.7
Netherlands	825	179	4.6	3.7
USA	15,774	3,788	4.2	2.0
Italy	2,019*	512	3.9*	3.8
Finland	181	57	3.2	2.0
Germany	1,819	749	2.4	1.6
Australia	245	245	1.0	1.4
UK	258	689	0.4	N/A

*Asterisked rates are for 1997.
**Kane's figures per 100 multiplied by 10.

25

per 1,000 live births. Kane refers to a "rate of adoption" per 100 births. Adoptions are seen as in some sense the equivalent to acquiring a child through birth (Andersson, 1986). In 1998, the adoption ratio in Norway was 11.2, which indicates more than one intercountry adoption for every 100 live births. In Sweden in 1978, the ratio was 17.4 per 1,000 – nearly two adoptions for every 100 live births. Table 1.5 contrasts the figures for 1997/1998 with those provided by Kane for 1989. As with the crude adoption rates in Table 1.4, standardisation shows the level of intercountry adoption in 1998 to be substantially higher in Norway and Sweden than in the USA. In most cases the level is higher than in 1989; substantially so in the case of Switzerland, France and the USA.

Standardised rates for States of origin

A crude adoption rate would show that the large numbers of children adopted from China are relatively small when set in context of total population size – so that the incidence of ICA per million population is much higher for South Korea or Guatemala than for China. But children under the age of five – the source of most adoptions – form a varying proportion of the total population of different States of origin: 15–16 per cent in Paraguay and Guatemala; 11–13 per cent in India, Vietnam and the Philippines; 7–8 per cent in China and Korea; but only 5 per cent in Russia, Romania and other Eastern European countries. For this reason, Pilotti (1990) suggested an age-specific adoption rate relating average yearly adoptions from 1979 to 1989 to the mid-period population aged 0–4. South Korea emerged as having the highest rate, followed by Colombia, with Chile, Guatemala and Sri Lanka well ahead of India despite the larger numbers from that country. A similar exercise using data from five countries in 1998 (see Table 1.6) shows that Bulgaria and Russia have the highest rates, closely followed by Korea, Romania and Guatemala. Analysis is limited to those countries sending at least 200 children to the five selected receiving states. The large numbers of children moving from China are seen to be modest in relation to the under-5s population in that country.

Table 1.6
Adoptions per 100,000 children aged 0–4: 1998 and 1995 (ICAs to USA, France, Sweden, Norway and the Netherlands) – States of origin sending at least 200 children to the five countries

Country	Annual number of adoptions 1998	Population under age 5: (millions) 1998	Adoptions per 100,000 aged 0–4 1998	Adoptions per 100,000 aged 0–4 1995
Bulgaria	319	0.38	83.7	55.0
Russia	4,763	7.00	68.0	25.6
South Korea	2,183	3.43	63.6	57.3
[Paraguay]	–*	0.76	–*	50.1
Romania	658	1.06	62.1	39.2
Guatemala	1,087	1.79	60.7	30.3
Vietnam	2,240	8.76	25.6	14.3
Colombia	1,023	4.79	21.3	28.2
Haiti	238	1.12	21.3	N/A
Cambodia	302	1.60	18.9	<5.0
China	4,621	98.57	4.7	2.3
Ethiopia	356	10.82	3.3	2.5
Philippines	237	9.69	2.4	3.5
Brazil	325	16.01	2.2	2.8
India	747	115.62	0.6	0.5

Source: Population data from UNICEF Country Statistics, at http://www.unicef.org

Notes
*Paraguay had no recorded adoptions to the five countries in 1998.
*Latvia and Lithuania sent less than 200 children in 1998 but have similar overall rates to Bulgaria, resulting from their low numbers in the under-5 population.

Standardisation against live births

As with receiving States an alternative is to standardise against births (an adoption ratio) which accentuates the gap between high and low birth rate countries, e.g. South Korea and India. I have used a ratio per 100,000 births to bring out the variations between different States of origin and facilitate comparison with the age-specific adoption rates in Table 1.6. Kane (1993) uses a similar measure for sending countries in 1989, calculating a "rate" per 100 live births.

Table 1.7 shows dramatically the changing pattern of intercountry adoption when seen from the point of view of States of origin. In 1989, the five countries with the highest levels of ICAs standardised against births were (in descending order) Korea, Chile, Colombia, Paraguay and Haiti. Only one of these – Korea – still features in the top five countries. The level of ICA has risen in Bulgaria, Russia, Romania, Guatemala, Vietnam and China, but has fallen in Korea, Colombia, the Philippines and Brazil. Chile, Paraguay and Sri Lanka, which had high levels of ICA in 1989, no longer feature in the top 15 countries.

Variations in birth levels are reflected in the under-5 populations unless there are dramatic differences in child mortality or recent changes in birth rates, so that in the tables presented the adoption ratio (Table 1.7) is between four and five times the level of age-specific adoption rates, which are based on the survivors of the previous five years' births (Table 1.6). As a consequence, the rank ordering of States of origin is similar whichever measure we use.

Discussion

Standardised rates can also be used to show the potential for ICA in both receiving States and States of origin. The estimated UK level of intercountry adoption is under 500 a year. If the UK experienced the 1995 rate of adoption in Sweden, the number would be over 5,000 a year. With the 1998 rate for Norway, this would rise to over 8,000. Likewise, if China were to experience the age-specific adoption rate of Russia in 1998, the number of intercountry adoptions to the five countries used in this analysis would rise to over 60,000! The rates also put into perspective the marginal demographic impact of ICA for most sending countries.

Table 1.7
Adoptions per 100,000 live births, 1998 (ICAs to USA, France, Sweden, Norway and the Netherlands)

Country	Adoptions in 1998	Births in 1998 (1,000s)	Adoptions per 100,000 births 1998	Adoptions per 100,000 births 1995	Adoptions per 100,000 births 1989***
Bulgaria	319	71	449	244	–
Russia	4,763	1,420	335	131	–
South Korea	2,183	682	320	277	540
Paraguay	–*	–	–*	225	200
Romania	658	202	326	185	<10
Guatemala	1,087	393	277	137	80
Vietnam	2,240	1,681	133	67	NA
Colombia	1,023	988	104	135	250
Haiti	238	253	95	<40**	110
Cambodia	302	364	83	<20**	–
China	4,621	20,134	23	11	<10
Ethiopia	356	2,652	13	10	<10
Philippines	237	2,064	11	16	<40
Brazil	325	3,340	10	13	50
India	747	24,671	3	11	<10

*Paraguay had no recorded adoptions to the five countries in 1998.
**Estimated figures: US figures less than 50 not reported by State Department.
***Kane's figures are derived from 14 countries – with 25 per cent more adoptions. In 1989, two of the highest ratios were Chile (300) and Sri Lanka (100), neither of which reached the minimum of 200 ICAs for inclusion in the table.

Demographic influences on intercountry adoption

Intercountry adoption is often seen as a humanitarian response to crises of war, famine and disease, which make it impossible for poor countries to provide for all their children. A Malthusian interpretation would see these crises as demographic in origin! It is, however, evident that, although ICA continues to be largely a move of children from poor to rich countries (Selman, 1998), the major sources are not always the poorest or highest birth rate countries, and that patterns persist long past the "crisis", and that demand for children is also a key factor.

Many States of origin are not high birth rate countries facing Malthusian population growth, but countries with total fertility rates below that of some of the major receiving states (see Tables 1.8 and 1.9). That South Korea, China and the former Communist states of Eastern Europe are sending children to the USA and Norway, when they have birth levels below replacement level and lower than in those two countries, must give pause for thought.

Table 1.8

Economic and demographic indicators: 1998 Selected States of origin

Country	Adoption ratio (1998)	Per capita GNP (US$) 1997	Total fertility rate 1998	Infant mortality rate 1998
Bulgaria	449	1,170	1.2	14
Russia	335	2,680	1.3	21
South Korea	320	10,550	1.7	5
Romania	326	1,410	1.2	21
Guatemala	277	1,580	4.9	41
Vietnam	133	310	2.6	31
Colombia	104	2,180	2.8	25
Haiti	95	380	4.3	91
Cambodia	83	300	4.6	104
China	23	860	1.8	38
Ethiopia	13	110	6.3	110
Philippines	11	1,200	3.6	32
Brazil	10	4,790	2.3	36
India	3	370	3.1	69

Sources: Population and Economic data from UNICEF country statistics.

The economic disparities in the per capita GNP are of course vast; US $20–36,000 for the receiving States; less than $3,000 for all the States of origin other than Korea and Brazil. Similarly, the differences in infant mortality are substantial: 4–7 per 1,000 for the receiving States; 110 per 1,000 for the States of origin. However, it must be noted that, of the 15 countries listed, only five had a per capita GNP less than US $1,000 for

Table 1.9

Economic and demographic indicators: 1998 Selected receiving States

Country	Adoption rate 1997/8	Per capita GNP (US$) 1997	Infant mortality rate 1998	Total fertility rate 1998
Norway	14.6	36,100	4	1.9
Denmark	11.8	34,890	5	1.7
Sweden	10.4	26,200	4	1.6
Switzerland	10.2	43,060	5	1.5
France	6.4	26,200	5	1.7
USA	5.7	29,080	7	2.0
Netherlands	5.3	25,830	5	1.5
Italy	4.6	20,170	6	1.2
Finland	3.5	24,790	4	1.7
Australia	1.3	20,650	5	1.8

Sources: State of the World's Children 2000.

a year in which the State of the World's Children gives the average for the 50 least developed nations as only US $256.

Demographic pressures and intercountry adoption

Three "sending" countries have dominated the story of intercountry adoption in the 1990s: Romania, China and Russia. Romanian adoptions are thought to have accounted for at least a third of all intercountry adoptions in 1990–1 (DCI, 1991), but this was short-lived as the Romanian government reacted to international criticism. But since 1995, it is China and Russia that have sent most children to the USA, accounting for more than half of the record number of 16,396 in 1999.

All three countries have experienced particular demographic pressures to which intercountry adoption has seemed to offer a relevant – if minor and inappropriate – response.

Romania after the fall of Ceausescu

The flood of children from Romania in the early 1990s was triggered by media images of desperately overcrowded institutions, but the crisis in those institutions had built up over the previous 25 years of rule by Ceausescu whose pro-natalist policies had banned legal abortion, leading to the highest rates of maternal mortality in the West. Following the fall of Ceausescu, abortion was legalised and within a year the number of recorded abortions was three times the number of live births (Hord *et al*, 1991). The demographic situation in Romania is made more complex by variations in birth rates by ethnic group.

By 1995, the total fertility rate (1.5) was well below replacement level and it has fallen further since (see Table 1.8). Despite this, the rate of adoption from Romania has been rising again in recent years; by 1996, Romania was fourth as a source of children in USA and for EurAdopt agencies. Renewed charges of trafficking in children (*Newsnight*, BBC2, 2 March 2000) may lead to tighter controls and so reverse this trend, as Romania was shown to lack the control over ICA expected of a country which has ratified the Hague Convention and which is applying for membership of the EU.

China's one child policy

China's "one child policy" has created a crisis in the rejection of girl babies. By 1990, there was talk of hundreds of thousands of "missing girls" as male/female sex ratios at birth rose to over 110 (Johansson and Nygren, 1991). This has been variously attributed to infanticide, selective abortion and non-registration of births (sometimes associated with *de facto* adoption). Johansson estimated that as many as half of the missing girls were "adopted" intracountry.

Intercountry adoption increased from 1990 and especially after the Adoption Law was implemented in April 1992 and had built up to 4,206 in the USA alone in 1998. However, even if the number of adoptions from China were to rise to 10,000 per annum this would be barely significant when set alongside the total number of annual births – 23 million in 1998 – or the under-five population – 99 million in 1998 (see Tables 1.6 and 1.7). Johnson *et al* (1998) note a rise in infant abandonment (predominantly female) in recent years, citing official (under)estimates of 100–200,00 a year with 8–10,000 domestic adoptions. There have also been reports of poor families "selling" unplanned babies to richer couples in China. Intercountry adoption from China is predominantly of girls and will therefore increase, however marginally, the already high sex ratio. Will there come a time when some young Chinese men, unable to find a bride in their own country, will turn to adopted Chinese women in North America as partners, as it is rumoured that in Korea there is a growing demand for Filippino brides, as young men in their twenties face the imbalance of gender resulting from selective abortion in recent years?

The Russian Federation after the fall of Communism
The recent rise of adoptions from Russia is associated with one of the most dramatic demographic reversals in recent times. Between 1989 and 1994, life expectancy fell from 73 to 65 and the number of male deaths rose from 762,000 to 1,226,000; deaths of men in their forties trebled over the same period. Like Romania, Russia has a low birth rate, but the recent rise in mortality has led to a situation in which annual deaths exceed annual births by 50 per cent. The Russian population is declining and in 20 years' time there could be a chronic labour shortage. So can Russia afford to send its children to the old enemy? In one sense, no – but nor can it afford the costs of the growing number of children in institutions. Children adopted from Russia include many abandoned by poor mothers and many of these have foetal alcohol syndrome (McGuinness, 1999).

What these three examples indicate is that a demographic history of adoption opens up the possibility of linking intercountry adoption to demographic crises in States of origin, as well as to demographic trends (e.g. a rise in legal abortion) in receiving States. But such crises may then establish a pattern that is hard to reverse even when the initial crisis is over, as has been argued in respect of our final example, Korea.

50 years of intercountry adoption from South Korea
Korea continues to be a sending country with one of the highest rates of ICA. Since intercountry adoption began in 1955, more than 120,000 children have been placed for adoption in other countries. Over 70 per

cent of these went to the USA, where the number of Korean "orphans" entering the country peaked at over 6,000 in the mid-1970s. Initially, many of the infants placed were of mixed parentage – the fathers being US military servicemen – but by the 1990s there were very few mixed parentage children placed for adoption.

Since the Olympic Games of 1988, there has been constant talk of a reduction and eventual end to ICA. In 1989, the Ministry of Social Affairs proposed a schedule which would have reduced the number of inter-country adoptions to 1,700 by 1995 and raised the number of domestic adoptions to 3,500. However, by 1998, ICAs were still above 2,000 per year and domestic adoptions below 1,500. A new 20-year plan was announced in 1997 to phase out ICA by the year 2020 (Sarri *et al*, 1998).

When intercountry adoption started, South Korea was devastated by war, had a low GNP per capita and a high birth rate. Today it is a prosperous country with a high level of education and sub-replacement fertility, but there is a continuing problem over the stigma of unmarried parenthood and, in the absence of a comprehensive welfare system, it is impossible for a poor single mother to keep her child. Sarri *et al* (1998) argue that ICA has discouraged Korea from developing an adequate child welfare programme. The example of Korea reminds us that the factors influencing ICA may change over time and that there may also be a factor of inertia, which makes it difficult to stop ICA.

Conclusion

I have argued that the number of intercountry adoptions is now at its highest ever level in global terms – confounding predictions from the early 1990s that ICA was a phenomenon that had peaked – and that the first years of the new millennium are likely to see even more children moving across national boundaries. Intercountry adoption remains – as it has always been – predominantly a movement of children from poorer to richer countries, but the level of adoption is determined by the demand for children in rich western countries as well as the availability of children in those countries afflicted by poverty and other ills.

In Chapter 5, Hoksbergen argues that the nature of intercountry adoption has changed over time and that the humanitarian motivation of the early years has given way to a demand from childless couples. However, he argues that for the Netherlands and Scandinavia there is unlikely to be a return to the level of international adoption occurring in the early 1980s. The picture emerging in the USA is very different, with numbers doubling in the last five years. Gailey (Chapter 17) goes further to argue that in the USA there is now an insatiable demand for young light-skinned healthy babies, which has led to a trade in children from and to countries where regulation of intercountry adoption falls far short of even the minimal standards sought by the Hague Convention.

Whatever the trends in individual countries, the recent rise in total numbers of intercountry adoptions makes the need for continuing research on the "epidemiological parameters" of the movement of children (Kane, 1993) and on the alternatives for children and birth families in the States of origin even more crucial than it was in the early 1990s.

References

Altstein H and Simon J (1991) *Intercountry Adoption: A multinational perspective*, New York: Praeger.

Andersson G (1986) 'The adopting and adopted Swedes and their contemporary society', in Hoksbergen R (ed) *Adoption in Worldwide Perspective*, Lisse: Swets & Zeitliger.

Apparao H (1997) 'International Adoption of Children: the Indian Scene', *International Journal of Behavioural Development*, 20:1, pp 3–16.

BAAF (1991) *Intercountry Adoptions: A survey of agencies*, London: BAAF.

Bean P and Melville J (1989) *Lost Children of the Empire*, London: Unwin Hyman.

Carstens C and Julia M (1995) 'Legal policy and practice issues for intercountry adoptions in the United States', *Adoption & Fostering*, 19:4, pp 26–33.

Defence for Children International (DCI) (1991) *Romania: The adoption of Romanian children by foreigners*, Geneva: DCI/ISS – also in Department of Health (1992).

Duncan W (1993) 'The Hague Convention on the Protection of Children and Co-operation in Respect of Intercountry Adoption', *Adoption & Fostering*, 17:3, pp 9–13.

Department of Health (1992) 'Intercountry adoption in the United Kingdom: a brief review', in *Interdepartmental Review of Adoption Law, Background Paper 3, Intercountry Adoption*, London: DoH.

House of Commons (1998) Health Committee Report, '*The Welfare of Former British Child Migrants: Government response to the Third Report from the Health Committee Session 1997–8*' (Cmn 4182) December 1998.

Hord C, Henry D, Donnay F and Wolf M (1991) 'Reproductive health in Romania: reversing the Ceausescu legacy', *Studies in Family Planning*, 22:4, pp 231–239.

Johansson S and Nygren O (1991) 'The missing girls of China: A new demographic account', *Population & Development Review*, 17:1, pp 35–51.

Johnson K, Banghan H and Liyao W (1998) 'Infant abandonment and adoption in China', *Population & Development Review*, 24:3, pp 469–510.

Kane S (1993) 'The movement of children for international adoption: An epidemiological perspective', *The Social Science Journal*, 30:4, pp 323–339.

McGuinness T (1999) *Risk and Protective Factors in Children Adopted from the Former Soviet Union*, poster presentation at International Conference on Adoption Research, University of Minnesota, 10–14 August.

Pilotti D (1990) *Intercountry Adoption: Trends, issues and policy implications for the 1990s*, Inter American Children's Institute.

Sarri R, Baik Y and Bombyk M (1998) 'Goal displacement and dependency in South Korean – United States intercountry adoption', *Children & Youth Services Review*, 20:1, pp 87–114.

Selman P (1989) 'Intercountry adoption: What can Britain learn from the experience of other European countries?' in Room G (ed) *Towards a European Welfare State*, Bristol: SAUS.

Selman P (1998) 'Intercountry adoption in Europe after the Hague Convention', in Sykes R and Alcock P (eds) *Developments in European Social Policy: Convergence and diversity*, Bristol: Policy Press.

Selman P (1999) 'The demography of intercountry adoption', in Ryvgold A, Dalen M and Sætersdal B, *Mine – Yours – Ours and Theirs*, Oslo: University of Oslo.

UNICEF (1999) *Intercountry Adoption*, Innocenti Digests no. 4; Florence: UNICEF International Child Development Centre.

Van Loon H (1990) *Report on Intercountry Adoption*, Hague: The Hague Conference.

Websites
National Adoption Information Clearinghouse (1997) *National Adoption Statistics*
http://www.calib.com/naic/whatsnew/stats.htm

National Adoption Information Clearinghouse (1997) *Intercountry Adoption Statistics*
http://www.calib.com/naic/adptsear/adoption/research/stats/intercountry.htm

UNICEF (1999) *Intercountry Adoption Information Portfolio*
http://www.unicef-icdc.org/information/portfolios/intercountry-adoption

Appendix 1

Table 1.10
Intercountry adoptions, 1994–1999: Selected receiving States

Country	1994	1995	1996	1997	1998	1999
USA	8,333	9,679	11,340	13,620	15,774	16,396
France	3,075	3,028	3,666	3,528	3,777	
Italy	1,712	2,161	2,649	2,019	–**	
Canada	2,045	2,022	2,064	1,799	–**	
Germany	1,491	1,643	1,567	1,692	1,819	
Sweden	959	895	908	834	928	
Switzerland	741	665	742	733	–**	
Netherlands	594	661	704	666	825	
Norway	541	488	522	583	643	589
Denmark	497	548	512	519	624	
Australia	222	224	274	269	245	
Belgium	173	193	217	216	254	
Finland	127	102	144	192	181	
UK	115	154	307	223	258	272
Ireland	39	40	54	51	120	

Note: **Figures from UNICEF (1999) – not available for 1998.

Appendix 2

Table 1.11

Crude adoption rates 1995–1999: Selected countries

Country	Annual no. of adoptions	Total Population (millions)	Crude adoption rate [per 100,000]
Norway 1995	488	4.3	11.3
Norway 1998	**643**	**4.4**	**14.6**
Denmark 1995	548	5.2	10.5
Denmark 1998	**624**	**5.3**	**11.8**
Sweden 1995	895	8.8	10.3
Sweden 1998	**928**	**8.9**	**10.4**
Switzerland 1995	665	7.2	9.2
Switzerland 1997	**733**	**7.3**	**10.0**
Canada, 1995	2022	30.4	6.5
Canada 1996	**2064**	**30.6**	**6.8**
France 1995	3.028	58.0	5.2
France 1998	**3,777**	**58.7**	**6.4**
USA 1995	9,679	263.3	3.8
USA 1999	**16,396**	**274.6**	**5.7**
Iceland 1995	10	0.27	3.6
Iceland 1998	**15**	**0.28**	**5.4**
Netherlands 1995	661	15.5	4.3
Netherlands 1998	**825**	**15.7**	**5.3**
Finland 1995	102	5.1	2.0
Finland 1998	**181**	**5.2**	**3.5**
Ireland 1995	40	3.5	1.1
Ireland 1998	**120**	**3.7**	**3.2**
Germany 1995	1,643	81.7	2.0
Germany 1998	**1,819**	**82.1**	**2.2**
Australia 1995	224	18.2	1.2
Australia 1998	**245**	**18.5**	**1.3**
UK 1995	154	58.0	0.3
UK 1999	**272**	**58.6**	**0.5**

Sources: State of the World's Children 1997; UN Demographic website.

2 The Hague Convention on Protection of Children and Co-operation in Respect of Intercountry Adoption
Its birth and prospects

William Duncan

William Duncan is Deputy Secretary General, Hague Conference on Private International Law, and Professor of Law and Jurisprudence, Trinity College, University of Dublin.

The Hague Convention of 29 May 1993 on Protection of Children and Co-operation in Respect of Intercountry Adoption is, at the time of writing, a robust child, supported by 39 Contracting States[1] within seven years of its birth and 41 by September 2000 (see Appendix I), certainly a record for Hague Conventions concerning children, outstripping in the speed of its development even the Hague Convention of 25 October 1980 on the Civil Aspects of International Child Abduction which is itself now approaching majority with 60 States Parties.

The vigorous early development of the 1993 Convention is due to a combination of factors. The careful preparatory work undertaken by the Permanent Bureau of the Hague Conference on Private International Law was an essential beginning.[2] The inclusion within the negotiating process of many States of origin which do not have a tradition of participation in the work of the Hague Conference secured the necessary

---

[1] For a full and up-to-date list of ratifying and acceding States, as well as details of Central Authorities and accredited bodies, consult the Hague Conference website at http://www.hcch.net. A bibliography on the Convention is also available on the site.

[2] See Van Loon J H A, *Report on Intercountry Adoption* (1990), in Hague Conference on Private International Law, *Proceedings of the Seventeenth Session,* Tome II, 1994, p 11. See also by the same author, 'International Co-operation and Protection of Children with regard to Intercountry Adoption', in *Recueil des cours de l'Académie de droit international de La Haye*, Vol. 244 (1993–VII).

balance of interests.[3] Despite the potentially sensitive nature of the subject matter, the early acceptance by the States involved that the starting point for all discussion should be the best interests of the child enabled bridges to be built between those States. The UN Convention of 1989 on the Rights of the Child provided a common point of reference. The Hague Convention may indeed be viewed as a practical expression of the fundamental principles set out in the UNCRC.

The fundamental principles and the UNCRC

The fundamental principles which underlie the Hague Convention are based on the best interests of the child and are drawn from the UNCRC, especially Article 21.[4] It is the Preamble to the UN Convention which provides the fundamental justification for intercountry adoption by recognising that 'the child, for the full and harmonious development of his or her personality, should grow up in a family environment, in an atmosphere of happiness, love and understanding . . .' Where the child's existing family no longer functions to meet the child's needs, Article 20 of the UNCRC requires the State to provide special protection and assistance to a child and 'to ensure alternative care for such a child'. That alternative care may include adoption.

It is Article 21 of the UNCRC which requires those States which recognise adoption to ensure that 'the best interests of the child shall be the paramount consideration'. Article 21(b) contains the principle that

---

[3] More than 70 States, five intergovernmental and 12 non-governmental organisations took part in the negotiations in three Special Commission meetings and a final Diplomatic Session. The Convention was adopted unanimously by the 66 States represented in May 1993 at The Hague. See the Explanatory Report by Parra-Aranguren G (1994), *Hague Conference on Private International Law – Proceedings of the Seventeenth Session,* Tome II, p 538.

[4] See further Parra-Aranguren G (1998) 'La tarea complementaria de la Convención de las Naciones Unidas sobre los Derechos del Niño realizada por las Convenciones de la Conferencia de La Haya de Derecho Internacional Privado', in *Revista de la Facultad de Ciencias Jurídicas y Políticas,* No 106, Universidad Central de Venezuela, Caracas, 1998, and Duncan W (1994) 'The protection of children's rights in intercountry adoption', in Heffernan L (ed), *Human Rights – A European Perspective*, The Round Hall Press/Irish Centre for European Law, p 326.

intercountry adoption may only be considered if there is no suitable alternative for the child in his or her country of origin. The Hague Convention, in its Preamble, slightly modifies this principle by recognising that intercountry adoption 'may offer the advantage of a permanent family to a child for whom a suitable family cannot be found in his or her State of origin . . .' Within the Convention this principle finds expression in the requirement, contained in Article 4(b), that the competent authorities of the State of origin must 'have determined, after possibilities for placement of the child within the State of origin have been given due consideration, that an intercountry adoption is in the child's best interests . . .'

Under Article 21(c) of the UNCRC, States Parties are required to 'ensure that the child concerned by intercountry adoption enjoys safeguards and standards equivalent to those existing in the case of national adoption'. The 'safeguards and standards' may be interpreted as applying both to procedures before an adoption order is made, and to the status of the child following the making of an order. The principle particularises the more general rule against discrimination set out in Article 2(1) of the UNCRC. One outcome of the negotiations at The Hague was the realisation that the differing and complex nature of intercountry adoption sometimes requires differences in techniques of protection. For example, the requirement of a probation period in the receiving State could not be insisted upon within the intercountry context. Also, the difference between full and simple adoptions required the formulation of special rules in Article 26[5] governing the effects

---

[5] *Article 26*

(1) The recognition of an adoption includes recognition of
a) the legal parent–child relationship between the child and his or her adoptive parents;
b) parental responsibility of the adoptive parents for the child;
c) the termination of a pre-existing legal relationship between the child and his or her mother and father, if the adoption has this effect in the Contracting State where it was made.

(2) In the case of an adoption having the effect of terminating a pre-existing legal parent–child relationship, the child shall enjoy in the receiving State, and in any other Contracting State where the adoption is recognized, rights equivalent to those resulting from adoptions having this effect in each such State.

(3) The preceding paragraphs shall not prejudice the application of any provision more favourable for the child, in force in the Contracting State which recognizes the adoption.

of the recognition of a Convention adoption.

Article 21(a) of the UNCRC requires States Parties to ensure that any required consent to adoption has been given, that the consent is informed and that it has been given on the basis of such counselling as may be necessary. These principles have been given effect in Article 4(c) of the Hague Convention. Article 12(1) of the UNCRC contains the principle that 'States Parties shall assure to the child who is capable of forming his or her own views the right to express those views freely in all matters affecting the child, the views of the child being given due weight in accordance with the age and maturity of the child'. This principle finds expression in Article 4(d) of the Hague Convention.[6]

Article 21(a) of the UNCRC requires States Parties to ensure that the adoption of a child is authorised only by 'competent authorities'. The Hague Convention is neutral on the question of whether this should be an administrative or a judicial body. Indeed, it is a general feature of the Hague Convention that, subject to a set of common fundamental principles, it does not attempt to lay down a uniform law of adoption, but

---

[6] *Article 4*

An adoption within the scope of the Convention shall take place only if the competent authorities of the State of origin –

c) have ensured that

(1) the persons, institutions and authorities whose consent is necessary for adoption, have been counselled as may be necessary and duly informed of the effects of their consent, in particular whether or not an adoption will result in the termination of the legal relationship between the child and his or her family of origin,

(2) such persons, institutions and authorities have given their consent freely, in the required legal form, and expressed or evidenced in writing,

(3) the consents have not been induced by payment or compensation of any kind and have not been withdrawn, and

(4) the consent of the mother, where required, has been given only after the birth of the child; and

d) have ensured, having regard to the age and degree of maturity of the child, that

(1) he or she has been counselled and duly informed of the effects of the adoption and of his or her consent to the adoption, where such consent is required,

(2) consideration has been given to the child's wishes and opinions,

(3) the child's consent to the adoption, where such consent is required, has been given freely, in the required legal form, and expressed or evidenced in writing, and

(4) such consent has not been induced by payment or compensation of any kind.

rather seeks to accommodate the many different systems of adoption operating around the world. The Convention is also neutral on the question of jurisdiction, that is, whether the authorities of the child's State of origin or the authorities of the country in which the child is received should have the right to determine whether the adoption may be made. The Convention provides for a division of responsibilities between the authorities in the two States concerned. The State of origin must ensure that the child is adoptable, that due consideration has been given to the possibilities for placement of the child in that State, that an intercountry adoption is in the child's best interests, and that the relevant consents have been freely given. The authorities in the receiving State must determine that the prospective adopters are eligible and suitable to adopt, that they have been appropriately counselled, and that the child will be authorised to enter and reside permanently in that State. Provided this division of responsibilities is respected, the Convention does not insist on the adoption being made in one or other State.[7]

Article 22(e) of the UNCRC requires State Parties to ensure 'that the placement of the child in another country is carried out by competent authorities or organs'. One of the most difficult questions to resolve during the negotiations leading to the Hague Convention was as to the role of independent persons, such as lawyers or doctors, within the adoption process. Should they be allowed to become involved in the making of arrangements for intercountry adoption other than in a capacity directly related to their professional competence? This is permitted in some States such as the USA but is prohibited or strictly limited in certain other States which take the view that only non-profit authorised agencies can provide the range of expertise and the necessary objectivity to protect the interests of children within the adoption process. The compromise which appears in Article 22 of the Hague Convention is that a Contracting State may permit the involvement of non-accredited persons or bodies in making arrangements for inter-country adoption within its territory, subject to supervision and provided

---

[7] Though see Article 28 and further comment in Duncan W (1993) 'Regulating intercountry adoption – an international perspective', in Bainham A and Pearl S (eds), *Frontiers of Family Law*, London: Chancery Law Publishing, p 46.

such persons or bodies 'meet the requirements of integrity, professional competence, experience and accountability of that State; and are qualified by their ethical standards and by training or experience to work in the field of intercountry adoption'.[8]

The phenomenon of globalisation

The 41 Contracting States to the Hague Convention (as of September 2000) are roughly equally divided between States of origin and receiving States. Among countries of origin, South and Central American States are strongly represented, but Eastern European States are less so. As in the past, Africa remains largely outside the global frame of intercountry adoption. Asian representation is patchy with as yet certain notable absentees such as India, China and Korea.

Ratifications of, and accessions to, the Convention seem likely to continue at a steady pace. There are an additional 12 States which have signed but not yet ratified the Convention (see Appendix I). Apart from the work done by the Permanent Bureau, the Convention is being supported and promoted in other international fora. The United Nations Committee on the Rights of the Child regularly recommends adherence to the Hague Convention in its reports on States Parties to the 1989 Convention. The Parliamentary Assembly of the Council of Europe has also added its weight.[9] There is strong support for the Convention among States of origin. Some, such as Paraguay, have indicated that they will only deal with the receiving States which are Parties to the Convention. Certain non-Party States of origin, such as Russia, are known to prefer to deal with receiving States which have ratified the Convention. The major receiving State, the USA, which is now taking in approximately 17,000 children per year through intercountry adoption (perhaps half of

---

[8] See Duncan W (1993) 'The Hague Convention on the Protection of Children and Co-operation in Respect of Intercountry Adoption', in *Adoption & Fostering*, 1993, 17:3, p 9.

[9] See Recommendation 1398 (1999) of 29 January 1999 inviting Albania to surround intercountry adoption with the protection of the 1993 Convention, and expressing the wish that all Council of Europe Member States would ratify the Convention. See also Recommendation 1443 (2000) of 26 January 2000 of the Parliamentary Assembly of the Council of Europe on 'International Adoption: Respecting children's rights'.

all children subject to intercountry adoption) is proceeding towards implementation. Legislation has been introduced into Congress. The fact that implementation has the support of a considerable body within the adoption community will probably ensure its success, despite some continuing discussions surrounding such matters as the appropriate body to oversee the accreditation process, access to birth records, and the requirements governing the eligibility of foreign adopters to adopt children who are resident within the USA. Ratification will probably not occur before 2002, primarily because it will take some time to establish the new accreditation procedures and to apply them to the many agencies concerned.[10]

The objectives and promise of the Hague Convention

It is worth recalling some of the practical objectives of the Convention, for it is against these that the promise of the Convention will come to be judged.[11] There were four hopes in particular surrounding its inception:

a) that the Convention would contribute to the elimination of various abuses which had been associated with intercountry adoption, such as profiteering and bribery, the falsification of birth documents, coercion of biological parents, the intervention of unqualified intermediaries, and the sale and abduction of children;

b) that the Convention would bring about a more "child-centred" approach within intercountry adoption. The process would become

---

[10] See Pfund S (1994) 'Intercountry adoption: The 1993 Hague Convention – its purpose, implementation and promise', in *Family Law Quarterly*, 28:1, p 53 for a discussion of some of the issues surrounding US ratification. The Bill (HR2909) to provide for implementation of the Hague Convention was passed by the House of Representatives on 18 July 2000.

[11] The objectives of the Convention, as set out in Article 1, are:

a) to establish safeguards to ensure that intercountry adoptions take place in the best interests of the child and with respect for his or her fundamental rights as recognized in international law;

b) to establish a system of co-operation amongst Contracting States to ensure that those safeguards are respected and thereby prevent the abduction, the sale of, or traffic in children;

c) to secure the recognition in Contracting States of adoptions made in accordance with the Convention.

less that of finding a suitable child for a childless couple and more that of finding a suitable family for a child;

c) that the Convention would improve the situation from the point of view of the prospective adopters, for whom lack of regulation and the absence of clear procedures were leading to delays, complications and often considerable costs;

d) that the Convention would bring about the automatic recognition in all Contracting States of adoptions made in accordance with the Convention and thus avoid the legal limbo of non-recognition in which many children who are the subject of intercountry adoption have found themselves in the past.

Some operational issues

Article 42 of the Convention authorises the Secretary General of the Hague Conference on Private International Law to convene at regular intervals a Special Commission to review the practical operation of the Convention. One such Special Commission was held in 1994. Implementation issues were considered, as well as model forms and certificates, the application of the Convention principles to refugee and other internationally displaced children and the development of the International Social Service Adoption Resource Center.[12] A second Special Commission is due to be held in November 2000. There is now enough experience of the implementation and operation of the Convention to make possible identification of some of the problem areas which are likely to be discussed at the next Special Commission.

a) Institutional framework (the co-operation structure)

The Convention in Chapter III provides for a system of Central Authorities in all Contracting States whose functions include co-operation with one another through the exchange of general information concerning intercountry adoption, and duties in respect of particular adoptions. (Several Central Authorities may be established within federal States.)

---

[12] Report of the Special Commission on the implementation of *The Hague Convention of 29 May 1993 on Protection of Children and Co-operation in Respect of Intercountry Adoption* (17–21 October 1994), drawn up by the Permanent Bureau, Hague Conference on Private International Law, March 1995.

These latter duties may be delegated to "accredited bodies" which are normally approved adoption agencies. As we have seen, there is also provision for some continued involvement by non-accredited individuals.

In practice, Central Authorities are usually located in ministries. One prerequisite for the successful operation of the Convention is that Central Authorities should be clearly identified so that communication among Central Authorities may be swift and simple. Already the Permanent Bureau of the Hague Conference has experienced some difficulties in obtaining basic contact information in respect of a small minority of States mainly situated in South America. The Hague Conference web site demonstrates the problem by the authorities listed or not listed therein.

b) The accreditation process

Article 10 states that 'accreditation shall only be granted to and maintained by bodies demonstrating their competence to carry out properly the tasks with which they may be entrusted'. Accreditation systems vary from one country to another, as well as the number of bodies accredited. For example, in Romania one hundred associations and foundations have been designated as accredited bodies by the Romanian Committee for Adoptions in accordance with Article 13 of the Convention, while Norway has designated only three. What constitute adequate accreditation criteria and a workable system for supervising accredited bodies require further examination and elaboration. The process of accreditation itself, the period for which accreditation is given, the qualifications of staff, the range of services available, matters of financing, management and accountability, and the provision of an effective system of review are some of the elements that need to be considered. It is not easy to reach common standards on all these issues among States with diverse administrative and legal systems. The effort, however, needs to be made in order to maintain the mutual confidence that is necessary for the successful operation of the Convention.[13]

---

[13] A continuing dialogue is important with respect to the more general principles underlying practice in intercountry adoption. An important recent contribution to this dialogue is International Social Service, International Resource Center for the Protection of Children in Adoption, "*The Rights of the Child*" in *Internal and Intercountry Adoption. Ethics and Principles. Guidelines for Practice*, Geneva 1999.

c) Improper financial or other gain

Under Article 8, Central Authorities are required to take 'directly or through public authorities, all appropriate measures to prevent improper financial or other gain in connection with an adoption and to deter all practices contrary to the objects of the Convention'. Article 32 of the Convention provides as follows:

1) No one shall derive improper financial or other gain from an activity related to an intercountry adoption.
2) Only costs and expenses, including reasonable professional fees of persons involved in the adoption, may be charged or paid.
3) The directors, administrators and employees of bodies involved in an adoption shall not receive remuneration which is unreasonably high in relation to services rendered.

One thorny issue is the practice adopted in many countries of origin of employing the intercountry adoption process as a means of securing certain contributions to the operation or development of child protection services within such States. For example, Romanian procedures introduced in March 1999 make a direct link between assignment of children for placement abroad with contributions to the development of child protection services within Romania. In various other States of origin, some of which are not Parties to the Hague Convention (for example, China), it is common knowledge that a charge is made which goes beyond the costs which are directly related to the specific adoption process. These practices raise difficult questions of interpretation in respect of Article 32, and particularly the rule that only costs and expenses may be charged or paid. It may be difficult to obtain at the international level full agreement on what constitutes an 'improper financial or other gain'. It appears that many persons working in intercountry adoption regard the making of some charges over and above the direct costs of a specific adoption as understandable and perhaps inevitable. Nevertheless, there should perhaps be movement towards an understanding of what constitute the reasonable upper limits of 'required contributions', on the need for clarity in the requirements themselves and for transparency in relation to the use to which such contributions are put. If intercountry adoption is not to become the privilege of the rich and if adopters are to be allowed some certainty with regard to the charges which they may face, some agreed parameters are necessary.

d) Simple adoptions

According to Article 2(2), the Hague Convention 'covers only adoptions which create a permanent parent–child relationship'. Excluded, therefore, are long-term transfrontier fostering arrangements, as well as the Islamic institution of *kafala* which, in the absence of adoption (according to most commentators prohibited under Islamic law), is an alternative method of providing long-term alternative family care.[14] However, the Convention does not exclude so-called "simple" adoptions, that is, adoptions which do not involve a complete severing of legal ties between the adopted child and the birth family. For those States which are familiar only with the idea of full adoption, the treatment of simple adoptions in implementing legislation has posed certain difficulties.[15] Where such a State is the receiving State, the problem may be overcome by providing that the adoption should be converted into a full adoption under the procedure provided for in Article 27 of the Convention.[16] However, the problem becomes more complex where a simple adoption is made in the country of origin and is recognised as such in the receiving State, but where subsequently the adoptive family move to another Contracting State in which simple adoption is an unknown institution. In this case, there is an obligation on the latter State under Article 26 to recognise the

---

[14] *The Hague Convention of 19 October 1996 on Jurisdiction, Applicable Law, Recognition, Enforcement and Co-operation in respect of Parental Responsibility and Measures for the Protection of Children* does, however, include foster care and *kafala* within its scope (see Article 3(e)), and provides in Article 33 some minimum regulations in respect of transfrontier placements. See Duncan W (1998) 'Children's rights, cultural diversity and private international law', in Douglas G and Sebba L (eds), *Children's Rights and Traditional Values*, Ashgate.

[15] See Department of Health (1996) *Adoption – A Service for Children* (March 1996). See also the Law Reform Commission (Ireland) Report on the Implementation of the Hague Convention of 29 May 1993 on Protection of Children and Co-operation in Respect of Intercountry Adoption, Chapter 5.

[16] This is essentially what is proposed for the United Kingdom.

adoption, but it is not easy to decide what effects are to be given to the adoption. Varying solutions have been proposed in different States.

e) Preservation of and access to identifying and other information

Under Article 16 of the Convention, the Central Authority of the State of origin is obliged to prepare a report on the child, including information about his or her identity, adoptability, background, social environment, family history, medical history, including that of the child's family, and any special needs of the child. Article 16(2) reminds the Central Authority, in transmitting this report to the Central Authority of the receiving State, to take care not to reveal the identity of the mother and the father if, in the State of origin, these identities may not be disclosed. Article 30 provides that the "competent authorities" of a Contracting State shall ensure that information held by them concerning the child's origin, in particular, information concerning the identity of his or her parents, as well as the medical history, is preserved. Some problems have already been experienced in interpreting these provisions. The identity of the "competent authorities" is not obvious. One view is that it is any authority that is authorised to hold records concerning the child. The issue of access to identifying information is also a very sensitive one. Although Article 16 allows the State of the child's origin to withhold identifying information where its law forbids disclosure, it is possible that authorities in the receiving State may come into possession of identifying information through other channels. For example, the consular authorities of the receiving State, located in the child's State of origin, may have made independent enquiries into the background of the child or when checking the validity of the consent given by a biological parent. As a result, they may have acquired identifying information. The issue of access to that information then becomes extremely difficult. The Convention makes it clear that it is the law of the State where the information is held that determines the conditions of access. The difficulty for a receiving State is to decide whether access should be permitted in circumstances where it is permitted under its domestic law but is prohibited under the domestic law of the State of the child's origin.

f) Miscellaneous questions

Examples of other issues which have arisen in practice and which may fall to be discussed at the Special Commission to review the operation of the Convention are as follows: who are the appropriate persons or bodies to give the consent under Article 17(c)? How can delays be avoided, especially where they are associated with the Convention's procedural requirements? What difficulties have arisen in respect of the requirement that information be obtained concerning the medical history of the child and his or her family? Is the system of issuing by competent authorities of certificates of compliance under Article 23 always working smoothly? How well are the provisions relating to consent and counselling operating in practice? What is being done in practice about post-adoption reporting, a matter which remains of concern to many countries of origin?

Concluding remarks

The conclusion of the Hague Convention of 1993 and its implementation in Contracting States is only the beginning of a long process. The Convention provides a secure framework but, if it is to operate effectively, that framework needs to be brought to life by a wide range of actors, from child care workers to health care practitioners to judges, who understand its philosophy and objectives and who are given the resources and training necessary to enable them to carry out their duties properly. The States of origin in particular deserve help in this regard. In this respect, it may be of interest to note that the Permanent Bureau of the Hague Conference is currently co-operating with the International Social Service in an ambitious project designed to provide training and support for Central Authorities, accredited agencies and others responsible for implementing the Convention. This is being done in the context of the Hague Project for International Co-operation and the Protection of Children which has been established to raise funding for a variety of activities in support of the Hague Children's Conventions.[17]

---

[17] Further information is available on the Hague Conference website at http://www.hcch.net.

3 In the best interests of the child?

Chantal Saclier

Chantal Saclier is International Programme Manager at the head-quarters of ISS (International Social Service) in Geneva, where she is responsible for planning and co-ordinating the activities of the ISS International Resource Centre for the Protection of Children in Adoption. After receiving a degree in Political Sciences and in Social Sciences, she travelled in the Americas and in Asia, and was then Programme Officer at the headquarters of the International Union for Child Welfare where she worked with Latin American and African countries. Then she co-founded and co-ordinated the Latin America and Caribbean Child and Family Network ("La Red") and lived for several years in Latin America. With ISS, she co-ordinated groups of experts who made an evaluation of the national situation of abandoned children and those at at risk of being abandoned in several countries and organised training sessions and seminars.

Introduction

I have lived for several years in developing countries, where I was able to observe the conditions in which poor families have to survive, in which numerous children live and are looked after in institutions, and where I had the opportunity to meet professionals involved in child welfare from both local non-governmental organisations (NGOs) and government organisations. Also, having worked for some time on matters relating to intercountry adoption while living in "receiving" countries, I can appreciate the complexity of the issues involved when considering the best interests and the rights of the child in intercountry adoption.

At present, a consideration of children's rights when talking about intercountry adoption forces us to confront a highly uncomfortable situation. In the name of the child, everyone raises his or her banner and simplifies the issues to the extreme, whereas in this field the rights of the children concerned are not always so clear-cut and obvious. The passions the topic unleashes, in both countries of origin and receiving countries, distort information, confuse people's thinking and make action difficult and risky. Often there is a tendency to consider only one aspect of the problem, filtered through the prism of the side of the planet on which one lives. Often ideology clouds judgement and is given priority over a real consideration of the best interests of the child. Often personal or organisational interests are masked under humanistic speeches. Everyone defends his or her personal convictions or interests, forgetting that at stake are the lives of human beings, and young and particularly vulnerable ones at that.

One might start by making two statements in terms of the interests of the children concerned. Adoption can offer a permanent and appropriate family to children who have been definitively deprived of their family environment or cannot, in their own best interests, be allowed to remain in it. Adoption is, then, an opportunity that should be offered to such children when it appears to be the right solution for them. Often, however, these two irrefutable statements are reinterpreted and transformed into the following highly questionable conclusion, one that can be used to cover up a host of practices that are contrary to the child's best interests: 'Since there are many children suffering in institutions in developing countries and many families keen to adopt in more privileged countries, international adoption should be encouraged and promoted.'

Institutionalisation of children

We are indeed facing a paradoxical situation. On the one hand, many thousands of children at present live in institutions in conditions that give great cause for concern. In a great number of developing countries, the physical condition of the institutions is highly worrying and has direct consequences for the children. Many institutions lack basic material necessities: buildings are unadapted; there is a shortage of clothes, beds, adequate food, heating, games, etc. The number of staff is insufficient and those employed are often poorly paid, inadequately motivated and not trained for the tasks they have to undertake. Moreover, the institution – even when material conditions are adequate – does not favour the human development of the child.

A child is a being who exists by virtue of relationships. The

54

satisfaction of his/her material needs is not sufficient to secure his/her development. From birth, the child is a person. For human development, the child needs to be able to look to a small number of adults who care for him/her permanently and on a long-term basis; to be loved, stroked and stimulated; to be personally recognised; and to be integrated into society as soon as possible in his/her life. Very few institutions are able to meet such needs. In an institution the child has scarcely the opportunity to attach to an adult in a stable, permanent, reassuring and positive manner. The relationships which are developed between the staff and the child are frequently not sufficiently personalised and affectionate. The greater proportion of children in relation to the staff, and the absence of awareness of the staff with regards to the importance of their attitude towards the children, can often lead to a situation in which there is almost no personalised human attention given to the children. Continuity in relationships and personal attention are not secured and children are often moved from one institution to another as they grow up.

The child who lives in an institution generally does not receive any explanation with regard to his/her situation. As a consequence, the child can then develop the feeling that he/she has no value and has never been desired and loved, which is a destructive feeling. This feeling can be exacerbated in those institutions where prospective adoptive parents are allowed to enter and to select their child: the children who are not chosen are sent back to their feeling of abandonment. In an institution it is difficult for the child to develop a sense of belonging or being valued, or to perceive the respective roles of the man (often absent from the institutions) and the woman, of the parents and the children, as well as the mode of relationship between themselves. It will then be difficult for a child who grows in an institution to become a spouse or a parent. It will also be most difficult to develop his/her capacity to integrate into the society. Consequently, in an institution, the emotional, psychological, social, intellectual – and sometimes physical – development of the child runs a high risk of being impoverished or even halted. Only a family is able to secure a normal and satisfactory progress for children.

For a proportion of these children, adoption (domestic and inter-country) is an option that ought to be implemented because they are in need of a permanent family environment. However, for many reasons, many remain in institutions and in a large number of countries there is no real political incentive to remove children from institutions and provide them with a family environment (whether in their own family or a foster home). There are several reasons why this may happen: in some countries, institutions are considered proper systems within the cultural or political tradition (this has been and is the case in Eastern Europe, China, etc.); staff working in these institutions may fear losing their jobs; professionals involved often do not face up to their individual responsibilities in the exercise of their duties and take refuge in bureaucratic attitudes; many of these abandoned children come from a sector of the population rejected by society, often as a result of religious, sexual or racial prejudices; or there is a fear of giving priority to the rights of abandoned children over those of abandoning parents.

Many children who are not orphans live in abandonment or de facto abandonment in institutions; they are not eligible for adoption in the legal sense and cannot be because of absent or non-consenting biological parents. Often there are gaps in the legislation covering this type of situation, which prevent such children becoming "adoptable". Generally speaking, all this is due to a lack of understanding or a failure to recognise the needs and the rights of the child. Furthermore, most developing countries do not have adequate structures, financial means and personnel, nor enough trained professionals to carry out the necessary investigations to determine and implement proper social and legal measures for the protection of these children. On the other hand, adoption, and particularly intercountry adoption, is the field of very questionable practices where the child is not always considered as a person with human rights and sensitivity.

The pernicious philosophy of the "right to a child"

Thousands of couples or individuals from "receiving" countries regard intercountry adoption as the only solution left at the end of a long, painful road that has typically included unsuccessful fertility treatment, applications for domestic adoption turned down or placement on a long waiting list. In the last two decades, intercountry adoption has progressively changed. From its initial purpose of providing a family environment for children, it has now become more demand-driven. Increasingly in industrialised countries, intercountry adoption is viewed as a way for childless couples to satisfy their desire for a child. Growing numbers of intercountry adoptions, in fact, involve countries where children can be found who correspond to criteria set by prospective adoptive parents: very young children whose physical appearance is as similar as possible to their own, and who have no physical or mental disabilities or serious illnesses. This trend has contributed to the development in the West of a pernicious philosophy of "a right to a child", which often goes so far as to violate the rights of the child.

To meet the demand for children, abuses and trafficking flourish: absence of support to the birth families at risk; psychological pressure on vulnerable mothers; negotiations with birth families; adoptions organised before birth; false maternity and paternity certificates; abduction of children from maternity hospitals or even from the street; children conceived specifically for adoption; political and economic pressure on governments...

Indeed, a booming trade has grown in the purchase and sale of children in connection with intercountry adoptions. It originates with the continuous pressure exerted by couples in economically advanced countries and the fact that they frequently can be induced to pay very large sums of money to satisfy their desire to have a child. All too often in these cases, adoption, whether intercountry or domestic, becomes an act of selfishness, an expression of an inability to accept being thwarted, a way of resolving a frustration by putting the burden on others who are less economically privileged. This trade also depends on the venality of officials, professionals and intermediaries who see adoption as a way of getting rich quick, either through corruption or by overcharging for services rendered. And it is fuelled by the lure of profit in populations destabilised by poverty or the breakdown of their societies.

The child whose rights are being stepped on has become an object, a tradable commodity. It is apparent that a growing number of children who have been adopted were not in need of a substitute family: children sought directly from within their birth family, who may or may not have passed through an institution; children who could have continued growing up in that family had it been given modest support – or had the demand from adoptive parents and the money they are prepared to pay not exerted pressure on birth parents and encouraged the development of abuses or other criminal acts; and even children who would not have been conceived were it not for the lure of money to be gained through intercountry adoption.

Certainly, the great numbers of children placed in institutions and kept there for years is one of today's most poignant tragedies. But adoption, and particularly intercountry adoption, can also turn into a tragedy for a certain number of children involved and their birth families. That is the reason why it is impossible to support the contention that intercountry adoption, per se, should be encouraged and promoted as being the solution for the many children suffering in institutions in developing countries.

Facing the challenges

Things are not so simple. When aiming at the best interests of those children, we have to face the following challenges:

- How can we ensure that those children who really need it can benefit from adoption? That is to say:
  - How can we ensure that children are not left without any prospect of family life?
  - How can we avoid a situation in which children are placed for intercountry adoption, when a solution could be found within their own biological family or their own community?
- How can we ensure that children who are placed in an institution do not stay there for a long period and that a plan for permanent placement is implemented which enables the child to return as soon as possible – with all necessary safeguards – to his or her birth family or, if this proves impossible, to be placed in an alternative family setting?
- How can we move children out of institutions and offer each of them a family environment which sees him or her first of all as a human person, with all that entails, and which meets his or her individual needs and characteristics?

We have to be aware of a host of factors. The majority of those who wish desperately to adopt – whether domestically or from abroad – would prefer to adopt a very young and healthy child. However, many of the children currently in institutions do not fulfill these requirements in that they are not babies; they have experienced a succession of traumatising situations which will require a lot of intelligence, comprehension, patience and solidity from the adoptive family; they often suffer from physical, psychological or mental health problems, generally related to their history. Moreover, a lot of institutionalised children are not legally adoptable. Some biological parents have disappeared or have never made a declaration of abandonment or given their consent to adoption. Others have entrusted their child to the institution but have not totally severed their links with the child, still contacting them periodically or exceptionally. It is far from the truth that all the children who are presently cared for in institutions are adoptable, either because the legal procedures to free them for adoption have still to be completed, or because the families who are able to take care of them and to accept them as they are, represent only a limited percentage of the prospective adoptive parents.

Some adopters idealise adoption, wishing to believe that love will solve any problem, but love does not appear automatically in a parent–child relationship and is not a long quiet river. Many of these prospective adopters refuse to admit that adoptive parenthood has to face additional difficulties in comparison to biological parenthood and that this requires greater capacities and the resolution of possible emotional problems related to infertility, celibacy or bereavement. All those who want to adopt are then far from able to be appropriate parents for those children who are really in need of a substitute family.

Children's best interests and rights in intercountry adoption

If children are to be set at the centre of all measures aimed at protecting them and respecting their rights, then several lines of action seem to me to need priority for children at risk or in a situation of neglect or abandonment.

1 Preventing abandonment and fighting for social justice nationally and internationally

Neglect and abandonment of children are mainly the consequences of poverty and destitution manifested in various forms: lack of education; absence of birth control; the breakdown of the nuclear family; a weakening of the role of the extended family; intrafamilial violence, alcoholism and drug addiction; and health problems. From a human rights perspective, it is impossible to consider adoption as a satisfactory answer for neglected or abandoned children. It is imperative that action be taken so that children are not abandoned but can remain with their families. Prevention of abandonment must be given high priority. This means:

- psycho-social support services and/or financial support for mothers or families in difficulty;
- conscious and responsible sex education and family planning;
- raising awareness of the importance of the father's role and responsibility in the development of his sons/daughters;
- training for parenthood and raising social awareness of the needs and rights of the child;
- the promotion and upholding of women's rights; and
- fair incomes and access to employment.

Implementing children's rights means fighting for national and international policies which bring about social justice, that is, those which improve the economic and educational level of impoverished populations and reduce global economic imbalances.

2 Favouring permanent family-based alternatives instead of institutionalisation

Throughout the world, and particularly in low income countries, placement in institutions often constitutes the automatic response to children in need of care and protection. This is not an initiative carried out solely by officials within these countries; when arriving in a country in crisis, the first action taken by many charities or NGOs from the industrialised world is to create institutions. This must be changed. It is clear that institutional placement has very adverse effects on the child's development, particularly when that placement is a prolonged one.

Priority must be given to family alternatives. Instead of creating new institutions, either temporary foster care or economical, psychological and social support to the biological families must be given key importance. The institution must be considered only as a temporary answer which offers protection to the child while his/her personal and family situation is clarified and plans are developed for a permanent placement in a family-based environment.

De-institutionalisation must become a main preoccupation in child welfare policies: searching for solutions within the nuclear and extended family of the child; developing the national foster care system in order to offer a temporary measure better adapted to the child's needs than institutional care; establishing obligations, delays and priorities for action in order to quickly study the personal situation of the children cared for in institutions and to propose a project of life for each of them and particularly the youngest. As soon as a baby or a very young child seems at risk of being abandoned in a maternity hospital, preventive measures must be taken and as soon as he or she enters an institution, an assessment must be undertaken in order to clarify his or her situation and to look for appropriate solutions.

Legislation should be modified in order to facilitate the legal "adoptability" of those children whose social and personal need for adoption has been established. In my opinion, this is equally applicable to industrialised countries where a certain type of open or semi-open adoption could allow more *de facto* abandoned children to benefit from permanent, reassuring and good family care without suffering a total severing of the child's relationship with his/her biological family.

We should also first be promoting a quality domestic adoption – and taking the necessary steps to improve the quality of intercountry adoption by tightening legislation, ratification of the 1993 Hague Convention, control of intermediaries, and a clear definition of reasonable fees and costs.

Some professionals are afraid to be involved in intercountry adoption because of the bad reputation it has acquired, preferring to accept maintaining children in institutions without the prospects of experiencing family life. But intercountry adoption is not bad in itself and is sometimes the only route to a family life. When it is well done, it can be a satisfactory solution for the child. Others are fiercely opposed to intercountry adoption on the grounds that children have a right to be brought up in their own culture, communities and country. On the basis of these rights, they are prepared to accept a situation in which children languish in institutions – where the right to remain in the culture and community is retained, but this is merely a theoretical embracing of these "rights" – what "culture" does an institutionalised child enjoy? Moreover, in an institution, a child's fundamental rights are often ignored or violated. In such cases, fear and nationalistic or political considerations rank before children's rights.

In a world where population movements are increasing, where intercountry adoptees are generally well accepted, is it not more respectful to offer a child a family that will help him or her to develop, in whatever country, rather than condemn that child to an "orphanage" culture? I consider that maintaining children for years in institutions without searching for a permanent family-based alternative is a violation of the rights of those children.

Implementing children's rights and caring for their best interests means fighting to raise awareness and to promote policies and promulgate legislation that favour family-based alternatives for children; limiting the role of the institution to temporary care aimed at facilitating the reintegration of the child into his or her family as a priority or, if this cannot be achieved, at seeking permanent placement in a substitute family; promoting and improving in-community and in-country adoption; and also monitoring and improving intercountry adoption procedures.

3 Reinforcing good practice in adoption and fighting against abuses and trafficking

Adoption, and particularly, though not only, intercountry adoption, can involve practices that generate high risks for children and their birth families (especially their mothers), abuses, trafficking and criminal acts such as the sale and purchase or abduction of children. All too often adoption is a means for couples and individuals (nationals and foreigners) to satisfy their desire for a child, but without giving paramount attention to the child's bests interests. Direct adoption arrangements from one individual or family to the other must be banned, except under extra-ordinary circumstances supervised by child protection services. Adoption is not an arrangement made between individuals. *It is a social and legal protective measure for children.* It should be considered and authorised with this sole aim in view and must be under the responsibility of the state. Adoption must be concerned with the children who are in institutions, not those who are living with their family.

The psychosocial and legal "adoptability" of the child must be established before starting the procedure of adoption. It has to be based on a study of the situation of the biological family (mother, father, siblings, grandparents, etc.) and sometimes the community this family is part of, as well as an assessment of the personal situation and needs of the child. This assessment must result in the definition of a project of life for the child, giving priority to the rehabilitation of the child into his or her family (or community) by bringing the necessary support to that family. The adoptability of the child should be confirmed only if it appears that the family of origin does not meet the conditions that ensure the psychosocial development as well as the physical and emotional integrity of the child. And importantly, poverty alone should not be a criterion for severing a child's bonds with his or her family of origin.

The psychosocial and legal eligibility to adopt of the prospective adoptive family must be established before starting the procedure of adoption. It has to be based on an assessment of the individuals wishing to adopt and of their family and social environment. The potential adopters must benefit from a thorough preparation to adopt *before* and after the eligility procedure, in order for them to consider adoption first as an answer to the child's needs and to be aware of possible problems the adoptee may experience and of the necessary abilities and commitment to manage them.

The matching between a child and a prospective adoptive family must take into account the characteristics and specific needs of the child and the characteristics and apparent ability of the family to meet those needs and to adapt in the long term to the child's characteristics in a satisfactory manner. The matching has to be based on both a detailed report on the child and his/her biological family, and a detailed report on the prospective adoptive parents, reports produced at the conclusion of the investigations mentioned above.

The periods of waiting and uncertainty that the child lives through must be reduced as much as possible. Continuity must be ensured in the care given to the child, and the transition between one life situation to another must be prepared and carefully supported in order to avoid disruption and distress. The way any decision about adoption becomes official must be established in law and must be respected. Where the adoption involves persons from two different countries and one or both of these countries has not ratified the 1993 Hague Convention, it is important to check that there are no contradictions between the legislations of each country before proceeding with the adoption. When private bodies or professionals are involved in some of the procedures related to adoption, they *must* be accredited to do so and supervised by competent authorities of the State. Criteria for accreditation must be reinforced and the good intermediaries supported. All the steps related to the preparation and the implementation of adoption must be entrusted to professionals and services competent in child and family welfare, with an ethical code compatible with human and children's rights. As far as possible, those professionals must receive training in understanding children's rights in adoption and the implications of this for their practice.

Rules must be established at national and international levels to monitor material aspects of adoption, and particularly of intercountry adoption. International Social Service (ISS) considers it essential that the following be quickly proposed and periodically updated in both receiving countries and countries of origin:

- a list of the steps involved in adoption procedures, or linked to adoption, that could justify a payment; and
- scales of emoluments, fees and the cost of services in adoption that could be considered reasonable.

Sanctions must be considered in the law and put into practice with regards to bad practice and unreasonable material gain.

Implementing children's rights involves the following:

- fighting against the growing philosophy biased towards the "right to a child";

- opting for adoption only when it is in the best interests of the child;
- improving ethical criteria;
- being exacting when accrediting and monitoring intermediaries;
- implementing procedures that ensure that the prospective adoptive parents match the child's needs and characteristics;
- improving laws and practices;
- training staff and judges involved in the procedures;
- creating psychosocial services to prepare children for adoption and to assist biological and adoptive parents as well as children after the adoption takes place;
- developing the exchange of information and experience throughout the world;
- taking very drastic measures to fight against profit-making in adoption-related matters and against the abduction of, sale of or trafficking in children.

All this is the responsibility of the receiving countries as well as of the countries of origin. The situation must improve in both. Moreover, the receiving countries must offer support financially and, when needed, professionally to the countries of origin for the implementation of global policies where priority is given to the prevention of abandonment and where procedures of adoption are organised in the best interests of the child.

Note

The International Social Service (ISS) has worked for many years on the question of intercountry adoption and has participated in international conventions on the topic. ISS is developing an International Resource Centre for the Protection of Children in Adoption (ISS/IRC), which aims to promote greater respect for children's rights (see Appendix II). The ISS/IRC offers documents of interest on the ISS website: www.iss-ssi.org under the heading "International Resource Centre". See particularly *The Rights of the Child in Intercountry Adoption*.

4 Intercountry adoption in the UK
Towards an ethical foreign policy?

Derek Kirton

Derek Kirton is Lecturer in Social Policy and Social Work at the University of Kent. His book, '"Race", Ethnicity and Adoption' (2000) was published by Open University Press. Apart from academic writing and research in relation to adoption, he has also been a social worker in the field of adoption and served as a member of an adoption panel.

Introduction

This chapter seeks to explore some of the ethical issues surrounding intercountry adoption (ICA) in the UK with two major foci. The first is that of comparison with debates on domestic transracial adoption (TRA), seeking to tease out their similarities and differences. A second is to consider the relationship between "public" and "private" aspects of ICA and the associated policy dilemmas. Any such exploration must entail acknowledgement of the heterogeneity of ICA in two senses. One relates to motivation on the part of adopters, which may derive primarily from humanitarianism or from childlessness. The other is that ICA is by no means coterminous with transracial adoption, either because there is a minority ethnic (in UK terms) match between the child and at least one parent, or because the child is white (in recent years usually from Eastern Europe). However, when ICA is transracial this clearly adds to its contentiousness and this situation will provide the main focus here.

Since the emergence of "same race" policies in the UK, opposition – real and perceived – to ICA on the part of UK adoption agencies (notably local authorities) has been presumed to rest on a similar rationale, namely that minority ethnic children are likely to suffer problems in relation to racial or ethnic identity and to face racism relatively unsupported by their adoptive families. Mirroring debate on domestic TRA, supporters of ICA tend to deem such arguments ill-founded and rooted in political dogma. More specifically, they are likely to advance one or more of three counter propositions. The first is that intercountry adopters can be, and often are, mindful of the importance of identity and cultural issues and able to meet their children's needs in these areas. A second is that, irrespective of the handling of identity issues, ICA is shown to be generally "successful" for children. The third proposition draws on the theme of "child rescue", contending that whatever problems the adopted child may face, they are relatively minor compared with those they would have experienced in their country of origin.

The major research spotlight in ICA has been placed upon the experiences of adoptees and their families, with the principal concern being that of whether ICA "works". The latter has been constructed largely in psychological terms of "adjustment" or "self-esteem", but sometimes also incorporating investigation of racial or cultural identity issues. This research has been effectively summarised elsewhere (see e.g. Triseliotis, 1993; Triseliotis et al, 1997, pp 181–207; Warren, 1999) and will not be considered in any detail here. The broad picture which emerges is that, while a majority of adoptions are "successful" in terms of family relationships and the psychological well-being of adoptees (and that problems are often unconnected to "race"), many adoptees experience difficulties related to questions of ethnicity and identity (McRoy, 1991, p 54; Triseliotis, 1991, p 48).

These difficulties are, in many respects, similar to those found in domestic TRA, although with important differences. They include the effects of visible difference from the adoptive family and often a desire to be white (Harper, 1994, p 22; McRoy, 1991, pp 57–8; Warren, 1999, p 20). Despite claims of ethnic sensitivity on the part of intercountry adopters, it is clear that, for most, assimilation remains the dominant paradigm, and that most adoptees are brought up with relatively limited input in terms of racial or cultural identity (Triseliotis, 1991, p 51). Yet such a strategy is vulnerable, not only to the effects of visible difference, but also the danger that experiences of racism will leave adoptees feeling isolated and unsupported within their families (Triseliotis, 1989, p 26; McRoy, 1991, p 58; Enrico, 1999, p 2). While disruption rates for ICA are generally low, it is also the case that the consequences of disruption may be more severe. Harper (1994, p 20) has suggested that adoptees' loss may be more "total", in that having acquired a new language and culture as well as a new family, disruption 'renders them a stranger in the world in which they find themselves, as well as in the world from which they came'. Finally, it is clear that, despite a tendency towards assimilation within ICA, adult adoptees tend to take a renewed interest in their country of origin. For instance, a recent survey of Korean adoptees in the USA found that while as children only 28 per cent had identified themselves as Korean(-American), this figure had risen to 64 per cent when they were adults (Enrico, 1999, p 2). This would seem to reflect first, a curiosity in identity and origins and second, absorption of a social reality within which minority ethnic identification by others renders a "white" self-identification untenable. However, taking on an identity from the country of origin is likely in many cases to lack content and "authenticity". This manifests itself most sharply and perhaps most poignantly in difficult interaction and strained relations with those of ostensibly "similar" ethnic background but raised within their own families or communities (Kirton and Woodger, 1999). Thus, Dalen and Saetersdal (1987) found that many Vietnamese adoptees in Norway not only felt marginalised within Norwegian society but also estranged from other Vietnamese people within the country.

While these issues and difficulties can be found in relation to both domestic TRA and ICA (especially when transracial), there are certain important differences between the two. These stem partly from the various "distances" involved in ICA, and partly from patterns of migration and settlement. By comparison with domestic TRA, ICA is liable to be characterised by greater distances – geographical, social, cultural, legal and administrative – between the child's birth family or community of origin and the adoptive milieu. In turn, this tends to pose greater challenges for adoptees in terms of integrating or managing different aspects of their lives and identities, with searching for birth relatives being one of the more obvious examples. Another important factor is whether ICA is the only route of migration between "sending" and "receiving" countries and hence whether the latter have communities of similar ethnic origins to intercountry adoptees. The existence (and location) of such communities will influence the ethnic politics of the country and the likelihood of intercountry adoptees interacting with those from their "community of origin". If, as noted above, such interaction can be difficult and even "threatening", it also offers opportunities for the development of ethnic identity and a potential source of support in the face of discrimination. Minority communities are also important in terms of a "voice" on ICA, a point to which we will return.

Identity needs . . .

While few would dispute that ICA can give rise to difficulties over identity, the question remains as to their seriousness – in short, do they matter? For those who would wish to play down their significance, the clearest evidence is taken to be that from studies of "adjustment", which generally show this to be high for intercountry adoptees (Feigelman and Silverman, 1983; Bagley, 1993; Rutter, 1998). I have offered a detailed critique of the focus on "adjustment" elsewhere (Kirton, 2000) and will make only a few brief points here. The first is that such measures operate on a "universalist" basis, which ignores social factors – including those of "race" and ethnicity – assuming that "adjustment" can be gauged independently of them. Second, this "universal" approach tends to enshrine conformity and assimilation. A third problem is that measures of adjustment are not necessarily well-placed to gauge inner experiences which lie behind the "presentation of self" involved in tests or research interviews. This is particularly relevant to the nuanced and often contingent experiences relating to "race" and ethnicity. Thus, a degree of scepticism is in order both in relation to measures of adjustment and to the oft-cited claim that it can be shown to be "independent" of ethnic identity (Feigelman and Silverman, 1983; Tizard and Pheonix, 1993). It is noteworthy that, despite the findings on adjustment, studies of ICA have often found greater than average incidence of mental health problems among adoptees, although this may partly reflect diagnostic issues (Carstens and Julia, 1995, p 30; Warren, 1999, p 20). Nonetheless, it is often argued that any difficulties arising from issues of "race" and ethnicity are relatively minor or transient and, in any event, outweighed by the benefits of ICA, in effect, a "price worth paying". As Simon et al (1994, p 68) put it, 'the bottom-line question that one should always ask is whether these children would be better off in their birth countries – in institutions, foster care, or even adopted – than they would be in the United States or Western Europe'.

... and the capacity of families to meet them

As with domestic TRA, the general pattern in ICA is that although a majority of adopters acknowledge in principle the significance of identity issues for their children, dealing with them in practice tends to be patchy and often limited. Claims that most adopters are able to meet the identity needs of their children (Bagley, 1993, p 79; Humphrey and Humphrey, 1993, p 7) appear sustainable only if a very low benchmark is set, for all empirical studies show the prevalence of limited parental input on issues of "race" and culture (Triseliotis, 1991, p 51). There seem to be a number of reasons for this. First, unless the adopters already have connections with the child's country (or community) of origin, it is questionable how far ICA will stimulate or sustain such efforts. Simon and Altstein (1987, p 109) have noted the waning of interest in "ethnic variety" over time, a finding supported by Feigelman and Silverman (1983, p 155).

Transracial or transcultural adopters always face a delicate task in relation to identity issues, granting them recognition without creating a sense of separation between the adopted child and other family members. If this balance does not flow easily from the family's situation and networks, the likely outcome is either waning interest or restriction to a "museum" view of culture which may do little to help the adoptee negotiate contemporary identity issues. Second, this problem is exacerbated by the fact that most intercountry adopters in the UK live in predominantly "white" areas, offering adoptees limited opportunity for interaction with others from minority ethnic backgrounds (McRoy, 1991, p 59). While group support from other intercountry adopters is clearly valuable in combating isolation, it is limited by comparison with the opportunities offered by more multiracial communities. Third, it is clear that a significant number of intercountry adopters see questions of "race" and culture as largely irrelevant. Feigelman and Silverman (1983, p 135) and Bagley (1993, p 198) have found intercountry adopters to give markedly less input on issues of culture than that provided by domestic transracial adopters, and itself often quite limited. While this is partly explicable in terms of the greater "distances" involved, there are also risks which flow from the nature of intercountry adoption itself.

The motivation of childlessness combined with the great practical difficulties of finding a child often renders the latter's country of origin largely incidental, as is evident in some of the titles – *Eventually . . . and so to Sri Lanka*, and *Colombia to the Rescue* – given to adopters' narratives (Humphrey and Humphrey, 1993). Similarly, undercurrents of "child rescue" can serve to minimise the importance of culture, often through an almost deliberate confusion of culture with the wretched conditions from which the child has been "rescued". 'Brazil is a beautiful country, and when the children are older we will take them to visit it. But it is extremely corrupt and has a great social divide. A rich minority, vast shanty towns, very little birth control, huge poverty-stricken families, drink and drug problems and thousands of children living on the streets. Is that culture? I don't think so' (Humphrey and Humphrey, 1993, p 54). There is, of course, a serious point being made here, that concern with culture might seem something of a "luxury" to street children or those in large institutions. Yet the argument seems to go further than this, to rationalise inaction over identity issues – surely "rescue" and a good Western upbringing are sufficient – and it is interesting to note that intercountry adoptees have often reported expectations of "gratitude" (Enrico, 1999, p 4). Finally, it should be remembered that some would-be adopters pursue the intercountry option in order to avoid what they regard as the unhealthy influence of "political correctness" (PC) over domestic adoption in the UK.

Ethical dilemmas in ICA

In this section, I consider more directly some of the ethical issues associated with policy and practice in ICA in the UK. Particular attention is paid to the relationship between its "public" and "private" aspects, and to the perceived threat of a "two-tier service", whereby the parties involved in ICA receive services inferior to those of their domestic counterparts. Any examination of ethics in relation to ICA must also look at the wider context within which it takes place. This "bigger picture" is particularly important in opening up discussion of what constitutes the "best interests" of children. Within the UK, developments such as the Hague Convention and the recent Adoption (Intercountry

Aspects) Act 1999 can be seen as attempting to use regulation to promote good practice in ICA, with a sub-text of resolving the conflict between unsympathetic, unsupportive local authorities and thwarted adopters some of whom engage in abuses of various kinds. The logic is that if good practice in ICA is facilitated, then war can legitimately be waged against bad practice and abuses eradicated. The argument advanced here is that while improved practice must surely be welcomed, there remain significant problems for which regulation and support must not be seen as a panacea.

Within the arena of adoption practice itself, many of these problems and challenges relate to the division of labour between "sending" and "receiving" countries (Caiani-Praturion, 1991). In many of the former, poverty may mean that adoption services are limited to struggle against the grosser abuses – kidnap, trafficking, bribery, corruption – and ensuring the legality of adoption. Aspects of what would be taken as "good practice" in the UK may receive less attention. These might include the quality of information and counselling offered to birth relatives, preparation for the child to move, and handling of the move itself (Harper, 1994, p 22). Contact between adopters and birth relatives is comparatively unusual and information on the latter often lacking (Greenfield, 1995). In these circumstances, forms of "openness" are relatively rare. Collectively, such practices may reflect one or more of several factors: lack of resources, norms of child care practice, social stigma, threats to birth parents, or legal proscription of contact (sometimes intended to prevent abuses such as bribery), and perhaps also the preference of many intercountry adopters for a "clean break". Recurring themes in the accounts given in Humphrey and Humphrey (1993) are those of the flying visit, a sense of horror at local conditions and the "escape" with the child. However "understandable" they may be, these features often found in ICA have a significant shaping influence upon it. They include the difficulties faced by adopted children in understanding their background or tracing birth relatives (Ngabonziza, 1988, p 39; Hill, 1991, p 21; Carstens and Julia, 1995, p 30). As to the latter, beyond occasional eulogies about the nobility of their sacrifice, the disinterest shown in their plight in relation to adoption within debates on ICA is striking. One small example of this is the way in which the UK's legal

72

requirement that consent to adoption should not be given in the first six weeks after birth is portrayed simply as an irritating obstacle and is sometimes flouted (Humphrey and Humphrey, 1993, p 38, p 68).

Within the UK as a "receiving" country, a major aim during the 1990s has been to place ICA on a similar footing to domestic adoption and to avoid any hint of a "two-tier" service (Department of Health, 1998, p 53). In principle, there is no reason why intercountry adopters should not be assessed on a similar basis to their domestic counterparts, with the important proviso that assessments do not take place after a child has been brought into the country and are not biased by the consequences of refusal. There are, however, more subtle pressures which may serve to undermine equality of treatment. While the popular perception is that assessments, carried out by workers suspicious or even antagonistic towards ICA, are "unduly rigorous" (Humphrey and Humphrey, 1993, p 9), there is an opposite danger, namely of less rigorous standards being applied. The context for this is that ICA frequently operates as a "safety valve" for pressures on domestic adoption and especially the shortage of healthy babies. Although this means that there are many "suitable" applicants who are unable to adopt babies in the UK, there are also those who may be rejected as domestic adopters – on grounds of age, health, or attitudes to childrearing – and turn to ICA as an alternative. Other possible sources of pressure include the making of a payment for assessment (although "private" home studies will be banned under the 1999 Act) and the "child" in the mind of the assessor. Although no-one is inclined to admit it, all assessments of adopters' suitability are influenced by perceptions of the circumstances and alternative scenarios for the child. In the case of ICA, there is an obvious potential for (perceived) conditions in "sending" countries to exert downward pressure on the threshold of suitability.

Coverage of identity issues linked to "race" and ethnicity is always likely to be the thorniest aspect of assessment. As noted above, there is often resistance on the part of adopters to acknowledging their signifi-cance. For instance, in most of the narratives edited by Humphrey and Humphrey (1993), more space is given to playing down the relevance of ethnic identity than to any efforts the adopters were making, or intending to make, to promote it. To see the editors offer middle-class background and education as "evidence" of racial awareness (1993, p 7) surely smacks of complacency, though it is perhaps revealing about the unwillingness of many prospective adopters to have their awareness and attitudes scrutinised by social workers.

What then are the implications of these challenges for policy and practice on ICA in the UK? Some can be located at the level of professional practice and its legal and policy framework and with efforts to avoid the pitfalls outlined above. These issues will be considered further below, but it would be dangerous to separate discussion of policy and practice from the wider context of ICA. In particular, it is important to consider the desirability of ICA, not only for the profound ethical questions this raises, but also because the "answers" given exert a powerful, if often unacknowledged, influence over policy and practice. Competing values and divergent constructions of children's "best interests" are central to this broader debate.

ICA and competing value systems

Support for ICA in the UK is closely linked to the values of liberal individualism, including its tendency to play down the salience of "race" and ethnicity. Mirroring arguments often advanced for domestic adoption, ICA is seen as an ideal solution, bringing together parents with homes, love and care to offer and children who (desperately) need families. Poverty and deprivation provide important underpinnings for this ideal solution, accentuating the extent of "need" on the part of the child(ren) and the compassion of adopters. Although there are occasional bold claims about the strategic importance of ICA in relation to child welfare in developing countries (Altstein and Simon, 1991, p 191), it is more commonly portrayed as making a modest but very worthwhile contribution. The power of individualistic constructions of children's best interests is evident in various ways. First, adoption is a highly specific form of "help" and raises awkward questions regarding the relationship between the few who are "chosen" and the many who are left (Triseliotis, 1991, p 25). Focusing on the former is certainly reassuring to many adopters, as when one couple states that the sight of street children begging confirmed to them that they were 'doing the right thing'

(Humphrey and Humphrey, 1993, p 51). This leads on to a second point, namely that the interests of children may be subsumed by those of the adopters, rendering ICA more a service for adults than one for children (Duncan, 1993, p 9). Critics argue that, despite the emphasis often placed on saving children from death, poor health or the horrors of institutional life, most adopters are seeking the closest approximation to healthy babies, with only a minority targeting the 'most needy' (Warren, 1999, p 13). The individual focus is likewise apparent in research interest, which has been overwhelmingly concerned with the development and wellbeing of children after adoption and neglectful of the impact of ICA upon other children, whether in "sending" or "receiving" countries.

By contrast, opposition to, and scepticism towards, ICA is characterised by a markedly more "collective" view of children's best interests. This emphasis is detectable in the weight given to the racial and ethnic identities of children adopted transracially or transculturally. More importantly, however, it also underscores views which are antipathetic to ICA as a phenomenon, seeing it as at best irrelevant, and at worst detrimental, to the interests of children in "sending" countries. This is partly a matter of scale, with ICA offering 'an immediate, idealised life for a very small number of children instead of addressing the need to build a global future for all children' (Ngabonziza, 1991, p 77). Where poverty is pervasive, ICA can be seen as an inappropriate response in two senses. At the individual level, poverty is often the reason for relinquishment, including situations where payments are used to help a birth parent look after their other children (Ngabonziza, 1988, p 37; Humphrey and Humphrey, 1993, p 17, p 114). Not only does this raise issues about the basis for *consent* to adoption, but it throws into sharp relief the fact that the cost of preventive assistance 'is amazingly low when compared to the amounts of money that the adopters are willing to spend on ICA' (Ngabonziza, 1988, p 40). Of course, the machinery through which such alternatives can be realised is complex, but what is clearly highlighted is how the "help" available is on the adopters' terms. At the wider societal level, it is equally clear that the sometimes substantial resources provided through ICA do little to alleviate poverty, very often simply rewarding the intermediaries who promote it (Pierce and Vitillo, 1991, p 139; Carstens and Julia, 1995, p 28). This leads on to the existence of a "market" in ICA and its effects, especially in relation to the wide-ranging abuses which have long been associated with ICA (Duncan, 1993, p 9). "Responsible" supporters, and pragmatists who believe that ICA cannot in any event be prevented, tend to see a closely regulated but not unduly restricted market as the best protection against abuses. Conversely, opponents or those who are sceptical of the potential for effective regulation, see the very existence of ICA as an encouragement to abuses, through pressures to match supply and demand, and the vested interests of individual and agency intermediaries (Triseliotis, 1993, p 122). Ngabonziza (1988, p 37) emphasises the complex links when he contends that abuses such as corruption, child prostitution and trafficking are 'both cause and consequence' of the ICA market. There is also the question of how to define abuse in the context of ICA. As has also been found in the case of surrogacy, the boundaries of improper financial inducement are extremely difficult to draw and equally so to enforce. In ICA, the gross material disparities between typical adopters and birth relatives add to the problems, creating a situation where payments modest by western standards may appear as a "fortune" to a poor recipient in a developing country. Thus, beyond bribery in one form or another, the process can also be seen as exploitative of the often vast inequalities involved and for Triseliotis (1989, p 25), still frequently amounts to the purchase of children. It is on this basis that ICA has been attacked as neo-colonialist, especially in Africa (Ngabonziza, 1991, p 80; Carstens and Julia, 1995, p 28).

Equally contentious is the relationship between the market in ICA and the development of services for children and families in "sending" countries. It is at least plausible that ICA, especially if widespread, acts as an alternative or even deterrent to the development of both preventive family support services and other forms of child placement, including domestic adoption programmes. Carstens and Julia (1995, p 28) argue that ICA has little effect on the development of domestic services, but Sarri *et al* (1998) contend that the flow of children from Korea, especially to the USA, has significantly impeded service development in the former. There are, of course, many permutations between domestic services and recourse to ICA. The latter's supporters rightly contend that resources would not necessarily flow to child welfare services if ICA were curtailed. There is also the question of curtailment "sacrificing" the current and pressing needs of children for long-term and hypothetical gains. Nonetheless, it seems highly unlikely that any country with well-developed services for children would also be a significant "exporter" of children through ICA. Thus, at the very least, ICA stands as a marker of the need to develop domestic services (Dickens and Watts, 1996; Sellick, 1997; Warren, 1999).

Questions over the conduct and desirability of ICA are not confined to "sending" countries. Issues connected with ethnic identity and vulnerability to racism have already been referred to, but there are also important factors relating to official treatment of ICA in the UK. While the popular perception is one of "disapproval" and obstruction, there is also a history of "facilitating" practices which must change if there is to be the type of effective regulation which is pivotal to the new "post-Hague Convention" order. Despite large numbers of adopters bringing children into the country without Home Office clearance or home studies, they have invariably been granted entry by immigration officers, although as we shall see, rather different standards have been applied to minority ethnic Britons (Triseliotis, 1989, pp 25–6 and 1991, p 47; Humphrey and Humphrey, 1993, p 9). Courts too have frequently shown a willingness to sanction breaches of regulations, including those on illegal placements and illegal payments, by granting retrospective authorisation (see e.g. Rosenblatt, 1995, p. 224, or re WM, Adoption & Fostering, 21:1, Legal Notes, pp 58–9). The usual justification given is that child welfare outweighs public policy, but this also creates a situation where child placement regulations are so poorly enforced as to lose any protective value. Van de Flier Davis says of the USA that, 'in some cases the penalty for littering is higher than the penalty for violating child placement regulations' (1995, p 27). Surely one of the disturbing cases in the UK has been that of Edita Keranovic, an orphaned victim of the Bosnian conflict "rescued" by a British family. The latter went on to pursue adoption despite knowing that members of the extended family were actively seeking her return, and by presenting false information to the authorities. Although condemning their 'appalling irresponsibility', the judge decided that Edita should remain with them, albeit as a ward.

Tellingly, the decision was praised by Barbara Mostyn of the Campaign for Intercountry Adoption as a ruling in favour of the child rather than the birth relatives (*The Guardian*, 18 February 1997).

While the dilemmas are as obvious as they are painful, such judgements are disturbing for various reasons. Of particular concern is their narrowness and, in some respects, ethnocentricity. Setting aside questions raised about the suitability of adopters, what is most striking is the way in which attachment is taken to override virtually all other considerations and that the wider implications of the judgements are ignored. Thus, the consistent message given is that abuses of process will be tolerated in all but the most extreme circumstances, offering a green light to unscrupulous adopters and putting children at risk. It remains to be seen how far judges will be prepared under new legislation to take a firmer line with those who flout the rules. Ethnocentricity is apparent in the ways in which "Western" norms are used to interpret "the best interests of the child". This applies not only to the particular elevation of attachment but also in interpretation of the (un)importance of religion and relationships with birth family. For example, it is clear that the Keranovic case was judged according to Western rather than Bosnian and Islamic criteria.

An amalgam of ethnocentricity and arguably institutional racism is also evident in the differential treatment meted out to white intercountry adopters and minority ethnic Britons attempting to bring children to the UK. While, as we have seen, the passage of the former tends to be smoothed by both formal and informal practices, the pathway for the latter is frequently strewn with obstacles. The immigration service's propensity for racialised mistrust is well-known, and it is not surprising that minority ethnic applications for ICA have often been challenged and/or rejected. Rosenblatt (1995) highlights a number of cases which ended in tribunals or court cases where the immigration service or the Home Secretary had challenged the genuineness of the adoption. (One can only speculate on how many applications are stopped before reaching the courts.) The grounds have varied, from challenges to the veracity of applicants' circumstances to claims that the adopter wanted someone to look after them in their old age, or that the major purpose of the adoption was to gain British nationality or bypass immigration controls. Of course, no doubt sometimes the allegations are well-founded and it should also be noted that the courts do not always support the officials against the adopters. Nonetheless, while there is ample evidence that the immigration authorities exercise their discretion in racialised ways, courts often choose or feel obliged to uphold their use of discretion in individual cases. Ethnocentric norms on the meaning of adoption are also influential in these processes. Many minority ethnic intercountry adoptions have involved older children and/or those who are related to the adopters, and this departure from stranger, baby/toddler adoption seems to add to the mistrust. Practices such as adoption by a childless aunt and uncle have often been challenged as "not genuine" on the grounds that the birth parents were able to look after their child (Rosenblatt, 1995, p 239, p 245 and p 247). The contrast between such attitudes and the readiness of Western countries to interpret terms such as "abandonment" or "orphan" extremely loosely to permit (white) ICA is striking (Ngabonziza, 1991, p 78; Humphrey and Humphrey, 1993, p 38).

Towards an ethical policy for ICA

It is argued here that the delivery of an ethical policy for ICA in the UK depends not only on issues of legal regulation and professional practice but also, crucially, on their underpinning values and wider contexts. There is no doubt that significant improvements will ensue from moving towards more closely regulated *and* supported ICA, along the lines of countries such as the Netherlands and Sweden (Selman, 1993). Better preparation for adopters, agency links to work more effectively with "sending" countries and to facilitate matching, and post-adoption support (especially in case of special needs adoptions), would all serve to improve the quality of adoptive experiences. It should go without saying that tackling abuses is vital, although it remains to be seen how far there is a genuine political will to do this.

Perhaps the most vexatious questions relate to how far ICA should be "promoted" and if so on what basis. It can be argued that the hitherto unsatisfactory situation regarding ICA owes much to its being "tolerated" so long as it remained a small-scale, private and almost clandestine activity. Prime Minister John Major, for example, talked of promoting

ICA even while his government was withdrawing funding from the Overseas Adoption Helpline (*The Guardian*, 4 December 1996). In relation to the promotion of ICA, there are broadly two alternative models which loosely correspond to the competing value positions outlined earlier. The liberal individualist approach would proffer legal and professional reform within the existing value framework. This would serve to leave ICA primarily as a service for (childless) adults, placing relatively little emphasis on issues of identity and significantly influenced by the assumptions of child rescue. There is, however, a second model, advocated in this paper, in which ICA could both better reflect Britain as a multiracial society and be part of a more strategic response to child welfare.

Domestically, the starting point lies with recognition of the importance of racial and cultural identities for intercountry adoptees. This in turn means that assessment of adopters must give due weight to their awareness and commitment in these areas, and crucially, their location and networks. Where the adoption is transracial, it is important that the adopters live in a multiracial area and have a significant degree of ethnic diversity within their close relationships. This links to a wider issue, namely the position and voice of minority ethnic Britons in relation to ICA. If emphasis within the latter is to shift towards it being more of a service to children, there are strong grounds for greater involvement of minority communities. Apart from encouraging minority ethnic ICA (or even removing some of the barriers to it), there is also the possibility of communities providing resources for adopted children of "similar" ethnic origin. Support for ICA from minority communities would also increase its legitimacy and help to allay concerns over its "imperialistic" tendencies. The value of support groups among those adopting from the same country has often been acknowledged (Humphrey and Humphrey, 1993, p 106; Selman and White, 1994, p 9). How much more powerful would be their link to families who had migrated from those same countries in recent times. If, on the other hand, such support is not forthcoming, this should raise serious questions for wider debate.

Equally important is the relationship between ICA and broader treatment of migrants, refugees or asylum seekers, children or adult (Argent, 1996; Jones, 1998). It is noteworthy that the Netherlands and

Sweden, often held up as offering good practice models in ICA, have also been more welcoming places to migrants than Britain in recent times. This wider link is important in two respects. First, it gives an indication of the extent of prejudice and discrimination which inter-country adoptees are likely to face. Second, it would surely be intolerable if ICA were to be treated entirely as a "special case" in terms of minority ethnic migration – a kind of swipe card through an otherwise impene-trable security. Thus, promotion of ICA should go hand-in-hand with a determined assault on institutional racism within immigration services and beyond.

Abroad, the differences of approach hinge on the nature of respon-sibility held or accepted for children in "sending" countries. In the liberal model, responsibilities are essentially individual, case-specific and "activated" when a child becomes linked to prospective adopters. The alternative, more collective model, would entail adoption agencies and government taking a wider responsibility for children's welfare in "sending" countries. If, as most would accept, the "need" for ICA reflects a combination of poverty and/or lack of domestic services, then the only ethical basis for it must be as a temporary measure, accompanied by *active work* to ensure that this "need" is reduced and ultimately elimi-nated. One obvious measure is more active promotion of alternatives to ICA, for example, sponsorship or forms of "adoption from abroad", which represent an incalculably more effective use of humanitarian resources and hence a more genuine service for children. There could also be creative ways of building on such schemes to develop close and enduring personal relationships without the total severance usually associated with ICA. Agencies involved in ICA should be required to contribute to wider child care provision in "sending" countries as part of any terms of approval, while governments in "receiving" countries such as the UK also have a crucial role to play in terms of both regulation and resourcing. With the UK government's much-vaunted "joined-up think-ing", there is considerable scope to ensure that any facilitation of ICA is closely linked to development of provision which will hasten its eventual disappearance. This is possible through aid programmes and co-ordination of non-governmental organisation (NGO) activity, but might also, for example, include bilateral agreements with "sending" countries to boost their (intercountry) adoption infrastructure if this is matched by commitment to development of domestic services.

It is difficult to be optimistic regarding how much of this more collective approach to ICA will be pursued in the UK (and it should be noted that the "post-Hague" framework remains firmly individualistic in approach). The liberal values which underpin support for ICA would tend to be antipathetic to the suggestions made above relating to assessment and approval, the involvement of minority ethnic communities and the wider view of responsibility for child welfare in "sending" countries. Instead, emphasis would be placed on the freedoms of prospective adopters to pursue ICA with a minimum of restrictions, and to legitimately utilise their favourable market position within the global economy. This "free market" pressure can be seen most clearly in the USA, but is also present to a degree in the UK. The impetus comes from ensuring the "supply" of children, and it is clear that those involved have no interest in removing the "need" for ICA. Although it may be pejorative to term this stance "imperialistic", there are three telling words within Simon *et al*'s (1994) "bottom line" referred to above "Or even adopted" makes clear that, for ICA supporters such as Simon, to be in the West is simply superior to anything developing countries have to offer. Beneath the child-centred language lies a hegemonic view that the children of other countries are "our children", but the partiality of the liberal view becomes clearer when it is realised that they are only "our children" when "we" want to adopt them. While successive governments in the UK have closely adhered to the liberal view, albeit largely by default, an ethical policy on ICA demands that if it is to have any long-term future, it must be firmly located within the context of broadly-based services for children in "sending" countries.

References

Altstein H and Simon R (1991) 'Summary and concluding remarks', in Altstein, H and Simon R (eds) *Intercountry Adoption: Multinational perspectives*, New York: Praeger.

Argent H (1996) 'Children in need: unaccompanied refugees', *Adoption & Fostering*, 20:1, pp 24–29.

Bagley C (1993) *International and Transracial Adoptions: A mental health perspective*, Avebury: Aldershot.

Caiani-Praturion G (1991) 'Intercountry adoption in European legislation', in Hibbs E (ed) *Adoption: International perspectives*, MadisonL International Universities Press.

Carstens C and Julia M (1995) 'Legal, policy and practice issues for intercountry adoptions in the United States', *Adoption & Fostering*, 19:4, pp 26–33.

Dalen M and Sætersdal B (1987) 'Transracial adoptions in Norway', *Adoption & Fostering*, 11:4, pp 44–6.

Department of Health (1998) *Adoption – Achieving the Right Balance*, LAC(98)20, London: Department of Health.

Dickens J and Watts J (1996) 'Developing alternatives to residential care in Romania', *Adoption & Fostering*, 20:3, pp 8–13.

Duncan W (1993) 'The Hague Convention on the Protection of Children and Co-operation in Respect of Intercountry Adoption', *Adoption & Fostering*, 17:3, pp 9–13.

Enrico D (1999) 'Korean adoptee and adoptive parent tells about the gathering of Korean adoptees', *Adopted Child*, 18:11, pp 1–4.

Feigelman W and Silverman A (1983) *Chosen Children: New patterns of adoptive relationships,* New York: Praeger.

Greenfield J (1995) 'Intercountry adoption: a comparison between France and England', *Adoption & Fostering*, 19:2, pp 31–6.

Harper J (1994) 'Counselling issues in intercountry adoption disruption', *Adoption & Fostering*, 18:2, pp 20–6.

Hill M (1991) 'Concepts of parenthood and their application to adoption', *Adoption & Fostering*, 15:4, pp 16–23.

Humphrey M and Humphrey H (eds) (1993*) Intercountry Adoption: Practical experiences,* London: Routledge.

Jones A (1998) *The Child Welfare Implications of UK Immigration & Asylum Policy*, Manchester: Manchester Metropolitan University.

Kirton D (2000) *"Race", Ethnicity and Adoption*, Buckingham: Open University Press.

Kirton D and Woodger D (1999) 'Experiences of transracial adoption', in British Agencies for Adoption and Fostering, *Assessment, Preparation and Support: Implications from research*, London: BAAF.

McRoy R (1991) 'Significance of ethnic and racial identity in intercountry adoption within the United States', *Adoption & Fostering*, 15:4, pp 53–60.

Ngabonziza D (1988) 'Intercountry adoption: in whose best interests?', *Adoption & Fostering*, 12:1, pp 35–40.

Ngabonziza D (1991) 'Moral and political issues facing relinquishing countries', *Adoption & Fostering*, 15:4, pp 75–80.

Pierce W and Vitillo R (1991) 'Independent adoptions and the "baby market" ', in Hibbs E (ed) *Adoption: International perspectives*, Madison: International Universities Press.

Rosenblatt J (1995) *International Adoption*, London: Sweet and Maxwell.

Rutter M (1998) 'Development, catch-up and deficit following adoption after severe global early privation', *Journal of Child Psychology and Psychiatry*, 39:4, pp 465–76.

Sarri R, Baik Y and Bombyk M (1998) 'Goal displacement and dependency in South Korean-United States intercountry adoption', *Children and Youth Services Review*, 20–1/2, 87–114.

Sellick C (1997) 'Developing professional social work practice in Romania', *Social Work in Europe*, 4:2, pp 49–52.

Selman P (1993) 'Services for intercountry adoption in the UK: some lessons from Europe', *Adoption & Fostering*, 17:3, pp 14–19.

Selman P and White J (1994) 'Mediation and the role of "accredited bodies" in intercountry adoption', *Adoption & Fostering*, 18:2, pp 7–13.

Simon R and Altstein H (1987) *Transracial Adoptees and their Families: A study of identity and commitment*, New York: Praeger.

Simon R, Altstein H and Melli M (1994) *The Case for Transracial Adoption*, Washington DC: American University Press.

Tizard B and Pheonix A (1993) *Black, White or Mixed Race? Race and racism in the lives of young people of mixed parentage*, London: Routledge.

Triseliotis J (1989) 'Some moral and practical issues in adoption work', *Adoption & Fostering*, 13:2, pp 21–7.

Triseliotis J (1991) 'Intercountry adoption: a brief overview of the research evidence', *Adoption & Fostering*, 15:4, pp 46–52.

Triseliotis J (1993) 'Intercountry adoption: in whose best interest?', in Humphrey and Humphrey (eds) op cit.

Triseliotis J, Shireman J and Hundleby M (1997) *Adoption: Theory, policy and practice*, London: Cassell.

Van de Flier Davis, D (1995) 'Capitalising on adoption', *Adoption & Fostering*, 19:2, pp 25–30.

Warren C (1999) *Intercountry Adoption: A social work perspective*, Social Work Monographs No 171, Norwich: University of East Anglia.

5 Changes in attitudes in three generations of adoptive parents: 1950–2000

Rene Hoksbergen

Rene Hoksbergen, married to the mother of his two children, studied social psychology and social pedagogics at University of Amsterdam. He was Senior Professor of Adoption 1984-2000 at the University of Utrecht, where he founded the Adoption Centre. He has written extensively on issues of intercountry adoption and modern procreation, and lectures in many countries. At present he is leading a research project titled "Romanian adoptive children".

Introduction

In most Western countries the phenomenon of adoption has existed for more than half a century. Freundlich (1998) estimates that between two and three per cent of the population of the USA has been adopted. The organisation, Americans for Open Records (AMFOR), estimates that half the population in the USA has an adoption in their immediate family (Carangelo, 1999). In the last three decades domestic – *intracountry* – *non-relative* adoption (excluding step-parent adoptions) has become much less important, particularly in mainland European countries. In the Scandinavian countries and the Netherlands, for instance, the number of domestic adoptions has dropped to the relatively low level of two to four children per one million inhabitants from 50 to 100 children three decades ago. The number of domestic adoptions in the USA has also decreased but remains much higher than in Europe.

During the same period *intercountry* adoption has grown in importance, but we must not forget that the movement of children between countries existed for two centuries before this. In the 1800s, following the Potato Famine, Irish children were sent to Canada and the USA (Kittson, 1968) and between 1866 and the close of 1915, children cared for in Barnardo's homes in the UK were sent to North America (Kittson, 1968). These "orphan trains" continued until World War II. Bean and

Melville (1989, p 1) see the process of "child migration" as starting as early as 1618 and continuing until 1967, involving 150,000 children moving to Canada, Australia, New Zealand and other parts of the British Empire.

In the USA, intercountry/transracial adoption developed as a consequence of World War II. Between 1948 and 1962, about 2,000 German and 3,000 Japanese children were adopted by American families (Silverman and Weitzman, 1986). In 1998 a total of 15,774 adoptive children arrived in the USA, most of them from the Russian Federation, China, South Korea and Guatemala (see Selman, Chapter 1 and Gailey, Chapter 17). In Western Europe, intercountry adoption started in the 1960s and, in some countries, it is now practically the only road to adoption.

Changes in society influencing the adoption phenomenon

If we want to understand why domestic adoption has decreased so drastically in the last three decades and why intercountry adoption has come into existence on a large scale, we must keep in mind that adoptive kinship is a pattern of social relationships firmly connected to the family system in the culture of the country (Kirk, 1985). In the countries concerned social relationships (and legal requirements) have changed considerably during the last decades. This means that modern adoption and changes in its character can best be understood when we see it as firmly connected to the evolving changes in culture and the structure of society.

Adoption used to be a taboo phenomenon and for that reason it was (and sometimes still is) often treated as a secret. In Western countries this taboo has vanished almost completely. Nowadays infertile couples as well as couples with biological children adopt, and transracial adoption is an accepted phenomenon in most societies. Although there is still a preference for healthy babies, the successful placement of disabled children is now well documented in the UK and USA (Glidden, 1990; Mason, Selman and Hughes, 1999).

The reality of the biological family and its importance for the adoptee is now often discussed in the process of preparing prospective adoptive parents. Open adoption is increasingly practised. Unmarried mothers are less stigmatised and their grief due to the relinquishment of the child is taken seriously by adoption agencies and modern adoptive parents (Triseliotis, Shireman and Hundleby, 1997; Grotevant and McRoy, 1998).

In this chapter I put forward an interpretation of some statistical and substantive changes in intercountry and intracountry adoptions, which are based on the hypothesis that, in Western countries in the second half of the 20th century, a pattern of three generations of adoptive parents has emerged. This hypothesis will then be used as a frame of reference for the interpretation of the changes in the motivation of adoptive parents, their value orientations and preferred characteristics in an adoptive child.

A pattern of generations

The hypothesis that a pattern of generations has emerged in Western societies was first developed in the mid-1980s and has been elaborated and tested since that time (Becker, 1985, 1987). The concept of a generation or "cohort" has been defined by Ryder (1965, p 843) as 'the aggregate of individuals, within some population definition, who experienced the same event within the same time interval'.

We hypothesise that since World War II three different generations of adoptive parents have emerged:

- the traditional-closed generation (adoptions between 1950–1970)
- the open-idealistic generation (adoptions between 1970–1985)
- the materialistic-realistic generation (adoption since 1985).

The hypothesis: three different adoptive generations

When we speak of an adoptive generation, we mean a cohort of parents who have adopted at least one non-related child, bearing in mind that adoptive parents are on average about eight years older than other parents (Hoksbergen, 1979; Feigelman and Silverman, 1983) but that there is often a maximum allowed age difference – in most countries between 40 to 45 years – between the eldest parent and the adopted child.

These, on average, somewhat older (adoptive) parents have different coping patterns in the adoptive parent–child relationship. They show a coping pattern characterised as either the *Rejection-of-Difference* attitude (RD), or *Acknowledgement-of-Difference* attitude (AD) (Kirk,

1963). In the past, most adopters seemed not to be able to acknowledge the difference between adoptive and biological parenthood. According to Kirk (1981) the RD attitude may help to assuage the pains of their own deprivation due to their involuntarily childlessness, but does not in the long run further the achievement of their family's integration.

When adoptive children are of the same "race" as the adoptive parents it is much easier to hide the fact of adoption and to maintain the illusion that your parenthood is not different from that of biological parents. However, since most adoptive children in mainland European countries today are of a different "race" compared with their adoptive parents, it is clear that the RD attitude is less easy to maintain.

Kirk's concept of different attitudes of adoptive parents, however, still has much relevance, primarily because some adoptive parents still may have the feeling and belief that the adopted child fully belongs to them, that their adoptee is really their child. As long as the adopted child, whether adopted intracountry or intercountry, is very young, this belief can easily be maintained. As soon as the adopted child enters school life, and later the stage of pre-adolescence, it will be much less easy to maintain the attitude of RD. Difficult questions from the child about his or her background, and reactions and questions from people outside the family might cause serious psychological problems in these adoptive families.

The "traditional-closed generation" adoptive parents: adoptions before 1970

The first large generation of adoptive parents in the Netherlands was born between 1920 and 1935, the pre-war generation. The majority of these parents adopted their first child between 1955 and 1970. This pre-war generation consists of parents for whom adoption was an alternative means to having a child. The first choice would have been a child of their own. Having an adoptive child was viewed as functional for the needs and wishes of the adoptive parents. Adoption was seen primarily as a service for childless couples, a way of providing them with a *substitute child*, to satisfy their emotional needs or to cement their marriage (Tizard, 1978). The main goal of these families was to replicate a birth family (Bussiere, 1998). According to this view, only infertile couples would be offered a child. It was assumed that a subsequent biological child would result in the rejection of the adopted child (Schneider, 1995). Research in the Netherlands (Geerans and Hoksbergen, 1991) confirmed Schneider's view that, on average, parents with adoptive and biological children encounter more deep and ongoing psycho-social problems in their families than full adoptive families.

The pre-war generation held conventional values about marriage, family life, law, sexual behaviour, and authority (Becker, 1985). This was reflected in the way in which they adopted a child. They followed the existing regulations and accepted the ideas, values and norms of the sometimes very authoritarian and dominating social workers. As soon as the child had been placed into the family the door was often closed to outsiders. Contacts with other adoptive parents were not especially encouraged by social workers (Reitz and Watson, 1992). If family problems developed after the arrival of the adopted child, adoptive parents often hesitated for a long time before asking for help from professionals in child and family care.

What the above suggests is a family system with a strong traditional, closed, internally-oriented character. Adoption plans were hardly discussed because the social environment surrounding the family had problems in dealing with the topic of adoption (Kirk, 1985). The social status of the biological parents was low and children with known pathology in their background were considered unadoptable (Cole and Donley, 1990). Unmarried biological parents, especially the mother, were advised to relinquish their baby and were promised secrecy and anonymity – they were even told by social workers that they would soon forget the whole affair (Marcus, 1981).

Adoptive parents were not given much information concerning the background of the child (Sokoloff, 1993). If the child had already been given a name, this was often changed by the new parents. The prevailing wisdom was that the child should be told about the adoption when it was four to six years of age, but this fact of life should not be stressed too much. It was thought desirable that the main attitude of adoptive parents towards their kinship was one of RD between their adoptive kinship and biological kinship (Kirk, 1985).

In Kirk's original study of North American domestic adoptions from

the 1960s, a majority of parents showed low scores on the AD difference measured on a six point scale about concern for the birth family
(Kirk, 1985, pp 43–44). We have replicated Kirk's investigation,
using data collected from a group of 87 Dutch parents who had
adopted a child from Thailand between 1974 and 1979 (Hoksbergen
et al, 1987). The supposition that the RD attitude prevailed in the
period before 1970 was tested by comparing Kirk's results (Kirk,
1981) with our results in the Netherlands (Hoksbergen et al, 1987)
where the AD attitude was dominant. In Kirk's group the mode (31 per
cent) was at 0 yes responses and in our data (29 per cent) at 4 yes
responses.

Role handicap for adoptive parents

Three to four decades ago the role of being an adoptive parent of a non-
related child or of being an adopted child was almost completely new in
society. Adoptive parents had to find out themselves how to deal with
their role as father/mother, and problems regarding the adoption status
of the parents and the child had to be answered and solved by the
individuals themselves. There was no script available for adoptive
parenthood. Kirk (1985, pp 8–9) calls this the "role handicap" of
adoptive parents.

Adoption professionals did not know very much about the social and
individual consequences of adoption and certainly not about the effects
for the representatives of the whole adoption triangle (Sorosky, Baran
and Pannor, 1984). The information that professionals would pass on to
the adoptive parents was highly influenced by their ideas about unwed
mothers, the importance of heredity and family life in general.

For many parents, one way to cope with their role handicap was to
adopt the RD attitude. They were convinced that this attitude would give
the child the best chances for attachment to and integration into the
adoptive family. Dealing with the background of the child, their biological parents and their roots was no issue at all.

Summary

The closed and traditional generation consisted for the most part of
infertile couples who adopted babies of the same "race". Adoption was

surrounded by an atmosphere of secrecy. There was a role-handicap for adoptive parents and the roots of the adopted person were ignored. The predominant attitude was one of rejection-of-differences between adoptive and biological kinship.

The open and idealistic adoptive parent: adoptions between 1970–1985

In the late 1960s and 1970s, many cultural values and norms changed. This cultural revolution has had a large influence on adoption practice, which can be seen in changes in the second generation of adoptive parents. This generation has been characterised as open, romantic, and idealistic. The critical changes included those relating to the place of women in society, ideas about sexuality and abortion, the decreased influence of the authorities, the emergence of the one-parent family, the impact of television, the growing social mobility and an emphasis on the influence of nurture over nature. In the 1960s, opinion was growing that the negative effects of social class differences, for instance on the level of school participation, could be conquered by influencing nurture.

Significant changes in adoption practice

In the field of adoption, the significant change has been the greater openness with regard to intimate subjects. Sexuality (including homosexuality), problems with fertility, marital problems, the effects of relinquishment for biological parents and those of adoption for adoptees – all these have become subjects of a more general discussion, not only for an educated elite. The belief that nurture (of adoptive parents) was of more importance than nature for the development of the personality has also been crucial.

An important consequence was that adoption has lost its secretive character. A much larger sector of society began to deem adoption a positive solution to infertility and an acceptable way to start or enlarge the family. For this generation adoption was seen more often as a form of *child care*, a way of rearing children whose biological family could not, or would not, look after them, although for most adopters the main motive continued to be to form or enlarge a family.

We see three main effects as a result of these changes in society.

- Many more couples, including fertile couples, wished to adopt a child.
- Relinquishment of a child by unmarried mothers was no longer the norm in Western countries.
- Intercountry and transracial adoption became an obvious, though not uncriticised, result following on from the first two effects (Hoksbergen, 1996).

One of the important consequences of the Korean War (1950–1953) was the large numbers of Korean children who became transracially adopted. In West European countries large numbers of children from Asia and South America first arrived in the early 1970s. In the US, Harry Holt established the first agency to find homes for children of mixed ethnicity (American-Korean). Similar European organisations were established ten to twenty years later (see Andersson, Chapter 19).

When the professionals in Western adoption organisations, full of enthusiasm and involvement, started their work with placing children from the Third World into Western adoptive homes, they first had to overcome bureaucratic inertia, the lack of adequate laws and procedures, and the scepticism of some authorities. But the social and cultural climate of society in these first years of intercountry adoption was ready for important changes in ideas about child welfare in the adoption field. The effect was that between 1970 and 1985 a growing number of parents in mainland Europe chose intercountry, and mostly transracial, adoption. In the Netherlands in 1970, over 80 per cent of non-relative adoptions involved Dutch children; a decade later this had fallen to about 11 per cent and by 1995 less than 8 per cent of adoptions were domestic. In Norway the proportion of domestic adoptions fell from 78 per cent in 1970 to 15 per cent in 1995 (Hoksbergen, 1998). A similar pattern is found in Finland, Sweden (see Andersson, Chapter 19) and other mainland European countries.

The increase in total numbers of intercountry adoptions stopped around 1985 (see Selman, Chapter 1) and in the Netherlands and Sweden we have seen a substantial decline since the late 1980s and early 1990s. However, in the USA the number of intercountry adoptions rose sharply in the 1990s, following a decline in the late 1980s.

Why these changes?

How did this change in the adoption field become possible? Western European couples who adopted a child between 1970 and 1985 looked at adoption differently from the first generation of adoptive parents. Official regulations were greatly improved during this period. The media, especially television, presented intercountry adoption as "help for children in need". Adoption was openly recommended as a last possibility for these children to survive and develop normally. As a result of this, politicians and authorities could not lag behind and formal barriers were levelled. The fact that research on intercountry and transracial adoption (e.g. Feigelman and Silverman, 1983; Hoksbergen, 1979) was showing positive results was also important in the promotion of intercountry adoption.

The AD attitude prevails

For the second generation of adoptive parents, one consequence of this research and the possible basis for their enthusiasm, was that they had little cause for feeling any doubts regarding their adoption plans. Therefore, the motives of these prospective adoptive couples were generally idealistic and expectations concerning their possibilities to educate an adoptee of any age were high. This open attitude toward children in need led to a great willingness, especially amongst parents with birth children of their own, to adopt older and disabled children – the so-called "hard-to-place" children.

The adoptive couples were predominantly middle and upper-middle class (Hoksbergen, 1979; Feigelman and Silverman, 1983; Verhulst *et al*, 1989, 1992). They were financially able to help children and wanted also to do something to address the problem of poverty in the Third World. Their motives for adoption were strongly influenced by factors external to the family. One of the results of their idealism was that millions of dollars collected by adoption agencies were sent to Asia and South America. The attitudes of this second generation toward adoption were marked by an *acknowledgement-of-difference* (AD).

However, there was another side to the story of adoption in this period. The pioneers and professionals of the adoption organisations did not seem to realise that adoptive families might have to encounter deep psychological and educational problems with their adopted child. During the 1980s, a number of studies found that the older the child at placement, the greater the probability he or she would exhibit problem s later (Hoksbergen and Walenkamp, 1991; Verhulst et al, 1992). This led to an increasing controversy in the Netherlands concerning the problematic aspects of foreign adoption (Hoksbergen, 1997). Research findings (Hoksbergen et al, 1988) revealed that a relatively large number of foreign adoptees were placed in residential care – 5 to 6 per cent of all foreign adoptees, which was five times the rate for Dutch-born children.

Between 1984 and 1987, the psychological problems of foreign adoptees became an important topic for radio and television programmes. An important consequence of the increased awareness that adoption of a foreign child might lead to intense family problems has been a large change in the composition of the group of adoptive parents, culminating in what I call the third adoption generation.

The third adoption generation: the realistic generation, 1985–the present

By the beginning of the 1980s, when large numbers of children adopted from abroad had reached adolescence, it became clear that many families were facing enormous psychological and emotional problems. In an extensive study by Verhulst and Versluis-den Bieman (see Verhulst, Chapter 7), adopted boys aged 12–15 were shown to have problem behaviours in areas such as delinquency (stealing, lying, destructiveness) and hyperactivity (poor concentration, nervousness, excessive activity, poor grades in school). Adopted girls of a similar age had problem behaviours relating to schizoid characteristics (hearing and/or seeing things that do not exist, strange behaviour, daydreams, nightmares, fearfulness) and cruelty (destructiveness, aggression, stealing, poor contacts with peers).

These and other psychological problems in the adoptive family were directly connected with difficulties in raising an adopted child (Jewett, 1982; Egmond, 1987; Hoksbergen et al, 1988; Verhulst and Versluis-den Bieman, 1989; Hoksbergen, 1997). As a result, the idealism and often high expectations characteristic of (upper) middle class families were met by much disappointment. In Belgium and the Netherlands adoptive parents who were facing these enormous problems even felt the need to organise themselves, because they had the impression that their problems were not taken seriously enough by adoption professionals and service providers. With the help of television, and the publication of accounts of their experiences in important newspapers, even a few biographies (Egmond, 1987; Grasvelt, 1989), these parents made it perfectly clear that there was a difficult side (Riben, 1988) to intercountry adoption.

The need for international rules

In addition to the need for more professionalisation of support services, there was also a great need for better international rules and greater international understanding of intercountry adoption. The enthusiasm of the pioneers, most of them adoptive parents themselves, sometimes led to carelessness. Other parents, tired of long waiting lists and bureaucracy, managed to get a foreign child on their own without considering too closely official procedures, laws and the amounts of money requested by lawyers and other mediators in the Third World.

In 1986, the General Assembly of the United Nations issued its Declaration on Social and Legal Principles relating to Adoption and Foster Placement of Children nationally and internationally. Intercountry adoption would be approved under certain conditions. On 20 November 1989, the United Nations' General Assembly approved the *Convention on the Rights of the Child*. In Articles 20 and 21 of the Convention special references were made for the first time to national and inter-country adoption.

A more realistic approach to foreign adoption

This third generation had much more scientific and clinical information at its disposal. These adoptive parents knew a lot more about the adjustment problems of children adopted from abroad. They also began to recognise the need of their adopted child, now adolescent or adult, to search for their background. A study by Storsbergen (1995) of the searching behaviour of adoptees adopted in the Netherlands from Greece showed that the vast majority (80 per cent) of them want to visit their country of origin and search for their biological family, and that 23 per cent had actually succeeded in meeting their birth parents.

The effect has been that the atmosphere around intercountry adoption has become more realistic in recent years and there is much less enthusiasm and idealism. The expectations of the parents are more in line with the reality of the behaviour of children with a difficult background. These expectations are definitely less romantic than those of the open-idealistic generation of adoptive parents; the latter's idealism and concern about the poverty in the Third World has decreased as well. Many projects in the Third World continue to receive support, but relatively less than a decade ago.

In the Netherlands and Sweden, the number of applicants for adoption has dropped dramatically since 1985. According to the Dutch adoption agencies it has become much more difficult to find families for older children and those with special needs. In contrast, in the USA the number of intercountry adoptions has increased – from 7,093 in 1990 to 15,774 in 1998. In the USA, although we see the same difficulty in placing older children, more older children than ever are being adopted, because the number of infants available for domestic adoption is decreasing and there are more organisations with programmes to expand the number of families willing to accept a special needs child, e.g. The Adoption Exchange (Van der Flier, 1994).

Fewer adoptions by parents with birth children

Another effect of the changes in this generation of adoptive parents has been that fewer couples with one or more children of their own apply for adoption. In Sweden, in the 1970s, amongst the families having adopted through the two main organisations, some 20 per cent had biological children (Johansson, 1976); the proportion is now about 12 per cent. In the Netherlands, less than 10 per cent of the first generation (up to 1971) consisted of couples with children of their own. For the second generation, the proportion of couples with birth children rose to 32 per cent, but for the third generation (since 1985) this number fell to 23 per cent in 1993.

Conclusions

The hypothesis that a pattern involving three distinct generations of adoptive parents has emerged in the 20th century in Western countries seems to correspond to important changes in the field of adoption. We have noticed major changes in the values of the last two generations of adoptive parents. Important changes – like the enormous decrease in domestic adoption and the replacement of these traditional adoptions by intercountry adoptions, of which most are transracial adoptions – can be more easily understood now. Our three generations of adoption – the traditional-closed, the open-idealistic and the materialistic-realistic generation – behave in ways that could be expected.

Looking at the last adoption generation we expect that intercountry adoption in Europe in the coming decades will never again become as popular as it was during the period of the open-idealistic generation. The number of adoptions to the US has increased, largely as a response to the opening up of adoption from China and Russia, but there is no indication that figures will change much in the Netherlands, Belgium and Scandinavia, although there has been a small increase arising from adoptions from China. Fewer fertile couples will adopt and more children, particularly older children, will become "hard to place". Modern fertility techniques will be very significant and will also lead to a decline in the number of parents seeking to adopt children. This is because couples formerly considered to be infertile will now have more reproductive technologies available to address their fertility problems and they will make more extensive efforts to have a child of their own.

This chapter is a revised and updated version of an article originally published in the journal, "Adoption Quarterly" (2:2 pp 37–55), under the title 'Changes in motivation for adoption, value orientations and behaviour in three generations of adoptive parents'.

Prof. Dr René A C Hoksbergen is affiliated to The Utrecht University. Address correspondence to R A C Hoksbergen, Hartmanlaan 20, 3768 XH Soest, The Netherlands
fax/tel. 31-35-6018069
R.Hoksbergen@fss.uu.nl

References

Bean P and Melville J (1989) *Lost Children of the Empire*, London: Unwin Hyman.

Becker H A (1985) 'Dutch generations today', *Netherlands Institute of Advanced Studies in Humanities and Social Sciences*, Wassenaar: NIA, Paper.

Becker H A (1987) *Generations and Social Inequality*, Utrecht: University.

Bussiere A (1998) 'The development of adoption law', *Adoption Quartely*, 1, pp 3–25.

Carangelo L (1999) *Statistics of Adoption*, Palm Desert: Americans for Open Records.

Cole E S and Donley K S (1990) 'History, values, and placement policy issues', in Brodzinsky D M and Schechter M D (eds), *The Psychology of Adoption*, New York/Oxford: Oxford University Press.

Egmond van G (1987) *Bodemloos bestaan: Problemen met adoptiekinderen (Bottomless Existence: Problems with adoptive children)*, Baarn: AMBO.

Feigelman W and Silverman A R (1983) *Chosen Children: New patterns of adoptive relationships*, New York: Praeger.

Glidden L M (1990) *Formed Families: Adoption of children with handicaps*, New York: Haworth Press.

Grasvelt C (1989) *Justo, een gekwetst kind. Ervaringen van een moeder met een ernstig verwaarloosd adoptiekind (Justo, a hurt child: Experiences of a mother with a seriously neglected adoptive child)*, Haarlem: de Toorts.

Grotevant H D and McRoy R (1998) *Openness in Adoption: Exploring family connections*, London: Sage Publications.

Hoksbergen R A C and Walenkamp H (1991) *Kind Van Andere Ouders (Child of Other Parents)*, Houten: Bohn, Stafleu, Van Loghum.

Hoksbergen R A C (1996) *Child Adoption – A guidebook for adoptive parents and their advisors*, London: Jessica Kingsley Publishers.

Hoksbergen R A C (1997) 'Turmoil for adoptees during their adolescence?' *International Journal of Behavioural Development*, 20:1, pp 33–46.

Hoksbergen R A C (1998) 'Changes in motivation for adoption, value orientations and behavior in three generations of adoptive parents', *Adoption Quarterly*, 2:2, pp 37–56.

Hoksbergen R A C (ed) Baarda B, Bunjes L A C and Nota J A (1979) *Adoptie van kinderen uit verre landen* (*Adoption of children from far-away countries*). Deventer: Van Loghum Slaterus.

Hoksbergen R A C, Juffer F and Waardenburg B C (1987) *Adopted children at home and at school*, Lisse: Swets en Zeitlinger.

Hoksbergen R A C, Spaan J J T M and Waardenburg B C (1988) *Bittere Ervaringen: Uithuisplaatsing van buitenlandse adoptiekinderen* (*Bitter Experiences: Placement in residential care of foreign adoptees*), Amsterdam: Swets–Zeitlinger.

Jewett C L (1982) *Helping Children Cope with Separation and Loss*, Harvard, Mass: The Harvard Common Press.

Johansson S (1976) *Tjänstledighet och Föräldrapenning för Adoptivföräldrar* (*Vacation and Costs for Adoptive Parents*), Sundbyberg: Adoption Centre.

Kirk H D (1963) *Shared Fate: A theory and method of adoptive relationships*, Port Angeles: Ben-Simon Publications.

Kirk H D (1981, 1985) *Adoptive Kinship. A modern institution in need of reform*, Port Angeles: Ben-Simon Publications.

Kittson R H (1968) *Orphan Voyage*, USA Country Press: Kittson.

Marcus C (1981) *Who is my mother? Birth parents, adoptive parents and adoptees talk about living with adoption and the search for lost family*, Toronto: Gage Publishing Ltd.

Mason K, Selman P and Hughes M (1999) 'Permanency planning for children with Down's Syndrome', *Adoption & Fostering*, 23:1, pp 21–8.

Reitz M and Watson K W (1992) *Adoption and the Family System*, London, New York: The Guildford Press.

Ryder N B (1965) 'The cohort as a concept in the study of social change', *American Sociological Review*, 30, pp 843–61.

Schneider S (1995) 'Adoption and ordinal position', *Adoption & Fostering*, 19, pp 21–3.

Silverman A R and Weitzman D E (1986) 'Nonrelative adoption in the United States', in Hoksbergen R A C and Gokhale S G (eds) *Adoption in Worldwide Perspective*, pp 1–21, Lisse: Swets en Zeitlinger.

Sokoloff B (1993) 'Antecedents of American adoption', *The Future of Children*, 3, pp 17–25. Los Altos: Center for the Future of Children, the David and Lucile Packard Foundation.

Sorosky A D, Baran A and Pannor R (1984) *The Adoption Triangle. Sealed or opened records: how they affected adoptees, birth parents, and adoptive parents*, New York: Anchor Press.

Storsbergen H E (1995) 'Geadopteerd zijn is . . .' Hoksbergen R A C, Storsbergen H E and Brouwer-van Dalen C, *Het Begon in Griekenland, Een verkenning van de achtergrond van in Griekenland geboren, geadopteerde jong-volwassenen en de betekchis van de adoptiestatus*, Utrecht: Adoption Centrre, pp 49–213.

Tizard B (1978) *Adoption: A Second Chance*, New York: Free Press.

Triseliotis J, Shireman J and Hundleby M (1997) *Adoption: Theory, policy and practice*, London, New York: Cassell.

Van de Flier D (1994) *Global Connections: Adoptions for US citizens abroad*, Denver: The Adoption Exchange.

Verhulst F C and Versluis-den Bieman H J M (1989) *Buitenlandse Adoptie-kinderen: Vaardigheden en probleemgedrag (Foreign adopted children: Capacities and problem behaviour)*, Assen: Van Gorcum.

Verhulst F C, Althaus M and Versluis-den Bieman H J M (1992) 'Damaging backgrounds: later adjustment of international adoptees', *Journal of the American Academy Child Adolescent Psychiatry*, 31:3, pp 518–525.

Section II
Research into outcomes of intercountry adoption

There is now a very substantial literature on the outcome of intercountry adoption, but this does not mean that we know all the answers – or even that we can begin to resolve questions about the rights and wrongs of intercountry adoption. There are a number of reviews of earlier research which are worth reading to get an overall feel for the area. Barbara Tizard and Ann Phoenix (1991) examine a number of studies carried out in Europe and the USA and conclude that overseas adoption has proved a success. June Thoburn and Marilyn Charles (1992) reviewed existing research for the Interdepartmental Review of Adoption Law, providing an excellent descriptive account, which avoids too much interpretation.

In an overview of the research literature for the BAAF International Conference on adoption in Edinburgh, John Triseliotis (1991) concluded that '. . . from the available evidence . . . children adopted intercountry generally do as well as own-country adoptions,' but that children were often brought up with little racial or ethnic awareness and that more research was needed on identity issues.

Other published reviews worth consulting include those by Rene Hoksbergen (1991), which covers a lot of the Dutch research not available in English, and Monica Dalen (1999) who has reviewed Scandinavian research and concludes that 'around 75 per cent manage well, without any sign of major problems' but that the remaining 25–30 per cent have 'problems linked to language, learning, identity and ethnicity' and that the teenage years are particularly demanding for adoptees and their families. There are also useful reviews of recent research projects in two issues of the magazine, *Adoption Quarterly* (Haugard *et al*, 2000a and 2000b). The article on Romanian adoptions is particularly useful in placing North American and Canadian research alongside that of Michael Rutter in the UK.

One consistent finding is that more persistent difficulties are experienced with children placed at older ages (Triseliotis *et al*, 1997) and those who have experienced long periods of institutional care. As with studies of transracial adoption, research into ethnic identity has been particularly contentious, especially where it has been carried out by white researchers from the host country. The four chapters in this section present findings on both the impact of institutionalisation and the complex issues of personal and racial identity.

Michael Rutter *et al* report on the early stages of his longitudinal study of children adopted into the UK from Romania. The study is as much about the development of children following profound deprivation in early life as about intercountry adoption, but clearly has many lessons for those involved in the adoption process. On one level this is clearly a remarkable success story with impressive gains both physically and mentally for a group of children arriving in very poor physical and emotional condition following varying periods of institutional care. Rutter's carefully planned study has a sound statistical base but can only provide a provisional picture of the progress of these children, who had reached the age of six years at the time of the reported findings. The findings present, in Rutter's words, 'a complex mix of spectacular success and worrying sequelae'. Already many parents are expressing concern over the long-term effects of institutional deprivation, a theme that is central to Verhulst's study in the following chapter, and Rutter ends by noting that his conclusions may need modification in the light of a further follow-up at age 11 years, which is currently underway.

Frank Verhulst starts with a general review of factors increasing risk of maladjustment in overseas adopted children and then reports on the latest stage of a longitudinal study of children adopted in The Netherlands. In contrast to Rutter's sample, most of the children were adopted transracially. They have now reached their mid and late teens and Verhulst shows that the gap between adopted and non-adopted adolescents is growing. His research relates this to the early experiences of the children, with those who had spent most time in institutions having the worst outcomes and suggests that the rise in problem behaviour may relate to issues of identity which become more relevant as the children enter their adolescent years. However, Verhulst stresses that most adopted children functioned well as adolescents and that he could find no clear correlation between the increase in problems and factors such as early deprivation or racist experiences. He concludes that 'transracial intercountry adoption may be a viable means of providing stable homes for children who would otherwise have had to endure many adversities'.

Malin Irhammar and Marianne Cederblad review Swedish research on overseas adopted persons. Much of the early research into physical and psychological development reflects both the optimism and the concerns of the studies by Rutter and Verhulst, but the most recent studies have not found the widening gap between adopted and non-adopted children highlighted by Verhulst. The latter part of their chapter concentrates on issues of identity and ethnicity and explores the differences between an "inner" and "outer" search. The picture that emerges is a complex one, which highlights the dilemmas facing children adopted transracially. A majority see themselves as Swedish – having what the authors term a 'Swedish self-identity' – but many also show a high degree of interest in their backgrounds. The authors stress that the Swedish identity seems important for successful overall adjustment but does not imply a denial of their ethnic origins and that the most successful adjustment was in children whose parents were open about these origins.

In their chapter, **Barbro Sætersdal** and **Monica Dalen** look at identity formation in international adoptees growing up in Norway and note a number of real problems arising from their ethnic and adoptive status. Of particular interest is the distancing of the adopted Vietnamese children from immigrants of a similar ethnic background. But the overall view of the authors is that the problems experienced by some international adoptees in Norway during their teenage years have eased by early adulthood. They conclude that questions of identity for persons adopted from overseas are very different from those experienced by native-born Norwegians, but also different from the children of immigrants in Norway who have been brought up within bilingual families and communities, more closely in touch with their culture.

No firm conclusions can be drawn from the chapters included here, but they all indicate the importance of continued high quality research and a careful reading of the findings. Despite the difficulties identified in adolescence, the majority of internationally adopted children have developed well, both psychologically and physically, overcoming the traumas of their early lives, and seem likely to make important contributions to their new countries.

References

Dalen M (1999) *The Status of Knowledge of Foreign Adoptions: A summary of the results of key foreign-adoption research projects in Scandinavia*, Oslo: Department of Special Needs Education, University of Oslo.

Haugard J, Wojslawowicz J and Palmer M (2000a) 'International adoption: Children predominantly from Asia and South America', *Adoption Quarterly*, 3:2, pp 83–93.

Haugard J, Wojslawowicz J and Palmer M (2000b) 'International adoption: Children from Romania', *Adoption Quarterly*, 3:3, pp 73–84.

Hoksbergen R (1991) 'Intercountry adoption: coming of age in the Netherlands', in Altstein H and Simon R (eds) *Intercountry Adopion: A multinational perspective*. New York: Praeger.

Ryvgold A, Dalen M and Sætersdal B (1999) *Mine – Yours – Ours and Theirs?*, Oslo: University of Oslo.

Thoburn J and Charles M (1992) 'A review of research which is relevant to intercountry adoption', in *Review of Adoption Law*, Background Paper 3 (DoH, January 1992) update in *Consultation Paper*, October 1992.

Tizard B and Phoenix A (1991) 'Intercountry adoption: a review of the evidence', *Journal of Child Psychology and Psychiatry*, 32, pp 743–756.

Triseliotis J (1991) 'A brief overview of the research evidence', *Adoption & Fostering*, 15:4, pp 46–52.

Triseliotis J, Shireman J and Hundleby M (1997) *Adoption: Theory, policy and practice*, 9, pp 187–195, London: Cassell.

6 Recovery and deficit following profound early deprivation

Michael Rutter, Thomas O'Connor, Celia Beckett, Jenny Castle, Carla Croft, Judy Dunn, Christine Groothues, and Jana Kreppner

The authors are all members of the English and Romanian Adoptees (ERA) Study Team, situated at the Social, Genetic and Developmental Psychiatry Research Centre of the Institute of Psychiatry, King's College, London. Michael Rutter has had an interest in the topic of maternal deprivation since the 1960s and published a seminal book on the topic in 1972. The team has undertaken studies of the effects of various forms of child rearing and has a special interest in adoption and fostering.

Introduction

The fall of the Ceausescu regime in Romania in 1989 was followed by extensive media coverage in the UK of the dreadful plight of the children in institutions and this, in turn, led many couples to apply to adopt children from the orphanages. The process constituted an important humanitarian endeavour but it also created a crucial research opportunity.

Two rather different sorts of research questions needed to be posed. First, what happens to the social and cognitive development of children who have experienced profound privation in early life but who are subsequently reared in well-functioning, normal families? To what extent do deficits persist and to what extent is recovery possible and, most crucially, what determines the progress of the children? What challenges are there for the children that derive from this major change in their life circumstances and what are the challenges for the parents taking on the adoption of children who have suffered in this way? Second, this massive change in life pattern provided a "natural experiment" that could be used to test environmental risk mechanisms. Because the vast majority of the children had been reared in institutions since the early weeks of life, there was no confound with family circumstances prior to admission.

Also, because the children had been admitted as tiny babies, it was implausible that psychological problems had constituted a reason for admission. Further, it seemed that scarcely any babies had been adopted or returned to their biological families before the regime fell. This was important because it meant that it was possible to study the effects of duration of institutional care without the bias created by the selective early adoption or return of the healthier children. The opportunity was, thereby, provided to examine in rigorous fashion the environmentally mediated effects of adverse rearing circumstances in poor quality institutions and, similarly, the effects of a major change of environment to somewhat above-average adopting families in the UK.

In order to take advantage of these opportunities and to address both sets of questions, the development of 165 adoptees from Romania was compared with that of 52 non-deprived English children adopted within the UK before the age of six months (Rutter et al, 1998). Systematic standardised assessments, using a combination of interviews, questionnaires, direct observations in the home and psychometric measures were used to study the children at the age of four years and again at six years. The children from Romania and the within-UK adoptees were studied in exactly the same way and, in both cases, there were comparable assessments of home circumstances. The children from Romania who entered the UK after the age of two years could not be studied at the age of four (because they were already too old for that to be done) but were studied in the same way at age six.

Psychological recovery

At the time of entry to the UK, most of the children were in a rather parlous state. Half were very severely malnourished with weights below the third percentile and over half were functioning developmentally in the retarded range. Both skin and intestinal infections were quite common (see Johnson, 2000) for a fuller account of the health and development of children in depriving institutions).

The first test of the effects of adverse institutional rearing was provided by comparison of the children's functioning at the time of UK entry and that as assessed at the age of four years (Rutter et al, 1998).

The catch-up with respect to weight and height was dramatic by four years; the vast majority of the children had heights and weights within the normal range, scarcely any were below the third percentile, and the means were only slightly below those for UK general populations.

Because no systematic standardised measures of developmental level were obtained at the time the children entered the UK, the assessment of developmental catch-up was necessarily less precise. However, the great majority of the parents had made detailed observations and notes and, frequently, videotapes. The parents were asked to complete a Denver Developmental Scale (Frankenburg *et al*, 1986) with respect to what the children could do at the time they came to the UK and again in terms of their functioning at age four years. The catch-up was equally dramatic. At the time of entry, the mean quotient was just above 60, whereas at four years, it was above 100. The meaningfulness of the latter assessment was shown by the good agreement with an individually administered standardised cognitive measure, the McCarthy General Cognitive Index (McCarthy, 1972). The validity of the retrospective assessment for the children's functioning at the time of entry was tested in a variety of ways and it was clear that, although imprecise, it was likely to be roughly correct (Rutter *et al*, 1998). Most of the children were not yet using language and many, too, were not yet walking despite being of an age when that might be expected. The extensive recovery following adoption into generally good UK families indicated that the major deficits at the time of UK entry had been due to some aspect of their early institutional rearing.

The extent of recovery, however, showed substantial individual variation and this provided another opportunity to examine environmental risk processes. Thus, of the 46 children from Romanian orphanages who came to the UK between the ages of two and three-and-a-half years, five (11 per cent) had scores in the severely retarded range at age six, but one child had a score of above 130, with most ranging in between.

Much the strongest predictor of cognitive outcome was the child's age at the time of leaving the institution to come to the UK. The children who came to the UK over the age of two years had a general cognitive index, on average, some 24 points below those who came to the UK under the age of six months (O'Connor *et al*, 2000a). The inference is that the duration of institutional care, and hence of psychological privation, constituted the key risk variable. Two points needed to be addressed, however, before that inference could be firm. First, perhaps it was the degree of malnutrition that mattered and not the duration of psychological privation. Multivariate analyses, examining the effects of several variables considered at the same time, showed that, although the degree of malnutrition (indexed by weight at UK entry) was of some importance, the children's age when leaving the institutions had a much greater effect. Of course, it is highly likely that malnutrition made children more vulnerable to psychological privation but the evidence suggested that the latter provided much of the risk. Developmental impairment was found even among the best-nourished children.

Because we had limited data on the quality of life in the institutions, and because the range of variations in patterns of institutional care was small (generally from poor to quite appalling) it was difficult to undertake rigorous tests to identify those specific aspects of institutional care that mattered most. However, with respect to cognitive functioning at age six years, the quality of individualised care in the institutions was shown to be relevant (Castle *et al*, 1999). Even after controlling for the children's age at the time of UK entry, those who had better individualised care tended to have higher cognitive scores at 6.

The second point was that it was necessary to separate the effects of duration of institutional privation from the consequences of how long the children had been in the adoptive home. Because, for the most part, the children went straight from the institutions to the adoptive home, the effects of the two could not be separated in relation to the assessments at age four. In other words, it necessarily followed that the longer the child had been in the institution, the shorter time they had been in the adoptive home, and vice versa. On the other hand, the two effects could be separated by taking into account the findings at both four and six years of age, studying changes over time. Thus, by standardising the scores between ages four and six, it was possible to take groups who had all been in the adoptive home for the same period of time, and then contrast them according to their length of institutional experience. This is shown in Figure 6.1 and it is clear that it was indeed the duration of institutional care that had the greatest effect. Children who had experienced prolonged

Figure 6.1

Effect of duration of privation controlling for time in adoptive home: McCarthy cognitive scores at age six years

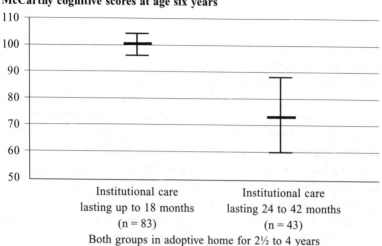

Institutional care lasting up to 18 months (n = 83)	Institutional care lasting 24 to 42 months (n = 43)

Both groups in adoptive home for 2½ to 4 years

NB: Regression used to equate four-year-old and six-year-old tests (because means differed)

privation in poor quality institutions tended to show a less complete cognitive recovery, although even with prolonged institutional care, cognitive catch-up was very substantial indeed.

This consistent dose response relationship between the duration of institutional care and cognitive outcome, and the evidence that this was not simply a consequence of malnutrition, strongly suggests that, insofar as there were continuing cognitive deficits at age six, these were a consequence of early institutional privation.

It was also important to consider how long the recovery process continued. Before we began the study, conventional wisdom had it that most recovery took place within the first few months. Our findings indicated that this was a mistaken view. Cognitive gains continued over quite prolonged periods of time. So far as we could judge, most catch-up was complete after some two- to two-and-a-half years in the adoptive home. On the other hand, for those children who continued to have low scores at age four, there was a significantly greater cognitive gain between four and six years than there was in the remainder of the group (O'Connor *et al*, 2000a).

Patterns of deficit

In our assessments, particular attention was paid to the children's socio-emotional and behavioural functioning. Previous studies of severely deprived children had paid very little attention to this aspect of psychological functioning and, hence, it was not clear what we should expect. Because the institutional care in Romania involved very little in the way of individualised interactions with either staff or other children, effects on the children's attachment relationships might be anticipated. These were assessed at both four and six years of age in various different ways. Detailed accounts were taken from the parents on the children's play and friendships, their relationships with their parents and with other adults, and their relationships at school. In addition, a modified form of Ainsworth's Strange Situation was used at home in order to assess children's responses to short separations from and reunion with their mothers and videotaped observations were made of their interactions with the investigators. As with cognitive functioning, many of the children seemed to be functioning entirely normally at both four and six years. Nevertheless, compared with the within-UK adoptees, there were some impairments and these were most likely to be present in the children who had stayed longest in the institutions. Both pretend and social role-play were significantly reduced in the adoptees from Romania (Kreppner *et al*, 1999) and physical contact-seeking with the investigators was increased during the observation session.

In keeping with our own observations, the parents also reported that the children were more likely than other children to show indiscriminate social approach to people whom they did not know, seeming to lack adequate social boundaries. Sometimes there were concerns that they might go off with a stranger because they seemed to lack the normal inhibitions against doing so. Overall, attachment disorder behaviours of this kind were substantially more common in the Romanian adoptees than the within-UK adoptees (see Figure 6.2) and, as with other outcomes, they were most likely in those children who had had the most

Figure 6.2

Attachment disorder behaviours at age six years according to duration of deprivation

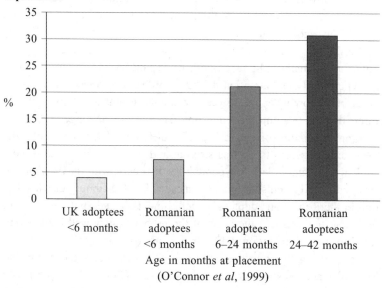

Age in months at placement
(O'Connor *et al*, 1999)

prolonged institutional deprivation (O'Connor *et al*, 1999, 2000b). The findings on social deficits seemed to differ in one key respect from those that applied to cognitive functioning. That is, with cognitive functioning, we were unable to find any cognitive deficits in those children who left Romania when under the age of six months. With social behaviours and interactive role-play, by contrast, although these were indeed much more frequent in those who had experienced prolonged institutional care, there were some impairments even in those who left Romania under the age of six months. The finding must be regarded as provisional at the moment, because the picture could look different when the children are older but the implication is that even when severe privation does not extend beyond six months of age, there may still be some deficits. If that proves to be the case, it will provide an important difference from the effects on cognition. The reasons for that difference, if it proves to be valid, warrant further research.

Our findings were also striking in showing the presence of two types of sequelae that have, hitherto, been thought to have a strongly biological basis, with genetic factors preponderant – namely, hyperactivity/inattention and autistic features. About a third of the children who came to the UK over the age of six months showed patterns of inattention and impulsivity accompanied by restless overactivity (Kreppner *et al*, submitted). There was no increase in those who came to the UK when younger. It remains to be seen whether this pattern has the same meaning as hyperactivity and attention deficit disorders as ordinarily diagnosed. A further follow-up at age 11 years, which is currently underway, should throw light on this important question. The data so far suggest, however, a complex mixture of similarities and differences. On the whole, the hyperactivity seems to be less striking and less pervasive than usually evident in attention deficit/hyperactivity disorders, with the problems of inattention and impulsivity more marked. Also, the finding that inattention in the Romanian adoptees tended to be associated with attachment problems suggests that the basis of the problems may well be different from "ordinary" attention deficit/hyperactivity disorders.

The finding that autistic features were much increased among the Romanian adoptees was even more unexpected (Rutter *et al*, 1999). The pattern was found in only a small minority, but about one in 16 of the children showed a pattern of autistic-like behaviour at age four that was closely comparable to that found in autistic children of the same age. Approximately another one in 16 showed somewhat similar features but to a much less marked degree. In terms of what had been found before with respect to the effects of poor quality institutional care, deficits in the domains of social relationships and communication are perhaps not unexpected. What was surprising, however, was the preponderance of quasi-obsessive and repetitive stereotyped behaviours. Thus, a number of the children were very preoccupied with sensations of smell or touch and a number had all encompassing preoccupations with objects such as lavatory cisterns, vacuum cleaners, watches, or shiny new £10 notes. Even at age four years, the autistic features were somewhat atypical in detail with respect to what is usually found in "ordinary" autism. For example, the children seemed to show more interest in social approach and there was a greater flexibility in their use of their limited communication skills. The most striking difference from "ordinary" autism, however, concerned the substantial changes that took place between four and six years of age. This is an age period when autistic symptomatology tends to become more marked. In sharp contrast, in the Romanian adoptees with this quasi-autistic pattern, there was substantial improvement. Their autistic-like features were not lost but they did diminish substantially in most cases. It is important that clinicians become aware of these unusual sequelae of profound early privation but, equally, it is crucial that they recognise that the prognostic implications may well be rather different from those associated with autism as found in other children. Also, it remains to be determined to what extent the mechanisms are different and the therapeutic needs not quite the same.

Overall patterns of normality and deficit

Because there is only modest overlap between the different forms of impairment and deficit that sometimes follow profound privation, it is important to go on to ask the extent to which there are children who seem to escape deficits completely in spite of their early adversities and the proportion who show multiple problems. Of course, the children are quite young at age six years and it would be misleading to suppose that the final outcome can be known at that age. There could be a modest further catch-up and also the development of more effective patterns of psychological and social coping. In addition, however, as children grow older, there are increasingly complex demands. Questions have to be asked as to whether their dramatic cognitive gains in the first few years after adoption can be translated into equally striking scholastic attainments. Will, for example, their educational progress be impeded by the behavioural difficulties that were present in some instances? Equally, it is good that so many of the children succeeded in forming attachment relationships with their adoptive parents and became sociable children. However, will they be able to make the crucial, and more difficult, transitions into lasting confiding peer relationships and, later on, to develop close selective friendships and love relationships? The further follow-up of the children at age 11 now underway will help to answer those questions but, in the meanwhile, some approximation can be obtained by looking at the range of problems as evident at six years of age (Rutter *et al*, in press).

Figure 6.3

Pervasive problems at age six years according to age at time of entry into the UK

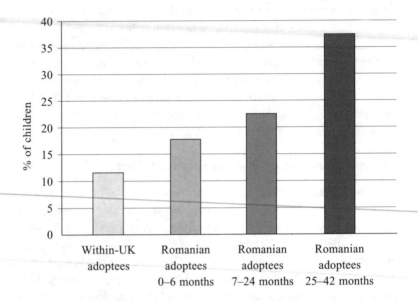

In order to undertake these analyses, the children's functioning was quantified in relation to seven different cognitive and socio-emotional-behavioural domains (attachment, peer relationships, attention/hyper-activity, conduct, emotions, cognition, and autistic features). The results were striking in showing that, although the rate of pervasive problems (meaning impairment on at least two domains) was much higher in the Romanian adoptees than within the comparison sample of children adopted within the UK, this was strongly connected with their age at the time of UK entry. Even within the group who were over the age of two at the time of entering the UK, over half did *not* show pervasive problems (see Figure 6.3). A somewhat comparable mirror image was obtained through a focus on the children who had essentially normal functioning – that is to say they showed no impairment on any of the seven domains. This designation of essential normality applied to just less than four-fifths of the within-UK adoptees but to substantially smaller proportions

Figure 6.4

Normal functioning at age six years according to age at time of entry into the UK

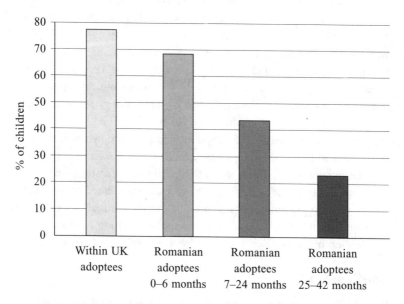

of the Romanian adoptees. Even so, of the children from Romania who came to the UK after the age of two years, over a fifth (22.2 per cent) showed no impairment (see Figure 6.4), and the proportion with normal functioning was much higher in those who left Romania at an earlier age (nearly half in those leaving between six and 24 months, and 70 per cent in those leaving under the age of six months).

Adoption experiences

At the time that these children were adopted (1990 to 1992), families adopting from abroad faced many difficulties (Beckett *et al*, 1999). Local authorities were generally unprepared for the influx of severely deprived children and some were hostile to intercountry adoption and refused to complete the work needed. Nearly half of the families had their home studies completed by independent social workers but most were required to have a second assessment. The authorities had to undertake welfare supervision before adoption but most families found what was offered unhelpful. It is evident that marked improvements in the procedures for handling intercountry adoptions were essential, as is now generally recognised. However, it is equally clear that, in the early 1990s, neither professionals nor parents adequately appreciated what was involved in helping children who had been as severely deprived as this group from Romania. Nevertheless, despite the very considerable challenges that were presented, and despite persisting difficulties in a substantial proportion of the children, the great majority of the adoptions have obviously been successful, however this is judged. By the age of six years, only two out of 165 adoptions had broken down, and the level of parental satisfaction was generally high at both four and six years of age (Groothues *et al*, 1999, submitted). Although family composition (with respect to features such as sibling spacing) seemed to play some role in relation to sibling conflict and the families' initial adjustment to the adoption, it was of marginal importance in relation to most aspects of adoption outcome (Beckett *et al*, 1998; Groothues *et al*, submitted).

Conclusions

Prior to this study, remarkably little was known about the long-term sequelae of profound and pervasive privation in early life. The findings have been informative in several key respects. First, the degree of developmental catch-up following adoption into well-functioning UK adopting families has been quite remarkable by any reckoning. At the time of UK entry, half were very severely malnourished and over half were functioning developmentally in the retarded range. By the age of four years, the group as a whole was, with only a few exceptions, functioning within the normal range. This progress was maintained over the next two years. Second, the view that prevailed in the 1980s that, if catch-up was to take place, it was largely complete within the first few months has proved to be mistaken. Gains often continued over as long as two- to two-and-a-half years, and in the case of children who still had deficits, more modest gains seemed possible over an even longer period.

The third point is that there were some continuing psychological deficits and impairments in some children. Much the strongest predictor of deficits was the overall duration of institutional privation. Those children who came to the UK over the age of two years had a general cognitive level some two dozen points below those who left institutions under the age of six months. The findings suggested that some of the risks derived from malnutrition (and probably, too, from associated infections and possibly from the excessive use of psychotropic drugs), but the evidence indicated that the main risks were likely to have stemmed from the psychological privation provided by the lack of play and conversation with caregivers, the lack of toys, the confinement to cots, and the general paucity of social and cognitive learning experiences.

Fourth, the social sequelae were as striking and as important as the cognitive deficits. Particularly among those children who remained in poor quality institutions beyond the age of two years, there was an increased incidence of attachment problems, of somewhat atypical patterns of inattention and impulsivity, and of quasi-autistic behaviour. Four aspects of these features warrant highlighting:

i)   possibly (although this has still to be confirmed) the sequelae were to a limited extent detectable even among those who left the institutions below the age of six months;
ii)   the patterns show many similarities with syndromes seen in non-deprived children but there appeared to be important subtle differences and it seems likely that the causal mechanisms may involve rather different processes;
iii)   the prognosis for these social impairments is at present unknown and further follow-up is needed to find out; and
iv)   although there are useful leads on how best to help children with these problems, there is a lack of evaluated interventions.

Fifth, the findings present a complex mix of spectacular success and worrying sequelae. It is unfortunate that the media have chosen to overemphasise only one or the other. Even in the group of children who came to the UK after their second birthday, three-fifths were free of pervasive problems and over a fifth were functioning without impairment in any of the seven domains assessed. Claims that early privation inevitably leads to "irreversible deficits" are clearly wrong. There can be no doubt that, from the point of view of the individual children, they have benefited enormously from adoption into UK families. The results speak volumes for the importance of environmental influences both in leading to deficits and in making recovery possible. There has not been space in this paper to discuss the role of the adopting families but our findings clearly document both their dedication and skilled loving care, and their persistence and ingenuity in coping with extremely challenging circumstances. It is very much a tribute to them that the rate of adoption breakdown has been so incredibly low. However, it is also necessary to appreciate that a substantial minority of the children are suffering continuing psychological and social difficulties of one kind or another. This is particularly the case for those who suffered psychological privation for the longest periods.

Sixth, although there have been no systematic studies of which forms of treatment are most effective, the findings offer some leads when considered in the context of what is known about the processes involved in normal psychological development. Because the children had been reared in a globally restricted environment, some had difficulties at first in coping with both a normal diet and a normal range of experiences and play opportunities. Thus, some seemed fearful of going outside and nearly all needed to learn to play with toys; many, too, had to learn how to chew solid food. Federici (1998) has warned of the problems for severely deprived children of going straight into a normal US or UK home because of the undue stimulation that it provides for those who have not previously experienced play, conversation, and family meals. Based on what we have seen of the approaches taken by families in our sample, we doubt whether the severely restricted environment he recommends is desirable for most children leaving institutions below the age of 42 months, but the message to provide a graded adaptation is clearly correct.

The indiscriminate social approach derives from children's lack of opportunity to develop selective attachments and the evidence on attachment development (see Cassidy and Shaver, 1999; Rutter, 1981) suggests that the remedy is likely to lie in part in the normal opportunities of close selective parent–child relationships. Indeed, that seems to have been the case with many of the children in our sample. Accordingly, we query the specific value of so-called holding therapy, which constitutes a key element in some attachment therapies (Keck and Kupecky, 1995), because it focuses on forced physical contact of a rather artificial kind. Although the "touchy" behaviour that often goes along with indiscriminate social approach is a problem when directed at peers and unfamiliar adults, it may be appropriate with family members. The children need to be taught selectivity, rather than generally discouraged from being physically affectionate.

Strongly directive physical control (as provided by behaviour modification methods) has been advocated for dealing with autistic-like behaviour, indiscriminate friendliness, hyperactivity and aggression (Federici, 1998). Clearly, behavioural treatments have a place but the real goal is for the child to learn self-control, not for the parents to bring about external control. In working towards that objective, the children need to be helped to pick up and understand social cues, to appreciate the effects of their behaviour on other people, and to learn what is socially unacceptable. Although the nature of the disorder is likely to be different, the treatment approaches used with autism (Howlin and Rutter, 1987; Rutter, 1985) may well be applicable to those with quasi-autistic features. On the whole, medication probably has only a minor role to play in the treatment of any of the problems associated with profound early privation. Methylphenidate (Ritalin) has helped a few children with marked overactivity but our experience is that often it does not help. Our findings suggest that this may be because the children's difficulties in maintaining quiet concentration in group learning situations derive from some aspect of social relationship difficulties rather than from a motor problem or cognitive deficit.

Although least emphasised in the literature, it is clear that decisions on schooling have been highly problematic for many families. It is partly because the mix of problems is unusual and partly because the children change so much during the early years following adoption. The great majority of the children in our study have coped with mainstream schooling (but a few have not) but many have needed a lot of individualised help and it has sometimes proved useful for the children to be placed in a class for those a year younger. It is evident that much has still to be learned about how to alleviate the children's social and cognitive deficits and research to address treatment needs should constitute a high priority.

Seventh, something of a rethink is required on how intercountry adoptions are dealt with. There is no doubt that the children benefited greatly from adoption. Adoption within their own country may well be preferable, but for most children in Romanian institutions this possibility was not on offer. Studies of children remaining in institutions indicate that a poor outcome is to be expected for many, and intercountry adoption provides the only realistic opportunity for improving their chances of normal development. Of course, it does not provide a remedy for the overall situation in institutions – that requires different actions – but it may offer hope for the individual child. Our findings so far provide no justification for the negative views among many social workers in the early 1990s. At our assessments at age 11 we are looking in more detail at the children's views and their patterns of identity and this should provide a fuller picture on the outcome of the adoption. Nevertheless, very few adoptions had broken down by age six, the children improved greatly and parental satisfaction was high. Proper procedures for assessing prospective adoptive parents are essential but the arrangements need to be made to function better and to be "family-friendly" in style. Also, it should now be possible to provide families with a much better idea of both the hazards and the potential than was available ten years ago. With respect to services during the period after coming to the UK and leading up to adoption, most families did not perceive what was on offer in the early 1990s as particularly helpful. It ought to be possible now to do much better and it is desirable that services be provided by workers with specific expertise in adoption. In the past, this pre-adoption monitoring role was often undertaken by general child care social workers who are more used to child protection issues.

There is then the further issue of possible help after adoption. That was generally not offered and, as a result of their sometimes unfortunate experiences with social services, many families would not have welcomed help. Of course, it should not be assumed that all families need assistance. It is striking how well most coped in the absence of much systematic intervention. We need to ensure that appropriate, well-informed services are readily available when required, but professionals need to appreciate that the children are tremendously varied and that the families differ, too, in what they need and want. With better regulated intercountry adoption and the signing up to the Hague Convention, it is to be hoped that arrangements in the future will work better (Parker, 1999) and that many of the difficulties faced by the families we have seen may not be an issue in quite the same way for future adopters.

Finally, it is essential to emphasise that the children whom we have studied were only six years of age at the time of the last assessment. We are currently undertaking a further follow-up at age 11 years and it may be that some of the conclusions in this paper will need modification in the light of what we find then.

Acknowledgements
Most of all, we are indebted to the families who have been so generous of their time in helping us with our study. We have also benefited greatly from discussions with them on the meanings of what we have found. In addition, we are most grateful for the willing help of professional colleagues too numerous to list here. However, we wish to note particularly our gratitude to the team members who played a key role in the early years of the study: Lucia Andersen-Wood, Diana Bredenkamp, Kathryn Ehrich, Alexandra Harborne, Dale Hay, Jessica Jewett, Lisa Keaveney, Julie Messer, David Quinton, and Adele White. The study was also reliant on generous funding from the UK Department of Health and the (British) Medical Research Council; we express our great gratitude to them.

References

Beckett C, Groothues C, O'Connor T and the English and Romanian Adoptees (ERA) study team (1998) 'Adopting from Romania: the role of siblings in adjustment', *Adoption & Fostering*, 22:2, pp 25–34.

Beckett C, Bredenkamp D, Castle J, Groothues C and the English and Romanian Adoptees (ERA) study team (1999) 'The role of social workers in intercountry adoption: an analysis of the experience of adopters from Romania', *Adoption & Fostering*, 23:4, pp 15–25.

Cassidy J and Shaver P R (eds) (1999) *Handbook of Attachment: Theory, research, and clinical applications*, New York, NY: Guilford Press.

Castle J, Groothues C, Bredenkamp D, Beckett C, O'Connor T G, Rutter M and the English and Romanian Adoptees (ERA) study team (1999) 'Effects of qualities of early institutional care on cognitive attainment', *American Journal of Orthopsychiatry*, 69, pp 424–437.

Frankenburg W K, van Doorninck W J, Liddell T N and Dick N P (1986) *Revised Denver Prescreening Developmental Questionnaire (R-PDQ)*. High Wycombe, UK: DDN Incorporated/The Test Agency.

Federici R S (1998) *Help for the Hopeless Child: A guide for families*, Alexandria, VA: Federici.

Groothues C, Beckett C, O'Connor T G and the English and Romanian Adoptees (ERA) study team (1999) 'The outcome of adoptions from Romania: Predictors of parental satisfaction', *Adoption & Fostering*, 22:4, pp 30–40.

Groothues C, Beckett C, O'Connor T G and the English and Romanian Adoptees (ERA) study team (submitted), *Outcomes and successful follow-up study of children adopted from Romania into the UK*.

Howlin P and Rutter M (1987) *Treatment of Autistic Children*, Chichester: Wiley.

Johnson D E (2000) 'Medical and developmental sequelae of early childhood institutionalization in international adoptees from Romania and the Russian Federation', in Nelson C (ed), *The Effects of Early Adversity on Neurobehavioral Development*, Mahwah, NJ: Erlbaum.

Keck G C and Kupecky R M (1995) *Adopting the Hurt Child: Hope for families with special needs kids*, Colorado Springs: Pinon Press.

Kreppner J, O'Connor T G, Dunn J, Andersen-Wood L and the English and Romanian Adoptees (ERA) study team (1999) 'The pretend and social role play of children exposed to early severe deprivation', *British Journal of Developmental Psychology*, 17, pp 319–332.

Kreppner J, O'Connor T, Rutter M and the English and Romanian Adoptees (ERA) study team (submitted), *Is inattention/hyperactivity a deprivation disorder?*

Lord C, Shulman C, Pickles A and DiLavore P C (1997) *Learning and not learning to speak: Examples from a longitudinal study of preschool children with autism-spectrum disorder*, Paper presented at the Society for Research in Child Development Biennial Conference, Washington DC, April.

McCarthy D (1972) *The McCarthy Scales of Children's Abilities*, New York, NY: The Psychological Corporation/Harcourt Brace Jovanovich.

O'Connor T G, Bredenkamp D, Rutter M and the English and Romanian Adoptees (ERA) study team (1999) 'Attachment disturbances and disorders in children exposed to early severe deprivation', *Infant Mental Health Journal*, 20, pp 10–29.

O'Connor T G, Rutter M, Beckett C, Keaveney L, Kreppner J M and the English and Romanian Adoptees (ERA) study team (2000a) 'The effects of global severe privation on cognitive competence: extension and longitudinal follow-up', *Child Development*, 71, pp 376–390.

O'Connor T G, Rutter M and the English and Romanian Adoptees (ERA) study team (2000b) 'Attachment disorder behavior following severe deprivation: Extension and longitudinal follow-up', *Journal of the American Academy of Child and Adolescent Psychiatry*, 39, pp 703–711.

Parker R (ed) (1999) *Adoption Now: Messages from research*, Chichester: Wiley.

Rutter M (1981) *Maternal Deprivation Reassessed* (2nd edn.), Harmondsworth, Middlesex: Penguin.

Rutter M (1985) 'The treatment of autistic children', *Journal of Child Psychology and Psychiatry*, 26, pp 193–214.

Rutter M, Andersen-Wood L, Beckett C, Bredenkamp D, Castle J, Groothues C, Kreppner J, Keaveney L, Lord C, O'Connor T G and the English and Romanian Adoptees (ERA) study team (1999) 'Quasi-autistic patterns following severe early global privation', *Journal of Child Psychology and Psychiatry*, 40, pp 537–549.

Rutter M and the English and Romanian Adoptees (ERA) study team (1998) 'Developmental catch-up, and deficit, following adoption after severe global early privation', *Journal of Child Psychology and Psychiatry*, 39, pp 465–476.

Rutter M O'Connor T G, Kreppner J and the English and Romanian Adoptees (ERA) Study Team (in press) 'Specificity and heterogeneity in children's responses to profound privation', *British Journal of Psychiatry*.

7 The development of internationally adopted children

Frank C Verhulst

Frank Verhulst is Professor and Director of Child/Adolescent Psychiatry at Erasmus University, Rotterdam, the Netherlands. His main research field is child/adolescent psychopathology with an emphasis on longitudinal research. He is joint editor of the Journal of Child Psychology and Psychiatry and has published books and articles in the English language.

Introduction

Adoption by non-relatives is an accepted solution for the rearing of children whose biological parents are not able or willing to provide for them. Adoption is also a solution for the adoptive parents who wish for a family life that they cannot have because of infertility or other reasons. In our contemporary society, adoption is incorporated in many mental health professionals' thinking as a good alternative for the rearing of unwanted children who might otherwise be raised in institutions. Because adoption involves the loss of the biological parents and family ties, and because factors related to adoption may place the child at various risks of developing subsequent problems, it is important to question what the impact is of adoption on the developing child. Although adoption seems to be in the best interest of children who would otherwise go on living under adverse circumstances, we need to know how adopted children fare in the long run, and how we can reduce the possible risks of them developing psychological problems.

Factors elevating the risk of maladjustment in adopted children

Adopted children are at increased risk of maladjustment because a number of factors known to be disadvantageous (Rutter and Garmezy, 1983) may exert their influence. These factors include:

Pre- and perinatal factors
- Maternal stress during pregnancy;
- Inadequate pre- and perinatal medical care;
- Malnutrition and infectious diseases in the mother during pregnancy.

Factors operating after birth
- Malnutrition and medical conditions;
- Discontinuous care-taking and poor adult–child relationships;
- Deprivation, abuse;
- Acquisition of behaviours that have a survival function but are maladaptive in the adoptive family;
- Influences from the adoptive family, school and social environment.

The biological mothers are often subjected to personal and social stress during and after pregnancy. These factors may be especially prevalent in women in developing countries who live under great economic and social stress. There may be a lack of antenatal care, and the children may be subjected to birth hazards such as low birth weight. Furthermore, the lack of medical care for mother and child may be further complicated by malnourishment.

Children often are subjected to negative environmental influences, such as separation from the natural mother, poor parent–child relationships, disharmonious family relationships, and discontinuous caretaking prior to adoption. Children may be deprived of influences that are crucial for a healthy development, such as adequate stimulation (especially linguistic), affection and opportunities for developing enduring attachments to others. Some children are subjected to abuse. Furthermore, children who have been institutionalised are prone to show disturbed social relationships and may have acquired interaction styles that are appropriate for surviving in the institution but that are maladaptive outside it. There is also the possibility of interactions between effects of biological vulnerabilities, such as physical disabilities or disease, and parental frustration and rejection leading to abuse and neglect.

127

Lastly there are factors operating after placement in the adoptive family. Relationships and expectations in the adoptive family, as well as psychosocial stress on the family, may increase the child's vulnerability to problem behaviour. Adopted children in adolescence may have concerns about their biological parentage and, in cases where they are of different ethnic background, their appearance may make them feel excluded from other family members or peers.

The factors listed above put adopted children at increased risk of developing problem behaviours. This is acknowledged by a number of authors (Brodzinsky, 1990; Bohman and Sigvardsson, 1980). However, most of our knowledge concerning the development of adopted children is not based on much empirical evidence. A majority of studies are based on casework and clinical observation (Brodzinsky, 1990).

From a theoretical point of view it is important to study the situation in which early deprived children are raised by usually highly-motivated parents. Such a situation can be regarded as a "natural experiment" concerning the vulnerability and resilience of children subjected to early negative environmental influences. Not only in developing countries, but also in wealthy Western societies, a substantial proportion of children are deprived or abused. Unless they are adopted, most of these children are chronically subjected to negative environmental influences, either in their own homes, or because they are institutionalised. In the case of adoption, however, an inadequate or damaging environment is replaced by an environment that usually provides sufficient care and stimulation. This situation makes it possible to investigate to what extent the possible damaging effects of negative early experiences can be mitigated by a much more favourable environment.

It is argued by a number of authors that the earlier the placement of the child in the adoptive home, the better (Bohman, 1970; Hersov, 1985). However, it is not clear which factors lead to children who are adopted at a later age being more at risk of a deviant development. One explanation is that the older the child at placement, the longer the child may have been subjected to negative environmental influences. Another factor may be that older children who have formed strong attachments to their caretakers have to cope with the trauma of loss which may influence their development. Also, it may be that adoptive parents have more difficulties in adjusting to an older child with habits and behaviours that are unfamiliar to them. Lastly, the older the child, the greater the adjustments the child has to make, such as learning a new language or adapting to new demands.

The Dutch International Adoption Study: method and design

From the existing literature, it is clear that a number of issues concerning the adaptation of adopted children from childhood into adulthood and factors influencing their development, remain unresolved. In 1986–87 we assessed the behavioural development of 2,148 adoptees originally aged 10 to 15 years and born in Korea, Colombia, India, Indonesia and Bangladesh. This survey was urged by the increasing concern about the overrepresentation of foreign adopted children in residential treatment. The results of the survey facilitated the study of the development of children who were often born and raised under adverse circumstances, and who, after being adopted, had to cope with adaptation to a new environment and with successive developmental tasks (see also Verhulst *et al*, 1990a,b, 1992, 1995; Versluis-den Bieman and Verhulst, 1995).

The first study

The original sample consisted of all children (N = 3,519) adopted from abroad by non-relatives in the Netherlands between 1 January 1972 and 31 December 1975 (see Verhulst *et al*, 1990a). Parents were requested to complete the Child Behavior Checklist (CBCL) (Achenbach, 1991a), a questionnaire for obtaining standardised parents' reports of children's competence and problem behaviours. In addition, parents were asked to provide information on a number of variables reflecting adverse environmental influences in the country of origin. Usable information was obtained from the parents of 64.9 per cent (N = 2,148) of the children who were aged 10 to 15 years at the time of the study. The age of the adopted child at placement ranged from a few days to 10 years, with the majority having been adopted before their fourth birthday. More than half of the children came from three countries (Korea 32 per cent; Colombia 15 per cent; and India 10 per cent), with the remainder coming from Indonesia, Bangladesh, Lebanon, Austria and other European countries. As in most adoption studies, the mean occupational level of parents of the adoption sample was much higher than that for the general population.

We compared the CBCL scores for the sample of adopted children with scores obtained from parents of 933 non-adopted children of the same age selected from a random sample of children from the general Dutch population (Verhulst et al, 1985).

The follow-up study

At follow up, in 1990, with a mean interval of 3.2 years since the first interview, parents of 2,071 subjects were requested to complete the CBCL, and a postal questionnaire with various questions about the early background and general functioning of their adopted children. We received usable information on 1,538 subjects (74 per cent), whose ages ranged from 14 to 18 years. The adolescents themselves were asked to complete the self-report version of the CBCL, the Youth Self-Report (YSR) (Achenbach, 1991b). Usable YSRs were obtained from 1,262 (61 per cent) of the young people approached.

Analysis of the characteristics of the dropouts revealed that there was a slight under-representation of older and problematic children in the sample. Subjects on whom parent reports were available (but no self-reports) were slightly older and functioned somewhat less well according to their parents, than subjects who co-operated. Findings from the follow-up study of adopted youths were compared with a sample of young people from our epidemiological follow-up of adolescents from the general population (Verhulst et al, 1990c).

Findings from the first study

Prevalence

The prevalence of problem behaviours in the original sample of 2,148 10- to 15-year-old intercountry adoptees was determined by comparing the CBCL scores for adopted children with those of 933 non-adopted children of the same age from the general population (Verhulst et al, 1990a). Parents reported more problem behaviours, especially externalising behaviours, for adopted rather than for non-adopted children.

More problems were reported for boys than for girls and for 12- to 15-year-olds than for 10-to 11-year-olds. The largest proportion of "deviant" children was found among 12- to 15-year-old boys, with more than twice as many boys with considerable problem behaviours in the adopted as in the non-adopted sample. Figure 7.1 shows the percentages of adopted versus non-adopted children scoring in the clinical range of the CBCL total problem score. The cut-off for the clinical range was set at the 90th percentile of the cumulative frequency distribution of CBCL total problem scores obtained for Dutch normative samples. Differences in mean total problem scores, indicating less favourable scores for the adopted children, seemed to be attributable to extremely high scores in a minority of adopted boys (see Verhulst, 2000).

At the syndrome level, the largest differences were found for delinquent and hyperactive behaviour in 12- to 15-year-old boys, with adopted boys showing more problem behaviour than non-adopted boys.

The gender difference in CBCL problem scores in the adoption sample was similar to that found for non-adopted children, with higher problem scores for boys versus girls. Adopted boys showed especially elevated

Figure 7.1

Percentage of adopted and nonadopted children scoring in the clinical range of CBCL total problem scores by sex and age group

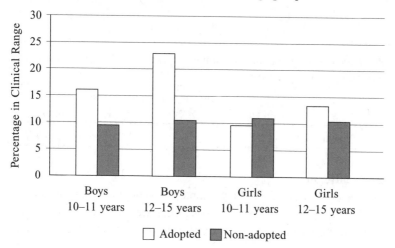

problem scores over non-adopted boys, although the scores for adopted 12-to 15- year-old girls were also higher than the scores for non-adopted girls (Verhulst et al, 1990a).

Unlike the gender difference, which was similar for adopted and non-adopted subjects, the higher CBCL problem scores for older children in the adoption sample contrasted with the slight decrease in CBCL problem scores with increasing age found for non-adopted children (Verhulst et al, 1985). It was not clear from the cross-sectional findings whether the increase of problems with increasing age in the adoption sample was truly developmental, or due to selection factors. Changing policies of governments in countries of origin, and variations in local selection procedures across time, may affect the characteristics of adopted children from year to year in unknown ways.

Age of child at placement

Age of the child at placement was significantly associated with an increased risk for later maladjustment, although the relationship was not fully linear. Children who were adopted within the first six months of their lives were at somewhat greater risk for later maladjustment than children who were adopted between seven and 24 months of age. However, this difference was not significant. After the age of 24 months, there was a gradual increase of the risk for later maladjustment with increasing age at placement.

Table 7.1
Percentage of adopted children scoring in the clinical range of the CBCL by age of child at placement

| | Age at Placement in months | | | |
	0–6	7–24	25–48	61–120
% in clinical range	14.0	11.5	17.5	20.5

Early adversity

A large proportion of the study sample for whom there was information on their early backgrounds had been subjected to adverse influences. Parents reported that in the country of origin children had been subjected

Figure 7.2

Percentage of adopted children scoring in the clinical range of CBCL total problem scores for different levels of early adverse influences

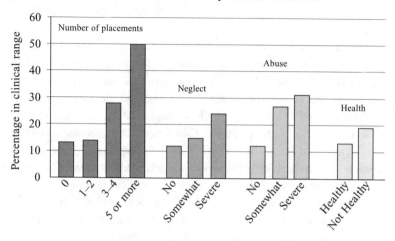

to neglect in 45 per cent of the sample, abuse in 13 per cent, and changes of caretakers in 54 per cent. Nearly six per cent of the children in the present sample had experienced three or more changes of care-taking environments. According to their parents, more than 43 per cent of the children in the sample were in poor physical condition when they joined their adoptive family. Although physical condition cannot be regarded only as a negative environmental influence but also a consequence of adversity, this variable was included in our analyses. As expected, the probability that a child showed maladaptive behaviours at a later age increased strongly when the child had been subjected to early serious environmental adversity. Figure 7.2 shows the percentages of children who scored in the clinical range of the CBCL for different levels of early adverse influences.

Fifty per cent of the children who experienced five or more changes in care-taking environment showed later maladjustment. Problem behaviour was also found in 24 per cent of the children who had been severely neglected and 31 per cent of the severely abused children.

Children who have experienced early negative environmental influences thus run a greater risk of developing problem behaviours than children with relatively favourable backgrounds. Early adverse experiences of neglect, abuse, and number of changes of care-taking environment, were all positively associated with the age of the child at placement. Age of the child at placement was so strongly associated with each of these variables that it did not add to the contribution of the early background variables in the distribution of children across the two categories of deviant and non-deviant behavioural functioning. In other words, the increased risk of developing later problem behaviours in children adopted at a later age could be explained by their having been subjected more to early adverse circumstances. In particular, evidence that a child had been abused was a potent predictor of later maladjustment. When these early influences are taken into account, the age of the child at placement as such is of lesser significance.

It was hypothesised that raising a child from his/her first months onward is easier than raising an older child who speaks a foreign language and has already acquired skills and habits and has a history of his or her own. However, the findings of the present study could not support this hypothesis. Children adopted at a relatively older age do not seem to run a greater risk of later maladjustment because they were adopted when they were older, but because of having been subjected to early adverse experiences.

It was found that, of the early adverse factors examined, the factor of abuse contributed most strongly to the prediction of later maladjustment. The effect of abuse in children's early histories was so strongly associated with later maladjustment that neglect and number of changes in the care-taking environment had no significant additional value in predicting poor outcome. In other words, if it was known that a child had been abused, this was sufficient information to expect a greater likelihood for later maladjustment.

More boys than girls showed high levels of problem behaviour. However, although boys run a greater risk of maladjustment than girls, this greater risk could not be attributed to a greater vulnerability to early adverse factors in boys rather than in girls.

The age at placement was associated with a higher risk of developing delinquent behaviour and depressive symptoms. The strong associations between age at placement and the early adverse factors indicate that early adversities put the children in the present sample at greater risk of developing behavioural problems and depression. This finding is informative with respect to the link between depression and early loss and other environmental adversities.

The results also demonstrated that the majority of children who had backgrounds known to be damaging seemed to function quite well. Apparently, the negative effects of early adverse influences can fade away under the positive influences of the adoptive family. Some children were able to escape the influences of early adverse experiences. Although the results indicated that adverse pre-adoption influences increased the risk of later maladjustment, later developmental aspects in the children's lives may also play an important role in the development of problem behaviours. The cross-sectional findings do not indicate in which direction future environmental factors will influence the adopted child's development. Problem behaviours resulting from early negative experiences may be ameliorated by later positive influences; or, if they are resistant to these positive influences, they may remain. It is also possible that certain developmental strains will exacerbate maladjustment. In particular, adolescence characterised by the developmental increase of cognitive abilities, independence, identity formation, and sexual maturation may be more stressful for adopted than for non-adopted children.

This was the starting point for the follow-up of adopted children's functioning into adolescence.

Results of the three year follow-up

Figure 7.3 shows the mean total problem scores at initial assessment and at follow-up for both sexes and four age groups separately.

As can be seen, there was a developmental increase in problem scores. Also, for the majority of syndrome scales, an increase was found. This was supported by statistical tests (Verhulst and Versluis-den Bieman, 1995). The largest increase was for the *Delinquent Behaviour* syndrome, followed by the syndrome designated *Withdrawn*. Apparently, withdrawal from contact and covert antisocial behaviours are of increasing concern to parents of internationally adopted children as they enter adolescence.

Figure 7.3

Mean CBCL total problem scores at initial assessment and follow-up for adopted children by age and sex

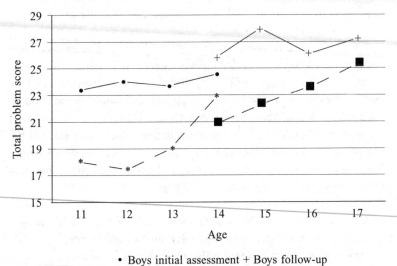

• Boys initial assessment + Boys follow-up
* Girls initial assessment ■ Girls follow-up

The increase in CBCL problem scores with increasing age contrasted with the results from our longitudinal epidemiological studies (Verhulst *et al*, 1990c) which demonstrated a slight decrease of CBCL problem scores with increasing age. The CBCL total problem score in the adoption sample showed a significant *increase*, from 21.4 to 24.8, whereas it showed a significant *decrease* in the comparison group of non-adopted children from 20.8 to 16.3.

The effects of early environmental influences

To test the effects of pre-adoption environmental factors on the developmental increase of CBCL problem scores, the following variables reflecting adverse environmental influences in the country of origin were assessed:

1) age of the child at placement;
2) medical conditions at the time of placement; and
3) neglect/abuse (any of the following three conditions in the past scored as present:
   a) at least three changes of care-taking environment,
   b) physical neglect,   ˙
   c) physical abuse).

The statistical analysis of the longitudinal data showed that early negative environmental influences as measured in the present study were *not* responsible for the *increase* in problems in our sample across time.

The effect of ethnicity
For the majority of European children, the adopted child and his or her parents were of similar ethnic background, whereas this was not the case for most of the children born in non-European, developing countries. The sample was divided into transracially adopted children born in non-European countries (N = 1,410), and intraracially adopted children from European countries (N = 128).

We tested the possible effect of ethnicity on the increase of problem scores across time. From our results we could not conclude that differences in ethnicity between the parent and their adopted child were responsible for the longitudinal increase in problems.

Self-reported problem behaviour
These findings from the CBCL were compared with the self-reported problem behaviour from the young people completing the YSR, in order to check that the CBCL results were not a consequence of adoptive parents' lower threshold for reporting problem behaviour. Using the YSR, we found much higher levels of self-reported problem behaviour in the adopted adolescents, the greatest difference being found in the YSR Delinquent Behaviour scale for boys, on which the adopted boys were six times more likely to score in the clinical range. The scale covers a total of 13 items, including self-reports of stealing, running away and going missing with other children who get into trouble. For girls the biggest difference was found on the Aggressive Behaviour

scale, where adopted girls were five times more likely to be in the deviant range.

Conclusions

A substantial number of the adopted children in the above mentioned study became increasingly maladjusted as their development progressed into adolescence. These findings do not confirm the much more favourable reports of the functioning of adopted adolescents by Bohman and Sigvardsson (1978, 1979, 1980) and Tizard *et al* (1974, 1975, 1978). Although these studies demonstrated the beneficial effects of adoption, the mainly white, and intraracially adopted children in these studies are unlikely to have experienced the extreme deprivation that many children in our Dutch survey of intercountry adopted children had suffered.

The adverse influences early in the lives of many of the children in the present study may have made them more vulnerable to the developmental stresses of adolescence. Compared with non-adopted children, the decline in adolescence of protective and supervisory influences exerted by the family (Larson and Richards, 1991) and school may have a stronger effect on adopted children who have experienced early loss than on non-adopted children. The prolonged pre-adoption exposure of many children in our sample to other environmental adversities such as weak and often disrupted adult–child relationships, deviant adult and peer models of behaviour, and poor discipline and supervision, may have made them more vulnerable to problem behaviours in adolescence with its decrease in environmental support and supervision. Although early environmental adversities were found to be associated with higher levels of later problems, the pre-adoption influences were *not* significantly related to the longitudinal increase in problem behaviours across time.

A factor possibly influencing the adolescent functioning of most intercountry adoptees is their ethnic background, which gives them a different physical appearance from that of their adoptive parents and their non-adopted siblings and peers. The adoption of children from Third World countries by white parents from rich Western countries has been a source of debate. Arguing that transracial adoption is a new form of colonialism, or that it can be seen as a form of cultural genocide (see

Silverman and Feigelman, 1990), some have strongly opposed the adoption of non-white children by white parents. Racial differences may put the adopted adolescent under undue stress with respect to establishing a satisfactory ethno-cultural identity and adequate self-esteem. Racism may also hamper the formation of adequate self-esteem, and social adjustment. However, our comparison of intraracially versus transracially adopted adolescents suggests that transracial adoption is not related to later maladjustment. This does not imply that racism may not cause considerable suffering for non-white adopted adolescents. Our results showed that possible racism does not affect the adopted adolescent's functioning to a degree that it can be regarded as deviant.

It must be concluded that factors other than the effects of childhood deprivation or racial antagonism are responsible for the majority of problems in adopted adolescents. It is possible that, with increasing age, adolescent adoptees become more and more prone to develop problem behaviours as a result of their increasing concerns over their biological parentage. Their increased cognitive abilities enable them to reflect on the meaning of being adopted. They are able to evaluate the lack of connectedness with their adoptive parents as well as with their biological parents. Their sense of loss of having once been abandoned, and their awareness of the lack of genealogical connectedness are evaluated in adolescence in terms of their developing identity (Brodzinsky, 1990). Emotional and behavioural reactions may result from this sense of loss, which is exacerbated by a loosening of the tie between the adolescent and his or her adoptive family, and by the adolescent's striving towards independence.

The adolescents adopted intercountry in our sample deviated more and more from their age-mates in the general population. This finding is a source of concern with respect to the adopted individual's future functioning. The adolescent's development towards adulthood with its greater independence, greater responsibilities, greater emphasis on stable sexual relationships, and even parenthood, may cause undue stresses, with still unknown consequences. It is important to evaluate how these adolescents develop in the future and to determine which factors influence their development, both in negative and positive ways. It also needs to be emphasised that the majority of adopted children, despite the many pre-adoption adversities and post-adoption stresses, seem to function well as adolescents. Our results support the view that transracial intercountry adoption may be a viable means of providing stable homes for children who would otherwise have had to endure many adversities.

References

Achenbach T M (1991a) *Manual for the CBCL/4-18 and 1991 Profile*, Burlington, VT: University of Vermont Department of Psychiatry.

Achenbach T M (1991b) *Manual for the YSR and 1991 Profile*, Burlington, VT: University of Vermont Department of Psychiatry.

Bohman M S (1970) *Adopted Children and their Families. A follow-up study of adopted children, their background, environment and adjustment*, Stockholm: Proprius.

Bohman M and Sigvardsson S (1978) 'An 18-year, prospective, longitudinal study of adopted boys', in Anthony J, Koupernik C and Chiland C (eds) *The Child in his Family: Vulnerable children*, London: Wiley.

Bohman M and Sigvardsson S (1979) 'Long-term effects of early institutional care: a prospective longitudinal study', *Journal of Child Psychology and Psychiatry*, 20, pp 111–117.

Bohman M S and Sigvardsson S (1980) 'A prospective, longitudinal study of children registered for adoption', *Acta Psychiatrica Scandinavica*, 61, pp 339–355.

Brodzinsky D M (1990) 'A stress and coping model of adoption adjustment', in Brodzinsky D M and Schechter M D (eds) *The Psychology of Adoption*, pp 3–24, New York: Oxford University Press.

Hersov L (1985) 'Adoption and fostering', in Rutter M and Hersov L (eds) *Child and Adolescent Psychiatry: Modern approaches*, pp 101–117, Oxford: Blackwell Scientific Publications.

Larson R and Richards M H (1991) 'Daily companionship in late childhood and early adolescence: changing developmental contexts', *Child Development*, 62, pp 284–300.

Rutter M and Garmezy N (1983) 'Developmental psychopathology', in Mussen P H (ed) *Handbook of Child Psychology*, Vol 4, pp 775–911, New York: Wiley.

Silverman A R and Feigelman W (1990) 'Adjustment in interracial adoptees: an overview', in Brodzinsky D M and Schechter M D (eds) *The Psychology of Adoption*, pp 187–200, New York: Oxford University Press.

Tizard B and Hodges J (1978) 'The effects of early institutional rearing on the development of eight-year-old children', *Journal of Child Psychology and Psychiatry*, 19, pp 99–118.

Tizard B and Rees J (1974) 'A comparison of the effects of adoptions, restoration to the natural mother, and continued institutionalisation on the cognitive development of four-year-old children', *Child Development*, 45, pp 92–99.

Tizard B and Rees J (1975) 'The effects of early institutional rearing on the behaviour problems and affectional relationships of four-year-old children', *Journal of Child Psychology and Psychiatry*, 16, pp 61–73.

Verhulst F C (2000) 'Internationally adopted children: the Dutch longitudinal adoption study', *Adoption Quarterly* (forthcoming).

Verhulst F C, Akkerhuis G W and Althaus M (1985) 'Mental health in Dutch Children 1; A cross-cultural comparison', *Acta Psychiatrica Scandinavica*, Supplement 323.

Verhulst F C, Althaus M and Versluis-den Bieman H J M (1990a) 'Problem behavior in international adoptees 1: an epidemiological study', *Journal of the American Academy of Child and Adolescent Psychiatry*, 29, pp 94–103.

Verhulst F C, Althaus M and Vesluis-den Bieman H J M (1990b) 'Problem behavior in international adoptees II. Age at placement', *Journal of the American Academy of Child and Adolescent Psychiatry*, 29, pp 104–111.

Verhulst F C, Versluis-den Bieman H J M, Van der Ende J, Berden G F M G and Sanders-Woudstra J A R (1990c) 'Problem behavior in international adoptees III. Diagnosis of child psychiatric disorders', *Journal of the American Academy of Child and Adolescent Psychiatry*, 29, pp 420–28.

Verhulst F C, Koot J M and Berden, G F M G (1990d) 'Four-year follow-up of an epidemiological sample', *Journal of the American Academy of Child and Adolescent Psychiatry*, 29, pp 440–448.

Verhulst F C, Althaus M and Versluis-den Bieman H J M (1992) 'Damaging backgrounds: later adjustment of international adoptees', *Journal of the American Academy of Child and Adolescent Psychiatry*, 33, pp 518–24.

Verhulst F C and Versluis-den Bieman H J M (1995) 'Developmental course of problem behaviors in adolescent adoptees', *Journal of the American Academy of Child and Adolescent Psychiatry*, 34, pp 151–59.

Versluis-den Bieman H J M and Verhulst F C (1995) 'Self-reported and parent-reported problems in adolescent international adoptees', *Journal of Child Psychology and Psychiatry*, 36, pp 1411–28.

8 Outcome of intercountry adoption in Sweden

Malin Irhammar and Marianne Cederblad

Malin Irhammar has a PhD in Psychology from the University of Lund in Sweden. Her thesis is concerned with issues of identity in adopted children.

Marianne Cederblad is Professor in Child and Youth Psychiatry at the University of Lund in Sweden. She has been researching the outcome of intercountry adoption for the past twenty years and has published many articles in medical journals.

Introduction

Swedish research regarding intercountry adopted children has focused mainly on somatic and mental health, and language and identity development. The first part of this review gives an overview of studies related to physical development, health and growth. It is followed by a similar overview of studies concerning language development, education, work and socialisation. The second part more closely reflects a larger study conducted by the authors concerning psychological development in respect of mental health and identity questions.

Physical development, health and growth

When intercountry adoption developed in Sweden in the late 1960s and in the 1970s, the first concern was about physical health and psycho-social adaptation. The first paediatric study comprised 144 pre-school children (Gunnarby *et al*, 1982). They were investigated when they arrived to their adoptive parents in Uppsala, one of the larger cities in the centre of Sweden. Seventy-two per cent came from Korea, India, Thailand and Ethiopia; 67 per cent were below one year of age when they arrived; 10 per cent were three years or above. The children were followed up in 1977 when most had been in Sweden 1–5 years, and their health status was compared with a reference group of 256 age-matched Swedish, non-adopted children. At arrival, 35 per cent had been physically ill or undernourished; 54 per cent had a very low weight and 64 per cent were much shorter than the Swedish reference group (they had values which only 2.5 per cent of a normal group have). Infections were common. At the follow-up all children were healthy and no child was undernourished. Even if weight and height had been normalised, 14 per cent were still far below the Swedish norm. The group did not differ from the Swedish reference group regarding psychomotor development but their language development was more delayed.

Another study (Tordai, 1982) comprising 153 adopted children from a city of similar size in central Sweden confirmed the findings about physical development. These were children who had arrived between 1965 and 1977. The medical records at the first paediatric investigation at arrival showed that only 21 per cent were totally healthy at the time of arrival; 13 per cent had needed hospitalisation, most often because of gastro-intestinal, skin or respiratory infections; and 60 per cent of the children were far below the Swedish norm for weight and height at arrival. Half of them were still small for their age after one year in Sweden.

The growth and development of Indian adopted children was further investigated by Proos (1992). This study comprised a retrospective investigation of 107 Indian adopted girls born before 1972 and a prospective two-year study of 114 Indian adopted children of both sexes, who arrived in Sweden in 1985. The study showed that the Indian adopted children were similar to average underprivileged Indian children with regards to clinical and anthropometric condition. Half of them were far below the Swedish norm for weight and height on arrival. The infectious diseases diagnosed at arrival were not serious; most of them could be treated or disappeared spontaneously. Those children who had a very low weight for their age at arrival had a higher rate of psychomotor retardation and anaemia. This improved quickly. Most children also grew rapidly during their first two years in Sweden. That was especially true for those children who also had a low height for their age. Linear catch-up growth dominated. In many girls this was cut short by early menarche. The median menarcheal age was 11.6 years, which was significantly earlier than for Swedish girls or for well-nourished girls in India. The group, which developed a very early puberty and eventually very short final height, consisted of girls who were very stunted at arrival, and who subsequently had a fast catch-up growth. The mean final height of the girls in the retrospective study population was one centimetre taller than females in an Indian general population (including less privileged groups), but did not attain the height of Indian girls from affluent families; 7.8 per cent of the girls attained only 134–145 centimetres as their final height, in spite of the favourable conditions in Sweden. Such low heights are associated with increased risk of obstetric and perinatal complications.

Language development

In a nationwide study of 207 adoptees, aged between 10 and 18 years, and their parents, Gardell (1979) noted that 47 per cent of the children in her study had problems with the Swedish language in secondary school. It was difficult for them to understand ordinary abstract concepts. Despite having difficulties in understanding education in school, they did very well in everyday life. These difficulties were most noticeable in the group of children aged between one-and-a-half and three years on arrival.

The significance of age at arrival has not been confirmed in other studies. De Geer (1992) compared five children adopted at different ages, during two years from their arrival to Sweden, and one Swedish born child. To map their linguistic and communicative development, the children were videotaped in their interaction with their mothers. The results show small differences between all the children, independent of age at arrival.

In another study of children referred to speech therapists, Thelander and Miske (1995) conclude that age and physical status at arrival were not related to language problems. However, their results show that the group of adopted children with disturbed language development had greater difficulties and were more often delayed in their language development compared with Swedish children. In their study of eight adopted children, now in their teenage years, Gillholm and Ivanov (1997) concluded that language difficulties cannot be considered as normal or expected just because the child is adopted. The authors suggest that, if adopted teenagers have learning problems, the adopted child's general and specific abilities should be tested.

The most comprehensive studies in this area have been conducted by Hene (1987, 1989, 1993). Her main results show, in accordance with Gardell, that the adopted children's language problems seem to be of lesser importance in informal situations compared to school situations.

When Hene compared language comprehension and production in a group of 24 adopted children, aged 10 to 12 years, with a group of 24 Swedish-born children of the same age, she found that the adopted children had special difficulties in understanding the literal meaning of words, and in some cases in understanding the sentence structure. The more advanced the tasks, the greater the differences between the two groups. Hene is of the opinion that it is more adequate to talk about a delay in the adopted children's language development. The results also show great differences *within* the group of adopted children which cannot be explained simply by their age at arrival. Such unevenness is not found in the Swedish-born group. Hene's explanation is that the adopted children's language development has not taken place in interplay with their motor, cognitive and social development.

Education, work and socialisation

In a survey of pupils from the ninth year of compulsory school and the sixth form of a grammar school (Moser, 1993), school-leaving certificates of 156 intercountry adopted children in one Swedish county were studied. The results were compared with those of Swedish pupils of the same ages and they were found to be practically identical. In the adopted group there were no differences between boys and girls. The school-leaving grades were not related to the parents' social class, as was the situation in the Swedish group. The adopted children who had arrived before three years of age had higher marks than those arriving at older ages.

In a follow-up study (Moser, 1997), 100 children from the original group were studied regarding their employment. Unemployment was significantly less common in the adopted group compared with the Swedish population in general. Among those who were in employment, a majority considered that it was easy for them to get a job. Most of them thought that their personal qualities, such as social competence, ability to adjust and a "go-ahead" attitude, had played an important role in increasing their chances of getting a job. Only a few had met negative attitudes related to their ethnic origin.

In an ongoing interview-study of young adopted adolescents from Latin America growing up in Sweden, Greiff (1997) asks how adoptees experience their situation as an adopted person, and how they understand the conditions in which they are growing up, and their life situations. She is also seeking to distinguish determining differences between the group of well-adjusted adoptees and those referred to residential care. The results are not yet published but will soon be in a doctoral thesis.

Psychological development, behaviour deviance and psychosocial adaptation

Early Swedish studies showed that pre-school children adapted well in their adoptive families (Cederblad, 1981). Many showed initial problems of adaptation such as regression and various crisis reactions (Cederblad, 1982), but both physical and mental health improved rapidly. Studies also showed that development during early school age seemed satisfactory (Gardell, 1979). Towards the end of the 1980s, when larger groups of adoptive children reached their teens, schools, social agencies and child psychiatric clinics reported seeing many problems in the adopted teenagers. Studies from child guidance clinics (Déry-Alfredsson and Katz, 1986; Cederblad, 1991) seemed to confirm these clinical reports. In both studies, foreign-born adopted children were more frequently found among the teenage patients than their proportion of the population in the catchment area for each clinic. In recent years, an over-representation of adopted teenagers has also been reported from schools for juvenile offenders (*NIA Informs*, 1996). It is, however, always impossible to draw conclusions about frequencies of disturbances in a population from studies of clinical groups. Many children with psychiatric problems never see a therapist while certain parents are more eager to ask for expert help than others when they confront different problems of upbringing.

The Cederblad and Irhammar study

In this section, we report on the findings of our recent research into the psychosocial development of young people adopted from abroad (Cederblad *et al*, 1993, 1994; Irhammar, 1997, 1998, 1999). In this research, all 181 families, living in one county in Southern Sweden, who had adopted children via the Swedish Adoption Centre during the period 1970–77, were invited to take part in a study of adoptees' identity development and mental health. A majority of the families (84 per cent) agreed to participate. The results reported in this section derive from interviews with the adoptees and their parents as well as from different self-rating instruments.

Seventy-three per cent of the adoptees were born in Asia and the remaining 27 per cent came from Latin America. At the time of the interview, all were aged between 13 and 27 years, with a mean age of 16.7 years. Their ages at arrival in their adoptive families ranged from a few months old to eight years, with a mean arrival age of 14.2 months. There were more women (59 per cent) than men (41 per cent) in the sample.

The study was partly designed to investigate if the teenage period was a time of increased adjustment strain for intercountry adopted young people. Interest in this question arose both from clinical reports on adjustment problems and from theoretical assumptions on possible increased identity demands.

Psychological adjustment and mental health
Methods of investigation
The mothers filled in the *Child Behaviour Checklist/4–18* (CBCL) (Achenbach, 1991). This well-known questionnaire covers 118 different problem behaviour and four competence scales. The single items have been factor analysed and constitute the eight symptom groups (or diagnoses) used in Table 8.1. "Externalising" is the sum of aggressive and delinquent behaviour groups; "internalising" is the sum of the

Table 8.1

Scores on the CBCL for adoptive children (Ad) and children from the comparison group (Co) in relation to age (two-way analysis of variance)**

	13 years		14 years		15 years		16 years	
	Ad	Co	Ad	Co	Ad	Co	Ad	Co
Number of children	8	165	35	140	52	147	38	77
Total score	**13.2**	**14.2**	**12.2**	**12.3**	**14.1**	**15.7**	**12.4**	**15.2**
Externalising	6.6	5.6	4.3	4.8	5.2	6.0	4.3	5.9
Internalising	3.9	4.4	3.3	3.6	3.8	4.8	4.2	4.2
Symptom groups								
Withdrawn	2.0	1.4	1.3	1.2	1.6	1.5	1.8	1.5
Somatic complaints[†]	0.6	0.6	0.4	0.6	0.6	0.8	0.6	0.8
Anxious-depressed	1.1	2.0	1.5	1.5	1.8	2.1	1.8	1.7
Social problems	0.6	0.6	0.9	0.6	1.0	0.6	0.8	0.6
Thought problems	0.0	0.1	0.0	0.0	0.0	0.3	0.2	0.2
Attention problems	1.2	1.5	2.1	1.5	2.5	1.6	1.9	1.7
Delinquent behaviour	0.9	1.2	1.2	1.0	1.1	1.4	0.9	1.7
Aggressive behaviour	5.8	4.4	3.2	3.8	4.1	4.5	3.3	4.2

**There were no significant relationships between the four age levels or between the adopted and control groups within each age level

[†] = items 56d and 56e were excluded from the syndrome because of differences between the studies in the coding procedure

withdrawn, somatic and anxious-depressed symptom groups. In all cases a higher score signifies more problems.

The CBCL is designed to be filled in by a parent. It has been translated into Swedish and used elsewhere in a large epidemiological study of Swedish school-children (Larsson and Frisk, 1999). The comparison group consists of a stratified, random sample of 529 adolescents from that study, who were aged 13 to 16 years and living in urban, semi-rural and rural areas in a county of Sweden.

The subjects aged 16 and over also filled in the *Symptom Check List [SCL-90]* (Derogatis *et al*, 1977). This is a widely used measure that contains a series of 90 factors referring to expressions of psychosomatic

Table 8.2

Scores on the SCL-90 for adoptive children (Ad) and children from the comparison group (Co) in relation to age in years (two-way analysis of variance)

	Age 17–19		Age 20–27	
	Ad	Co	Ad	Co
Number of children	39	63	27	55
Total score	**41.3**	**36.0**	**44.4**	**42.4**
Diagnostic categories				
Somatisation	3.3	4.8	4.9	5.5
Obsessive-compulsive**	7.1	4.9	6.5	5.2
Interpersonal sensitivity	5.1	4.6	4.3	5.7
Depression	7.1	5.9	7.8	7.9
Anxiety	5.2	4.5	5.7	5.8
Hostility	2.6	2.1	3.3	2.8
Phobic anxiety	1.1	1.1	2.0	1.1
Paranoid ideation	3.2	2.4	3.0	2.9
Psychoticism	3.0	2.1	2.8	2.1

**The difference between adopted and comparison groups at each age level was significant for this category [$p < 0.05$]. Otherwise, there were no significant differences between the adopted and control groups within each age level – or between scores for each group at the two defined ages.

and emotional distress. The results are presented as a total score and nine diagnostic categories (see Table 8.2). The results of this inventory have been briefly presented elsewhere in Swedish (Cederblad *et al*, 1993). The SCL-90 had earlier been used on adolescents of comparable ages in a child psychiatric epidemiological study in Sweden, which was used as a comparison group (Cederblad and Höök, 1991). The comparison group consists of a stratified, random sample of 118 adolescents/young adults, 18–21 years of age, in urban, semi-rural and rural areas in a county of Sweden.

All youngsters filled in the self-report inventory 'I think I am . . .' (Ouvinen-Birgerstam, 1984). The inventory measures different aspects of self-esteem and acceptance of one's own looks and body, performances, psychological well-being, family relations and relations to others, for example, friends. The inventory has been standardised for Swedish youngsters.

Good mental health in the group of adoptees

Table 8.1 presents the problem behaviour scores on the CBCL for the adoptees compared to a Swedish epidemiological study (Larsson and Frisk, 1999). The mental health of the adopted children was as good as in the comparison group. There were no significant differences between the four age levels. Girls in both the adopted and the control groups had higher scores on "internalising" as well as on the separate "withdrawn", "somatic complaints" and "anxious-depressed" symptom groups. Twelve per cent of the adopted children and eleven per cent of the comparison group had scores in the clinical range.

Table 8.2 presents the total scores and the scores of the diagnostic categories for the older age-groups investigated with SCL-90 compared with a Swedish born comparison group (Cederblad and Höök, 1991). The mental health of the adoptees was as good as that of the control group, except that the adoptees had significantly higher scores on "obsessive-compulsive" symptoms. There was no difference between the age groups. In both groups, girls had higher scores on the total score as well as on "somatisation" (experience of psychosomatic aches and pains), "interpersonal sensitivity", "depression" and "anxiety". The percentage of severely disturbed subjects did not differ between the adoptees and either of the comparison groups.

On the self report inventory, 'I think I am', the adoptees reported a higher total score of self-esteem than the Swedish norm (a high score indicates good self-esteem): the same scores as the Swedish norm on the components "looks and body", "performances", "psychological well-being" and "family relations" and a higher score on "relations to others" ($p< 0.001$).

The impact of the adoptees' pre-adoption experiences

The effect of age at arrival and the pre-adoption situation on the adopted group was analysed using the CBCL scores as outcomes (Table 8.3). The situation of the child before adoption seemed to have more impact

Table 8.3

Scores on the CBCL for adoptive children in relation to the age of arrival and the pre-adoption situation (two-way analysis of variance)

| | 0–12 mths | | 13–45 mths | | Statistical significance | |
	pre-1	pre-2	pre-1	pre-2	Age on arrival	Pre-adoption situation
Number of children	114	10	11	10		
Total score	**12.2**	**20.3**	**8.6**	**18.8**	—	**
Externalising	4.2	7.0	4.3	5.9	—	—
Internalising	3.6	6.7	2.5	5.4	—	*
Symptom groups						
Withdrawn	1.6	2.5	1.4	3.2	—	**
Somatic complaints	0.6	1.4	0.0	0.3	**	—
Anxious-depressed	1.5	3.0	1.1	2.0	—	—
Social problems	0.8	1.5	0.2	1.9	—	**
Thought problems	0.1	0.1	0.0	0.7	—	—
Attention problems	2.0	3.5	1.3	3.8	—	**
Delinquent behavior	1.0	1.1	1.0	1.1	—	—
Aggressive behavior	3.2	5.9	3.3	4.8	—	—

pre-adoption situation = length of time in orphanage + fosterhome in the country of origin:
pre-1 = 0–6 months, pre-2 = 7 months or more.
— = not significant, *= $p < 0.05$, **= $p < 0.01$

than age at arrival. Those who had spent seven months or more in an orphanage or foster home prior to arrival had significantly higher total problem scores and higher scores on "internalising" and on three of the symptom groups – "withdrawn", "social problems" and "attention problems". It was not possible to analyse care in orphanages and foster homes separately.

Conclusion

To summarise, our study has shown that this group of adoptees had good mental health as assessed through parental interviews and self-reports. The subjects reported higher self-esteem overall and in respect of relations to others. We therefore conclude that the mental health of the group investigated was as good as that of Swedish non-adopted individuals of comparable ages investigated with the same investigation instruments (see also Cederblad *et al*, 1999).

Identity reflected through meaning of biological and ethnic origin

In the study described above, adoptive parents and adoptees were also interviewed separately using semi-structured interviews. The focus of the interviews was on the adoptees' biological and ethnic origins. The adoptees were asked about memories of, knowledge about, thoughts of, and interest in searching for information about their origin and about their communication with the adoptive parents concerning their biological and ethnic background. They were also asked about their ethnic self-identity, how they experienced their physical appearance, and how others perceived them in relation to their ethnic background. They were also asked about their perceptions of similarities and dissimilarities between themselves and the adoptive parents in different respects. In the study, interest in biological origin i.e. interest in their birth family, is distinguished from interest in ethnic origin. A distinction is also made between an *inner* search (thoughts about their biological family) and an *outer* search (a more active search for information about the biological family).

The adoptive parents were asked about their knowledge of, thoughts about, interest in, and ways of handling issues relating to the children's biological and ethnic origins. The study examines how the adoptive parents' handling of these issues related to their adopted children's own interest in their origins.

As described above, different instruments were also used to measure mental health and self-esteem among the adoptees. A standardised instrument to measure family relations in the adoptive family was used as well (FARS, Family relation scale; Höök and Cederblad, 1992). The material has been statistically analysed, using Chi square, variance analyses and logistic regression (Irhammar, 1997 and 1999). In this chapter, the statistical results are not described in detail but the level of significance is indicated where appropriate.

Thoughts about the biological family: an inner search

One way of exploring biological origins is to think about the biological family. The majority of the adoptees (70 per cent) in this study do think about their biological family, women significantly more often than men. An explanation can be that it is most often the mother who has had to make the decision to give up the child, and it can be easier for women to identify with this situation.

About half of those adoptees who have their biological family in their thoughts, had talked to their adoptive parents about them, and a further 14 per cent had talked to somebody outside the family. This means that more than one third had kept their thoughts to themselves. Variables *not* related to thoughts of the biological family were age at adoption, age at interview, memories before the adoption, knowledge about the biological family, experiences of similarities between the child and adoptive parents and the adoptive family composition. Furthermore, family relations were *not* related to whether or not the adoptees thought about their birth families.

Most often the adoptees thought about who they looked like and whether they might have siblings in their birth country. They would typically say that they missed pictures and stories from this first period in their lives, stories which could help them to create continuity in their life. This can be interpreted as a search for a *mirror* in which they can reflect themselves. Some of the older adoptees were concerned for their parents' life situation and their decision to leave their child. Sometimes these adoptees can feel a responsibility for the family they once had to leave.

However, a small group (seven per cent) was more intensively pre-occupied by such thoughts. This group had, according to the total score on the test 'I think I am', a significantly lower self-esteem compared to those who thought less often – or never at all – about their biological family. It is only the sub-scale measuring psychic wellbeing that explains the differences. These more intense thoughts of the biological family seemed to be related to poorer mental health. In this group with more intense thoughts about their birth family, the inner search seemed to be less a search for a mirror than an expression of an unsatisfactory life situation.

An outer search: the quest for information about the biological family

Another way of exploring the biological origin is through a more active, *outer* search for knowledge. More than half of those who thought about their biological family also wanted to try to get more information about the family. Although women seemed to have a greater interest in their biological family as expressed by an *inner* search, there are no statistical differences between women and men in respective of an *outer*, more active search.

Openness in the adoptive family to the child's origin is related to the adoptees' interest in their origin. In those families where the adoptive parents had an ongoing contact with the child's orphanage or someone who was involved in the adoption in the country of origin, the adoptees were significantly more interested in searching for information about their biological family ($p<.05$). Experience of divorce of adoptive parents also contributed to an increased interest by adopted persons in their biological origins ($p<.01$).

Those who had a higher self-confidence regarding contacts outside their family seemed to be significantly more prepared to search for information about their biological family ($p<.05$). This higher degree of "sociability" seemed to reflect a more outgoing, open, information-seeking approach, and also a more general "coping" strategy.

Neither age at adoption, age at interview, memories, nor actual knowledge (two-thirds knew something about their background) were related to interest in searching. It might be expected that actual knowledge of their background would be related to adoptees' search interests, but this is not the case. An explanation may be that many of the adoptees who do know something about their biological family have so little information that the difference between knowing and not knowing is not a determining factor. Most adoptive parents had told their children what there was to know about the child's history, but usually there was very little information to pass on. Often it had been difficult to get information from the orphanage or hospital, given the circumstances in which the children had been left.

Experiences of similarities between the child and adoptive parents and the adoptive family composition did not seem to influence the adoptees' interest in searching. Likewise, family relations, mental health and self-esteem were not related to interest in a more active search. However, those who thought about their biological family, but had no interest in searching, were found to have a poorer mental health.

Internal and external ethnic identification

Most of the adopted persons in this study (88 per cent) have a Swedish ethnic self-identity, which means that they experience themselves as Swedes, with a Swedish cultural practice. A "Swedish" self-identity was related neither to mental problems nor to low self-esteem for this group, as has been claimed by opponents of transracial adoption in the Anglo-American debate (see e.g., Gaber, 1994; Small, 1986). On the contrary, individuals with a Swedish self-identity had a significantly *better* mental health status than those with a "non-Swedish" self-identity ($p<.05$). One explanation of this could be that a "non-Swedish" self-identity does not reflect a sense of belonging to an ethnic group, but rather a sense of being *different*. Ethnic self-identity was not related to the gender of the child or to age at adoption or interview, nor to the adoptive parent's openness toward the child's origin, family relations or the attitudes the adoptees met in their social environment.

About two-thirds of the adoptees reported experiences of being externally identified as immigrants. The older the adoptees are, the more common these experiences are. For most of them, these situations were connected with some sort of conflict, either through the attitudes they met or through their own feelings of embarrassment, when their appearance attracted attention. One common strategy to counter this was to stress their Swedish language, which gives them a Swedish legitimacy. Others tried to explain and defend themselves, while others used some form of avoidance strategies, sometimes even expressed as negative attitudes to immigrants. However, many of them had no specific strategies to handle these situations, and behaved in a more passive way.

Interest in ethnic origin

It is important to note that a Swedish self-identity does not imply a denial of their ethnic origin. One third of this group did take an active interest in their ethnic origin.

In order to assess interest in ethnic origin, an index was created from four variables:

1) Reading about their birth country and its culture;
2) Listening to music from the country;
3) Wanting to learn the language;
4) Wanting to visit the country of origin.

Adoptees were given a score from 0–3 in relation to their interest in each area, giving a total of 0–12 on the index, a higher score indicating a greater degree of interest.

The interest factor was divided into a more active interest (6–12) and lack of interest (0–5) respectively. Even in the group which did not express any strong interest in their ethnic origin, there was often a wish to visit their country of origin.

Adoptees who had a more active interest in their ethnic origin were more likely to have come from Latin America than from Asia ($p<.001$). They had also more often been adopted after one and a half years of age ($p<.01$). They also had significantly lower self-esteem according to the sub-scale measuring psychic wellbeing ($p<.05$).

It is probably not the continent per se that influences a more active interest in ethnic origin. When controlling for variables related to country of origin, it was found that families with children from Latin America were less likely to have had contact with the orphanage or someone who had been engaged in the child's adoption in the country of origin. Further, those adopted from Latin America showed lower self-esteem on the sub-scale measuring physical appearance: i.e. they were less satisfied with their appearance ($p<.01$).

Where the adoptive family showed little interest in the child's origins, there was a more active interest in ethnic origin amongst the adoptees themselves. When controlling for ethnic self-identity, we found an inter-correlation between ethnic self-identity and interest in ethnic origin. Those with a "non-Swedish" self-identity were more interested in their ethnic origin. Because of this, separate calculations were made for the two different identity groups (i.e. those with "Swedish" and "non-Swedish" self-identities). A lack of identification with the adoptive

parents was, in the case of those with a Swedish self-identity, significantly related to an interest in their ethnic origins. Those who experienced themselves as Swedes but could not find any similarities between
themselves and their adoptive parents were more likely to show a higher
interest in their ethnic origin. Gender, age at interview, family conditions
and external identification were of no importance in explaining the
young person's interest in their ethnic origin.

It is important to note that a lack of identification with the adoptive
parents was only associated with an interest in ethnic origins, not with
an interest in their biological families, whether reflected in an inner or
outer search.

Finally, the group (70 per cent of those interviewed) who reported
thinking about their biological family, those with an *inner* search, were
divided into four sub-groups in respect of their interest in an *outer* search
for their biological and/or ethnic origins; i.e those who thought about
their birth families and showed an active interest in finding out more
about:

1) Both biological and ethnic origins (30 per cent);
2) Biological but not ethnic origins (31 per cent);
3) Ethnic but not biological origins (10 per cent);
4) Neither biological nor ethnic origins (29 per cent),

Further analysis, using these four categories, showed that the small group
who thought about their biological families, but only wanted to search
for their ethnic origins (group 3), were significantly more likely to have
a poorer mental health and lower self-esteem when compared with
the other three groups ($p < .01$). They were also more likely to live in
families with disturbed relationships ($p < .05$). This may be interpreted as
indicating that an ethnic interest can sometimes be a substitute for an
interest in the birth family because the issue may be seen as less
threatening.

Summary and conclusion

A high interest in ethnic origins seems to be related to three main factors:

- The adoptive parents' lack of openness about the child's origins;
- The child's lack of identification with the adoptive parents;
- The adoptee's dissatisfaction with his/her appearance.

This can be interpreted as a sense of being *different*. If so, this sense of being different may lead to a disequilibrium, which results in an active interest in ethnic, rather than biological origins.

But, where there is openness and interest in the child's origins on the part of the adoptive parents, this is associated with a higher self-esteem and seems to encourage an active interest in the birth family, while lessening the adoptee's interest in their ethnic origins. The adoptive parents' openness can not only contribute to their child's knowledge of their background, but also confirm those origins in a positive way and so reduce the experience of being different.

The adopted persons in this study were often reminded of their special situation as "visible" adoptees compared to non-adopted young Swedes. Two-thirds had had the experience of being regarded as foreigners. However, although the study showed that there was a relation between identity problems and mental health, the majority of the subjects seemed to cope well with their special outsider situation since the group as a whole was well adjusted. To live with a Swedish inner identity but a foreign external appearance is probably an inevitable dilemma, which is the cost of having been adopted transracially. The benefit is that most of the time the individual will have good mental health and a high self-esteem despite this deviant life situation.

A more detailed account in English of the research described in the second half of this paper can be found in Irhammar, 1999.

References

Achenbach T M (1991) *Manual for the Child Behavior Checklist/4–18 and 1991 Profile*, Burlington, Vermont: University of Vermont, Department of Psychiatry.

Cederblad M (1981) 'Utländska adoptivbarns psykiska anpassning' (Foreign adopted children's psychological adjustment), *The Swedish Medical Journal*, 78, pp 816–819.

Cederblad M (1982) *Utländska Adoptivbarn Som Kommit till Sverige efter Tre Års Ålder (Foreign Adopted Children Arriving in Sweden after Three Years of Age)*, NIA-The Swedish National Board for Intercountry Adoption, Stockholm: Sweden.

Cederblad M (1991) ' "Hög" ålder vid adoption – största risken för att utveckla anpassnings-problem i tonåren' (High age at adoption – greatest risk for developing adjustment problems in adolescent), *The Swedish Medical Journal*, 88:12, pp 1081–1085.

Cederblad M and Höök B (1991) *Östgötastudien: Stressreaktioner och Beteend-Estörningar hos Barn på 80-talet i Östergötland (The Östgöta study: Stress reactions and behaviour problems in children in the1980s in Östergötland)*, Save the Children, No 1, Stockholm, Sweden.

Cederblad M, Irhammar M, Mercke A M and Höök B (1993) 'God psykisk hälsa hos utländska adoptivbarn' (Good mental health among adoptive children of foreign origin), *The Swedish Medical Journal*, 90:16, pp 1537–42.

Cederblad M, Irhammar M, Mercke A M and Norlander E (1994) *Identitet och Anpassning hos Utlandsfödda Adopterade Ungdomar (Identity and Adjustment in Adopted Youth Born Abroad)*, Research about Children and Families, no 4, Department of Child and Youth Psychiatry, Sweden: University of Lund.

Cederblad M, Höök B, Irhammar M and Mercke A M (1999) 'Mental health in international adoptees as teenagers and young adults an epidemiological study', *Journal of Child Psychology and Psychiatry*, 8, pp 1239–1248.

De Geer B (1992) *Internationally Adopted Children in Communication: A developmental study*, Working Paper no 39, Department of Linguistics, Sweden: University of Lund.

Derogatis L R, Lipman R S and Cleary P A (1977) 'Confirmation of the dimensional structure of the SCL-90. A study in construct validity', *Journal of Clinical Psychology*, 33, pp 981–989.

Déry-Alfredsson I and Katz M (1986) *Utländska adoptivbarn på PBU (Foreign adopted children at child guidance clinics)*, Department of Psychology, Sweden: University of Stockholm.

Gaber I (1994) 'Transracial Placements in Britain: A History', in Gaber I and Aldridge J (eds), *Culture, Identity and Transracial Adoption: In the best interest of the child*, London: Free Association Books, pp 12–42.

Gardell I (1979) *A Swedish Study on Intercountry Adoptions*, Stockholm: Allmänna Barnhuset.

Gillholm I and Ivanov A (1997) *En Kartläggning av Språkförmåga hos åtta Utlandsadopterade Tonåringar (A Survey of Language Ability in Eight Foreign Adopted Adolescents)*, Department of Logopedics and Phoniatrics, Sweden: University of Lund.

Greiff von K (1997) 'Sverige som socialisationskultur: En studie av utlandsadopterades syn på sina uppväxtvillkor och sin livssituation' (Sweden as socialization culture. A study of foreign adoptees' view of their upbringing and life situation), in Forsten-Lindman N (ed) *Proceedings*. The 3rd Nordic research conference concerning adoption 23–25 May 1997, Department of Psychology at Åbo Academy, Finland: University of Åbo.

Gunnarby A, Hofvander Y, Sjölin S and Sundelin C (1982) 'Utländska adoptivbarns hälsotillstånd och anpassning till svenska förhållanden (Foreign adopted children's health and adjustment to Swedish conditions), *The Swedish Medical Journal*, 79, pp 1697–1705.

Hene B (1987) *De Utländska Adoptivbarnen och deras Språkutveckling (The foreign adopted children and their language development)*, SPRINS-report 36. Department of Linguistics, Sweden: University of Gothenburg.

Hene B (1989) '*Proficiency in a New Native Language: An investigation into the proficiency in Swedish in intercountry adoptees between 10 and 12 years of age*'. Institute of Child Language Research, No 4, pp 59–66, Department of Linguistics, Sweden: University of Lund.

Hene B (1993) *Utlandsadopterade Barns och Svenska Barns Ordförståelse. En jämförelse mellan barn i åldern 10–12 år* (Foreign Adopted Children's and Swedish Children's Word Comprehension: A comparison between children in the age of 10–12 years), SPRINS No 41, Sweden: University of Gothenburg.

Höök B and Cederblad M (1992) *Familjerelationsskalan (FARS): Forskning om barn och familj nr 1.* (Family relation scale (FARS): Research about Children and Families, No 1). Department of Child and Youth Psychiatry, Sweden: University of Lund.

Irhammar M (1997) *Att Utforska Sitt Ursprung: Identitetsformande under adolescensen hos utlandsfödda adopterade. Betydelsen av biologiskt och etniskt ursprung (Exploration of Origin: Identity formation during adolescence in adoptees born abroad, meaning of biological and ethnic origin)*, Dissertation Thesis, Department of Psychology, Sweden: University of Lund.

Irhammar M (1998) 'Ursprung och identitet', *Invandrare och Minoriteter, 4.* (Origin and Identity). *Scandinavian Migration and Ethnic Minority Review.*

Irhammar M (1999) 'Meaning of biological and ethnic origin in adoptees born abroad', in Ryvgold A, Dalen M, Saetersdal B (eds) *Mine – Yours – Ours and Theirs*, Oslo: University of Oslo.

Larsson B and Frisk M (1999) 'Social competence and emotional/behaviour problems in 6–16-year-old Swedish school children', *European Child and Adolescent Psychiatry*, 8, pp 24–33.

Moser G (1993) *Adoptivbarns Skolprestationer och val av Studieväg: En studie av barn från utomeuropeiska länder som adopterats i Kronobergs län åren 1971–1980 (Adopted children's school performance and choice of studies)*, Institute of Education, Department of Education, Sweden: University of Stockholm.

Moser G (1997) *Ett Perfekt Svenskt Uttal Lugnar de Flesta Arbetsgivare: En studie av unga internationellt adopterades utbildning och arbete (A perfect accent reassures most employers: A study of education and work in a group of international adoptees)*. Unpublished master's thesis, Institute of Education, Department of Education, Sweden: University of Stockholm.

NIA Informerar 1996:2. (NIA Informs 1996, p. 2). The Swedish National Board for Intercountry Adoption, Sweden: Stockholm.

Ouvinen-Birgerstam P (1984) *Jag tycker Jag är – En metod för studier av barns och ungdomars självuppfattning* (Manual. I think I am – A method to study children's and adolescent's self-esteem), Stockholm: Psykologiförlaget.

Proos L (1992) *Growth and Development: Indian Children Adopted in Sweden.* Dissertation Thesis, no. 363. Faculty of Medicine, Sweden: University of Uppsala.

Small J (1986) 'Transracial placements: Conflicts and contradictions', in Ahmed S, Cheetham J and Small J (eds), *Social Work with Black Children and their Families*, London: Batsford, pp 81–99.

Thelander U and Miske E (1995) *Frän Chile to Kil: En jämförelse av språkavvikelser hor en grupp utlandsfödda adoptivbarn och en grupp svenskfödda barn (From Chile to Kil: A comparison of language discrepancy in a group of foreign adopted children and a group of children born in Sweden).* Research Reports No. 5, Centre for Public Health Research, Sweden: County Council of Värmland.

Tordai G (1982) 'Utländska adoptivbarn i Norrköping', I: *Internationella adoptioner*. Delegationen för Social Forskning, nr. 4. (Foreign Adopted Children in Norrköping, in *International Adoptions*. Delegation for Social Research, no 4), Sweden: Stockholm.

9 Identity formation in a homogeneous country
Intercountry adoption in Norway

Barbro Sætersdal and Monica Dalen

Barbro Sætersdal and Monica Dalen are both professors at the Institute of Special Needs Education at the University of Oslo.

Introduction

Norway, with its 4.5 million inhabitants, is one of the countries with the highest number of foreign-born adopted persons in relation to its population size. The country currently has around 15,000 children adopted from about 20 different countries, mainly in Asia and Latin America. Recently, with the fall of communism in Eastern Europe, children have also been adopted from Poland, Romania and Russia. Most of the foreign-born adoptees in Norway are still quite young or of primary or lower secondary school age, but some of the first adoptees from Korea, Vietnam and Colombia are now grown up and in their 30s. Around 5–600 children are now adopted from foreign countries annually, equivalent to one per cent of all the children born in Norway each year. Norway now has one of the highest rates of overseas adoptions per 100,000 population (Haugland, 1999). This figure has remained high despite the fact that artificial-insemination methods have become more and more advanced and common as a form of treatment for infertility. Statistics on intercountry adoptions over the past 20 years are provided in the Appendix to this chapter.

Adoption policy and procedures in Norway

Norway ratified the Hague Convention on 25 September 1997. The Central Authority is the Governmental Office for Youth and Adoption in Oslo. The system is similar in many ways to that found in Sweden and the Netherlands, but private adoptions are not permitted. A new Adoption Act in April 1999 lays down strict and thorough procedures for all applicants. The Ministry for Children and Family Affairs requires that all those wishing to adopt must have good physical and psychological health, be under 45 years of age, married and living with their partner for at least two years or a single person with particular and broad experience of children (Haugland, 1999). Adoption by unmarried heterosexual or lesbian or gay couples is not permitted, but these groups' rights are on the political agenda and have been hotly debated in recent years. Norwegian adoption agencies have pointed out that none of the countries they are working with would consider placing children with lesbian or gay couples.

Adoption from overseas is possible only through one of the three authorised agencies named as accredited bodies: Adopsjonsforum (Adoption Forum); Verdens Barn (Children of the World); and InorAdopt. In 1998, there were 643 intercountry adoptions, 96 per cent of which were mediated by the first two organisations. In that year, over 60 per cent of the children came from three countries (China, South Korea and Colombia). Since 1998, the two largest organisations have also offered new preparatory courses for prospective adoptive parents in many parts of the country, but these are not compulsory as in the Netherlands (see Duinkerken and Geerts, Chapter 20).

Home studies are carried out by local authorities, whose social workers have to prepare a report with recommendations for approval or rejection, which is sent to the Governmental Office for Youth and Adoption. If applicants are rejected they have a right of appeal to the Ministry for Children and Family Affairs. Those approved then apply to one of the authorised agencies described above.

There is a government grant of 22,000 kroner (about £1,800) towards the costs of the adoption and families have full access to all benefits and welfare services. Older adopted children get extra language classes and other special tuition if Norwegian is not their first language.

Intercountry adoption is fully acceptable in Norway and breakdown rates are very low (Dalen, 1999a). Most people regard adopting a foreign child as a private, personal matter, and as an acceptable, alternative, but "next-best" way of having children. Domestic adoptions are very rare in Norway and domestic *transracial* adoption is virtually non-existent.

Race, migration and adoption in the Norwegian context

The intense political discussions that have characterised debates about transracial and intercountry adoption in the UK have been more or less absent in Norway, which has historically been ethnically homogeneous, apart from the small minority of Lapps who live in the northern part of the country. The immigration of labourers from southern Europe in the 1950s and 1960s, which affected much of Northern Europe, never reached Norway. In the early 1970s – at much the same time as overseas adoption was starting – emigration from the Third World began and has been growing steadily. This means that Norway still does not have the old well-established minority ethnic communities that are found in England or Germany. Today, there are 165,070 people with foreign citizenship registered in Norway, most of them Europeans, but that figure does not include the growing number of people from the Third World who have obtained Norwegian citizenship. About 20 per cent of all pupils in the lower grades of inner-city schools are from families originating in the Third World. In this context most Norwegians find it hard to understand the passionate debates about racial identity in the USA and Britain or to see any relevance for Norway.

The development of identity of foreign born children adopted in Norway

In this chapter, we will concentrate on how the identity of Norwegian children who have been adopted from abroad develops and describe their attitude to their own ethnicity. What is it like to grow up in a homogeneous society as a "coloured" Norwegian? What is their attitude to the culture and background they left behind when they were adopted? Do they feel they belong in the society in which they have grown up or do they find themselves in a mental and cultural vacuum?

In the following discussion, we will differentiate between how the adopted children *themselves* feel they belong (ethnic self-identification) and how *those around them* categorise them (external identification). If these are the same, such as they are for Norwegian-born children in Norway, then there is no problem. Ethnic Norwegians are, feel they are, and are treated as being, "Norwegian", without any questions being asked as to where they belong. This becomes more of a problem if a foreign-born adoptee feels Norwegian but, because of his or her different appearance, is often treated as being non-Norwegian. A conflict then arises between the child's ethnic self-identification and the external identification.

In discussing these issues we draw on a recently completed study (Sætersdal and Dalen, 1999; Dalen, 1999b), in which Vietnamese and Indian adoptees and their adoptive parents were interviewed separately using semi-structured interviews. Different self-rating instruments were used to study mental health, self-esteem and family relations. The interviews were recorded and transcribed. The focus of the interviews was on the adoptees' biological and ethnic origin and their attitudes towards immigrants and refugees in Norway. They were also asked about their ethnic self-identity, how they experienced their physical appearance, and how they were perceived by others in relation to their ethnic background.

What does ethnicity mean in a homogeneous society?

The concept of ethnic identity is used in many adoption studies. Although the discussion about "roots" and "a black identity" has been an important theme of international research into adoption, this concept has rarely been defined. "Black identity" is an Anglo-Saxon, political concept which arose from colonialist oppression and the slave trade. The argument itself presumes that there is a homogeneous, classless "black" background culture, which is separate and different from an assumed "white" majority culture. Tizard and Phoenix (1989 and 1995) discuss this in relation to the UK debate on adopting foreign children and their "black identity":

The notion that there is a black culture which must be transmitted to transracially adopted children is unconvincing, given the plethora of British lifestyles. The belief that there is a "positive black identity" which must be acquired by black children is oversimplified and prescriptive and fails to take into account the way in which black parents and children describe themselves. (1989, p 436)

The concept of a "black identity" is basically problematic, as are the concepts of "coloured" or "mixed" identity. It is also puzzling that concepts such as social class, gender and context are rarely included as important factors in analyses of foreign-born adoptees' identity formation. Those who have been adopted from other countries and ethnic backgrounds have not only travelled from one culture to another, they have also crossed class boundaries – from poverty to prosperity.

How complicated the concept of adoption and ethnic identity is in a society like the Norwegian one can be illustrated by some examples from our surveys of Vietnamese and Indian teenagers and adults who have been adopted in Norway (Dalen and Sætersdal, 1987; Sætersdal and Dalen, 1999). What aspects of ethnic identity would the two groups have in common with each other? Should Indian adoptees' ethnic identity be based on the reality they originally come from, i.e. usually low-caste groups? Should the starting point be Indian history as it is imparted through literature and art, i.e. a high-caste culture, or Indianness as it is perceived by small groups of low-caste Indians who have emigrated to Norway quite recently? Should the adopted Vietnamese children's ethnic and cultural identity be based on war-time conditions, present-day refugee camps in Hong Kong or refugee groups in Norway, or on successful, well-integrated immigrants or on gangs of young criminals who have settled in Norway over the past decade? What about adoptees from Colombia, Korea, China, Russia and Ethiopia? What do these groups have in common, apart from having being adopted by wealthy, middle-class Norwegian parents and coming from poor developing countries?

Attitude to appearance

The adoptees' appearance is the *ethnic marker* that sets them apart from their own families from the start, and which later puts them in the category of being "alien" – like immigrants or foreigners. Other markers that otherwise distinguish minority ethnic communities, such as language, accent, dialect, body language, clothes, cultural and behavioural norms, etc, will not be any different from those of the adoptees' adoptive families or other Norwegians around them. Their appearance is the reason why they are often assumed to be immigrants or refugees. These are groups with which the adoptees themselves do not identify and that have a low status in our society, thus sometimes making life problematic for them. It is not so much their *appearance in itself* that is at the heart of the problem, but the fact that their appearance sets them apart from their family, siblings, relatives and friends. Their appearance is the visible marker that stamps them as "different" and non-Norwegian.

Attitude to culture and background

Foreign-born adoptees are more accepting of their background than they are of their appearance. However, for some, their ideas about their cultural background are strongly linked to their thoughts about the adoption itself and their own biological family. They do not want to think constantly about a past that no longer feels relevant to them: 'It's best not to think about such things.' Several of them also refrain from raising any questions about this because they care about their parents – and are afraid of hurting them with their statements.

An important delineation in this connection is the division between their "inner" and "outer" search for their biological family (Irhammar, 1997; see also Irhammar and Cederblad, Chapter 8). An "inner" search can be defined as ideas about their biological parents – 'do they think about me?', 'I think they had me adopted because . . .'. This may be an expression of the fact that those who are adopted and whose origins are completely different to those of their adoptive families want *someone in whom they can see themselves reflected;* a biological mirror in which they can receive confirmation of whom they resemble, and also a glimpse of what they will be like when they are older. The "outer" search, on the other hand, symbolises the adoptees' active, deliberate tracing of and contact with their biological families in their native countries, an activity which many of our older adoptees had undertaken. However, their desire to have contact and belong may conflict with their fear of being confronted with a brutal reality. Sometimes one's imagination is easier to cope with than reality.

Attitude to immigrants and refugees

Teenagers who have been adopted from foreign countries have a varied, ambivalent, complex attitude to both their own ethnic group in Norway and other immigrants. In two large, recently completed research projects (Brottveit, 1999a; Sætersdal and Dalen, 1999), these teenagers stated in different ways and more or less covertly that they wanted to distance themselves from immigrants and refugees. Such a distancing could be physical or psychological. They distanced themselves physically from immigrants in the school playground, on buses, at social events and in public places. The distancing was also psychological at times. Even though many had had immigrants in their class at school, very few of them had any friends who were immigrants.

It may be understandable that this is the case for children adopted from India and Vietnam, who have the same ethnic background as the largest groups of immigrants and refugees in Norway. However, children adopted from Colombia and Korea, who have few compatriots in Norway, expressed the same fear and displeasure that they might be taken for immigrants. Brottveit (1999b) claims that immigrants have a culturally stigmatised minority position comparable to that previously held by Lapps, who now have their own parliament which deals with questions concerning their situation as an ancient Norwegian minority.

Although opinion surveys show a relatively positive attitude to immigrants – especially on the part of younger people – Brottveit claims that these factors mean that foreign-born adoptees have problems defining themselves. Brottveit calls this an "ethnic role disability". However, by distancing themselves from immigrants and refugees, they also distance themselves from their background and origins. There is a risk that they will develop self-hatred and double communication. Some of the older teenagers were aware of this and stated that they did not like their own reactions.

In our own follow-up study of 41 Vietnamese adoptees in Norway (Sætersdal and Dalen, 1999), most of the young adults, who had been interviewed previously ten years earlier, seemed to have found a success-ful psychological balance between their Norwegian identity and feelings of belonging to their country of birth. In 1987 we found that many of the

Vietnamese adoptees (then adolescents) seemed to deny or minimise their feelings of being different and dismiss the importance of ethnic identity, but ten years later, these young adult adoptees seemed more secure in their dual identity. This was combined with a positive and mature interest in their country of birth. In 1987 Vietnam was a closed country, but since then, many of the adoptees had visited Vietnam or were planning to do so. Some had gone with friends or partners, some alone, some with refugee friends or other contacts. One had worked in the orphanage where she had lived as a child.

Few reported any serious discrimination at work or in their private lives. They seemed to have learned how to handle occasional remarks in the streets or at discos without any great difficulties. Those who had married had all married Norwegians and reported that they had been well received by their families-in-law. The adult adoptees had achieved this balance over the years as part of a process of maturation. The contrast with their ambivalent attitudes – towards their past and towards immigrant groups in Norway – when we interviewed them as teenagers ten years earlier, was remarkable. Now many of them seemed to have met the additional challenge of integrating their history as an adopted person into their overall identity. Many of them seemed to have accepted their multiple identities.

Their problems in 1997 were more related to *social* problems, learning difficulties, education and work, rather than to their ethnic origin and racism, findings which we believe are of great importance for post-adoption services. Much more effort should be concentrated on solving the various special educational and psychological problems of inter-country adoptees. This will be a great challenge to researchers and post-adoption services in the years ahead.

Norwegian membership

From their statements, it is clear that membership of the group of "foreign-born adoptees" is of minor significance to both the teen-agers and their parents, while "Norwegian" membership is very important. We have included assertions of belonging with family, friends, boyfriends/girlfriends and other primary social groups in the

171

concept of Norwegian membership. The parents primarily define their adopted children on the basis of their own social class and status. They believe it is particularly important for those who "look like" immigrants to get an education. A high social status is a strategy for avoiding racism.

The adoptive parents' concerns do not seem to be linked to any general anxiety about increasing racism in Norway, but to a fear that the adopted children will be confused with immigrants. Adoptive parents are worried that racists will "make a mistake" and discriminate against their children. This is an indirect admission that racial discrimination that affects one's own child is worse than that which affects immigrants with different cultural backgrounds. This fear is also to be found in the teenagers: 'I can't wear clothes that may result in me being confused with an immigrant'. Such feelings are also reflected in Danish and Swedish surveys of adults who were adopted as children (Irhammar, 1997; Røhrbech, 1989). Individual preferences as regards friendship and love were what was most important, not political solidarity with other adoptees or with immigrants or refugees from their own native countries. It was also clear that the teenage foreign adoptees who identified themselves as being mainly Swedish or Danish had fewer psychological problems and greater self-esteem, as measured by interviews and assessment scales.

Strategies for coping

When they are young, foreign adoptees are relatively protected against discrimination by strangers. On the whole, their schools and local environments have shielded them because they were accepted and recognised as members of Norwegian families. However, the protection and shielding provided by the adoptive family during childhood disappears once the child becomes a teenager and has to face many situations alone. Strangers may not identify them as Norwegian and may treat them as immigrants or refugees, with all the discriminatory attitudes that this involves. The young foreign adoptee is defined as "belonging" *inside,* while teenagers are often defined as being *outside* the context with which they identify themselves. Sometimes they belong, and sometimes they do not – depending on how those around them define them. Their position is marginal, or rather *"double-marginal"* because of both their adopted status and their ethnic origins, which do not define them as either "Norwegian" or immigrants. They do not belong to a clearly defined cognitive or cultural category.

Brottveit (1999b) describes Korean and Colombian adoptees' attitudes to their own ethnicity as three different ways of relating to this: the "Norwegian", the "double-ethnic" and the "cosmopolitan". He feels that the "Norwegian" identity has to be *confirmed*, the "double-ethnic" identity can be said to build on an additional identity that must be *discovered*, while the "cosmopolitan" one is an identity that has to be *created*.

In Brottveit's view, all three solutions are compatible with the adoptees having a good self-image and secure identity, including as regards their own appearance, which is crucial for being able to deal with external categorisation when this conflicts with their own self-image.

In our interviews with young and adult foreign-born adoptees (Sætersdal and Dalen, 1999) we identified two types of strategies for coping that resulted in harmonious personal developments. The first type is characterised by an active exploration of the adoptee's adoptive status, ethnic identity and biological and cultural backgrounds. This is a process of increasing awareness that results in the adopted person recognising his or her situation in life as a foreign-born adoptee. It can be described as "Black is beautiful – and I am me".

But we also found another, more defensive and non-exploratory process which also seems to result in good psychological and social adaptation. Unlike the first type, this is not characterised by exploration and a process of increasing awareness, but on the contrary by a *denial* of the significance of the adoptee's own genetic and cultural background, i.e. a Norwegian re-interpretation of the concept of identity. In order for such an identity interpretation to succeed, the foreign-born adoptees must be recognised and accepted as Norwegian by those around them. One can look on such a defensive process as a sad compliance with a homogeneous society's pressure to assimilate.

A Norwegianised, satisfied foreign-born adoptee is also at variance with established theories on the importance of roots in developing a harmonious personality. However, our earlier research results (Dalen and

Sætersdal, 1987) confirm that this way of "solving" identity problems is often an effective strategy for coping during the teenage years, since it gives foreign-born adoptees a longed-for feeling of being included in the community and being (almost) like everyone else. As they grow to adulthood, the adopted person seems more able to take on board the complexities of a "double-ethnic" identity (Sætersdal and Dalen, 1999).

The main problem – particularly during the teenage years – is to do with the difference between other people's and the adopted person's definition of identity and belonging. The most important factor for teenage and adult foreign-born adoptees is for them to receive confirmation that they really belong, both as a member of their nuclear and extended families and as a member of the society in which they have grown up and of which they have become a part. The considerable mental energy expended by many of them to mark the fact that they belong in Norwegian society bears witness to their uncertainty regarding their own social position. But it is also an indication that racist ideas have gained a foothold in Norway.

Adoption policy and identity

The adoption policy goals of cultural and ethnic awareness are based on theories developed from research into minority ethnic communities, sometimes carried out with strongly moral and political undertones. This reflects the trend in international research into minorities and identity, which has mainly focused on the relationship between the majority and the minority, while less interest has been devoted to relationships between individuals and groups within the same ethnic group. The significance of differences in gender, class and status and of different political and religious groups within particular ethnic minority communities is rarely analysed. But ethnic identity and a feeling of belonging are not just an intra-psychic, individual process. They are also socio-psychological, inter-personal processes that depend on the historical, political and social contexts and the stratification of both the individual minority group and society as a whole. It is therefore puzzling that the question of whether it is realistic to have a connection with the immigrant and refugee environments in Norway, and on what terms any such contact should take place, is rarely discussed.

I am who I have become, not who I was or who I could have been

The social anthropologist John Knudsen has discussed the situation of Vietnamese refugees in Norway in several studies (Knudsen, 1988a, b). In one of them he analyses how Vietnamese refugee youths are integrated in Norway, and underlines how the situation of being in exile is closely linked to the Vietnamese family's situation, irrespective of whether the family lives in Norway or in its native country. The family plays a central role, not least as regards the individual's self-image and perception of himself or herself as a socially valuable person.

Knudsen shows how difficult it is for Vietnamese teenagers who are on their own in their exile existence, and how marginal their position becomes if they do not have any family or relatives in this country who can confirm their identity. His survey shows how Vietnamese refugees in exile seek to reconstruct a hierarchically arranged social and cognitive system, with people who were previously of high rank trying to retain their (lost) positions. They seek confirmation of their personal identity using the formula: 'Who I *am* is not who I have *become* but who I *was*'. As a consequence, in this system, relationships with strangers, both Norwegians and young single Vietnamese refugees, become more remote and superficial. This is because they may represent a threat to the more established Vietnamese refugees' own, often fragile adaptation to Norway.

What actual chance is there that teenagers adopted from Vietnam will be likely to form closer links with the Vietnamese refugee society? And what about those adopted from India? And the Koreans, Chinese, Colombians and all the others? The foreign adoptees' formula is really the direct opposite: 'I *am* who I have *become*, not who I *was* or who I *could have been*'.

Towards a new freedom

In Norway, we can identify two parallel development processes in society. On the one hand, there is an idealisation of what is one's "own" and reinforced boundaries against what is "alien". This is particularly noticeable in youth environments – where various sub-cultures exist alongside each other and where originality and marginality compared to other groups are aspired to – and marked. On the other hand, new identities arise across established boundaries between the sexes, nationalities and racial differences. The latter reflects general trends in postmodern urban society developments and is characterised by ethnic diversity, religious pluralism and international cultural patterns. Youth culture, especially in the towns, is now greatly affected by global fashion, food, music and lifestyle trends. It is clear that this also allows for new identification opportunities. Internationalisation is not just a dangerous, one-way force; it can also give young people with quite different backgrounds a new opportunity to develop more freely than previous generations, when children's lives were staked out in advance from the cradle to the grave: like father like son.

Adoption must be viewed as a normative, a natural, rather than a pathological situation with special challenges due to the children's background and origins. There is a danger of obscuring or denying adopted persons the right to develop complex and multiple identities as individuals – a danger of forcing a rigid identity pattern upon them. To stress the adoption aspect of the adopted person, or to force a specific and politically defined meaning upon them, might impair their personal growth and development and drive them into a marginal position. This might be even more dramatic in homogeneous societies, such as in Norway, where there are few or no established ethnic minorities to relate to.

The new research findings described in this chapter show that foreign-born adoptees develop their identities in significantly different ways to Norwegian-born and immigrant teenagers. A person who has been adopted has had a more definite break in his or her life history than most of the immigrant youths. They have undertaken a long journey to a new culture and class and they do not have a return ticket. Unlike immigrant children, they do not grow up in a bilingual environment in contact with their biological family, relatives and friends in their native country. Nor do adopted teenagers have to struggle to relate to two different cultures and different family traditions like immigrant youths do. The problems they have in liberating themselves from the parental generation are more like those of Norwegian-born teenagers. However, they have an additional struggle to arrive at a harmonious understanding of their identity as regards who they are and how they want society to define them. That is why the eternal existential question: 'Who am I?' has a deeper, more complicated meaning for them than for many others.

The authors may be contacted at:
Department of Special Needs Education,
Faculty of Education, University of Oslo,
PO Box 1140, 0317 Oslo, Norway
Telephone: + 47 2285 8148
Fax: + 47 2285 8021
E-mail: barbro.satersdal@isp.uio.no
monica.dalen@isp.uio.no

References

Brottveit Å (1999a) *Jeg ville ikke skille meg ut!* (*I didn't want to look different!*) Oslo: Diakforsk.

Brottveit Å (1999b) 'Negotiating ethnic identities: Intercountry transracial adoptees' strategies facing external categorisation', in Ryvgold A, Dalen M and Sætersdal B (eds) *Mine – Yours – Ours and Theirs*, Oslo: University of Oslo.

Dalen M (1999a) The *Status of Knowledge of Foreign Adoptions*, Oslo: Department of Special Needs, University of Oslo.

Dalen M (1999b) 'Interaction in adoptive families', in Ryvgold A, Dalen M and Sætersdal B (eds) *Mine – Yours – Ours and Theirs*, Oslo: University of Oslo.

Dalen M and Sætersdal B (1987) 'Transracial adoption in Norway', *Adoption & Fostering*, 11:4, pp 41–46.

Haugland V (1999) 'Official opening', in Ryvgold A, Dalen M and Sætersdal B (eds) *Mine – Yours – Ours and Theirs*, pp 8–11, Oslo: University of Oslo.

Irhammar M (1997) *Identity Formation during Adolescence in Adoptees Born Abroad: Meaning of biological and ethnic origins*, Doctoral dissertation. Department of Psychology, Sweden: Lund University.

Knudsen J (1988a) *Vietnamese Survivors*, Doctoral dissertation, Department of Social Anthropology, University of Bergen.

Knudsen J (1988b) *The Position of Cognitive Models in the Structuring of Life Stories*, Department of Social Anthropology, University of Bergen.

Røhrbech M (1989) *Mit Land er Danmark (My Country is Denmark)*, Socialforskningsinstituttet (Social Research Institute), Report 14, Copenhagen.

Ryvgold A, Dalen M and Sætersdal B (eds) (1999) *Mine – Yours – Ours and Theirs*, Oslo: University of Oslo.

Tizard B and Phoenix A (1989) 'Black identity and transracial adoption', *New Community*, 15:3, pp 427–537.

Tizard B and Phoenix A (1995) 'The identity of mixed-parentage adolescents', *Journal of Child Psychiatry and Psychiatry*, 36:8, pp 1399–1410.

Sætersdal B and Dalen M (1999) *Hvem er jeg? Adopsjon, identitet and etnisitet (Who am I? Adoption, identity, ethnicity)*, Oslo: Akribe Forlag.

Appendix

Statistics for Intercountry adoption in Norway: 1979–1998

Table 9.1
Annual numbers of adoptions of foreign born children

Year	Number	Year	Number
1979	243	1989	490
1980	384	1990	500
1981	442	1991	442
1982	463	1992	520
1983	458	1993	519
1984	535	1994	541
1985	507	1995	488
1986	439	1996	522
1987	513	1997	583
1988	491	1998	643
Total		1979–1998	9,723

Table 9.2
Major countries of origin of children

1980		1990		1998	
Korea	163	Colombia	118	China	162
Colombia	62	Korea	113	Korea	121
India	62	India	56	Colombia	110
Indonesia	54	Philippines	34	Ethiopia	41
Sri Lanka	14	Brazil	33	India	40
		Peru	15	Romania	40
Total from *all* countries					
	384		500		643

Source: Norwegian Governmental Office for Youth and Adoption

Section III
Intercountry adoption in the UK

We saw in Chapter 1 that the number of intercountry adoptions in the UK is much lower per head of population than that found in the USA, Scandinavia and other mainland European countries such as France and Switzerland. Although domestic non-relative adoptions have fallen in number, there are still many more than in most countries of mainland Europe and the placement of special needs children is more widespread. Domestic adoption services, though subject to criticism, are well established and there is a flourishing post-adoption service in the non-governmental sector.

In contrast, services for intercountry adoption are far behind those available to prospective adopters in Europe and America and even today, a majority of such adopters have to do the bulk of arrangements themselves. There has, however, been some progress and examples of good practice are emerging. What is missing is a unified system that is accepted by prospective adopters and maximises the chances of adoption being in the best interests of the child. In this section of the book, we look at the current position in the UK from the perspective of a number of organisations involved in the intercountry adoption process.

Michael Brennan outlines current progress towards ratification of the Hague Convention. Mark Oaten's Private Member's Bill received Royal Assent in July 1999 and the Adoption (Intercountry Aspects) Act 1999 will enable Britain to ratify the Convention in late 2000. Brennan shows clearly that the UK has made considerable progress over the last five years. The new legislation will make it clear that all local authorities will be required to provide an intercountry adoption service, that private home studies will not be permitted, and that it will be an offence to bring a child into the UK for adoption, where the requirements of legislation have not been met. Much of the detail of the legislation will become clear only as regulations and guidance are issued and both of these were subject to consultation at the time the chapter was written.

Jan Way and Kathy Mason describe the growth of parents' groups over the past 25 years, a period during which prospective adopters have until recently found little support – and not a little hindrance – from official services. *STORK*, founded in 1986, has now changed its name to *AFAA* (The Association of Families Adopting from Abroad). Several smaller groups operate only in relation to one country e.g. *Children Adopted from China* and *Family Thais*. Today *AFAA* has become increasingly involved in post-adoption support, an area widely acknowledged to be one of the biggest gaps in provision for overseas adoptees and their families (Selman and Wells, 1996). The authors stress that most intercountry adopters do not see adoption as a panacea and are not against regulation and assessment, as long as it is fair and informed.

One of the greatest needs in improving services for intercountry adoption is the provision of accurate information about how to adopt from overseas and about any State of origin from which a child is sought. **Gill Haworth** describes the history of the *Overseas Adoption Helpline* from its formation in 1992. Despite the withdrawal of government funding in 1997, the Helpline has continued to grow and now deals with more than 1,700 enquiries a year. Haworth shows clearly the desperate need of prospective adopters for informed advice from an independent source and reminds us also of the problems facing those wishing to adopt relatives – a much ignored group.

Another important source of advice for many prospective adopters is *OASIS* (the Overseas Adoption Support and Information Service), a charitable organisation led by adoptive parents. **Julia Fleming** is a committee member and herself the mother of four children adopted from abroad. Her chapter describes the work of the service, which has a current membership of over 1,000 families. As with AFAA and OAH, OASIS has increasingly become aware of the need for post-adoption support.

Responsibility for home studies in the UK lies with local authorities, whose social workers have received much criticism for their lack of expertise and – in some cases – manifest lack of sympathy for those wishing to adopt from abroad. **Cherry Harnott** looks at the experience of one local authority, Hampshire, which has developed a comprehensive service for those seeking to adopt from overseas. Since 1990, Hampshire has dealt with over 9,000 inquiries and a total of 95 children have come from abroad for adoption. Harnott readily acknowledges the problems for those authorities with only a handful of overseas adoptions, but argues that there is no reason why a quality service of advice, preparation and assessment should not be available throughout the country, even if this entails the development of regional consortia (see Selman and White, 1994). She also touches on the vexed problems of "charges" and the need for these to be directly related to service costs.

The nature of assessment in home studies for intercountry adoption is discussed in detail by **John Simmonds and Gill Haworth**, drawing on work undertaken for the Department of Health and Children in the Irish Republic. They note the wide range of responsibilities social workers have: to the children and their birth parents; to the applicants; to their own and other agencies; and to the child's State of origin which will depend on their judgement of the suitability of the prospective adopters. The authors identify the criteria which should inform any such judgement, while reminding us of the importance of not setting a standard that most people having a family of their own could not be expected to achieve. Above all, they point to the dynamics of power and loss in any home study and the need for all involved to be aware of this.

The new legislation will make private home studies illegal, but permits – and indeed encourages – the participation of voluntary organisations, subject to their approval by the DoH. To date most of the larger voluntary bodies – such as Barnado's – have been unwilling to get involved in overseas adoption, but one smaller agency, *Childlink*, has been approved for work in overseas adoption. In Chapter 16, its Director, **Caroline Hesslegrave**, explains how the organisation came to be involved in home studies on an agency basis and later developed its own service. Work in the area has been extended to offering preparation groups in conjunction with OAH and Hesslegrave speculates about future moves into mediation. In her conclusion she argues for the need for 'high-quality, child-centred practice in the interests of children whose only chance of a family upbringing is through adoption across national, and in many cases across ethnic, cultural and religious boundaries'.

It will become clear from reading this section that provision for intercountry adoption has been very poor in the past and that even now access to support varies considerably across the country. Fees charged for home studies also vary considerably and are often not clearly related to actual costs and the availability of preparation courses is also unpredictable. A major gap in current provision is the absence of any "mediating" agency – whether a public authority or an "accredited body" – which has links with States of origin and so can take prospective adopters through all the stages of an intercountry adoption (Selman and White, 1994). Such agencies are found in most countries of mainland Europe (see chapters by Andersson and Sterky in Section IV) and in some – Denmark, Finland and Norway – it is illegal to adopt from abroad unless the applicants go through one of these organisations. Agencies also flourish in the USA, but standards vary considerably, and private/independent adoptions still comprise a majority of ICAs (Gailey, Chapter 17). The need for "mediating" agencies with well-established links with States of origin is raised by a number of contributors to this section and will be further explored in the conclusion to the book.

The UK is a late entrant on the intercountry adoption scene and still has a much lower level of overseas adoption than most other receiving countries. It is, therefore, perhaps not unexpected to find that our services are less developed. The chapters in this section show clearly the potential for services which meet the expectations of countries ratifying the Hague Convention and the ethical standards outlined by Saclier and Kirton in Section I.

References

Selman P and Wells S (1996) 'Post adoption issues in intercountry adoption', in McWilliams E and Phillips R (eds), *After Adoption: Working with adoptive families*, London: BAAF.

Selman P and White J (1994) 'The role of "accredited bodies" in intercountry adoption', *Adoption & Fostering*, 18:2, pp 7–13 [Reprinted in Hill M and Shaw M (eds) *Signposts in Adoption*, London: BAAF, 1998].

10 Creating a framework
A view from the centre

Michael Brennan

Michael Brennan is a Principal at the Department of Health responsible for adoption policy. In 1993 he was the UK co-representative at the Hague Conference on intercountry adoption.

Introduction

Intercountry adoption is usually described as the adoption of a child resident in one country by adopters living in another. Intercountry adoption, therefore, encompasses private international law as well as the relevant adoption legislation of the child's country of origin and that of the prospective adopters. This assumes, therefore, that a State of origin invariably engages in a process by which consideration is given as to whether a child should be permitted to leave his or her own country to live permanently with new adoptive parents in another. It also presupposes that in each receiving State the prospective adopter has been assessed by a competent authority as suitable to adopt a child from abroad and that the authorities in the child's State of origin are satisfied that adoption by the applicant is in the child's best interests.

Regrettably, the history of intercountry adoption has not always been so structured. In his report on intercountry adoption (van Loon, 1990) prepared in April 1990 as a preliminary document for the Hague Conference, the then First Secretary of the Hague Conference, Hans van Loon (since appointed Secretary General), referred to three main areas of child trafficking in relation to intercountry adoption: buying and selling of children; parental consent obtained through fraud and duress; and child abduction.

1993 Hague Convention

It was against the background of child trafficking that the Hague Conference began its work in 1990 to prepare a Convention that would

185

protect children from such abuses, inviting all Member States and extending invitations to all other interested countries to consider the issues and prepare a framework for intercountry adoption to take place. This framework cannot be uniform throughout Contracting States since their substantive adoption laws will differ, but this is not necessarily a weakness of the Convention since many States will have in place more than what is minimally required under the Articles of the Convention.

The full title of the Convention concluded in May 1993 is the **Protection of Children and Co-operation in Respect of Intercountry Adoption**. The two key words in that title are **protection** and **co-operation**. In terms of protecting children, the one essential principle made paramount by the Hague Conference was that the Convention should be effective in safeguarding the interests of the child, protecting his or her welfare throughout the entire adoption process. About this, the Conference was uncompromising. The other key word, **"co-operation"**, is the ultimate test of the effectiveness of the Convention and will in part be measured by the degree of co-operation achieved among Contracting States. Central Authorities will play a key role in achieving this. The greater the co-operation, the more effective the protection available to children, adoptive parents and birth parents. Ratification of the Hague Convention, therefore, is seen as the most effective means yet for safeguarding the welfare of children in intercountry adoption.

Publication of the Convention marked the end of the work of the Hague Conference on intercountry adoption, at least for the time being. The Convention was intended to act as a springboard for countries to begin the task of looking critically at their existing adoption law and practice, compare them to the requirements of the Convention and then take the necessary steps to enable them to ratify in due course.

In its Preamble, the Convention makes specific reference to two important international agreements:
- the UN Declaration on Social and Legal Principles relating to the Protection and Welfare of Children, with Special Reference to Foster Placement and Adoption Nationally and Internationally (December 1986); and
- the UN Convention on the Rights of the Child (November 1989).

These two documents were regarded by the Hague Commission as the bedrocks in its general approach to consideration of the welfare of children in intercountry adoption and well as being important declarations of principle. The UK ratified the 1989 UN Convention in December 1991.

The Hague Convention is essentially a framework of minimum standards for regulating intercountry adoption, placing responsibilities on both the State of origin and the receiving State to ensure that an acceptable and effective range of measures are in place for the protection of the child throughout the adoption process. The Convention includes provision for the automatic recognition of Convention adoptions in other Contracting States. As in the case of the UK, countries intending to ratify the Convention will be required to introduce the necessary legislation to absorb certain articles within their own substantive child care and adoption laws.

Adoption (Intercountry Aspects) Act 1999

The passing of the 1999 Act marked an important milestone in adoption legislation as well as a vital stage in progress towards the UK ratifying the Hague Convention. The Act places intercountry adoption on a sound legal footing for the first time, making provision for intercountry adoption to be regulated in both Convention and non-Convention cases. The Act enables the UK to ratify the Convention; it amends the Adoption Act 1976 and the Adoption (Scotland) Act 1978 in respect of intercountry adoption.

Sanctions

The 1999 Act introduces sanctions to deal with unacceptable practices in intercountry adoption and includes measures for the protection of children, including placing a restriction on bringing children into the UK for the purposes of adoption. For example, the 1999 Act inserts a new section after s.56 of the Adoption Act 1976 making it a criminal offence for a person habitually resident in the British Islands to bring to the UK for the purposes of adoption a child who is habitually resident outside these islands unless they comply with requirements to be prescribed in regulations. The offence, of course, does not apply to a parent, guardian or relative of the child.

Following enactment, the Government took the opportunity to make a Commencement Order with effect from 31 January 2000, which puts beyond all doubt that a privately commissioned home study report for the purposes of adopting a child resident abroad is an offence. Such reports are already unlawful under s.11 of the 1976 Act relating to restrictions on arranging adoptions and placing children for adoption where the children are resident within the UK. The 1999 Act ensures that this protection extends to a child living abroad. To do otherwise would leave the UK open to the justifiable accusation of applying double standards.

New subsection (3A) therefore extends the interpretation in the 1976 Act relating to arrangements for adoption by providing that, in relation to the proposed adoption of a child resident outside the British Islands, references to arrangements for the adoption include references to arrangements for an assessment for the purpose of indicating whether a person is suitable or not to adopt a child.

The effect is to make clear that in intercountry cases, a home study assessment report for the purposes of adoption must be prepared by or on behalf of an adoption agency. The amendment should be read with s.11 and s.56 of the 1976 Act which deals with restrictions on arranging adoptions and prohibitions on making certain payments in connection with the adoption of children. This section prohibits privately commissioned home study assessments. There are several sound reasons why this should be so. In general terms, any system of regulation must be based on an acceptance that intercountry adoptions, like other adoptions, cannot be regarded as an entirely private matter. It is incumbent on society to take the necessary steps to protect the welfare of children for whom failure of the adoption would be a tragedy. There is a legitimate public interest in the success or failure of intercountry adoptions: the cost of supporting such adoptions and dealing with the consequences of breakdowns falls on public services. The enforcement of law and the proper management of adoption are the responsibility of national governments. Particular objections to privately commissioned home study assessments include:

- such assessments are not permitted in relation to the adoption of children residing in the UK and therefore should not be permitted for the adoption of children living overseas;
- private assessments are commissioned and paid for by the prospective adopter, thereby establishing a direct financial relationship between the prospective adopter and the social worker – such an arrangement cannot be conducive to providing an objective report;
- entry clearance for the child to enter the UK will not be sanctioned by the Home Office on the basis of a private home study, therefore in such cases children are brought to the UK without authority;
- the privately commissioned social worker cannot take any responsibility for a child once he or she enters the UK;
- there is no management supervision of privately commissioned social workers, the method of assessment or the quality of their reports;
- privately commissioned social workers cannot obtain police reports on prospective adopters to comply with The Children (Protection from Offenders) (Miscellaneous Amendments) Regulations 1997.

During the progress of the Adoption (Intercountry Aspects) Bill through both Houses of Parliament, the Government gave a commitment that regulations be introduced and be subject to a consultation process before being presented to Parliament. The Department of Health aims to complete the consultation stage on the draft regulations and accompanying guidance before the end of 2000 and thereafter prepare for ratification of the Convention.

Care Standards Act 2000

This recent and important piece of legislation is concerned with the regulation of private and voluntary healthcare in England and for the regulation and inspection of social care and healthcare services in Wales. The Act establishes a new, independent regulatory body for social care in England, to be known as the National Care Standards Commission. The regulatory body will be required to inspect the relevant functions of the various bodies.

In the context of the provision of an adoption service, the relevant functions subject to regulation and inspection are those concerned with making arrangements for the adoption of children, i.e. approval of prospective adopters, preparation of children for adoption and the making of adoptive placements. Regulations and sanctions governing adoption procedures will continue to be under the 1976 and 1999 Act, as amended by the 2000 Act. Voluntary adoption agencies will be required to register with the Commission. For the first time, local authorities will be subject to inspection and, in concert with voluntary adoption agencies, required to meet the same national minimum standards. These standards will apply to all voluntary adoption agencies including those providing only an intercountry adoption service.

Central Authorities

The identification of a Central Authority and accredited bodies is the necessary foundation within each State for creating a new, or improving an existing intercountry adoption structure to make the Convention work. This has to apply equally to both the State of origin and the receiving State. In protecting children, the articles of the Convention also ensure that prospective adopters and birth parents receive the measure of protection to which they are entitled.

An essential task of a State intending to ratify the Convention is to establish one or more Central Authority within that State. A Central Authority is a body within a political boundary or country which is responsible for implementing the Convention. The 1999 Act provides for the functions of a Central Authority to be discharged separately in England and Scotland by the respective Secretary of State and in Wales by the National Assembly for Wales. Northern Ireland intends to introduce the necessary legislation to ratify in due course. Designating the respective health departments as Central Authorities makes sense since these departments already carry out functions under current adoption legislation not dissimilar to those required of a Central Authority under the Convention.

In the development of the Hague Convention since 1993, the appointment of a government or public authority to act as a Central Authority is a common feature in most, if not all Contracting States. We are fortunate that in the UK we already have a legal and administrative adoption structure which mirrors very closely the framework envisaged by the Hague Conference. The 1999 Act fills the legal gaps in adoption legislation to enable the UK to meet the requirements of the Convention.

Roles and responsibility

A Central Authority must review its procedures to satisfy itself that their functions comply fully with the Convention. In several areas, this work has already begun in the UK. To ensure that the Convention will work effectively in practice, there is the important element of providing information and training for judges, lawyers, social workers and administrators so that they may become familiar with the Convention, know how its procedures are to work and understand the implications for their particular disciplines. This aspect of preparation is currently being developed. Because it is charged with responsibility for intercountry adoption, the Central Authority will normally be the first point of contact with other Contracting States. International liaison, therefore, will be an important feature of its work.

Each Central Authority will maintain a register of adoption applications made under the Convention and introduce a system for monitoring the progress of these applications. Should prospective adopters meet unforeseen difficulties abroad, it may sometimes be necessary to assist prospective adopters directly, which may require the intervention of the Central Authority through the usual diplomatic channels to help complete the adoption process.

Where there is evidence of non-compliance by another Contracting State, a Central Authority will be expected to take appropriate action under Article 33 to try and resolve the difficulty. A Central Authority will also be an important link with the Permanent Bureau of the Hague Conference, keeping them informed of changes to accredited bodies, adoption legislation and any cases where matters of non-compliance cannot be resolved.

As a government department, each Central Authority will be responsible to their Secretary of State and will act in concert with other government departments, particularly the Home Office, which will continue to have responsibility for immigration, and also the Foreign and Commonwealth Office.

Accredited bodies

Section 2 of the 1999 Act provides for an approved adoption society to act as an accredited body for the purposes of the Convention.

The relationship between a Central Authority and accredited bodies is essentially one of partnership – two important halves of the inter-country adoption structure working together to make the Hague Convention work effectively. It is intended to be a process in which all parties to the intercountry adoption process can have confidence.

Article 10 is clear about the principle to be applied to bodies seeking accreditation: 'Accreditation shall only be granted to and maintained by bodies demonstrating their competence to carry out properly the tasks with which they may be entrusted'. By operation of the 1999 Act, each local authority will have the statutory responsibility to provide an intercountry adoption service. Local authorities therefore do not require accreditation under the Convention. A voluntary adoption body which is successful in its application to the Secretary of State for approval to provide an intercountry adoption service will be given automatic accreditation under the Convention. To date, four voluntary adoption agencies have been approved to provide an intercountry adoption service: Childlink, Parents and Children Together (PACT – formerly the Oxford Diocesan Council for Social Work), Doncaster Adoption and Family Welfare Society and Norwood Jewish Adoption Society. These agencies are approved for domestic and intercountry adoption. A voluntary body, however, may apply to the Secretary of State for approval to provide *only* an intercountry adoption service. Approval would allow the agency to carry out all aspects of an intercountry adoption application without reference to a local authority except in obtaining the necessary police reports required under the Children (Protection from Offenders) (Amendment) Regulations 1999 (as amended).

Section 104 of the 2000 Act amends s.155 of the Police Act 1997 by providing for enhanced criminal record checks to be carried out in relation to persons being considered as suitable to become adoptive parents. Enhanced criminal records certificates are to be made available only to a local authority or voluntary adoption agency that is carrying out an assessment of a person's suitability to adopt. Part V of the Police Act 1997 enables an approved adoption agency to apply direct to the Criminal Records Bureau to obtain information which could indicate that a person has been convicted of, or received a police caution for, certain prescribed offences. This facility extends the availability of criminal record checks to all child care organisations, including the voluntary and private sectors. In order for these organisations to be able to use this facility, they will be required to register with the Criminal Records Agency and to abide by a Code of Practice (not yet finalised).

Each Central Authority will be responsible for managing the accreditation of voluntary bodies through a process of inspection against established standards and criteria. These standards and criteria encompass Article 11 that a body must be non-profit-making, directed and staffed by persons qualified by their ethical standards and training or experience, and be subject to supervision by competent authorities of the State as to its composition, operation and financial situation. If the inspection is satisfactory, approval to operate as an intercountry adoption agency will be given by the Secretary of State. So far as the UK is concerned, each body must be registered as a charity or be an incorporated body before accreditation can be considered.

Article 22(2) permits certain functions to be carried out by individuals who meet the requirements of integrity, professional competence, experience and accountability of that State, and are qualified by their ethical standards and by training or experience to work in the field of intercountry adoption. The essential condition to this particular article is that the individual may only function 'to the extent permitted by the law and subject to the supervision of the competent authorities of that State'. This particular Article was included in the Convention as a compromise to meet the requests of one or two countries which license private individuals to make arrangements for adoption.

So far as the UK is concerned, the protection of children to be adopted from overseas is far too important to be left to private transactions. The 1999 Act makes clear that only local authorities and approved adoption societies will be permitted to make arrangements for the adoption of children living in the UK or residing abroad. Adoption must be viewed primarily as a service to meet the needs of children – never as a means of finding children to satisfy the needs of prospective adopters.

A person, therefore, who wishes to be approved to adopt a child living abroad must apply either to a local authority or to an accredited body which will provide counselling about the nature and implications of adopting a child from a particular country and, equally important, point out the implications for a child to be adopted and brought to the UK, where language, culture, diet and general way of life are likely to be in marked contrast to the experience of a child, particularly an older child. Procedures for adopting from a particular State of origin and any special requirements to be met in that State will also be explained.

Where an authority or body decides that a person may be eligible to be an adoptive parent, it must carry out a thorough assessment on that person – his/her background, lifestyle, motives for adopting, social environment, ability to undertake intercountry adoption, the age of the child which the applicant wishes to adopt, and much more. The authority or body must also obtain written reports from personal referees, a report on the health of the applicant from a registered medical practitioner and a report from the police authority. In 1997 the Government introduced regulations that prohibit an authority or adoption agency accepting an adoption application from a person who has been convicted of, or been cautioned by the police for, a specified offence against children. The Children (Protection from Offenders) (Miscellaneous Amendments) Regulations 1999 (as amended) place a duty on an adoption agency to ensure an adoption application is not accepted from any person who has a conviction or caution for a specified offence under these regulations.

Looking ahead some years at how the role of an accredited body might develop, there may be opportunities for them to employ representatives of their agency in certain countries. The function of these representatives could include, for example, being available to assist competent authorities in States of origin to complete the adoption process; act as a mediator between a competent authority and the accredited body in the UK; and on their arrival in the State of origin, provide a "hand holding" service for prospective adopters through the final stages of the adoption process. I would expect such representatives to be fluent in the local language as well as familiar with that country's adoption procedures.

Clearly, there are advantages – for the accredited body, prospective adopter and the competent authority in the State of origin – in an accredited body having a representative abroad; this has been a feature in the operation of many approved intercountry adoption agencies in Europe for some years. Such a development would, of course, be a matter for an accredited body to decide; consideration is likely to include, for example, the volume of applications to a particular country. The appointment of a representative abroad will also have an effect upon the fees charged by the body.

Certificate of approval

If the authority or body is satisfied that a person is suitable to adopt a child from abroad, it will send the application and relevant papers to the Central Authority in compliance with Article 15. Before sending the adoption application and other papers to the State of origin, the Central Authority must add an important document to the application papers in compliance with Article 5 – a Certificate of Approval. This certificate provides assurance to the competent authorities in the State of origin, including the court, that the applicant is eligible and suitable to adopt a child from the particular country of choice; has received appropriate counselling; and that the child to be adopted will be permitted to enter and reside permanently in the UK.

This certificate was introduced by the Department of Health in 1993. It is the only certain means by which an authority or court in a State of origin can be assured that the application before them has been completed according to UK legislation. The certificate, therefore, not only gives assurances about the suitability of the prospective adopter but is also an important measure for the protection of the child. Without this certificate, no child from a Contracting State can be given entry clearance to enable him or her to live permanently in the UK. The Central Authority will also be responsible for obtaining the necessary notarisation and legalisation of the relevant documents.

Information on the child, sent to the Central Authority from the State of origin under Article 16(2), is passed to the authority or accredited body that made the assessment. That authority or body will consider the information on the child and, if satisfied that the adoption should proceed, will send it to the prospective adopters and arrange to discuss its contents with them. If the prospective adopters are agreed, they inform the Central Authority in the child's State of origin of their wish to adopt the child. At this stage, the UK insists that each prospective adopter must visit the child before giving their final consent to adopt the child matched to them.

Under recently revised arrangements concerning entry clearance for adopted children, agreed between the Department of Health and the Home Office, the Department can now link directly with the Entry Clearance Officer in the child's State of origin. Entry clearance can therefore be given without delay, provided that the application has been made and the necessary information and documents, including the adoption order, are presented to the Officer at the appropriate British Embassy or Consulate in the child's State of origin. This arrangement was agreed to avoid prospective adopters having to wait days or even weeks before entry clearance was given; in many cases, because of the delay, prospective adopters chose not to wait but take the child out of the State of origin before entry clearance was given. This revised arrangement has been the subject of a pilot scheme in a few countries and has proved to work very successfully. This is one way in which the Department of Health has been able to introduce improvements to streamline procedures and reduce delay to a minimum.

Linking with States of origin

It will be the responsibility of a Central Authority of a receiving State in each case to send to a State of origin the completed adoption application, duly notarised and legalised. Thereafter, it may be the case that a competent authority in a State of origin wishes to seek clarification about the application or obtain further information and make contact direct with the local authority or accredited body in the receiving State, as opposed to the Central Authority, that approved the applicants.

There can be no objection to such contact. Indeed, it is envisaged that once the 1999 Act is implemented in full and has had time to bed down, local authorities and accredited bodies will feel confident about making direct links with their opposite number in the State of origin that is currently processing an application prepared by them. The development

196

of such direct links, once the application has been processed and dispatched by the Central Authority, will help establish good working relationships between both countries.

Entry to the United Kingdom

Once the required legislation is in place and the Convention ratified, a child adopted in a State of origin according to the Convention will be able to enter and live permanently in the UK. Also, by the act of making the adoption order in that State, the child will receive British citizenship automatically, by an amendment to the British Nationality Act 1981, provided that at least one of the adoptive parents is a British subject at the time the adoption order is made. The making of the adoption order completes the adoption process and it becomes recognised in all Contracting States as a Convention adoption according to Article 23. Since a Convention adoption conveys the effects of an adoption order made in the UK, it will no longer be necessary for adoptive parents to make further application to a UK court.

Adoption from non-Convention countries

Most of this chapter concentrates on looking at the future framework for operating the articles of the Hague Convention under the 1999 Act. However, prospective adopters will continue to choose to adopt from their country of choice, whether it is a Convention or non-Convention country. It is likely that adoptions from non-Convention countries will continue for years to come; not all countries will have ratified or acceded to the Convention by the time the UK does so and some countries may not ratify at all. There is no question, therefore, of taking the opportunity of the 1999 Act to somehow impose limits on the range of countries of choice to Convention countries.

Procedures for dealing with non-Convention applications within the UK will follow as closely as possible the procedures that are to apply to applications for Convention countries. This means, for example, that the process of preparation, assessment and approval of prospective adopters by adoption agencies will be the same, irrespective of their country of choice. Clearly, once the adoption application leaves the UK, the procedures applied in non-Convention countries will vary. It will still be incumbent upon a Central Authority in the UK to adhere to the principles of the Convention; for example, the Authority will need to be satisfied about the circumstances of a proposed adoption in a non-Convention country as are identified in Article 4 of the Convention.

There will continue to be differences in the effects of an adoption order made in a State of origin that has ratified or acceded to the Convention, and an adoption made in accordance with its articles, and an adoption order made in a non-Convention country. For example, whereas British nationality will be conferred automatically as one of the effects of a Convention adoption, this will not be the case in a non-Convention adoption. Also, an adoptive parent will be able to obtain entry clearance for the adopted child once the Entry Clearance Officer has confirmation of the Convention adoption. Except for those countries currently included in the Adoption (Designation of Overseas Adoptions) Order 1973, there will be no necessity, unlike a non-Convention adoption, for entry clearance to be confirmed by a Central Authority in the UK.

The "designated list"

A draft of the regulations to implement the 1999 Act will be prepared in 2000 and made available for consultation along with a draft of the accompanying guidance. Among the issues to be consulted upon will be the future of the designated list. There appears to be a general consensus among those involved in intercountry adoption, both agencies and professionals, that the list needs amendment. Several options are likely to be put forward in the consultation document, including that:

- the list should remain unchanged;
- the list should be amended by reducing the number of countries to those with whom the UK has formal adoption agreements;
- certain conditions should apply (for example, a prospective adopter must have been approved by a local authority or approved adoption agency) before the effects of an adoption order made in a designated country can be recognised.

It has also been suggested that the 1973 Order should be repealed in its entirety; This would have at least one advantage in that there would be only two types of adoption: Convention and non-Convention. However, repealing the Order would have adverse implications for those adoptions from the People's Republic of China, which the Department of Health would want to avoid.

Adoption of relatives

Where the 1999 Act regulates the intercountry adoption process concerning the application and assessment of a prospective adopter's suitability to become an adoptive parent, it will apply to an adopter who wishes to adopt a relative who is residing abroad. The process of preparation and assessment will be the same, although in the case of a relative adoption, the child is usually already known to the prospective adopter. The requirements of the Home Office for a child to enter the UK to join a parent or relative will continue to apply. These requirements are set out in Appendix 1 to the information leaflet on intercountry adoption prepared by the Immigration and Nationality Directorate, Apollo House, 36 Wellesley Road, Croydon, Surrey CR9 3RR.

Conclusion

This chapter provides only a brief outline of the framework for making the Convention work. A more detailed picture will emerge once draft regulations and accompanying guidance have been prepared and made available for public consultation and comment.

A persistent and major "balancing act" faced by the participating delegates of the Commission when working on numerous drafts of the Convention was that its articles had to be sufficiently robust to achieve its objectives and, at the same time, contain sufficient flexibility for it to be workable and therefore acceptable to all participating States. Delegates were committed to producing a document which would be both realistic and worthy of those objectives.

It is my belief that, so long as that commitment to the Convention can be sustained by all Contracting States in the spirit of co-operation, the Convention should not fail in its principal objective of protecting children.

References

Brennan M (2000) 'The Adoption (Intercountry Aspects) Act 1999', *Representing Children* (ed) 12:4, National Youth Advocacy Service.

Van Loon J H A (1990) *Report on Intercountry Adoption*, The Hague; Permanent Bureau of the Hague Conference.

Appendix 1
Overseas Adoption in the UK: Adoption applications (Home-study Reports) received by DoH – by child's State of origin

Table 10.1
33 countries with 3 or more children between 1993 and 2000 (in descending order of number of home studies)

Country	1993	1994	1995	1996	1997	1998	1999	2000	1993–2000
China	3	17	59	206	110	123	149	136	803
India	16	20	22	29	21	22	19	10	159
Guatemala	2	3	12	16	26	20	15	20	114
Romania	22	14	9	10	5	17	18	13	113
Thailand	4	10	5	10	10	13	21	38	111
Russia	1	4	4	3	3	13	10	9	47
USA	4	0	8	4	5	8	5	12	46
Paraguay	8	16	6	1	1	0	0	0	32
Brazil	3	3	7	4	4	3	4	1	29
Phillippines	7	2	1	5	4	4	1	3	27
Sri Lanka	4	6	3	2	3	0	2	2	22
Colombia	3	1	1	4	4	7	0	0	20
Pakistan	1	2	3	1	3	2	0	0	20
Bulgaria	2	3	0	2	0	4	4	3	18
Vietnam	0	1	1	1	3	2	2	7	17
Chile	1	1	1	0	4	4	0	0	11
Poland	2	1	2	1	1	2	2	0	11
Nepal	1	1	1	1	1	2	0	0	7
Ukraine	2	0	1	0	0	2	1	1	7
El Salvador	1	3	1	0	0	0	0	0	5
Hungary	1	1	1	0	1	0	1	0	5
Albania	1	1	1	1	0	0	0	0	4
Bolivia	1	0	1	0	0	0	2	0	4
Mexico	0	0	1	0	0	2	1	0	4
Peru	1	0	0	0	1	1	0	1	4
Belarus	0	0	0	0	1	1	1	0	3
Estonia	0	0	0	0	3	0	0	0	3
Iran	0	0	0	1	0	0	1	1	3
Jamaica	2	0	0	0	1	0	0	0	3
Jordan	0	0	0	0	1	0	1	1	3
Lebanon	0	2	0	0	1	0	0	0	3
Morocco	0	0	0	0	0	0	0	3	3
Turkey	1	1	1	0	0	0	0	0	3
Sub-total for 33 countries	94	113	152	302	217	252	268	266	1,664

33 other countries sent one or two children to the UK over the period 1993–September 2000. These were (in alphabetical order):

Algeria	Ghana	Lithuania
Armenia	Greece	Madeira
Bahrain	Guyana	Mauritius
Barbados	Haiti	Nicaragua
Belize	Honduras	Panama
Burundi	Hong Kong	Serbia
Cambodia	Indonisia	Sierra Leone
Czech Republic	Israel	Singapore
Egypt	Japan	Taiwan
Eire	Kazhakstan	Tanzania
Ethiopia	Latvia	Yugoslavia

Table 10.2

Total numbers for all 63 countries over the seven year period

1993	1994	1995	1996	1997	1998	1999	To Sept 2000	1993–2000
101	115	154	308	223	258	277	271	1,707

Of the total of 1,707 applications between 1993 and September 2000

47 per cent involved one country: China.

29 per cent involved four countries: India, Guatemala, Romania and Thailand.

13 per cent involved eight countries: Russia, USA, Paraguay, Brazil, the Philippines, Sir Lanka, Colombia and Pakistan.

11 per cent involved the remaining 53 countries.

Overall, 13 of the 66 countries listed accounted for 89 per cent of all applications.

11 Growth and turbulence
A history of a parent support group

Jan Way and Kathy Mason

Jan Way is a social worker who has specialised in intercountry adoption since 1987. She is the parent of a child adopted from overseas and was chairperson of AFAA from 1990–94. She is also an adopted person.

Kathy Mason is an ESRC funded doctoral student based in the Social Policy Department at the University of Newcastle upon Tyne. She has worked as a research associate on several adoption-related projects.

Introduction

The history of intercountry adoption (ICA) in the UK extends back only over the last 30 years, in contrast to countries such as the USA and Sweden where adoption of children from overseas was well developed by the 1960s (Andersson, 1988; Cederblad, 1982; Dalen and Saetersdal, 1987; Geerars, 1996; Hoksbergen, 1984; Rorbech, 1990; Zaar, 1991). As statistics in relation to children adopted from overseas have not, until recently, been reliably maintained in the UK, it is hard to estimate with any accuracy when the process began in earnest. However, parent groups indicate that, with the exception of a handful of children entering the UK per year, it was not until the 1980s that intercountry adoption became an issue worthy of policy and professional discussion. As the numbers of white baby placements declined (Department of Health, 1993) leaving older and "hard to place" children as those primarily requiring placement, and as ideological changes within the social work profession in the UK discouraged professionals from considering white adopters as being suitable parents for black and mixed heritage children, intercountry adoption began to be considered by potential adopters as a possible way to found a family. The main countries of origin were ex-Commonwealth countries such as Sri Lanka, and Central and South American countries. In 1990, the collapse of the Ceausescu regime in Romania and the discovery of large numbers of children, of varying ages, living in atrocious conditions within the state orphanage system led to many prospective adopters from the UK seeking to adopt such children, moved by their obvious plight, ably presented by the media. Three years later this was followed by the "opening up" of relations with China, and the realisation that China had many children abandoned by parents, living in state orphanages and in need of a permanent family, primarily as the result of the "one child policy". Thus it became possible, and was indeed encouraged by the Chinese authorities, for potential adoptive parents from the West to apply to adopt these children.

Consequently, over the last two decades the numbers of children entering the UK as a consequence of overseas adoption has increased, although, in real terms, the numbers are still small in comparison to the number of placements in other countries (e.g. Norway or USA) and in comparison to domestic placements. Nevertheless, alongside this increase in numbers there has been an increase in awareness in the public, professionals and policy makers. The latter two groups have also been strongly influenced by the Hague Convention on Intercountry Adoption, concluded in 1993 and now in the process internationally of being ratified by member States, and in the UK, in particular, of being incorporated into new adoption legislation.

The ideological debate in the UK

Intercountry adoption in the UK has always been a highly contentious area in the field of adoption, with an ongoing ideological debate based upon the rights and wrongs of transracial placements (Chestang, 1972; Chimezie, 1975; Silverman and Feigelman, 1981; and Simon and Altstein, 1977) raging within both professional and lay circles. As the numbers of children being placed through ICA increased during the 1980s, the arguments intensified. The history of this debate and its impact upon professional thinking and placement practice domestically within the UK has been well documented by Gaber and Aldridge (1994) but the practice implications have also had a profound impact upon families and individuals considering the adoption of a child from overseas. The International Bar Association Report in 1991 (IBA, 1991) graphically illustrated the parents' experience in the 1980s, when many local authorities in the

UK, responsible for both counseling and assessment of prospective adopters, were openly "hostile" to enquirers, with heavy emphasis being placed upon the fact that transracial placements were damaging to children, even though some research indicated that this was not necessarily the case (Dale, 1989). Whilst a few local authorities were prepared to assess and work alongside overseas agencies, many were not.

Equally, the fact that the UK had no clear policy or system for dealing with ICA deterred many reliable, child-centred agencies overseas from considering UK couples wanting to adopt. The reality for many UK individuals who wished to explore and pursue ICA was that they were on their own, both in terms of working with the country from which they wished to adopt a child and in terms of preparing themselves and their documentation. A considerable number of such adopters chose to employ independent social workers (professionals who worked outside of the statutory adoption authorities, often called private social workers), relying upon their knowledge and skills to support them during the adoption process. Whilst there has been considerable criticism of independent social workers in this field, notably from the Department of Health (1992), it is important to note that during the 1980s they were, in many areas, the only professional social work service for overseas applicants, operating at a time when both central and local government were either burying their heads in the sand or providing a service that can at best be described, in the majority of cases, as obstructive!

The development of a parent support group

The early years
It was in 1986, at a time when the numbers of children being placed in the UK was increasing, that the first parent support group was founded. Prior to this, prospective adopters and families who had successfully completed an adoption, tended to link with PPIAS (now Adoption UK[1])

---

[1] Adoption UK, re-launched in May 1999, formerly PPIAS since 1971, has a broad remit of 'supporting adoptive families before, during and after adoption'. They have available information sheets about adopting from overseas and are able to facilitate contact between experienced overseas adopters who are able to share information about their adoption experiences.

a voluntary organisation founded in 1971 by domestic adopters. They provided a small service to members in the form of a fact sheet and a telephone link to experienced adoptive families. Information concerning agencies or individuals abroad willing to work alongside UK couples was handed down primarily through telephone links, with previous adopters' experiences often being the only source of UK based information upon which prospective adopters could rely, other than the UK-based embassies, some of whom were highly supportive of applications being made to their countries. The need, however, for a specialist support group was evident and in 1986 a core of adopters with children recently adopted from overseas came together to form STORK.

STORK's aims, perhaps naïve in those early days, were twofold: firstly, to offer support to families and their children post adoption and secondly, to actively promote ICA as a valid way of founding a family. All those involved in the Steering Committee were well aware of the ongoing implications of an overseas and transracial adoption and there was a strong sense that not only would the adults benefit from ongoing contact with other adoptive parents with children from overseas but, as the children grew, they too would benefit from contact with each other. The second aim of promoting ICA grew as a direct response to the negative stance adopted by local and central government, and again was child-centred, in that if the negative view of ICA remained, what impact would that have upon the self-esteem and worth of children adopted through that route?

STORK's membership grew rapidly (25 per cent per year during its first four years of existence) aided by the launch of a quarterly newsletter which offered individual stories of the adoption experience, detailed books, conferences etc., as well as publishing articles of professional interest. Membership was open to anyone who had adopted from overseas and a wide number of countries were, and still are, represented including Thailand, India, Sri Lanka, Russia, Turkey, Romania, China, Nepal, Ethiopia, Sudan, Japan, USA, Honduras, Guatemala, El Salvador, Colombia, Ecuador, Bolivia, Paraguay, Argentina and Chile.

In the autumn of 1987 the first Annual General Meeting was held. Families travelled from all over the UK to attend this first meeting in

Bedfordshire, confirming the need for ongoing links, and this annual meeting with its party atmosphere has been an ongoing feature of STORK ever since. The parents, however, wanted more, primarily the opportunity to explore within adult circles the issues surrounding post adoption issues and the following year STORK held its first parents' seminar in London. These too have become an annual event, with a different focus each year and topics include exploring adoption with children, handling racism and discrimination in school and community and, in 1998, the experience of returning to the birth country and reunions with birth families. Within this framework, smaller workshops have become a popular feature, giving people the chance to discuss in an open way their personal experiences of these issues. A further spin off has been the development of country specific groups within the main body, such as the Peru Support Group, and of regional groupings, with each area of the UK having their own co-ordinator, a model borrowed from our friends at Adoption UK.

Balancing pre- and post-adoption demands

STORK also, however, found that there were other demands upon its limited voluntary resources in the late 1980s, primarily from prospective adopters still unable to obtain advice and support from professional sources. The initial response was to set in place a helpline staffed by members who had adopted from different countries, offering a limited service to non-members who sought advice prior to adoption. However, as STORK became better known, the demands upon individuals in their own homes became onerous and in 1989 a formal helpline was established, staffed by an able volunteer with a telephone and a computer! The Helpline began to collect and collate information about procedures within different countries, producing country specific fact sheets, as well as offering advice and support to prospective adopters throughout and during the adoption process. In essence the helpline co-ordinator became a telephone "buddy" to many prospective parents, offering both practical and emotional support at a time when professional support was limited, either because of lack of resources or social work dogma, in both quantity and quality.

Throughout this time, considerable effort was made to forge links with individual social services departments to both promote the organisation and to influence social work views and thinking about ICA. STORK was a founder member of both CICA,[2] the Campaign for Intercountry Adoption, and of BABICA, the British Advisory Board for Intercountry Adoption, now renamed NICA,[3] the Network for Intercountry Adoption, sharing the views of parents with the professionals and academics within the network. It is interesting to note that, in contrast with other countries, parents have played a critical role in challenging the status quo, through the establishment of groups such as CICA, which acts as a pressure/lobbying forum to promote change both in legislation and process in relation to ICA. Parents from STORK also played an active role in BABICA. Equally, the media was targeted and STORK began to be regularly approached as a spokesperson in matters concerning intercountry adoption. This resulted in several lively TV debates in the late 80s and early 90s, as well as numerous magazine articles.

Conflict and separation

It was perhaps inevitable, however, that once STORK became more widely known amongst both professionals and the public, it too would come under attack and become the target for individuals who remained ideologically opposed to ICA. Thus in the late 1980s and early 1990s, considerable criticism was leveled at the pre-adoption

---

[2] CICA is a group of adoption professionals and interested parties with representatives from the legal profession, AFAA, OASIS, adoptive parents and academia who lobby Parliament in an effort to advise and influence policy decisions, guidelines, civil service practice, and local social service activity.

[3] NICA, formerly BABICA, is an independent group composed of those who have an interest in and/or experience of intercountry adoption. The membership is as wide-ranging as possible in order to encompass a diversity of experience and professional discipline. The group has four main aims which are, 1) to promote the paramountcy of the child's interests in all matters relating to intercountry adoption, 2) to promote the exchange of information and to encourage research, 3) to propose and pursue improved standards and services in intercountry adoption and finally 4), to ensure that an agreed ethical base underpins all intercountry adoption.

helpline, which was viewed as aiding and abetting individuals to pursue adoptions from overseas and circumvent official procedures. The fact that clear and efficient procedures for ICA in the UK had still not been developed seemed irrelevant to critics, whose opposition to adoption from overseas seemed intransigent. As an organisation STORK responded by looking carefully at its procedures and information systems. Certainly within the organisation there were instances of adopters not following the "correct procedures" but for the most part this was a result of an inability to obtain advice and guidance from statutory bodies. There were, as within all organisations, others whose motives for circumventing the system were less clear-cut but, as a voluntary organisation, it was impossible to police members and equally impossible to screen the information that was passed by word of mouth.

As the number of prospective adopters and established families increased during the early 1990s (the Romanian crisis not only focused attention on adoption from that country but also raised the possibility of overseas adoption per se in the minds of many applicants who had previously considered it unattainable), it became increasingly hard as a group of volunteers to service the needs of pre-adopters and post-adopters. In order to allow pre-adopters to attend post-adoption seminars, an affiliate membership system was developed, allowing access to some but not all events, a situation reflecting membership anxiety that events could become dominated by pre-adoption issues. Separate workshops were held for pre-adopters, many of whom were desperate to share their experiences of the pre-adoption process and to seek support during the assessment stage.

In 1993 the situation was alleviated by the creation of the Overseas Adoption Helpline (OAH) headed by Gill Haworth. Reception to the new Helpline within STORK was mixed, with some members viewing it as an organisation that could eventually replace the STORK helpline, leaving STORK to focus on post adoption issues, and others feeling that the Helpline, funded at that time by the Government, would not offer impartial advice and would "toe the party line". Ultimately the two views were irreconcilable and the STORK helpline split away from the main body, forming a new organisation, OASIS, the Overseas Adoption Support and Information Services (see Fleming Chapter 13).[4]

From STORK to AFAA: the maturer organisation

There was now an opportunity to revamp and re-market STORK, focusing almost exclusively upon post-adoption issues, although retaining affiliate membership to allow access to seminars for pre-adopters who wished to explore the kind of issues that would be of importance to them in their adoption lifetime. A series of post-adoption leaflets were published, focusing upon the basics of exploring adoption with children, coping with racism, adoption bereavement (loss of birth parents) and maintaining cultural links. A strong link was forged with the OAH to which all enquiries for factual information were referred, and which reciprocated by encouraging their enquirers to join STORK.

The change of focus also provided the opportunity to rethink the organisation name and logo. The name STORK had always had limitations, conjuring images of babies being carried from overseas into the arms of joyful parents. As many of our STORK members had adopted older children, this image neither reflected the reality nor conveyed the kind of image the organisation wished to present. Thus the Association for Families who have Adopted from Abroad (AFAA) came into being in 1994.

Since then there have been numerous developments worthy of note. Membership continues to grow steadily (about five per cent per annum) with both pre and post adopters joining, and in 1996 AFAA was awarded a lottery grant to develop its membership information systems.

---

[4] OASIS was set up by founder members Coral Williams and Julia Fleming in February 1995 with the main objective being to offer support and information to couples and single people considering adoption from overseas. This was to be done by the production and distribution of uptodate fact sheets describing the adoption procedure in various countries and via the telephone helpline. At the present time, OASIS has approximately 650 members and has broadened its remit which now includes linking families around the country who are then able to support each other during the adoption gprocess and maintain links, if they wish, following the adoption. They have also obtained charity status, and funds raised from the sale of fact sheets and membership fees are donated to support orphanages and street children in countries from which members have adopted.

This is of particular relevance to the children, many of whom are now in their teens and for whom the ability to link with fellow adoptees, both nationally and internationally, will be of enormous benefit. Social events, both regional and national, continue to be a feature, as do the seminars for parents and the quarterly newsletter. We maintain strong links with other parents' groups such as ARC (The Association of Romanian Children),[5] OASIS, Children Adopted from China[6] and with newer organisations such as PNPIC (The Parent Network for the Post Institutional Child).[7] Equally, links with older friends such as Adoption UK continue, such links ensuring that we can all benefit from each others' experiences and knowledge. AFAA continues to be a presence in the lobbying field, with parents involved in CICA and NICA, and being an active voice in the campaign to ensure that the new Adoption (Intercountry Aspects) Act 1999 reflected the parent's voice as well as the voice of the professionals.

Perhaps the greatest move forward has been in the forging of links with professionals. As the professional attitude towards ICA has mellowed in the UK, with both local authorities and voluntary agencies now undertaking the assessment work, so the views and expertise of the parents have begun to be viewed as being of value and worth hearing.

---

[5] ARC was founded in 1988 and presently has a membership of approximately 130 families. There has recently been a split within the organisation because of disagreements as to the purpose of the group and the significance of possible effects of institutionalisation of the adopted child's future development. ARC considers its main purpose is to provide support and information for its members and NOT to be a campaigning organisation or pressure group. Members who felt these two latter objectives were an important role for a parents' group have formed an alternative group, BIR (Born in Romania). Those who wanted a greater acknowledgement and information about the consequences of institutionalisation set up a subgroup of PNPIC (Parent Network for the Post Institutionalised Child).

[6] Children Adopted from China began in 1995 with 25 families. However, membership now exceeds 200 families. The main objective is to share experiences and knowledge about adopting children from China and to learn about Chinese culture.

[7] PNPIC (Parent Network for the Post Institutionalised Child) started in England in 1996 (the USA in 1993), and has a mailing list of approximately 1,000 families concerned about issues of institutionalisation and the impact this may have on the lives of children who have spent part of their life, however short, in an institution.

AFAA members now sit on several local authority adoption panels, and contribute to pre-adoption workshops run by agencies, often working alongside the OAH in order to offer both pre- and post-adoption input. Individual social workers and social services departments can now join AFAA as Associate Members entitling them to Association literature and newsletters. AFAA now has meaningful and positive working relationships with organisations such as BAAF, the British Agencies for Adoption and Fostering. While there remain some ideological differences, the fact that as a parent group AFAA is seen as having a valid contribution in the professional arena reflects a shift from both sides towards a more mature stance.

Ultimately, both professionals and parents are seeking similar goals related to the well being of children. Intercountry adoption brings with it many challenges, and it is not the perfect solution for children who cannot be cared for by their birth families in their country of origin. However, it is one way to ensure that such children are loved and nurtured within a family where differences can be celebrated, and where they can develop a sense of self worth with which to move out into the wider world. For many abandoned children overseas, there may be no other option to ensure quality of life.

A view of the future

While AFAA anticipates continuing to offer the core services developed, it must also look to the future and to the changing needs of the families and children within. Mention has already been made of the developing internet facilities which will enable teenagers to link with other adoptees both nationally and internationally, and issues related to returning to the birth country and tracing the birth family are assuming significance. The Catholic Children's Society Project 16–18 (1999), in which Gill Haworth interviewed a group of overseas adoptees in young adulthood, gave clear evidence of the importance to children from overseas of developing roots and connectedness to their country of origin, and sometimes to their birth families, and of the practical and emotional difficulties of this journey. Within AFAA, the young adults and their families are undertaking different journeys, with some returning to their countries to holiday, and others returning to seek out and participate in reunions with their birth families. This new stage in the lives of the children and of their families is a new challenge for AFAA, and it is perhaps conceivable that the organisation, either on a formal or informal basis, might itself become involved in participating in returner visits, much in the same way that Parents' groups in other European coutnries have done.

A further challenge relates to the need for all of the parent groups in the UK to develop further links between them. Perhaps the time is approaching for the groups to unite under a consortium, where individuality could be retained, but skills, ideas and resources could be pooled. Such sharing would also bring with it added strength and lobbying power, vital to obtain limited resources.

On a broader note, looking overseas to organisations in countries where ICA is longer established, parents' groups have played a key role in the professional development of the adoption service. Many members of AFAA would like to see the full service agencies that exist overseas, in existence here in the UK, where prospective adopters are not only prepared for the task of adopting, but assessed, facilitated and supported during the waiting, matching and introductory period, and offered post adoption support and guidance through workshops and seminars throughout the life of their child; in essence, centres of excellence for ICA, where the knowledge and skills of both professionals and parents can be brought together for the benefit of children. Such an agency could well build links with a smaller number of countries initially, with parents' groups who have adopted from those countries having an input not only into the preparation of prospective adopters but contributing to the Panel and to post-adoption services, akin to the developments in Belgium where parent groups have been active in developing such agencies.

In the long term, a number of such agencies could be established, based either within an existing voluntary agency with a mix of domestic and intercountry work, or with specialist agencies, where intercountry work is the focus. It seems that whilst local authorities do now undertake the work, very few have sufficient resources, or indeed sufficient numbers of applicants seeking an adoption service, to be able to truly develop specialist skills in this area. Voluntary agencies, usually smaller and more flexible in nature, can often be innovative and creative in ways which are impossible for larger more bureaucratic bodies and could be an ideal basis for such a specialist venture. During the short history of AFAA, there have been several efforts to achieve this aim, the driving force behind each attempt being parents. While such projects are often viewed with scepticism within the Government, it is of importance to note that parents' groups are often well placed to instigate regulated change – our commitment is to our children. Parents want their placements, and the placements of all children from overseas, to be successful and to continue into the future. To place children with ill-prepared adopters, with the risk of disruption, is not only a disservice to the child, but to all of the children already in the UK. Contrary to popular belief, adopters do not see adoption as the panacea for all ills and feel that preparation and assessment are vital components in the adoption process, provided the systems are fair and removed from social work dogma.

Conclusion

Those parents who have battled in the UK to prevent intercountry adoption being demonised, and have fought to place it on the agenda and have it recognised as an acceptable option for some children, feel that at last we are coming of age. Ironically, it is at about the same time that those of us who began the Odyssey in the 1980s have children literally coming of age. As parents, children and professionals we have all learnt together about the challenges, the joys and the difficulties of working through our differences. Looking to countries such as Sweden and the USA, whose history of intercountry adoption is longer than ours, shows that we have still a great deal to learn, but as a parent group, and maybe as a country, we are now on the way.

AFAA can be contracted at: www.afaa.mcmail.com

References

Andersson G (1988) *The Adopting and Adopted Swedes and their Contemporary Society*, Sweden: Sundbyberg.

Catholic Children's Society Project 16–18, (1999) *Adoption in My Life: The intercountry experience*, Nottingham.

Cederblad M (1982) *Children Adopted from Abroad and Coming to Sweden after Age Three*, Solna, Sweden: NIA.

Chestang L (1972) 'The Dilemma of Biracial Adoption', *Social Work*, 17:3, pp 100–105.

Chimezie A (1975) 'The Transracial Adoption of Black Children', *Social Work*, 20, July.

Dale D (1989) *Denying Homes to Black Children*, Social Affairs Unit Research Report 8.

Dalen M and Sætersdal B (1987) 'Transracial Adoption in Norway', *Adoption & Fostering*, 11:4, pp 44–46.

Department of Health (1992) *Review of Adoption Law, Discussion Paper No 4. Intercountry Adoption*, London: DoH.

Department of Health (1993) *Adoption: The future*, London: HMSO.

Gaber I and Aldridge J (1994) *In the Best Interest of the Children: Culture, identity and transracial adoption*, London: Free Association Books.

Geerars H *et al* (1996) *Adoptees on their Way to Adulthood*, Netherlands: Utrecht University.

Hokesbergen R A C *et al* (1984) *Adopted Children at Home and at School*, Lisse: Swets & Zeitliger.

International Bar Association (1991) *The Intercountry Adoption Process*, IBA Education Trust.

Rorbeck M (1990) *Denmark – My Country*, Copenhagen: Danish National Institute of Social Research.

Silverman A and Feigelman W (1981) 'The Adjustment of Black Children Adopted by White Families', *Social Casework*, 62:9, pp 529–536.

Simon R J and Altstein H (1977) *Transracial Adoption*, New York: Wiley.

Zaar C (1991) *Intercountry Adoptions: What is the state of research and what new fields need to be investigated?* Stockholm: NIA.

12 Overseas Adoption Helpline
Helping people through the maze

Gill Haworth

Gill Haworth is Director of Overseas Adoption Helpline. She has been a qualified social worker for over 20 years and has an MSc in Social Work and Social Administration and a CQSW from the London School of Economics. Gill was an adoption practitioner as well as team manager of a fostering and adoption section of a London Borough before joining The Bridge Child Care Development Service as principal social work consultant. Her focus on intercountry adoption began with her appointment in early 1992 as Director of the initially government-funded information and advice service.

Introduction

The idea of an information and advice service on intercountry adoption, independent of the adoption authorities whose role it is to assess and approve adoption applicants, was first introduced by the *Campaign for Intercountry Adoption* (CICA) parliamentary lobby group. In 1992, in response to increased interest in adoption from overseas, the government provided Department of Health (DoH) funding to The Bridge Child Care Consultancy Service (now The Bridge Child Care Development Service) to host an Overseas Adoption Helpline as an experimental project; between May 1992 and March 1997, it responded to over 14,000 enquiries.

Despite the change in the government's priorities, which resulted in a termination of funding, there remained an evident need for such a service among adoption professionals, prospective intercountry adopters and established adoptive families. The service was reconstituted, as an independent voluntary organisation, by staff and volunteers who had been instrumental in running the previous helpline. Overseas Adoption Helpline (OAH) was granted charitable status in January 1998 (see Appendix II).

The legal background

The absence of a legal framework for intercountry adoption has been keenly felt by adoption professionals and prospective intercountry adopters alike. The lack of clarity that follows from a reliance on domestic adoption law, regulations and guidance also undermines confidence that children's interests are being protected. Adoptive families are acutely aware of the lack of consistency throughout the UK concerning the availability and quality of preparation, assessment and other services and the fees that will be charged.

It is important to emphasise that, despite these observations, considerable development in intercountry adoption services and their delivery has taken place in the UK since the beginning of the 1990s. The effects of the Hague Convention are to some significant degree anticipated in the body of guidance issued by central government since 1990. For example:

- At the beginning of the 1990s few local authorities, if any, provided a home study in advance of a specific child being identified overseas for adoption. Now such a service is provided UK wide and increasingly local authorities aim to offer a service comparable to domestic adoption at the pre- and post-adoption stages.

- Some voluntary adoption agencies have elected to apply for, and have been granted, approval to operate an intercountry adoption service in their own right. Previously, they could operate a preparation and home study service only on behalf of local authorities (see Hesslegrave, Chapter 16).

- Immigration procedures have been streamlined and applications are no longer, as a matter of routine, processed by both the Home Office and the DoH. The waiting time for the visa to be issued is thereby shortened (from months to weeks) as in practice it has largely become integrated into the adoption process.

OAH – The new organisation

OAH is unique in the UK and, so far as OAH has been able to determine, in intercountry adoption services elsewhere in the world. Its uniqueness stems from its status as a service staffed by social workers with several years' experience of UK and intercountry adoption, yet separate from organisations which prepare, assess, recommend or endorse adoption applications. It is also separate from the associations of families who have adopted whether in the UK or from abroad. At the same time, close links are maintained with adoption agencies and organisations of adoption professionals and of adoptive families. This is amply reflected in the structure of the organisation and in the growing number of co-operative activities in which OAH is engaged. The trustees and an advisory panel of experts bring a diversity of professional and personal connections and expertise.

The staff team includes salaried and volunteer members and all those involved with the organisation, whatever their role, volunteer some of their time, as do a growing number of volunteers who have adopted a child from overseas.

Advice and information

OAH has a team of five advisers who work on a sessional basis responding to callers and are also involved in consultation, training and in writing OAH publications. If callers prefer to use the advice line[1] in a language other than English, telephone appointments can be made for them to do so in one of several European languages or in Hindi.

Joint initiatives are also undertaken with key professionals and organisations, including some of the self-help groups. These include AFAA (The Association of Families who have Adopted from Abroad); Project 16–18, Catholic Children's Society (Nottingham) an approved adoption agency (non-governmental organisation – NGO); Family Thais (an association of families who have adopted from Thailand); Childlink Adoption Society; and adoption and child welfare agencies in India.

OAH has a constantly up-dated database of information on the policies, procedures and criteria for adoption in over 100 countries as well as lists of relevant organisations and bodies in those countries. Information is gathered from other agencies in the UK, agencies overseas and adoptive families.

---

[1]The advice line is the core service of the organisation, although now it comprises just one part of the charity's work. OAH had responded to 19,300 enquiries from its inception to the end of 1999.

Consultation Days

For those users who may wish to receive more than telephone advice, OAH has designed Consultation Days for prospective adopters, which are intended mostly to benefit people at the pre-assessment stage. Originally piloted by the former Helpline, in conjunction with Childlink Adoption Society, these have become an important and developing activity. Consultation Days are led by OAH staff and one person who has adopted from overseas, and are run on a small group, experiential basis.

Services for agencies

Agencies subscribe to OAH in order to be kept up to date with current issues in intercountry adoption, to have access to relevant information and to receive training and consultation. In the year 1999/2000, 30 agencies subscribed at an annual fee of around £500 to £1,000, according to the agency status and size (i.e. voluntary adoption agency, unitary authority or a county authority).

Use of OAH services

Use of the advice line

Although many who call the advice line are comfortable giving full details about themselves, others, for a variety of reasons, are reluctant to do so. The service therefore can be accessed anonymously if that is the user's wish.

As a matter of routine, advisers will ask for basic information but it will be a matter for their judgement whether, and how much, additional detail is sought. OAH contact statistics should, therefore, be understood in this context.

- Of all contacts, 85 per cent were from members of the public and at least 20 per cent from repeat callers. As might be expected, contact peaks when intercountry adoption – or some disaster overseas – is in the headlines.
- The advice line is primarily used as a source of information and advice, or as a sounding board, very early in the process, as part of an initial exploration. Initial enquiries represented about 82 per cent of all contacts from the public in 1997/98 and about 91 per cent in 1998/99.

- People wanting to adopt relatives accounted for 8 and 9 per cent of enquiries respectively in 1997/98 and 1998/99.
- Another identifiable group comprises people who wish to apply to adopt an abandoned or relinquished child from their own, or their family's, country of origin. This group accounted for 8.6 per cent of enquiries in 1997/98 and 4 per cent in 1998/99.

The call to OAH's advice line is, for many people, the first move they make to find out about intercountry adoption: Does it happen? Is it legal? Where do you start? How much does it cost? How long does it take? The user is generally satisfied at this stage by the verbal information they receive and go on to to request our publications.

There are others who have found a number of sources of information first and wish to check things out with OAH. They may also have specific queries which they wish to discuss outside an assessment situation and before they become too committed to the process.

In the UK, the home study assessment must be undertaken in respect of an application to one stated country and this can pose some difficulty for prospective adopters if they have no obvious links with any country. OAH's publications offer some pointers to factors that might influence the applicants' decision, and provide some information about the profile of children for whom intercountry adoption is considered and how children come to need adoption by foreign applicants.

The advice line is frequently used by prospective applicants to compare the realities of the children who might be placed with them to the child they had imagined they might parent. Understandably when prospective adopters are contemplating adoption of an infant or young toddler, perhaps as first-time parents, they may not readily project years ahead to the potential needs of the adopted person as a young adult. However, OAH aims to introduce this dimension from the outset as it should influence the choice of country to which applicants apply. Where intercountry adoption is transracial adoption (as most is) this provides a context within which applicants can begin to examine for themselves their capacity and readiness, for example, to:

- put in place as much as they can to assist their child should he or she wish to visit the country of origin, to trace and have access to adoption papers (if permissible) or to seek to reunite with birth family members or other significant people;

- stand with the young person when he or she encounters racism;
- keep the child's knowledge of and connection with the country sufficiently alive to give some real choices in adulthood about forging or maintaining their own individual relationship with that country and its peoples. Consultation Days offer another setting in which these issues can be explored.

There are some issues which are raised less frequently than in the past:

- Questions about the acceptability of privately commissioned home studies (assessment reports which applicants commission individual social workers to prepare). These are no longer commonplace but do still get asked from time to time, especially in the context of adoption applications to designated countries, principally the USA. There has, however, been a recent cluster of calls as a Commencement Order under the new legislation made it an offence, with effect from 31 January 2000, for home studies to be prepared other than by or on behalf of an adoption agency (statutory or NGO).
- Concerns about, and requests for assistance to overcome, prolonged delays in obtaining entry clearance for the child have declined in respect of non-relative adoptions, although they remain a consistent feature in respect of relative adoptions.

Others have become more frequent.

- Complex questions associated with increased geographical mobility of applicants and, in some cases, the children to be adopted. For example, EU nationals who hope to adopt from overseas whilst living temporarily in the UK.
- Contact from people who have learnt about ICA on the internet, usually from USA web sites, and who may not be aware of the differences between UK and USA adoption practice.

There is a significant group of users who do not have a specific country in mind. Even so, during each of the years 1997/98 and 1998/99, OAH was asked about adoption provision, procedures and requirements in respect of 96 countries.

The DoH statistics for the nearest comparable period (January 1997 to June 1999) show that 607 applications were received in total, distributed between 41 countries. There will be other factors contributing to the disparity between OAH patterns of interest and DoH patterns of application, including:

- delay in taking applications further;
- applicants counselling themselves out, being counselled out or having their application rejected;
- applications to countries that do not routinely require them to come via the DoH;
- applications by relatives in respect of over 60 different countries, some of which are likely to have been processed outside the intercountry adoption procedures.

Adoption professionals may contact the advice line on behalf of their clients or for themselves:

- to obtain or check out information for themselves or their agency/ organisation;
- to understand the role and expectations of their agency and the procedures to be followed;
- to seek specialist services and resources, e.g. lawyers, therapists, counsellors, interpreters, research references and relevant publications;
- to be linked with colleagues in other agencies/authorities who may have faced similar problems or matters of policy.

In addition to providing advice, and often written materials as well, OAH advisers have referred around six per cent of all advice line users to the organisation they might expect to process their application or to other organisations for additional specialist services.

Consultation Days and the issues most often raised by prospective adopters

Ten Consultation Days were held between September 1998 and December 1999 which, taken together, catered for 103 prospective adopters (40 couples and 23 single applicants). None of the participants was considering the adoption of a related child. Participants in Consultation Days had, by the time they attended, usually identified a country about whose adoption policies they wished to know more. Issues that they most commonly wanted to explore included:

- cross-cultural adoption and racism from the perspectives of the child and the whole family, and the impact for the child of growing up with parents of a different "race";
- increased understanding of the special needs of the child adopted from overseas;
- the effects of early deprivation and orphanage life;
- how to help the child adapt to change;
- links to the child's country of origin and access to possible support there once the application has been sent;
- how to avoid the alleged pitfalls in the overseas country and to be sure a child is genuinely free for adoption.

Consultation Days have reinforced the messages received through the advice line about just how much anxiety is carried by applicants about all the complexities of intercountry adoption and, in particular, about the home study assessment process. Applicants are apprehensive about the response they are likely to receive when they first make contact with the local authority or adoption agency. Some prospective adopters express tremendous concern about being rebuffed at the outset, or not being considered up to the task. Regrettably, this has remained a consistent concern since 1992. It is unsatisfactory for even one applicant to feel that an enquiry about adoption was unwelcome but it is OAH's perception that in reality most people find that they have worried needlessly. However, this apprehension is understandable, engendered as it is by:

- adverse comments in all sections of the media about adoption in general, and transracial adoption in particular, and whether or not it is acceptable. Just as in domestic adoption, people are fearful of being judged too old, having too low or too high an income, having too few or too many books – and so on;

- the awareness that adoption has a life-long impact for all concerned and, in this context, a concern that intercountry adoption cannot readily afford the adopted person continued contact with the country, language, culture and other more subtle norms of the child's original country;

- the professional awareness that there are more children in the UK needing adoption than there are families to adopt them,[2] and yet families are turning overseas to adopt children who are younger, but whose birth family heritage and pre-adoption experiences may in fact make them more challenging to adopt than their UK counterparts.

OAH'S own publications and those of AFAA provide an introduction to the home study process and details of what it entails. But for most prospective adopters, it is the people who have experienced the process themselves who are the source of greatest reassurance. Accordingly, OAH links new users, if they wish, with adoptive parent volunteers and ensures they are aware of the various associations of families who have adopted, both from the UK and from overseas.

Applicants who have prior strong links with the country of origin

It is an agreed principle that a child's interests are better served by an adoptive placement with a family in his or her original country. However, it seems that there is a tendency to see intercountry adoption as a second choice, after domestic adoption, for adoptive applicants as well. This is not the case, and between May 1997 and March 1999, around 600

---

[2]When adoption agencies and social workers are working directly with children for whom they know they are unlikely to find families, they are perhaps least receptive to arguments about a mis-match between the UK families wanting to adopt and the UK children waiting. It is OAH's impression that, while some prospective intercountry adopters would also consider the placement of older children waiting in the UK, or younger children with special needs, most would not.

contacts (about 15 per cent) with OAH were about adoption from a particular country in preference to domestic adoption, for one of the following reasons:

- there is a wish to adopt a child who is known to them (perhaps, but not always, a relative);
- applicants who are not white British wish to adopt from their country of origin, or from a country where the children may reflect the applicants' ethnicity;
- the applicants have a special knowledge of or connection with the country, e.g. they were adopted from that country themselves; they have siblings who were adopted from that country; they have spent their formative years living in that country.

Applications from relatives

I would like to make particular comment on the position of prospective adopters who are related to the parents of the child they hope to adopt. Between May 1997 and March 1999, 351 contacts (8.75 per cent) concerned prospective or actual "adoption" by relatives. Members of this distinct group are from minority communities and most often enquire about the adoption of young relatives from India, Pakistan, Philippines, Jamaica, Thailand, Nigeria, Ghana and China. Relatives who contact OAH may have no knowledge of the UK adoption services and procedures and will usually be without the peer support that family associations provide for non-relative adopters. It may also be that English is not their first language and, if so, someone else may be acting for them. It would not be unusual for callers to tell OAH that they consider they have been ill served by immigration advice and assistance given informally, or otherwise. Many, therefore, will anticipate the need to meet certain requirements in the child's country of origin but may not anticipate having to follow procedures and meet requirements in the UK as well. They often only become aware of the existence of UK adoption requirements when application for the child's entry to the UK has been made or refused.

The prospective adopters (and if old enough, the child) usually have the emotional pressure of knowing that they are "there for each other". The child may have been conceived for the applicants or given as a "gift" to an infertile relative consistent with traditional cultural norms. It may be that, whether by traditional ceremony or court process, the applicants have already assumed parental responsibility for the child in his or her country of origin.

So far as UK adoption is concerned, it is open to birth parents to place their child for adoption with a relative, as defined by the adoption legislation, without the involvement of an adoption agency. Furthermore, the Children Act 1989 is explicit about the important part relatives, and other people who are significant to the child, might play in providing supplementary or alternative care when a child is separated from his or her birth parents.

In OAH's experience, there is a stark contrast between the approach taken to in-family placements in domestic and intercountry adoption. The current situation lends itself to differing but equally unsatisfactory scenarios.

- It is mandatory for applicants who are related to the parents of the child first to make application, within the immigration rules, for the child to come to the UK to join them on the grounds that there are serious and compelling family or other reasons.

  This may be an appropriate and speedy resolution to a family crisis but it may be at odds with the adoption and emigration procedures in the child's state of origin. It may also serve to propel the relatives through an immigration process without access to pre-placement advice, preparation and assessment which is integral to adoption. The latter could be especially important to family and child(ren) in the early stages of their adjustment to family life together especially if the child(ren) has experienced loss or other trauma prior to placement.

- More commonly, OAH hears stories with a very different outcome. Of course we cannot know how many applications, which at one stage appear to be meeting insurmountable difficulties, are ultimately resolved satisfactorily. But there are numerous examples of applicants continuing for two years or more in their attempts to bring a related child to the UK for adoption.

It would appear that the immigration requirement that causes relatives most difficulty is that which states the child should have lost or broken ties with the original family. Some kinship patterns and traditional family structures militate against this requirement being met, for example, where extended families live together in joint households. Whatever the reasons for the transfer of parental responsibility, intercountry adoption applications by relatives point to some incompatibility between the principles of immigration control and the practice of in-family care for children. Continuity of care and phased introductions are prized elements of domestic adoption placement practice but may be a bar to a child's eligibility for entry in many intercountry relative adoptions.

After adoption

The OAH advice line is used far less after adoption than at the early stages of the process, and our post-adoption service needs to be developed. But from the contacts OAH does receive, we are aware of the extra challenges intercountry adopted people experience growing up, particularly if they wish to find further information about their own adoption or re-unite with birth family members. OAH, therefore, valued the opportunity to work in collaboration with Project 16–18, Catholic Children's Society (Nottingham) on *Adoption in My Life – the intercountry experience* (Jardine and Samwell-Smith Chapters 27 and 28).

Although the numbers of young adults in the UK who have been adopted from overseas may be relatively small, their number is set to grow substantially. There are many issues common to domestic and intercountry adoption, but from what young adults are telling us of their experiences, there is an evident need for services that take account of the unique issues arising out of intercountry adoption.

The additional ways in which people adopted from other countries feel, or are in fact, different are likely to magnify in significance and complexity as the adopted person grows older. While post-adoption provision might appropriately be made available to the adoptive parents in the early phases of intercountry adoption placements, priority is properly shifted to the needs of the adopted people themselves as they grow towards adult independence.

One or more return visits to the child's country of origin may represent an essential feature of the post-adoption phase, both for the child and for other members of the adoptive family. Who will counsel and support them should they intend to make a journey to their original country? Who will prepare, counsel and support them in their search for information? Where will they find interpreters if they are hoping to reunite with birth family members? Where will they find the finance to enable this to happen? What about those young people who will never have access to information about their adoption, or who find out that their records have been falsified or destroyed – to whom might they turn?

Issues for consideration

People who use OAH's services appreciate that more services are available to them than were to their counterparts ten years ago. Nevertheless, they make a strong argument for UK adoption agencies to offer a full service from pre-adoption to post-adoption.

OAH services, amongst others, may go some way to inform prospective adopters in advance of their application, and the preparation and assessment services will take the process further, but applicants regret that there is still a strong "do-it-yourself" element in respect of arrangements with the child's country of origin. Where it is consistent with the policies and procedures in the child's country of origin, some UK applicants are engaging the services of "full service" agencies based in yet another country (usually the USA) to provide support and assistance in the overseas country.

The need for this is reflected in reverse by adoption authorities in some of the overseas countries of origin of children placed with UK applicants. There is an often-stated preference for developing a working relationship with a small number of adoption agencies in the UK, rather than having the Central Authority as their single consistent point of contact.

Some question how it can be that UK intercountry adopters are prepared and assessed by UK adoption agencies only to be referred on to agencies in another country (or, still worse, having to rely on their own resources) to undertake the linking with a child. They must then return to the UK for the scrutiny and support of the UK adoption agencies in preparation for an adoption application to the UK court. Is this really the most effective system?

It is to be hoped that the new legislation (see Brennan, Chapter 10) will provide the impetus for the development of specialist agencies and the funding to sustain them. However, given the broad spread of countries to which UK applicants apply, as illustrated by the DoH statistics of received home studies referred to above, it is unrealistic to expect specialist agencies to offer a service which embraces them all. Whatever the future framework for intercountry adoption, there must be more emphasis on services after adoption.

Were full service agencies to be established in the UK, they might over time encompass post-intercountry adoption services as core activities. In the meantime, there is a growing body of young people for whom the focus of post-adoption services, which have developed in the domestic context, may not be entirely relevant to their experiences, issues and concerns.

Conclusion

The last ten years have seen greater openness towards statutory and NGO co-operation and involvement in intercountry adoption services. As has been the case for some time in UK domestic adoption, intercountry adoptive parents and young people have begun to be involved in programmes of adoption awareness, preparation for prospective adopters, membership of agencies' adoption panels and post-adoption support. This is a welcome development but has scope for even wider application.

Relative adopters need recognition as a distinct group of adoptive applicants about whom little information or research appears to be available. People applying to adopt a young relative living overseas appear to OAH to be particularly vulnerable, comparatively unsupported and faced with enormous complexities when attempting to negotiate immigration and adoption procedures.

There is continuing support among prospective adopters, adoptive families, adopted people, and adoption professionals for a source of information, advice and consultation separate from the assessment and approval processes.

The fact that demands on OAH have been sustained over time, whatever changes have taken place in the services provided by the local authorities, adoption agencies and central government departments, is indicative of the need for an information and advice service that stands apart from the bodies that assess/approve and endorse applications. A separate service such as OAH provides a neutral and confidential setting in which applicants can really explore their greatest hopes and worst fears without being judged.

Local authorities and NGO adoption agencies are geared to the needs of waiting children in the UK, and to the preparation and assessment of domestic and intercountry adopters within their area of operation. OAH is a service to which they too can refer. OAH is dedicated to receiving enquiries UK wide from people with general queries, and it can act as an instant referral service for all adoption agencies in the statutory and voluntary (NGO) sectors.

OAH can, and does, also keep statistics and compile information, which can be disseminated and used towards improving services. In due course, people adopting from overseas should be able to receive a service at least as comprehensive as people adopting domestically, and one which is fully tailored to the needs not only of the adopters, but above all to those of the children concerned.

13 OASIS – The Overseas Adoption Support and Information Service

Julia Fleming

Julia Fleming is an OASIS Committee member and mother of two Chinese-born and two Vietnamese-born children.

What is OASIS?

OASIS is a parent-led information service dedicated to helping institutionalised children throughout the world (see Appendix II). We actively seek families willing to adopt internationally as well as financially supporting deserving projects around the globe.

Why a parent-led information service?

The Overseas Adoption Support and Information Service (OASIS) was formed in 1995 and was granted charitable status the same year. The original Oasis committee set the service up for a number of reasons, primarily that there was a need for accurate, reliable and up-to-date information from people who had actually been through the process of adopting internationally.

This was important for two reasons. First, in the early 1990s, the profile of children being adopted into the UK began to change radically. Instead of young, fostered children with known birth parent(s) and relatively accurate medical information, families began bringing home abandoned, institutionalised children with no known medical details. The average age of the adopted children began to climb as well. Although these types of adoptions had always occurred from some sending countries, they were now firmly in the majority. The parents experiencing these types of adoptions first hand were frustrated by the lack of information available in the UK and the apparent lack of interest from well-established adoption support groups.

It was obvious that prospective parents needed good information about the effects of institutionalisation, the incidence of hepatitis B and C (and treatment), the warning signs of Foetal Alcohol Syndrome/Effect

(FAS/FAE), drug-resistant TB, feeding issues associated with extremely malnourished children, the correct medical tests to be performed on arrival home, and many other issues not being adequately tackled by existing support groups or social services departments at that point in time. Secondly, we felt that there should be some place in the information network for parents, the very people who had "been there, done that". Much of the information from other sources was misleading. A particular country may indeed have statutes on the books allowing international adoption but that does not mean that adoptions actually occur. Another country might allow infants to be adopted but what may not be obvious to someone reading a government fact sheet is that *infants* are only actually available for domestic adoption.

OASIS felt that information from returning parents should be collated and shared with others. In this way, we could (and can) offer families information on the accuracy of medical information in various countries, non-adoption related expenses, the types of children available for adoption and current length of time to be matched and then travel to adopt, as well as many other nuggets of information. Nor did we feel that individuals who have *not* parented an adopted child (particularly a transracially adopted child) could adequately answer pre-adopters' questions on issues like racism, self-esteem difficulties, adverse family reactions, facing awkward questions from the public, fostering a multi-cultural identity, return trips to birth countries, birth parent searches and the like. Traditionally, these had been seen as post-adoption issues. OASIS felt that these issues, and others, needed to be explored in depth at the pre-adoption stage. As is always the case, hearing from someone who has walked in your shoes and has shared your dreams and fears is invaluable.

Of course, we do not underestimate the value of input from professional social workers but felt strongly that parents' voices needed to be heard.

What do we believe?

The ultimate goal of our organisation is to find families for children rather than children for families. We strongly believe that a child's birth family is always the first choice for that child. We believe it wrong to place a child for intercountry adoption if an alternative family in the child's birth country can be found. We believe that international adoption should only result from genuine need. Institutionalisation is a tragedy. It can cause intellectual, physical and emotional damage. Even children living in well-run, caring institutions deserve a family. Each and every child born in this world deserves a childhood. Every child needs to feel a parent's loving embrace, hear kind words and experience love and affection. All children deserve parents who will love them, advocate for them and guide them into adulthood. Institutions rob children of all these things. Because of that, OASIS firmly believes that it is wrong for a child to languish in an institution when there are families around the world willing and able to offer them a new start.

We believe that choosing to place children internationally is not only a caring but also extremely brave and difficult decision on the part of sending countries. Countries that allow international adoption are giving a great deal to all concerned. It is imperative that adopting families recognise this and obey the laws of the sending country. Families must be willing to adopt not only the child but the country as well. Adopting families do not become British families with internationally-adopted children, they become a multicultural family. This must be understood and family life must change to reflect the reality of the new family unit.

OASIS believes that no family should act from a position of cultural imperialism. It is not acceptable to say that poor children in underdeveloped countries would be better off in Britain. International adoption is not a goal in and of itself. Instead, we say that all children deserve a family.

Anything else?

Yes! We believe that prospective adopters have the right to timely, accurate information. We believe that all adopters have the right to an affordable home study performed by specially trained social workers. Also, home studies for international adoptions should be presented to appropriately trained panels and those panels should include international adopters.

Is there more?

Yes, we believe in the Convention on the Rights of the Child developed by the United Nations. However, we would like to see this taken one step further. We would like children's institutions the world over to be subject to a set of minimum standards (much like the Geneva Convention for prisoners of war) and mandatory inspections performed by a voluntary body. It seems ridiculous to have to state the obvious but children are human beings. As we enter the new century, there are myriad pressure groups and human rights' organisations that care for adults. There are also many aid organisations working with needy children around the world. Too often it is the most vulnerable of all – the institutionalised child – that has no voice.

What does OASIS do?

We serve our members in the following ways. Currently, Oasis subscribes to nine adoption journals and informally swaps newsletters with a half a dozen other adoption support groups. Before PNPIC (Parent Network for Post Institutionalised Children) became active in the UK in 1997, OASIS sent delegates to the main PNPIC conferences in the USA in order to learn, establish information networks and disseminate information to our members.

We have been using the internet to source information since 1994 (and have had our own website (www.oasis.ndirect.co.uk) for several years) and have watched the explosion of this medium in the adoption world with great interest.

We disseminate information to our members by way of our helpline (phone lines, fax lines and email), fact sheets, quarterly newsletter and annual seminars. All helpline operators distribute information within strict guidelines using only approved sources of information. Considerable time and money is expended checking information at source, hiring translators as required.

OASIS is represented on CICA and NICA. As we have become more well known, our committee members have been asked to join adoption panels, present information to pre-adopters at preparation classes and give seminars to local authority adoption panels. On several occasions,

235

we have been approached by social services to use our network to help find homes for children available domestically.

All OASIS committee members and helpers are volunteers. This means that the bulk of our revenue can be sent to help the children left behind. Since inception, OASIS has sent £48,500 to children in need around the world. The money has primarily gone to institutionalised children. Children in 16 different countries have benefited.

OASIS and other groups

OASIS maintains friendly links with many country-specific as well as regional support groups. OASIS members often belong to four or five different support groups (OASIS, a regional group, regional Adoption UK group, country-specific group and AFAA). OASIS welcomes all support groups but actively encourages members to join non-country specific groups. We feel this is important for a number of reasons. Intercountry adoption is subject to trends: one country closes, another opens; one country becomes designated, another calls a moratorium, and so on. With the exception of Thailand, most children from any particular country tend to be clustered together in age.

Parents with young children need to be able to seek advice and support from those a little further down the line. For instance, the majority of Chinese adoptees in this country are under five. In order to understand issues that arise in school, parents should be talking to families with children from Sri Lanka, Romania, Thailand, El Salvador, etc. Parents with children in their middle teens could ask parents with children from Hong Kong and Vietnam about issues that surface in young adulthood.

Additionally, it is beneficial for children to see a broad spectrum of adoptees. It helps them to know that adoptees of all ages, both genders, and many different ethnic backgrounds, needed to be adopted for a variety of reasons and are from many different countries. Understanding adoption as a global phenomenon will not only help children understand what has happened to them but also understand that their birth country was not the first nor the last to make the decision to send children overseas. Joining multi-country support groups is also a step in the direction of true multiculturalism. OASIS believes that families must actively demonstrate an acceptance of all cultures, not just British and that of the birth country of their adopted child.

The future

All of us working in the field of intercountry adoption in the UK are united in the belief that we desperately need international adoption agencies. Although we lag far behind the rest of the world in this regard, in some ways it might be a blessing. It means that we can study the systems in place in Europe, the USA and Australia (many of which are described elsewhere in this anthology) and choose the best of those systems. OASIS believes that whichever type of agency emerges, parental and adoptee involvement is a necessity. It is hard to imagine a valid agency operating without the input of these two groups. We also believe that an agency should be staffed by those with not only a genuine understanding of all the issues but a deep and abiding passion for the children who wait.

OASIS at the turn of the century

Our belief that a parent-led advice and information service was needed has been amply rewarded. At the end of 1999, OASIS had a membership of just over 1,000 families. We also have individual social workers and social services departments who subscribe to OASIS. The bulk of our membership do not 'move on' after adoption so our newsletters and seminars now encompass post-adoption issues as well. OASIS has distributed information to both personal and professional enquiries from all parts of the UK and Germany, Canada, Dubai, Bahrain, Spain, USA, Trinidad, Hong Kong, Singapore and New Zealand.

At the last count our members had adopted children from 27 countries ranging in age from their late 20s to early 60s, are both married and single (male and female singles) and have families ranging in size from one child to seven children. Many of our members adopt several times and many choose to adopt from more than one country. A significant proportion has birth as well as adopted children. Our adopters come from all walks of life and all income brackets. Our children range in age from infancy to adulthood.

Many of the children arrived in the UK as babies but others are welcomed into their new families as toddlers or school age children. Some come home healthy and others arrive with known or unknown special needs. Most families adopt one child at a time but some adopt sibling groups. In short, we are an extremely disparate group with only one thing in common – the belief that we can offer a child in need a second chance at a life of love and happiness. We know the road our families travel can be long and fraught with difficulty but together we rejoice in our children and search for solutions to any difficulties they and we face along the way.

14 Developing services for intercountry adoption
A local authority perspective

Cherry Harnott

Cherry Harnott is the Adoption Manager for Portsmouth City Council and was previously employed in a similar capacity by Hampshire County Council from 1989 to early 2000. She was responsible for setting up the intercountry adoption service in Hampshire in 1990, and chaired the intercountry adoption panel from 1990 to 1995.

Introduction

It was in response to the many enquiries that were received in 1990 following the Romanian crisis that the decision was made to set up a specialist intercountry adoption service that did not compete with Hampshire's domestic adoption service. The intercountry adoption panel was established in 1990, and two part-time intercountry adoption social workers were appointed to prepare and assess applicants.

The aim of this chapter is to describe the setting up of the intercountry adoption service and outline the procedures followed in Hampshire. I shall end by looking at the outcomes for children adopted over the past decade and consider the policy implications for the UK as it prepares to ratify the Hague Convention.

A statistical overview

Applicants
In the ten years from January 1990 to 31 December 1999, a total of 901 enquiries were received, many of which were in response to extensive media coverage of children living in difficult circumstances in institutions overseas. There were 225 enquiries received in respect of Romania in 1990 and 1991, as well as 88 enquiries in respect of Bosnia alone in 1993. During the last five years there have been approximately 50 enquiries per year.

Eighty-nine per cent of those making an initial enquiry did not proceed to request a formal interview, but most of the remainder went through the assessment process. Ninety-seven applications have been considered by Hampshire during the past 10 years, of which 92 were approved and five rejected. Full details of enquiries and outcome of applications can be found in Table 14.1 in the Appendix.

Children

In the past ten years a total of 95 children from overseas have entered Hampshire for the purpose of adoption, ranging in age from one week to 17 years (see Table 14.2 in the Appendix).

Setting up the intercountry adoption service

Intercountry adoption social workers

Given the high number of enquiries anticipated, it was clear that the intercountry adoption social workers' role should be confined to that of preparing and assessing applicants, rather than being overloaded with the additional responsibilities of adoption welfare supervision after children have entered the UK. Once the application has been dealt with by the intercountry adoption panel and agreed by the agency decision-maker, the applicants are transferred to a local family placement worker, to support them while they are waiting to be matched with a child and throughout the adoption process.

On the rare occasions when service demand has been limited over the past ten years, the intercountry adoption social workers have carried out assessments on domestic applicants. This has enabled the workers to transfer appropriate skills and knowledge to the task in hand. On occasion, when service demand for intercountry adoption has been particularly high, other family placement workers have assessed inter-country adoption applicants.

Although a number of enquiries have been received from people living in other areas of the country asking for Hampshire to provide them with a home study report, to date it has not been possible to expand the service to such applicants.

The intercountry adoption panel

Hampshire's intercountry adoption panel was set up in 1990 and was chaired by the adoption adviser from 1990 until 1995. The majority of panel members had previously served on domestic adoption panels. For the first five years this panel dealt exclusively with intercountry adoption cases. It was considered to be the best way of developing a pool of expertise quickly, given the sharp learning curve for all those involved. The legal adviser has played a significant role in advising panel members on the complex and varied issues associated with intercountry adoption.

During the first year, part of each panel meeting was devoted to training and team building; this enabled panel members to debate a whole range of issues with which we are all confronted when considering intercountry adoption. It is evident that such opportunities for debate are essential if panel members are to work together effectively and pursue a consistent approach when dealing with such different cases. Indeed, what has emerged from the first five years is a panel "philosophy" which has now been incorporated into a statement of principles and a code of conduct for panel members. It is a requirement for new panel members to accept the statement of principles and agree to abide by the code of conduct prior to their appointment.

More recently the intercountry adoption panel has also considered domestic applications. This has had the benefit of increasing panel members' experience, helping them to remain child-focused, and giving them opportunities for comparison. This has proved beneficial for both domestic or intercountry adoption applications.

When the intercountry adoption service was first set up it was anticipated that the intercountry adoption panel members and workers would be able to transfer their skills and knowledge of domestic adoption work to the intercountry adoption task. There is no doubt that this has happened. However, the reverse is also very true: we have learned a great deal from our intercountry adoption work, aspects of which have been incorporated into domestic policy and procedures to the benefit of all concerned. An example of this is the importance of ensuring that referees expressing any concerns about the applicants are sent a copy of the report of the record of the worker's visit to them, so that they can confirm in writing the accuracy of the comments attributed to them.

The intercountry adoption process

Initial enquiries

Most enquiries come through a central point where advice is given about domestic adoption as well as intercountry adoption, eligibility criteria, preliminary checks and references, process and procedures, timescales, costs and the roles of the adoption agency and the Department of Health (DoH) in the whole process. Enquirers are also sent an extensive information pack about domestic and intercountry adoption. They are advised to make further enquiries of the embassy of any country in which they are interested, to ascertain eligibility criteria and information about adoption procedures, to contact the Home Office and the DoH, and to ensure that they are aware of immigration requirements for the UK. They are also advised to make further enquiries of people who have already adopted a child from the country to which they intend to make their application. The adoption adviser often facilitates such links, and applicants also tend to approach OASIS (Overseas Adoption Support and Information Service) and the Hampshire Intercountry Adopters Group, which was set up by adoptive parents to provide advice and support for those who either have adopted, or intend to adopt, a child from overseas.

After having obtained the information suggested, enquirers then request a formal interview with an intercountry adoption social worker. Our experience shows that it is more effective for people to make their own enquiries, without feeling "over influenced" by social services: indeed we have found that 89 per cent of those who first enquire, decide for themselves that intercountry adoption is not for them. Consequently, those who do come back to us are better informed about adoption in general, and intercountry adoption in particular. This also provides a more effective launching pad for the preparation and assessment process.

Costs

The current charge for the preparation and assessment of intercountry adopters is £3,600 and is based upon very detailed calculations of each step in the process by those involved, from the agency decision maker to the administrative support worker who types and photocopies documentation for the adoption panel in respect of a relatively straight-forward application. No charge can be made for the initial counselling interview, or for work undertaken after the child enters the UK, such as adoption welfare supervision.

There is a facility for the Director of Social Services to reduce or waive a fee in exceptional circumstances: this facility has been used on three occasions.

The charge levied by adoption agencies for intercountry adoption is but a small proportion of the overall costs of adopting a child from overseas: Hampshire families tell us that is usually costs between £10–15,000 to achieve. The cost of intercountry adoption is a factor in the high drop out rate of enquirers, many of whom are unaware that it is necessary for them to go through the adoption process in the child's country of residence before they will be permitted to bring the child into the UK.

Preliminary checks and investigations

It is Hampshire's policy to complete all checks and references prior to the start of the preparation and assessment by an individual worker. These checks include police, probation, DoH Consultancy Index, NSPCC, confirmation that rental/mortgage payments are up-to-date, health, education (where the applicants already have children of school age), social services, child and family guidance service, and SSAFA Forces Help (where appropriate). Medical reports are also obtained on the health of each applicant. Two independent personal references and one from a family member are obtained in respect of each applicant. All referees are sent a questionnaire to complete at this stage. Should any significant concerns be raised by a referee, he or she will be interviewed at an early stage by the social worker. A report of that visit will be sent to the referee who will be asked to confirm in writing the accuracy of that report.

There have been a number of occasions on which applicants have forgotten that they have a conviction for criminal offences, and therefore have not disclosed them. It is a policy requirement to seek written legal advice in respect of applicants who have been cautioned or convicted for any offences. It is important for us to address these issues early on in the process, to learn about the circumstances prevailing at the time the offences were committed, to examine the applicant's subsequent behaviour and to consider any implications for the adoption process. Where any information received is likely to jeopardise the outcome of the application, it is our practice to seek panel members' advice about whether the application should proceed to full assessment, in line with DoH Guidance [LAC (97) 13].

It is not uncommon for serious health issues to be raised during early medical examinations; such cases are always subject to full panel debate. Only where the applicant's condition is life-limiting, or has serious implications for the care of a child, are adoption panel members likely to recommend that the application is rejected at an early stage. In such cases it is not uncommon for the applicant to be unaware of the full implications of his or her condition, and therefore the utmost care is taken to work with the applicant's General Practitioner to determine how best to inform the applicant of the situation.

Once the decision has been made to accept the application, a letter is sent to the applicants asking them to complete a written undertaking to:
- pay the charge (currently £3,600) in full in advance;
- obtain an entry clearance certificate for the child, if the application is endorsed by the DoH; and
- permit a social worker to visit their home to see the child, should the authorities in the child's country of origin require post-placement or post-adoption progress reports.

Preparation groups

When the intercountry adoption service was set up, special preparation groups were arranged for intercountry adoption applicants. However, over time, views have changed in recognition of the fact that it is all too easy to concentrate on intercountry adoption issues and fail to address adequately the central issue for all adopters – the adoption task.

Applicants are now invited to join a domestic adoption preparation group, and later to meet with other intercountry adoption applicants for a day, or several evening sessions, to address issues of particular relevance to intercountry adoption. Applicants at all stages of the process attend the latter group, all of whom benefit greatly from sharing views and experiences, as well as making abiding friendships that will serve them well throughout the adoption process and beyond.

Assessment by an individual social worker

The assessment process is not always well understood by applicants who may find the process irksome and intrusive, especially if they are not clear about the reasons why particular issues are raised. It is incumbent upon adoption agencies to explain to applicants the purpose and value of the preparation and assessment process, and the relevance of individual topics that need to be explored. There is much work yet to be done in bridging this gap.

The most important objective must be to prepare applicants for the life-long responsibilities they seek to take on through adoption, and to ensure that they have a good understanding of the adoption task in general, as well as the specific intercountry adoption task. The home study report is a product of this preparation process, and it should not be regarded as an end in itself.

Children who have tremendous life changes imposed upon them through intercountry adoption, not the least of which is to leave their country of origin, have a right to expect that we will place them with people who are suitable and equal to the task. There can be no substitute for the thorough preparation of applicants for the profound and enduring responsibilities of intercountry adoption.

There are many issues which need to be addressed in the preparation and assessment process, in addition to those relevant to domestic adoption, the most important of which include:

- the capacity of each applicant to manage the "unknowns" of intercountry adoption;
- the applicant's understanding of the risks involved, especially the health risks, given that some health problems may not be diagnosed or treated until after the child enters the UK;
- the effects of institutionalisation and severe deprivation on children and how this may affect their capacity to form close emotional relationships;
- the need to be conversant with techniques for promoting attachment, especially eye-to-eye contact, to enable children to develop an awareness of social communication and cues;
- an understanding of the types of behaviours the child is likely to exhibit and to help applicants feel confident in managing such behaviour;

- the process of a child learning a second language;
- the need for the applicants to "be there" for the child to facilitate the bonding process, especially during the first year of placement.

Adoption agencies are advised to use the new BAAF Form F3 (*Assessment of prospective adopters adopting a child from overseas*) which has been designed specifically for use in intercountry adoption applications. When the home study report is complete it is sent to the local family placement team who arrange for a worker to carry out a "second opinion" visit. This provides an opportunity for a family placement worker who has not been involved with the case to visit the family concerned, having identified any issues from the home study report which require further exploration. The report of the "second opinion" visit is sent to the applicants, and forms part of the documentation sent to panel members, and later, to the DoH.

Role of the adoption panel

It is the role of the adoption panel to determine each applicant's suitability as an adoptive parent for a child from a specific country, and to recommend the age and characteristics of the child for whom the applicant is considered suitable.

Where panel members consider an application to adopt a specific child, every effort is made to obtain social and medical reports about the child. A "linking" report is also required, similar to that for domestic adoption, outlining the child's needs, how each applicant is likely to be able to meet the needs of the child concerned, and a post-placement and post-adoption support plan. In such cases the role of the intercountry adoption panel is to determine the suitability of the applicants as prospective adoptive parents for the specific child under consideration.

Panel members receive copies of the home study report, questionnaires completed by the applicants, a declaration by the social worker naming any individual who has expressed reservations about the application, a health and safety check, details of the characteristics and background of a child for whom the applicants are best suited, a report from the leaders of the preparation groups, a report from the "second opinion" social worker, a statement of financial circumstances, all checks and references, reports of visits to referees, photographs of the applicant's home, and information about the laws and procedures of the country concerned.

Where there is an application for a specific child, panel members would also expect to receive a statement from the child's birth parents or guardian outlining why the child is being relinquished for adoption (if available) or an abandonment certificate, a linking report containing a list of the child's needs with reasons for believing that the prospective carers have the potential to meet this child's needs, and all background information made available by the authorities in the child's country of residence.

The recommendation of the intercountry adoption panel is highly specific in terms of the age, characteristics and needs of a child for whom the applicants should be approved. After having read the documentation presented to panel members, and having considered carefully the minutes of that meeting, the agency decision maker will then, if satisfied, confirm the authority's decision in writing.

Role of the medical adviser

The intercountry adoption medical adviser makes a vital contribution to the totality of Hampshire's intercountry adoption service. When applicants first enquire about adoption the medical adviser writes to the applicants to give them any information about the health of children likely to be made available for adoption in the country concerned. Applicants are also advised about any immunisations needed before travelling to the country concerned.

The medical adviser sends a letter to each applicant's GP requesting a medical examination, enclosing an information sheet about intercountry adoption issues. Once the completed medical reports are received, the medical adviser will be expected to make whatever investigations are considered appropriate in order to obtain sufficient information about the health of each applicant and any health risks, including those associated with life-style.

The medical adviser routinely attends the intercountry adoption preparation groups to give further advice on medical issues; this provides an opportunity to develop a professional relationship with applicants long before a child is identified.

Matching process

As soon as information from the authorities in the child's country of residence is received (which may be either before or after the adoption panel meeting), it is considered by the adoption adviser and the medical adviser. Such information is often very limited.

Where an application is being made for a specific child, this information is supplemented by the applicants themselves who are encouraged to take photographs and videos of the child in his or her usual surroundings, engaged in various activities throughout the day. Video footage is seen by both the adoption adviser and the medical adviser and is particularly valuable in showing how the child relates to familiar children and adults, giving an indication of the extent of the child's mobility and general development, the effect of any major medical conditions, and an insight into the child's likely future needs.

The medical adviser then sends an analysis of the information available to both the applicants and to the adoption adviser. At this stage the medical adviser may recommend further tests take place in the child's country of origin, for example, for growth measurements (height, weight and head circumference) to be repeated, or for further blood tests to be carried out.

If there are concerns about the child, the medical adviser will contact the applicants in person to discuss the matter further, and may suggest that they also discuss the concerns raised with their own GP.

When the applicants have reached a decision about whether they wish to proceed with the child matched with them, the adoption adviser sends written confirmation to the DoH that the child is within the age group for which the applicants have been approved and that, from the medical reports provided, the agency considers that the applicants are able to meet the needs of the child concerned.

After entry into the UK

As well as being supported by their own local family placement worker, intercountry adopters who need to go through the adoption process after bringing the child into the UK, are also allocated a children's social worker, whose primary responsibility is to carry out adoption welfare supervision duties.

All applicants are encouraged to take the child to be examined by the medical adviser, irrespective of whether or not the applicants need to adopt the child in the UK. The intercountry adoption medical adviser will examine the child, advise the applicants on any health issues, and ask the GP to arrange for further tests and immunisations, as appropriate.

Where the child concerned has special health or educational needs, a strategy meeting is held to include the prospective adoptive parents, the child's GP, the health visitor, the intercountry adoption medical adviser, the child's head teacher, the social worker(s) concerned, a senior manager, the adoption adviser and any other relevant colleagues. The aim of this meeting is to ensure that everyone involved is fully aware of the child's needs. Together we identify the resources required to meet the child's needs, and develop a plan of action to support the adoptive parents in their task of caring for the child.

Role of the adoption adviser

The adoption adviser's responsibilities include the day-to-day management of the intercountry adoption service, data collection, monitoring new enquiries, and advising the adoption panel and the agency decision maker. Policies and procedures were developed by the adoption adviser, which include a statement of principles, a code of conduct for workers and panel members, as well as quality standards and performance indicators.

Another important role fulfilled by the adoption adviser has been to support the applicants at various stages throughout the adoption process. It is particularly important to ensure that a senior representative of the adoption agency is available to assist applicants after they are matched with a child and as they go through the adoption process in the child's country of origin. A number of applicants find that additional documentation is required and they need urgent assistance to comply with the requirements of the authorities in the child's country of origin. The adoption adviser is able to assist with this task and liaises directly with the overseas adoption agencies and occasionally the relevant foreign court.

When the applicants return to the UK with their adopted child, the adoption adviser invites the applicants to take their child to see the medical adviser, and sends them an information sheet about the next stage of the process, including adoption welfare supervision duties, the role of the two social workers involved, and the court process.

All post-placement progress reports are forwarded to the agency in the child's country of former residence by the adoption adviser. Some countries require reports for several years after an adoption order has been made in the UK.

The Adoption Agencies Consultants' Group on intercountry adoption aims to enable managers of adoption agencies throughout the UK to share information and knowledge, to promote strategies for co-ordinating child-centred intercountry adoption work, and planning for future developments.

The court process

Most applicants find the court process bewildering and highly stressful: both they and the children concerned express fears and anxieties about having to attend court. An important contribution can be made by both the child's and the applicant's social workers to help prepare the family for the court process and the hearing. A preliminary visit to the court building does help to reduce their anxiety, especially if they can be shown the layout of a room where adoption applications are usually heard.

The judiciary can also play its part, and the more enlightened approach of some judges is most welcome when an unhurried, meaning-ful discussion takes place with both the child and his or her adoptive parents. One local judge usually gives a personal "congratulations" card to the child with his or her new name already on the envelope, and another judge presents the child with a signed certificate which is tied with a ribbon. There are also occasions on which adoptive mothers have been presented with a bouquet of flowers. These gestures, although small, add the human touch to an important ceremony which serves to emphasise the difference between adoption and other less positive proceedings which take place within the court environment.

Post adoption

As most intercountry adopters in Hampshire tend to live in "clusters", very effective informal networks exist in the area. These are positive and supportive and endure through time. Nevertheless, all intercountry adopters need to know what support is available in their locality, from both the adoption agency and other support groups. This will enable them to make an informed choice as to whether or not they wish to participate.

Intercountry adopters are invited to attend support groups provided by the adoption agency for all adopters in their locality, including an annual barbeque for adoptive parents and their children. In addition, workshops are provided to assist adopters in the task of explaining to their adopted child the circumstances surrounding the adoption.

There is also a central adoption telephone helpline for anyone involved in the adoption process, no matter how long ago the adoption took place. Those involved in intercountry adoption are encouraged to make use of this facility.

All adoption files on children who have been adopted from overseas are stored in a place of special security for 75 years. Should such children, as adults, seek information from the agency about why they were placed for adoption, help and support will be made available to them.

Outcomes: the adoptive parents

There have been many examples of adoptive applicants gradually getting to know the child before going through the legal processes overseas. This has been achieved in a variety of ways including exchanging photographs, letters, telephone calls and regular visits to see the child concerned for extended periods of time.

Applicants have taken on board with enthusiasm the need for information about why the child became available for adoption, as well as the context in which the intercountry adoption took place. Some applicants have gone to extraordinary lengths to find details about the child's family of origin, including travelling to remote villages, and making extensive enquiries from the local inhabitants and those in positions of authority. All this information, if transmitted age-appropriately and with due sensitivity as the child grows up, will assist greatly in the child developing knowledge and understanding of why he or she came to be placed for adoption in a foreign country.

As long as nine years after the placement has been made, some adoptive parents still exchange information and photographs with their adopted child's family of origin, and others remain engaged in humanitarian aid programmes. These activities keep adopters in touch with the children's homes and other institutions from which the children were placed. A number of children have also been taken back to visit their country of origin and are able to maintain strong and positive links with their roots. The level of parental satisfaction has remained high, long after the adoption took place. Indeed, nine families adopted more than one child, another nine families have come back to us to adopt a second child, with one family seeking to adopt a third child.

Outcomes: the children

A total of 95 children have been brought into Hampshire for the purpose of adoption over the past ten years, with an age range from one week to 17 years (see Table 14.2 in the Appendix). The vast majority of children have come from institutions where they had previously spent significant periods of time ranging from a few weeks to eight years. Children were often kept in poor conditions with a lack of warmth, food, hygiene, physical care and individual attention.

The medical and social histories of many of these children were very limited, as were details about their health and development, immunisation history, and medical treatment given to them in their countries of origin. In a significant number of cases, health problems were neither diagnosed nor treated until after the children were examined in the UK. On several occasions the children's dates of birth were invented for the purpose of the adoption.

Many children have experienced difficulties adjusting in the early stages of placement, particularly with regard to sleeping, bathing and eating arrangements. Many were distressed at having to sleep on their own, some were frightened of water and bathing. Others would eat secretly and voraciously, especially when tasting unfamiliar foods for the first time.

Although many children were quick to learn the rudiments of a new language, initially much of the speech and language was composed of learned sentences, and it became apparent that their comprehension was limited. This problem was often masked by the speed with which the new language was apparently acquired.

In spite of behaviour difficulties exhibited by many of these children, including being excessively noisy, boisterous, having no sense of danger and few boundaries, there was no doubt that teachers were enthusiastic about the children joining their schools, and there was a high degree of tolerance shown by other children in the school and teachers alike.

Some intercountry adopters reported difficulties in bonding with their child, particular in the early stages of the placement. Adoptive parents needed to develop an awareness of techniques for promoting attachment, especially eye-to-eye contact, and to provide sustained stimulation in order to assist the bonding process.

The majority of children made very substantial progress by the time that the adoption order was made in the UK, and their health improved over time as would be expected with better nutrition and individual care. No placement has yet disrupted, as far as we are aware.

The future

All adoption agencies need to make preparation for the ratification of the Hague Convention, given that the Adoption (Intercountry Aspects) Act 1999 has been given Royal Assent. It is likely that there will be a small increase in the number of requests made to local authorities for home study reports in view of the fact that all privately commissioned intercountry adoption home study reports were prohibited by the Adoption (Intercountry Aspects) Act 1999: Commencement Order which entered into force on 31 January 2000.

Particular consideration needs to be given to the fact that the UK will become a "sending" country and it is likely that a considerable number of requests will be made by people living overseas who seek to adopt a child from the UK. Indeed, Hampshire has already received a number of requests from people living overseas who would like to adopt a child from the UK.

Implications for adoption agencies

Policy

- All agencies need a statement of shared principles which provides a solid basis for an intercountry adoption service, as well as quality standards and performance indicators by which that service can be assessed and reviewed.
- Eligibility criteria, agency policies and procedures need to be clearly set out, accessible to all and easily understood. A charter is a helpful way to provide some of this information for service users.
- A charging policy for intercountry adoption must be directly related to service costs, and should be among the information given to those making their first enquiry about intercountry adoption.

Support

- Intercountry adoption applicants can easily feel isolated, especially when they are adoption "pioneers" with regard to a country from which very few children have previously been adopted by applicants resident in the UK. Applicants need support throughout the process at a level with which they feel comfortable.
- Agencies need to ensure that interagency partnerships work effectively to provide services that are sensitive to the needs of the child concerned, as well as to those of their adoptive parents, especially with regard to health and education services.
- Applicants need to be able to contact an identified senior officer employed by the adoption agency when going through the adoption process in the child's country of origin, so that all information required can be provided within the timescales of the authorities in the country concerned.

- Intercountry adopters, as well as domestic adoptive parents, need written confirmation of the post-placement and post-adoption support for which they are eligible, and how to access those services.
- The agency's medical adviser plays a valuable role in the intercountry adoption service and is best placed to co-ordinate the health support services needed for particular children. The medical adviser is also best placed to collate information available on health issues in various countries to form a database for the intercountry adoption service.

Training

- Each agency should ensure that sufficient training is available for panel members, social workers, family placement workers and managers so that they are able to meet the expectations of service delivery. The agency needs to keep up to date on developments in intercountry adoption, especially those to which the UK is committed upon ratification of the Hague Convention.
- It is essential to provide opportunities for debate about the contrasting views of individuals who are part of the intercountry adoption process. This is especially true of adoption panel members, who need to be able to debate these issues outside the confines of particular applications under consideration.
- The managers of adoption agencies need to share their knowledge and experiences, and seek opportunities to enhance their understanding of the issues involved in intercountry adoption if they are to make significant improvements in service delivery.

Conclusions

In an ideal world, the children at the heart of intercountry adoption should, of course, be given the opportunity to grow up in their own families, in their own countries of origin, where they are supported by health care systems, education systems, and benefit systems which can sustain them effectively where available. However, many countries do not have the choices that we have come to take for granted; neither do they have the number and range of substitute families to provide viable alternatives for all children currently contained in institutions, let alone families who reflect precisely each child's ethnic, cultural, religious and linguistic heritage.

We must confront reality and recognise that there is a place for intercountry adoption for a small number of children, where the authorities in their countries of origin confirm that there is no prospect of placing them in a family, and where it is considered appropriate to place them for adoption in foreign countries.

If we are to provide a credible intercountry adoption service, it is important for us to recognise that our primary responsibility is to enable people to make an informed decision about whether or not intercountry adoption is right for them, and then to prepare them for the life-long responsibilities they are about to undertake.

It is equally important for us to maintain a positive approach, and to recognise that intercountry adopters are as entitled to post-placement and post-adoption support services as are domestic adopters. If we are to plan our services effectively, we need to work in partnership with other agencies such as health and education. As with all adoptive parents, those who choose to adopt a child from overseas need to know the level and source of support they may expect after they return to the UK with their adopted child, and thereafter. They are entitled to be given information about service provision, and must be given the opportunity to access services available in their area. Above all, they are entitled to a positive and welcoming response.

Appendix

Table 14.1

The applicants

Outcome of intercountry adoption enquiries from 1990 to 1999

Category	Joint	Single	Total applications	No. of persons	Percentage
General enquiries	**901**				**100%**
Enquirers who decide not to proceed	804				89%
Applications considered by agency	94	3	97	191	11% of all enquiries received by agency
Applicants rejected	4	1	5	9	5% of those considered
Applicants approved by agency	90	2	92	182	95% of those considered
Applicants with children placed	74	2	76	150	82.6% of approved applicants
Applicants approved and waiting for a child	7	0	7	14	7.6% of those approved
Approved applicants who have withdrawn	9	0	9	18	9.8% of those approved
Total approved	**90**	**2**	**92**	**182**	**10% of all enquiries**

Table 14.2

Children entering Hampshire for the purpose of adoption 1990–1999

Age of children	1990 – 1994	1995 – 1999	Total
Under 1 year	24	18	42 (44%)
Between 2–5 yrs	19	17	36 (38%)
Between 5–9 yrs	10	0	10 (11%)
Over 10 years	6	1	7 (7%)
TOTAL	**59**	**36**	**95 (100%)**

15 The dynamics of power and loss in home study assessments

John Simmonds with Gill Haworth

John Simmonds is Head of Development at the British Agencies for Adoption and Fostering (BAAF). He has extensive experience as a university teacher and in practice and research in child care. He was the author of the Guide to Practitioners referred to below.

Gill Haworth is Director of Overseas Adoption Helpline (OAH), an information and advice service on intercountry adoption matters.

Introduction

The following chapter is adapted from material in the *Guide to Practitioners* published by the Department of Health and Children in Eire. The Guide is part of the implementation of the Department's Standardised Framework for Intercountry Adoption Assessment. It was accompanied by a six-session preparation course for applicants.[1] Central to the approach in the new framework was a belief that applicants need access to knowledge and information that enable them to assess themselves as ready (or not ready) for the particular issues that adoption and intercountry adoption presents them with. This will inevitably include the impact that adoption might have on their past life experiences as well as the availability of material, emotional and social resources in their current circumstances.

The introduction of a coherent and comprehensive set of materials is part of the Irish government's preparation for the ratification of the Hague Convention.

---

[1] Throughout we have used the term "applicants" to refer to both single and joint applicants.

The role and responsibilities of social workers in home study assessments

Social workers have a number of diverse responsibilities when undertaking home study assessments in intercountry adoption. The objective of this chapter is to discuss the different dimensions of this role and the impact that these have on the process and the responsibilities that go along with it. In doing so, it will focus particularly on issues of power and loss.

Role and responsibility are two key characteristics of being a social worker. Integral to these are issues of power and authority. At their best, power and authority enable individuals, groups and political systems to take action to provide structures that facilitate people in living and leading their lives in a safe and effective manner. What this means in practice is complex as individuals, groups and political systems will have their own ideas about what makes for a "good life" and what measures they need to take to bring this about. Central to this are many issues about who has responsibility for what when it comes to raising children. What the state takes responsibility for, what power it has to exercise this responsibility, what individual families take responsibility for and what power they have to exercise this responsibility are critical parts of the political structure and process of every country. The practice of intercountry adoption has to steer a very precarious route through these issues. The relationship between the different parties will undoubtedly confront the people involved in the process with complicated questions about their own definitions of what might be needed to raise children and what power and responsibility they have in relation to these. They will also be confronted with the reality that many individuals, groups and political systems do not have the power, resources or sometimes even the will to provide structures that can enable people to live their lives in a safe and effective manner. This is so particularly in relation to children.

There are fundamental inequalities in the distribution of power throughout adoption practice and this is particularly so in intercountry adoption. The role and responsibility of an assessing social worker will be continually influenced by these issues of power and the unequal access that the different parties have to both power and resources. Everybody involved in the process of assessment will have their own thoughts and feelings about these issues of power. They will also react to their own experience of the process depending on the position that they find themselves in. This can have significant consequences for the process of home study assessments. Rather than being a focussed, objective exploration of the preparedness of the applicants to adopt, it can become influenced, and in some cases dominated by, the participants' reactions to the relative power or powerlessness of the parties involved. It is possible for people to find themselves experiencing fear, resentment, anger and distrust. This may involve feelings of being persecuted or of feeling victimised. It may involve wanting or needing to rescue a child from his or her dangerous or unsatisfactory circumstances or, for the couple, of each other from their childless state. At times, it may involve wanting to persecute others when they do not come up with the right answers to the problems people are trying to solve.

Key responsibilities of social workers in the assessment process

Before exploring these themes further, it may be helpful to set out the seven principal responsibilities that assessing social workers have in the process of intercountry adoption.

The first responsibility is towards the child who may be placed with the applicants. They are the most powerless and vulnerable in the whole process, easily exploitable and in no position to change anything. It is the social worker's legal responsibility to safeguard their welfare. In intercountry adoption this issue is made difficult because of the circumstances in which the child may have been born and in which he or she may be currently living. The child may already have suffered significant harm and, in extreme cases, be at significant risk including real danger to their life. While this may be a reality and creates a real sense of urgency, particularly for the applicants, it cannot be allowed to compromise the social worker's responsibility to undertake a thorough and professional assessment and to complete the process as set out in law and procedure.

The second responsibility is towards the child's biological parent or parents. Their circumstances may put them equally at risk and they may also, in some cases, have suffered significant harm including dangers to their life. The assessment process is intended to play its part in not further adding exploitation or danger to them by putting their child at risk. It is meant to provide a guarantee to them that, in giving up their child for adoption in a foreign country, their child's welfare will be of paramount consideration in their new family and country.

The third responsibility is towards the applicants. Their desire to create a new family or expand an existing one may have taken a painful, uncertain and anxious pathway. For most, they will not have chosen this as a first preference and are unlikely to have predicted this as a part of their life course. Although they are not as powerless as the child or the birth parents, and indeed in many areas of their life may have significant power through education, social position and economic resources, they are still vulnerable and open to exploitation by insensitive bureaucratic or legal processes.

The fourth responsibility is towards the agency that is accountable for the home study assessment. Their policies, procedures, priorities and plans will be the framework within which the social worker has a role and will be performing the assessment task.

The fifth responsibility is towards those other agencies that will be using the social worker's assessment to make decisions and provide approval and certification. They will be relying on the assessing social worker's professionalism, which will be the outcome of who the worker is as a person – their education, training, experience and commitment to a socially responsible position.

The sixth responsibility is towards the country of origin that will be asked to agree to approve the applicants as suitable to be the family that raises one of their children. While having the power that goes along with being a state, the fact that it is unable to provide the services to the child's biological parents that enable them to keep their child or to provide services that enable the child to be looked after in their birth country is unlikely to be a matter of choice for that country.

The seventh responsibility is the social worker's responsibility to him or herself as a professional. What the social worker brings to the assessment process will be the product of their life path, their experiences, advantages, resilience and anxieties. Although not as powerless as the child, the birth parents or the applicants, they will have their own vulnerabilities and worries. A critical part of this will be how they are supported and how they look after themselves professionally and personally.

Although these are the seven principal parties to whom social workers have a responsibility in intercountry adoption, there may be others who play their part in the process and will need to be added to the list. However, what should be clear is that the process of application, approval and placement in intercountry adoption involves a responsibility towards individuals, groups and political systems that are in a complex relationship with each other.

The impact of power and loss on the assessment process

Each party in the process is defined by the characteristics of the systems that give them access to power. For social workers it will be the characteristics of their profession, the agency that employs them and the state systems to which they report such as the legal system. For the applicants, it will be their personal circumstances, their status as citizens and their values, knowledge and skills which enable them to engage in this complex process. Throughout the whole system of relationships, there is an unequal distribution of power because of actual or perceived differences in resources, role and responsibility. This inequality will exist at many different levels. At one level, it will involve the historical and global position of some of the parties when it is an issue of the relationship between states. At a more intimate level, it will involve the applicants and their assessing social worker with their differential access to individual, economic, personal, social and political resources. But whatever significant differences exist in this relationship, they cannot compare to that of the children who might be available for adoption from overseas and to the birth parents of these children.

At the centre of this complex process is the problem of managing responsibilities towards vulnerable people who are trying to improve or change their circumstances. While the intention in the whole system of intercountry adoption is to change things positively, there are actual and potential experiences of loss throughout the process. The birth parents will lose a child, the sending country will lose a citizen, the child will lose his/her birth parents and probably his/her culture, language, nationality and religion. Any individual or organisation in the above list faces the possibility of losing some of what it already has to another party in the hope of gaining something else. In the process of trying to create gains and positive change therefore, individuals and organisations also have to face the losses involved. In doing so, they are likely to try to defend their current position if the threats from these losses seem too great and threaten to overwhelm them. When individuals or political systems try to change, defend or improve their positions through using or acquiring power, there is enormous potential for stirring up strong feelings. The feelings involved and the action taken will affect different parties in different ways depending on their perception or position of power.

In the process of home study assessments, therefore, the defence by any of the parties involved of what one already has is as important as the hoped for gains. Although it is difficult to be precise for any particular applicants, the potential loss of face at having to confront both the reality of childlessness and exposure to the home study process has to be balanced against the potential gains of being in a position to become the parents of an adopted child. The applicants are involved in a risky balancing act where issues of power and control are critical. While having power in some areas of their lives, they may not have had the power to create their own children. They may have experienced considerable powerlessness, maybe over many years, in being confronted with this and having to deal with the consequences of it. Physically, emotionally, socially and probably financially they will have had to develop strategies for managing the losses. These strategies will inevitably have involved ways of maintaining a positive sense of identity and self-esteem and the power that they have to do this will have been very important. Similarly, the risk of being turned down as an adopter threatens not only to deprive the applicants of something they want, it is a matter of enormous emotional and psychological significance also involving loss and, in many circumstances, feelings of humiliation and shame.

The applicants' relationship with their social worker is a key part of the process in home study assessment. Social workers have the power to grant or deny the applicants access to a child they want to adopt. The applicants are dependent on the social worker and the social worker has some control over access to something they need and want. However, the social worker is also part of a system of social services with limited resources and competing priorities. They have marginal power to change this and indeed are dependent on the decisions and actions of others who do have some power to change this. In this sense, the social worker may well feel vulnerable and out of control when having to represent an agency that appears to be inactive, unresponsive or insensitive in allocating the necessary resources to undertake the assessment that the applicants have applied for. Although both the applicants and the social worker are in quite different positions in terms of their role, they also share the experience of being dependent on others who control access to the resources they need in order to work on the things they are responsible for.

However, whatever they share, they have different responsibilities associated with their respective task. Each will tend to view their responsibilities from their own perspective – their needs, desires, and anxieties – and will understand the responsibilities of others from within this perspective. The issues at stake for the applicants and the dynamic processes involved can be as great in home study assessments as in a territorial dispute between countries. Yet the relationships that each have with the other in order for the process to work involve and indeed require trust, dependency and respect. Throughout the process then, this primary requirement of trust, as in territorial disputes, always carries the potential or actual threat of vulnerability and exploitation.

While loss may be familiar as a concept to social workers, the impact of the dynamics of power described above is far less so. Territorial disputes are not generally what social workers like to think of themselves as engaged in. Power struggles are for the more politically minded! However, when access to and the use of power fuel the process of intercountry adoption, there is also the risk of it seriously damaging the process when it is not properly harnessed. The culture of social work emphasises partnership, co-operation, support, understanding and growth. But it is an inescapable factor that understanding and managing the dynamics of power are a critical part of a social worker's ability to engage with their role and discharge their responsibilities.

Over the course of the assessment, each of the different areas of responsibility and the various relationships between the people involved will have to be kept in mind and most particularly the power dynamics that they generate. Indeed if the assessment seems to have become stuck or embroiled in misunderstanding, struggle or conflict, then it may be helpful and appropriate to think about the relationship between the various parties and of their power dynamics.

When people are clear about their tasks and roles, the dangerous misuse of power is lessened. But it is important not to forget that from within their respective roles, each party has its vulnerabilities. However, the co-dependence in these relationships is dependent on respect, trust and openness. If these relationship values permeate the role, tasks and responsibilities of assessing social workers, then this will be the greatest facilitator in managing the complexity of intercountry adoption home study assessments.

The aims and purpose of home study assessment – the child-centred principle

The task of undertaking a home study assessment involves a number of different functions. Firstly, it is part of a legal process both in relation to the "receiving" country as well as the "sending" country. This involves interaction between domestic adoption law, the domestic law of the sending country and international law and conventions (see Brennan, Chapter 10). These set out various and detailed requirements in terms of the information required about the applicants, the processes and pro- cedures which they will have been required to complete and, in the UK, the legal and administrative certification required in approving them to adopt a child from a foreign country. Although practitioners and appli- cants will need to familiarise themselves with these legal requirements in detail from other sources, the primary requirement is to ensure that the child's needs are of paramount consideration.

Protecting and safeguarding a vulnerable child is among the most demanding and responsible activities that an adult can engage in. Yet as the discussion above highlights, when adults try to co-operate together when there are significant inequalities of power in the relationship, there may be real difficulties in keeping the needs of vulnerable children in mind. It is all too easy to create a dynamic where the desire to protect the child also becomes the means by which adults engage in conflict with each other. However, as a powerful and important principle, it is not a reason for unwarranted or inappropriate intrusion on the part of professionals into the lives of applicants. It is also not a reason for unco-operative or pressured behaviour on the part of applicants. While the process of home study assessment may seem complex and can feel lengthy, there is good reason for it when it is properly carried out. Throughout the process therefore, whatever anxiety, difficulty or stress that may be encountered, as indeed it may, both social workers and other professionals involved as well as the applicants themselves should return to this child-centred principle if they have any doubt about the focus of the process that they are engaged in.

Making predictions in assessment – the nature of the evidence

One of the real difficulties in assessment is the complex question:
> On the basis of what we know at this point in time about the applicants and their life experiences to date, what can we predict about their likely capacity and competence to parent not just in the future in one set of circumstances but to parent as the child grows and circumstances change?

The significance of information

The professional task for social workers is not just about making a prediction about the future parenting capacity of the applicants based on what is known now but of realistically appraising what it is possible to know now given that it is largely based on soft or social information. There are important issues therefore not only about the quantity of the information available but of its status as social information. Soft or social information has a very different quality to hard information. Hard information might be what we collect from police record checks, bank statements, birth or marriage certificates or educational or professional qualifications. We either have this information or we don't. It is either acceptable or it isn't. It is there objectively before our eyes and there is little controversy in verifying this.

Social or soft information is quite different. Its meaning is derived from the construction that an individual places on it. This will be derived from the context within which the information is generated – what does it mean to the person concerned given the current circumstances they find themselves in and the purpose for which the information is to be used? Over the course of time, this meaning may change and individuals may have a different sense of the event to that which it had originally. This will depend on what has happened in the meantime and the new context within which they currently find themselves. For example, an applicant may view a part of their life experience as relatively unprob- lematic – past experience of "recreational drug use" when they were at College was just something that everybody did. In their current life context, it has little meaning because they have moved on. However, in relation to home study assessment, this experience may feel as if it has quite a different meaning – in fact a possible reason for being rejected. The applicants may therefore suddenly find themselves in a quite different relationship with this experience given the context of the home study assessment and the meaning that this may have for the social worker. They may decide they want to say nothing about it but then be concerned about the possibility of it being referred to by one of their personal referees. An event that has one kind of meaning in one context may have quite a different meaning in another.

This issue is of enormous practical importance because the context within which the applicants are discussing their life history is signifi- cantly affected by their desire to adopt a child from overseas. Are they going to be approved or are they not? Are they going to be able to resolve the issue of their childlessness and their desire to create and establish a family with children by adopting a child from overseas? Their relationship with the assessing social worker is the key to resolving this problem.

It is important not to set a standard for applicants that most people embarking on creating a family could not reasonably be expected to achieve. For most people, producing biological children is not particularly difficult – indeed quite the opposite. It can be done with varying degrees of planning, thoughtfulness, knowledge and insight. Indeed, it can be done with no thought at all and the parents still turn out to provide the child with a nurturing, safe and meaningful family life. Whatever the circumstances of conception, the reality of what actually happens when babies are born, develop and grow can be very different to a parent or parent's plans or expectations.

Giving and discussing soft or social information which is open to interpretation when you don't know the rules and there is much at stake is a very difficult thing for anybody to do. In the best of circumstances people will try to manage the information in such a way as to ensure that the interpretation that the assessor puts on it best serves the objectives in mind. If this gives a picture of applicants being devious or manipulative or unable to conduct themselves in a fair or representative manner, then this is not the intention. Although for a few adoption is the first choice, the greater majority of applicants will have not entered the process freely or by choice. It will have been something that they "chose" to do because circumstances dictated that it was a solution open to them in their circumstances.

Infertility, where this is a part of the applicant's motivation to adopt, may be one of the first experiences where they really felt out of control and unable to change the circumstances of their lives. So while most people will have had some experience of things not turning out as they would have wished, the power and control that they exercised in relationships, in choice of education, occupation or profession, of having money and choosing how, when and where to spend it, etc. may well have not prepared them for what, for example, infertility brings and what intercountry adoption will confront them with.

The dynamics of power, the nature of the information involved, and the difficulty of making accurate predictions have a significant impact on both the nature and process of the home study assessment. In order to address these issues there needs to be a clear and explicit set of criteria against which the preparation course and the home study process is conducted. The applicants need to be empowered by having access to full and proper information provided through a thorough preparation course prior to the home study assessment. They also have to become fully engaged in the process which means taking responsibility for gathering the information they need and assessing its meaning for them given their life history, current circumstances and future plans. It is not the case that anybody can successfully adopt from overseas. In particular, nobody should adopt from overseas where there is evidence that they might put a child at risk at any point during their childhood. But with strong motivation, sufficient information, preparation, resilience and adequate support, a wide variety of people can provide a loving home in which a child will grow and thrive. It is a primary responsibility for social workers not to support applicants who are unsuitable but with that accepted, the role is to provide information, preparation and support and to help people think through the journey that they are about to embark on.

In this sense, therefore, the recommendation that applicants are suitable to adopt is not a prediction in any absolute sense but rather the outcome of an exploration of the available evidence, some of which may be reasonably clear and may indeed exclude some applicants but most of which will be indicative of the way that the applicants' past and present experiences, circumstances and resources are likely to impact on the processes involved in, and their preparedness for, both intercountry adoption and of establishing and raising a family. In terms of social information, therefore, the role of the social worker is not primarily to accurately predict the future or to sit in judgement on the capacity of the applicants to parent a child but to take on an exploratory and supportive role in relation to their experience and resources. A respectful stance in the spirit of inquiry is far more likely to help people make sense of their experiences and the way that this might prepare them for what they are planning to do than anything that too readily suggests that the "social worker knows best". In most cases, adults, like children, do best when they feel confident to explore their environment rather than feel fearful of it.

The framework standards for home study assessments

In Eire, the standardised framework requires that applicants complete a six session preparation course before proceeding to the home study assessment. The preparation course is primarily focused on helping applicants to gather the information they need, educate themselves in some of the issues that they might be faced with and explore what this might mean to them. The home study assessment is primarily focused on helping applicants to explore the implications and meaning that the preparation course has had for them as an individual or couple. It is a matter of their maturity, strengths and resilience and of the resources that are available to them that enables them to overcome the gap between expectation and reality. However, it is clear that the demands placed on an individual or couple in intercountry adoption demand a level of resilience, resourcefulness and adaptability that is not normally required of parents who produce their own biological children. It is essential that applicants are both prepared for this and that it forms a significant part of the home study assessment.

Both the assessing agencies and the applicants use the following standards from the initial inquiry through to the recommendation. They form a framework for thinking about what the process of intercountry adoption involves and the responsibilities that will need to be exercised.

1. The applicants' capacity to safeguard the child throughout his or her childhood.

2. The applicants' capacity to provide the child with family life that will promote his or her development and pay due regard to their physical, emotional, social, health, educational, cultural and spiritual well being. The resources that families can draw on will vary from family to family and may change over time. Whatever circumstances the family find themselves in, the applicants will be able to demonstrate their understanding of the importance of maintaining an ongoing and meaningful relationship with their child.

3. The applicants' capacity to provide an environment where the child's original nationality, "race", culture, language and religion will be valued and appropriately promoted throughout childhood. This will include the capacity of the parents to recognise the differences between themselves and their child within these areas and to recognise and try to combat racism and other institutional and personal oppressive forces within society.

4. The applicants' capacity to recognise and understand the impact of

the child as an adopted child from an overseas country on the development of the child's identity throughout both their child and adulthood. This will include the capacity to understand the importance of tracing the many dimensions of the child's roots in their birth country and the incorporation of this in a meaningful way into the child's identity.

5. The applicants' capacity to recognise the need for and to arrange for appropriate support and intervention from health, social services, educational and other services throughout the child's childhood. Where relevant, it may also include the capacity to recognise their needs in relation to themselves as adults

In Eire, these five standards are initially assessed through the various checks and references on the applicants – their nationality, domicile, marital status, health evaluation including physical and mental health, criminal record checks, and employer and personal references. Following this, the applicants participate in a preparation course with both information and a range of exercises and tasks critical to understanding the nature of intercountry adoption.

Applicants will also be asked to evaluate the learning and meaning that these sessions have for them in the plans they have to adopt.

The standards will also form the focus of the interviews undertaken in the home study. This has the strong advantage of both social workers and applicants understanding what is significant in their discussion. This transparency in the standards lessens the possibility of a secret or mysterious agenda dominating the assessment.

Creating an effective working relationship with the applicants
Much of what has been discussed previously has highlighted some of the complexities facing social workers and applicants in the home study assessment. These might be summarised as:

- the length and complexity of the intercountry adoption process;
- the nature of the information that makes up the assessment;
- issues of power;
- the importance of emotions – particularly anxiety and uncertainty, hope and expectation;
- the history of intercountry adoption– facts and myths.

The way that these issues are handled in the context of the primary task of the home study assessment will depend on the skills and professionalism of the social worker. Key to this will be the development of a positive working relationship with the applicants. What is outlined below are some of the factors that will enable this to happen. They draw on both training and experience. They should also form part of the agenda for supervision.

Engaging the applicants in the home study assessment
If the home study assessment is to meet its objective, it is essential that the applicants are engaged in the process. Although there is no foolproof way of ensuring that this happens, there are a number of important considerations and conditions that will help.
- The social worker is clear what the purpose of the home study assessment and how each stage contributes to this.
- The social worker and the applicants are clear about their respective roles, responsibilities and tasks.
- There is an opportunity to explore the above two issues at the beginning of the home study and at any time during it, when there is any doubt or uncertainty about these issues or when something appears to one of the parties to have changed.
- There is a need for the acknowledgement of the unequal distribution of power in the relationship including factors such "race", culture, class, religion, and language.

In addition to this, there are a number of other factors that can influence the social worker's approach to assessment.
- The social worker approaches the applicants with an openness and genuine desire to help them explore and formulate their views on how they have prepared themselves to adopt a child from an overseas country. In particular, social workers should remember that many of the issues for discussion and exploration are of a personal and sensitive nature. Applicants will not feel able to be open about these issues if they feel coerced, threatened or fearful. Even expectations or the hope that the applicants trust the social worker may be unrealistic given the limited time available for a relationship to develop and the

issues that are at stake for the applicants.

- The social worker endeavours to plan the home study from where the applicants currently find themselves. It might be helpful to think of intercountry adoption as a journey. A home study assessment should not be confused with the journey itself but considered to be part of the toolkit that equips the applicants for the journey. As a journey, it has to start at the beginning. Like a true journey of adventure, rather than a routine trip to work or a highly organised package holiday, there will be undiscovered or unanticipated experiences that may sometimes be unbelievably beautiful or exciting and sometimes threatening. The applicants have to be trusted to make his or her own journey without unnecessarily exposing the child to undue risk or hazard.
- Social workers should not expect applicants to be able to articulate neat explanations of complex personal and social experiences. Many applicants will not be familiar with the language of loss, trauma and attachment – and may find it difficult to understand why social workers put so much emphasis on them. However, it does not necessarily mean that, in the course of the journey, the applicants will not be able to relate to the experiences this language describes in a meaningful way.
- There is no attempt to create a mystique about the home study process or the preparation of the final assessment report.
- The applicants are not being judged against an undefined picture of the "ideal" parent.
- The social worker has well-developed skills of accurate empathy with the applicants, clear and transparent communication and a non-possessive warmth.
- The social worker is reliable and predictable in the arrangements that they make and the way that they conduct themselves.

Conclusion

In both domestic and intercountry adoption, the process of assessment and approval is controversial, complex and often painful. Intercountry adoption brings its own difficulties because of the distance, the heightened complexity of international boundaries and arrangements, and the considerable uncertainty. The Irish government has approached and managed this by, in part, establishing a national and standardised framework with accompanying guidance to practitioners and applicants. In so doing, the issues of loss and power so central to the process will not go away. But what has been created is an opportunity for addressing these difficult areas in a manageable way, as it should be in all countries. It is for the adults involved, whatever their respective role and responsibilities, to remember who this framework was created for.

Acknowledgement
Permission has been granted by the Department of Health and Children, Eire, for extracts from 'Towards a Standardised Framework for Inter-country Adoption Assessment Procedures: Guide to Practitioners' to be quoted in this chapter.

16 The role of accredited bodies in preparation and assessment

Caroline Hesslegrave

Caroline Hesslegrave qualified as a social worker at Edinburgh University, and has specialised in adoption and fostering since 1980. Following 15 years working within various local authority settings, she joined the Childlink Adoption Society as Intercountry Adoption Manager in 1991. She has been Director of Childlink since 1992.

Introduction

Ten years ago, a small adoption agency based in south London took its first tentative steps into the sphere of intercountry adoption (ICA). A decade on, the agency operates a busy ICA project alongside the continuing delivery of its domestic (incountry) adoption services. This chapter charts the development of Childlink's practice in preparing and assessing prospective intercountry adopters. It also explores some of the wider issues which Childlink has confronted as a voluntary adoption agency working in the changing context of intercountry adoption.

The agency

The Childlink Adoption Society is a voluntary adoption agency (a non-governmental organisation (NGO)) approved by the Secretary of State for Health under the provisions of the Adoption Act 1976. Previously known as the Church Adoption Society, the agency was founded in 1913 by a Canon of the Church of England. For many years its primary functions were to offer a service to birth parents (usually mothers) who found themselves unable to keep and raise their babies, and to recruit and approve adoptive parents for the infants who were relinquished.

The well-documented changes in UK adoption trends dating from the 1970s prompted the agency to review its future role and to decide whether to diversify its activities. By 1990, it had acquired its new name and assumed a non-denominational basis of operation. It had broadened its role to include the provision of adoptive families for children looked after by local authorities, and was on the verge of launching its specialist intercountry adoption project.

The ICA project

At the start of 1990, few local authorities were providing preparation and assessment for prospective intercountry adopters in advance of specific children being identified in their countries of origin. Childlink had long been concerned about this gap in agency adoption provision. At the heart of its concern was the conviction that children adopted from abroad had the right to be protected by safeguards and standards equivalent to those applied in relation to UK domestic adoption practice.

Following extensive consultations with a range of interested individuals, organisations and bodies, Childlink decided to offer a preparation and assessment service for couples and individuals seeking to adopt from overseas. On the advice of the Department of Health (DoH), it was agreed that access to this service would be routed via the applicants' local authorities, on whose behalf the agency would carry out the required work.

The launch of Childlink's ICA project coincided with the aftermath of the Christmas revolution in Romania. Guidance issued by the DoH in the autumn of 1990 included the requirement that prospective intercountry adopters be approved by their local authorities prior to placement. Subsequent guidance has reinforced this requirement, clarified procedures, and set out principles to be applied in considering applicants' suitability.

Local authorities were permitted to commission approved adoption societies to carry out the necessary preparation and assessment on their behalf. Three London authorities commissioned Childlink on this basis in 1990, and the first referrals followed. During subsequent years a further 13 authorities (12 London boroughs and one English county) set up similar arrangements with the agency. Childlink calculated its preparation and assessment costs as being similar to those incurred in its domestic adoption work – then set at £2,500 by the nationally applied formula for interagency reimbursement of domestic adoption costs.

Almost all the referring authorities required the prospective adopters to meet Childlink's costs in full, which the agency recovered in three stages.

To date, Childlink has processed some 150 intercountry adoption applications to completion and consideration by the Adoption Panel, on behalf of referring local authorities. Table 16.1 (see Appendix) details the number of applications made in respect of each overseas country, how many applicants shared the ethnic heritage of the children they were seeking to adopt, and how many had identified named children in advance of commencing the home study process.

In 1998, the agency decided to take up the newly available option of applying to the Secretary of State for approval to provide ICA services in its own right. This approval was granted and the following year, after a six-month period of notice, the existing arrangements with referring local authorities were terminated. Prospective intercountry adopters living within Greater London are now free to apply direct to Childlink for preparation, assessment and approval to adopt from overseas.

Getting started

Although intercountry adoption represented uncharted territory for the agency in 1990, many aspects of its domestic adoption practice and expertise were directly transferable to the work of the ICA project.

Its staff had long experience of working directly with adoptive parents from the point of initial recruitment through to legal adoption and beyond. The profiles of the children for whom these adopters were coming forward increasingly involved backgrounds of poor early care, disrupted attachments and special needs in relation to health and development. The relinquishing birth parents with whom the agency was still working included a significant number with roots of heritage in overseas countries.

The users of the agency's post-adoption service also offered insights into the outcomes of placements arranged during earlier decades. Of particular relevance to the ICA project were the perspectives of the adopted adults who approached the agency for information about their birth origins, especially those who had been placed across ethnic, cultural, religious and/or linguistic boundaries; and those of the birth mothers who had felt compelled to relinquish their babies by the social, cultural, religious and/or economic pressures prevailing at the time.

Notwithstanding this reservoir of experience, the agency had much to learn about intercountry adoption in a short space of time. Approaches made to a range of UK government departments, overseas embassies and adoptive family associations, in particular PPIAS (Parent to Parent Information on Adoption Services, now Adoption UK) and STORK (now AFAA, the Association of Families who have Adopted from Abroad), produced a wealth of information and additional contacts to assist the ICA project.

Developing ICA practice

The first group of applicants, referred to the project shortly after the issue of the 1990 DoH guidance, were prospective adopters who had already identified children in Romania. They were naturally anxious to complete the formalities at the earliest opportunity. Adoption workers were allocated to undertake their home studies as a matter of urgency.

Agency practice with domestic applicants normally involved a number of stages prior to the assessment process: initial information giving; preliminary counselling; and group preparation. Although there was no inherent reason for replicating the domestic model in relation to future ICA applications, this is in fact how the operation of the project has evolved over the years, as outlined below. Childlink's domestic adoption practice has developed over the same period, and cross-fertilisation between the two strands of the agency's pre-adoption work has benefited both.

Several underlying principles have remained constant:

- that, first and foremost, adoption is a service for children;
- that the desire to parent a child or children through adoption is valid;
- that thorough preparation and assessment lay strong foundations for successful adoptions;
- that adoption practice should be continually reviewed in the light of placement outcomes; and
- that work with prospective adopters has the most constructive impact if it is based on respect, openness and empowerment.

Initial information giving

The requirements and procedures underpinning intercountry adoption to the UK are complex. Applying for approval to adopt a child can also be experienced as an intrusive and disempowering process, particularly if it follows years of unsuccessful fertility treatment. From the earliest days of the ICA project, Childlink has endeavoured to be as open and clear as possible about the overall requirements and about its own policies, practices and procedures. As a first step, all prospective adopters enquiring about the agency's ICA service are sent an information pack which addresses these themes.

The contents of the pack have grown over time in the light of changes in regulations and guidance, alterations to agency procedures, advice from government officials, and feedback from users of the project's services. Additions have included: an outline of the criteria applied by the agency in considering preliminary applications and completed home study reports; a breakdown of the agency's costs in working with ICA applicants; and guidelines about making representations and complaints. Information about the Overseas Adoption Helpline has also been featured since its establishment in 1992, and all enquirers are encouraged to make use of its services.

Preliminary counselling

From Childlink's point of view, the preliminary interview plays a crucial part in introducing the agency's philosophy and style of working. While the individual starting points of ICA applicants may prove decisive (for example, if it is clear that they will not be able to satisfy the prevailing requirements for approval), the agency accords equal importance to their willingness to use the process of preparation and assessment as an opportunity for learning. The applicants are welcomed to the agency and respected in their wish to adopt from abroad. Many have acknowledged their appreciation of this approach, and have been reassured to learn that the agency provides prompt and open feedback about concerns that emerge during assessments.

The initial counselling interview is offered as an opportunity for mutual exploration. Key themes raised with applicants are why they wish to adopt from their country of choice rather than domestically; whether they are able to satisfy the prevailing requirements of the overseas country and the UK; and how far they appreciate the range of issues and needs they will be called on to address as intercountry adoptive parents. They are given additional information about the preparation and assessment processes, and are advised about any identified factors that may have an adverse effect on the outcome of their application.

Group preparation

First-time applicants with whom the agency considers it appropriate to proceed are sent a checklist of activities they can undertake by way of individual preparation. They are also invited to attend a series of ICA preparation groups. A feature of the groups on which they frequently comment – usually favourably but sometimes as a criticism – is the prominence given to the perspective of the child. This is an accurate reflection.

The over-riding purpose of the groups is to highlight themes which are universal and lifelong for intercountry adoptees, and to offer prospective adopters appropriate frameworks and strategies for addressing them. Emphasis is placed on the significance of loss, displacement, difference, racism, birth heritage and identity. The perspective and importance of the birth family are also explored and particular attention is paid to the impact of heredity and early experiences on the subsequent health, development and behaviour of adopted children.

Group preparation for intercountry applicants, which mirrors but is offered separately from domestic adoption preparation, was introduced early in the life of the ICA project. The content has been developed and expanded in response to requests and suggestions received from applicants and their assessing workers. The process, however, has retained its original objectives of active participation and experiential learning. The impact of personal and video testimony from adult adoptees, relinquishing birth parents and experienced intercountry adopters has been invaluable.

The groups are currently spread over three full days and (places permitting) are open to applicants being assessed by other agencies and local authorities. In normal circumstances, Childlink applicants attend prior to embarking on the assessment process, which is enhanced as a result. Each series of groups has been unique, given the active part played by the prospective adopters. The presence of applicants who are hoping to adopt from their country of heritage (whether white European or representatives of minority ethnic communities) has invariably resulted in broader and deeper consideration of the adoption issues raised.

Assessment

Intercountry applicants approach the agency from a wide range of backgrounds, prompted by a variety of motivations. They may already have experience of caring for children, existing connections with the overseas country concerned or the same ethnic heritage as the child they are seeking to adopt (over 25 per cent of Childlink's ICA applicants falling into the latter category). As well as differing strengths, they also have differing areas of vulnerability and learning needs. No two assessments are the same. Nor does Childlink have a "blueprint" of a suitable intercountry adopter.

However, there is a range of baseline qualities and attributes which the adoption panels expect applicants to have demonstrated by the end of the assessment process. These include the time, space and emotional resources applicants are able to devote to the adopted child; their realism, adaptability and capacities in relation to the child's anticipated needs; and the knowledge, experience and networks on which they can draw in addressing issues around child's birth origins and identity needs. As stated earlier, these criteria are included in the current version of the initial information pack.

The agency also follows a consistent checklist for assessments. This is set out for applicants in a self-assessment questionnaire, developed in the early 1990s to demystify the assessment process. The applicants receive a copy of the questionnaire prior to the preparation groups, and are invited to consider one or more sections in advance of each assessment interview. Although many find it daunting, they have valued the foreknowledge it has offered them. Most, including those for whom English is not their first language, have produced written responses for the agency records.

At the heart of the assessment process is the profile of the child the applicants hope to adopt, including: his or her background and birth origins; his or her known or likely genetic inheritance, early experiences and special needs; and the factors leading to his or her abandonment or relinquishment for adoption. The assessing worker evaluates the applicants' motivation, expectations, experiences, supports and attitudes in relation to the child's projected needs and development throughout childhood and beyond. He or she also considers the applicants' openness to looking at themselves, to learning, and to taking seriously the potential stresses and setbacks – alongside the rewards and joys – of adoptive parenting.

Approval and beyond

When the overall volume of Childlink's pre-adoption work necessitated the creation of a second adoption panel, it was decided that each panel would consider a mix of domestic and intercountry applications in the interests of equivalent standards and safeguards. Additional intercountry adopters, adoptees and professionals were recruited as panel members. Joint panel training addresses intercountry as well as domestic adoption issues, and the panels routinely contribute to the development of agency practice and the production of associated guidelines.

During the life of the ICA project, Childlink has processed inter-country applications to numerous countries in the Americas, south and east Asia, north Africa, the Middle East, Eastern Europe and the former USSR (see Appendix, Table 16.1). The adoption panels have not been in a position to develop detailed knowledge of all these sending countries. As an alternative, they have asked that applicants supply an appendix to their home study reports, providing a range of information about their countries of choice. Undertaking the necessary background research has almost always enhanced the applicants' preparation.

Until recently the agency's formal role ended on completion of the home study process, although for several years one of the referring local authorities appointed Childlink as its agent in carrying out welfare supervision of the ensuing placements (nine in all) and preparing the necessary court reports for the UK adoption proceedings. This arrangement, for which the local authority paid, offered Childlink a useful picture of early ICA placement issues, as has the return of 16 applicants seeking approval to adopt a second child from overseas. Many other intercountry adopters have kept in touch with the agency on an informal basis, and some have recounted their experiences to applicants attending the agency's preparation groups.

The overall picture gleaned from these post-placement contacts has been a positive one. While a significant number of the adopters have described issues and challenges – both foreseen and unanticipated – in connection with their children's health and/or adjustment to adoptive family life, most have taken these in their stride and their children have flourished. To the agency's knowledge, no placements have disrupted, although one couple who adopted a four-year-old child eight years ago have sought advice concerning her disturbed behaviour, which has tested them severely over the years.

The precise implications of Childlink's free-standing status as an ICA agency, as affected by the recently-enacted UK intercountry adoption legislation, have yet to be clarified. There is no doubt, however, that the agency's intercountry role and duties will be extended to encompass aspects of the matching and post-placement stages. The development of post-adoption services for intercountry adopters and their adopted children will also feature as an important priority for the agency. These developments will raise significant issues for the agency – including the recovery of associated costs – as highlighted briefly below.

Reflecting on the ICA service

A number of other voluntary adoption agencies across the UK provide intercountry adoption services, and Childlink's ICA project staff have valued the opportunity to network and collaborate with colleagues from these agencies, as well as from local authorities and organisations such as the Overseas Adoption Helpline and International Social Services. Continuing links with ICA family associations and other ICA groups and working parties have also benefited the work of the project. There exists a rich diversity of perspective and expertise across the country on which Childlink continues to draw in developing its intercountry adoption work.

In the summer of 1999, Childlink conducted a postal survey of all the prospective adopters it had prepared and assessed for intercountry adoption during the preceding three years, to elicit their evaluation of the ICA project. Of those who responded, the majority expressed satisfaction with the practice elements of Childlink's service. However, a number highlighted frustration around the interlinked issues of choice, costs and waiting times. All had been directed to Childlink as their only option for accessing a home study service, and almost all had been expected to pay the costs in full. Many had wanted to commence and complete the home study process at a high speed.

Although counselling interviews were offered promptly, and although Childlink had recruited and trained a sizeable group of experienced sessional adoption workers who could take up assessments at short notice, the uneven pattern of referrals meant that some applicants had to wait several months before attending preparation groups and commencing their assessments. Some argued that the home study process was unnecessarily detailed and lengthy, although all accepted the importance of a degree of scrutiny in the interests of the children. They rarely took issue with the agency's need, as a registered charity, to recover its costs in providing ICA services. However, some regarded these costs as too high and a number argued that ICA home studies should, in any event, be financed from public funds rather than by applicants.

Since the ICA project started operating on a free-standing basis, there has been no decrease in demand for its services and the agency still needs to recover its costs from the service users. However, the dimension of choice now available to applicants has gone some way towards decreasing the resulting tensions. Childlink remains available to the local authorities on a consultancy basis to advise and assist them in developing their own intercountry adoption services. Many of them still recommend Childlink to their residents who enquire about adoption from overseas.

The local authorities are hard pressed to find adoptive families for children in their care, and concern is sometimes expressed that each application to adopt from overseas represents the loss of a potential placement for a child waiting for adopters in the UK. In fact, an increasing number of people approaching Childlink about intercountry adoption have chosen to apply for domestic adoption on learning about the numbers and types of UK children who need adoptive families. Some of these enquirers had mistakenly understood – or been inaccurately advised by local authorities or other voluntary adoption agencies – that domestic adoption would not be a viable option for them. A number of excellent domestic adoption placements have flowed from the work of Childlink's ICA project.

Looking to the future

The 1990s saw a significant and steady increase in the number of children adopted from overseas by people living in this country. Simultaneous developments occurred in the provision of ICA services within the UK, informed by the principles underpinning the Hague Convention on Intercountry Adoption. It is argued – not least by the intercountry adopters themselves – that much remains to be achieved, including the establishment in the UK of "full service" intercountry adoption agencies.

The current absence of agencies fulfilling a linking and matching role in liaison with the overseas sending countries is experienced by many adoptive families as a serious void. Childlink supports the view that ICA provision would be improved through the development of specialist agency-to-agency placement mediation services. Whether the mediation function would most appropriately be undertaken by the agencies and authorities that provide pre-approval preparation and assessment, or whether the development of separate post-approval agencies each linking with one or more overseas countries would be preferable, is a matter of debate. Either way, there will be a cost dimension that will need to be addressed.

The full service model of domestic adoption in the UK has much to commend it, providing as it does a continuity of contact and support for the adopters, and first-hand involvement with placement outcomes for their approving agencies. Whether it would be realistic and practical to seek to transfer this model to intercountry adoption, however, is less clear. Childlink, as a small voluntary adoption agency whose core adoption services relate to domestic adoption, would not be in a position to operate a full service model in respect of every potential sending country – nor, in all probability, would the local authorities.

The requirements and preferences of the sending countries are also worthy of consideration in this regard. A number already prefer to liaise with only one or a few identified agencies in each of the countries receiving their children for adoption. Some insist on this and therefore do not accept applications from people living in the UK. A system whereby all UK local authorities and voluntary adoption agencies liaised on behalf of their respective approved adopters might not be looked upon with favour.

A more viable option would perhaps be to locate a "generic" preparation and assessment function within local authorities and those voluntary agencies wishing to undertake such work, and to develop a network of separate mediation agencies each specialising in one or a small number of sending countries. The benefits of such a model would include well-informed, ongoing liaison with agencies in the overseas countries; increased support and assistance for UK adopters while in these countries; and a source of country-specific advice and assistance after adoption, in response to the needs of the children placed. Statutory responsibility for post-placement supervision, when required, and the provision of post-adoption services could either revert to the approving agencies or be allocated to the mediation agencies, depending upon central government regulations and guidance.

Childlink's domestic adoption work with prospective adopters, from initial recruitment to legal adoption, includes routine contact with children in need of adoption, both before and after placement. This contact has been central to the agency's practice development. In whatever way ICA provision develops within the UK, the agency considers that some direct involvement with children – whether in the UK or overseas – will be a vital dimension for any agency providing ICA services.

Conclusion

There has been much debate and controversy in the UK about the rights and wrongs of intercountry adoption as a solution for children, about who should provide and control the associated services, and about the criteria that should be applied in evaluating the eligibility and suitability of prospective adopters.

Childlink has been perceived in some quarters to be a promoter of intercountry adoption. This is not the case. What the agency has sought to promote through its ICA project is high-quality, child-centred practice in the interests of those children whose only chance of a family upbringing is through adoption across national, and in many cases across ethnic, cultural, religious and linguistic boundaries.

The final arbiters of the appropriateness and effectiveness of the UK's intercountry adoption services will be the children themselves. It is to be hoped that the circumstances that give rise to the need for intercountry adoption will be well on the way to resolution by the time children currently being placed come of age.

Acknowledgment
The section of this chapter describing the development of Childlink's ICA practice draws on the contents of a paper commissioned by the Post Adoption Centre (London): 'Practice Paper F: Intercountry Adoption – Pre and Post Adoption Practice and Procedures' (1996) was co-authored by Gill Haworth and Caroline Hesslegrave, who retain joint copyright. The author is grateful to Gill Haworth for her permission to adapt the relevant material.

Appendix

Table 16.1

ICA applications taken through to completion by Childlink, broken down by applicants' country of choice

Country	Number of applications	Applicant(s) sharing ethnic heritage of child applied for	Child already identified
China	58	7	–
India	21	19	
Romania	14	–	7
Guatemala	7	–	1
Thailand	7	1	1
Russia	6	–	2
Brazil	4	–	–
USA	4	1	–
Paraguay	3	–	–
Sri Lanka	3	3	2 (1 related)
Iran	2	2	1
Pakistan	2	2	1
Peru	2	–	–
Philippines	2	–	–
Vietnam	2	–	–
Armenia	2	1	–
Bolivia	1	–	–
Bulgaria	1	–	–
Chile	1	–	–
Colombia	1	–	–
Croatia	1	1	1
Hong Kong	1	–	1
Lebanon	1	–	1
Morocco	1	1	1
Poland	1	1	–
Singapore	1	1	–
Yugoslavia	1	1	–
Total	150	41	19

Section IV
A worldwide perspective: experience from other countries

If the UK is to ratify the Hague Convention with honour, it is vital that we move quickly to a structure of services that can not only ensure that intercountry adoption is carried out in the spirit of the Convention, but can also offer good support to adoptive families. In doing this, we have the advantage of being able to learn from the experience of other countries where ICA is more common and services have been developed over a longer period. We also need to learn from the States of origin about what they expect and need from the countries to which they send children.

The chapters in this section explore the experience of other countries. They are not meant to provide a comprehensive or balanced account of ICA worldwide, but rather a series of insights to challenge preconceptions we may hold about ICA and some possible lessons – both positive and negative – for those involved in developing services in the UK.

We have seen that the USA takes more children through intercountry adoption than any other country – although the "per capita" level remains well below that found in Sweden and Norway. It has also been the focus of much of the concern over "trafficking" and the prevalence of substantial independent adoption alongside agencies of varying quality has made many cautious of seeking lessons. In her chapter, **Christine Gailey** shows how issues of "race", class and gender permeate thinking about intercountry adoption in the US through a trenchant analysis of its development over time. Gailey also offers a critique of current American policy and practice. One of the key criticisms she makes is that the State Department continues to refer in all its statistics to "orphans", a terminology which enables parents to see adoption as an act of "rescue", where the birth family is off the scene. Like the UK, the USA is belatedly moving towards ratification of the Hague Convention and Gailey ends with some suggestions for the changes needed if such a step is to be made.

Australia resembles Britain in being a late arrival on the intercountry adoption scene, but has moved more rapidly to ratification of the Hague Convention in 1998 and has recently established a number of new structures to aid implementation. Australia has followed the USA in encouraging full-service agencies, though not in permitting adoptions arranged by individual attorneys, but, like the USA, it has a federal structure so that caution has to be exercised in talking about the Australian experience. **Jonathan Telfer** focuses on the development of services in one state – South Australia – where a full-service agency was established in 1992. He raises a number of issues central to the development of intercountry adoption in Australia, including important questions about the respective roles of public authorities and accredited bodies. Many of the issues raised are highly relevant to current discussions in the UK. His chapter also draws on anthropological research into adoptive parents, which shows clearly the need to understand and respect the experiences and struggles of couples seeking intercountry adoption, while ensuring that the interests of the child come first.

The next three chapters concentrate on the experience of Europe, and in particular the Netherlands and Scandinavia, where levels of intercountry adoption are comparatively high and services well established. These latter countries share a similar structure (Selman, 1998), with home studies the responsibility of statutory authorities and adoptions mediated mainly by non-governmental agencies: in contrast to the full-service agencies discussed in the previous two chapters.

Gunilla Andersson writes from the experience of thirty years involvement with the *Adoption Centre,* Sweden's largest adoption organisation. She describes changes in the nature of adoption over that period, a pattern which reflects the generational changes described by Rene Hoksbergen in Chapter 5: the shift from humanitarian motives to overseas adoption as an answer to childlessness and the more recent recognition of the real problems involved. These changes have been accompanied by a gradual refinement and expansion of the services relating to ICA, with a strong central direction, skilled assessment, and the emergence of organisations with strong links to States of origin. One interesting development in

Sweden has been the emergence of groups formed by adoptees. Many of these consist of young people adopted from a single country, but more recently, adoptees from several different countries have come together to form a 24th branch of the Adoption Centre itself.

Albert Duinkerken and Hilda Geerts discuss the introduction in the Netherlands of compulsory attendance at preparation courses *before* prospective adopters can seek approval for overseas adoption and see this as a result of growing concern over the outcome of intercountry adoption and an awareness of how ill-prepared most adopters were for the challenges many of their children presented. The courses are run by an organisation called Bureau VIA, which is independent of the local authorities which carry out assessment and the agencies which link prospective adopters to the States of origin. The chapter also outlines the content of the six-session course, which provides many stimulating ideas for anyone wishing to develop a preparation course in this country. Most of those attending found the sessions useful, although many said the information depressed them and made them have doubts about inter-country adoption. The authors conclude that the preparation groups have been a success and that those who proceed to assessment and placement are both better informed and more confident in negotiating these later stages of the intercountry adoption process.

Kerstin Sterky looks at the need for structures above a national level which can bring professionals together to learn from each other. EurAdopt is a forum for adoption organisations working directly with agencies in States of origin, which has done much to raise and maintain standards in Europe. There is a biennial meeting of member agencies to which Central Authorities and other interested parties are also invited for an open day. Sterky also identifies a number of ongoing issues for mediating agencies, many of which overlap with the concerns raised by Duncan in an earlier chapter. The organisation is dominated by agencies from the Nordic countries and, in an appendix to this chapter, **Lars von der Leith** contributes a brief piece on the *Nordic Adoption Council,* founded in 1996, but building on a much longer history of co-operation between the Nordic countries. Member organisations include a parents' group, placing agencies and organisations that are involved in arranging adoptions but also have adoptive parents as members.

All that we have discussed so far is from the perspective of receiving States and has looked primarily at their responsibilities in respective of the assessment and preparation of parents and the after care of parents and children. In the final two chapters of this section, we look at the experience of a sending country, India.

Nilima Mehta and **Andal Damodaran** present the view from the States of origin by looking at the responsibilities of the countries sending children. They explore the history of intercountry adoption in India, the expectations that sending countries should have about receiving States, and cite some important examples of where intercountry adoption can go badly wrong. They also identify the immense task facing poor countries in developing their own adoption and fostering services – which should one day make intercountry adoption unnecessary – and the role of the developed world in helping that day to come sooner.

Neena Macedo's chapter tells of the experience of one Indian agency, the *Delhi Council for Child Welfare,* through its children's home, PALNA. Two points emerge of importance to the debate on intercountry adoption. Macedo clearly sees a role for intercountry adoption in Indian child welfare, especially in respect of children with special needs, including sibling groups, who are "hard to place" for domestic adoption, but also stresses why PALNA prefers to work with only a few countries and why the UK is not one of those. In an appendix to her chapter there are some short letters written by Indian children placed in Italy.

17 Race, class and gender in intercountry adoption in the USA

Christine Ward Gailey

Christine Ward Gailey is Professor of Anthropology and Chair, Department of Women's Studies, University of California, Riverside.

Introduction

Although intercountry adoption accounts for only a small proportion of all adoptions in the USA – an estimated five per cent in 1992 (Flango and Flango, 1995) – like domestic transracial adoption, it attracts disproportionate media coverage and thereby helps to shape adoption discourse far beyond the actual numbers involved. Both international and transracial adoptions highlight the way family formation is conceived in the USA and raise issues of identity and claims to children in a context of racism, and cultural and class domination. In this chapter I shall explore four central issues:

1. the historical and political-economic patterns which have influenced the countries from which children have been adopted by US parents;
2. the "orphan" myth – how US international adopters conceive of their children's origins;
3. infertility and the right to a "child of one's own";
4. kinship ideologies and how they affect the ways adopters construct relationships with their children (Kirk, 1985; Modell, 1994).

In discussing these issues I shall draw on interviews with intercountry adopters, which formed part of a larger project (Gailey, forthcoming 2001). I end with some suggestions for policy changes in relation to intercountry adoption in the USA.

Adoption and kinship

Adoption potentially poses the most subversive challenge to what David Schneider (1980) has called the core tenet of American kinship ideology, that "blood is thicker than water"; i.e. that people believe that genetic connections or "shared substance" underlie the strongest familial attachments, with all other relationships reflecting a diluted degree of commitment and sense of belonging (see Telfer, Chapter 18).

Because intercountry adoption generally does not involve "blood relatives", it is a particularly good lens through which to view two key dynamics. One is the way intercountry adoption articulates and embodies racial, ethnic, national, gender, and class discourses at different times. The other is the way a dominant ideology of kinship and family can be reconstituted within or alongside the fact of adoptive connection. Since many intercountry adoptions are transracial adoptions, intercountry adoption can also provide insight into shifting racial ideologies and colour hierarchies in the USA.

The process of adopting from abroad in the USA

US citizens wishing to adopt from other countries have two options: to work through specialist private agencies, or to work through lawyers whose practices focus on intercountry adoption and who are associated with particular orphanages and lawyers in specific countries. For most adopters the largest single expenses are the approved home study by a licensed adoption agency and the airfares to the child's country of origin. The cost of adopting internationally is given by the National Adoption Information Clearing House (NAIC) as ranging from US$10,000–US$30,000, but costs can be much higher if prospective adopters work through private adoption lawyers (Gailey, 1999). Intercountry adoption costs are not subsidised by the Government as in some European countries, although there are modest tax benefits to defray a portion of adoption expenses.

The scope of US intercountry adoption

The numbers of intercountry adoptions in the USA have grown steadily over the last decade from about 8,000 in 1989 to 16,396 in 1999. These figures mark the US numerically as the largest "importer" of adopted children in the world (see Selman, Chapter 1). Published data are broken down by country of origin, but do not indicate the marital status of adoptive parent(s), whether the adoption is privately arranged through adoption lawyers or through a US-based adoption agency, or whether the adoptions are by military personnel. There are of course many other things we do not know about intercountry adoptions: the outcomes of these adoptions over time; the rates of mental institutionalisation or juvenile detention; the number of attempts made to return children to agencies or countries of origin (Gailey, 1999).

Policy and practice in states of origin

Within sending countries, policies and practices vary widely regarding how (and sometimes if) official termination of birth parental claims is mandated, the length of time a child has to be in state or private care prior to adoptive placement, the length of time adopters must reside in the country prior to finalisation of the adoption, and the required characteristics of acceptable adopters. The discrepant political and economic conditions and practices in sending countries leave open the possibility in many that children may be kidnapped or taken from their birth mothers by other relatives to be sold for adoption (Perlez, 1994; Granelli and Reyes, 1984; Sharp and Punnett, 1982; Haberman, 1990; Brooke, 1994).

The role of courts and lawyers in sending countries is sometimes well delineated and regulated by the government, as in Colombia, and sometimes so vague that none of the parties may be sure when the adoption is ready to be finalised (Nash, 1992). When sending countries realise that intercountry adoptions can be a lucrative local source of hard currency, they generally move to regulate it, but sometimes the infrastructure, as throughout the collapsed Soviet bloc, makes this impossible. This may lead to a cyclical pattern in which relative ease of outflow of children is followed by drastic government restrictions on the number of permitted adoptions, and then an increase in the outflow under greater state control (*New York Times*, 1995; Trimborn, 1983). The outbreak of scandals, rumours or documentation of child trafficking or kidnapping, or demands from domestic adopters for access to infants has led some countries to place a moratorium on international adoptions (Stanley, 1997; *New York Times*, 1990).

International efforts to regulate intercountry adoption

In the past decade there have been important international efforts to regulate intercountry adoption. The focus has been on regulating the ways children come to be available for intercountry adoption, the treatment of relinquished or abandoned children within sending countries, and the process of legal relinquishment of birth parent claims. Similarly, efforts have begun to standardise legal processes and thereby reduce graft and illegal payments. Still others are attempting to assess in a more systematic way the parenting potential of proposed adopters. The widespread condition of hard currency borne by prospective adopters from the North and endemic poverty and underpaid professionals in the South has led in many cases to what can only be called a market in children. The Hague Convention on Protection of Children and Co-operation in Respect of Intercountry Adoption is the most important attempt, in the words of the US State Department, to 'prevent illegal child trafficking'. The US signed the Convention in March 1994, but has still not ratified it, although a Bill has now been introduced (see Duncan, Chapter 2).

Racial and colonial overlays in US intercountry adoption

The history of intercountry adoption in the US cannot be disassociated from the history of US military operations. In the second half of the 20th century, the patterns are closely linked to the consequences of US covert operations and Cold War activities. What is unusual about the US as a conquering state is the aftermath: often the US has attempted to assimilate or incorporate the "enemy other". The zeal with which the US as an imperial power attempts to promote what is termed "the American way of life" or "democratic society" (i.e. a particular configuration of capitalism with a non-welfare state apparatus, particular forms of gender hierarchy, and beliefs in individualism) is widely recognised.

The first transcultural/transracial adoptions can be seen as dating back to the early history of the British colonies that later would become the US. Missionary groups and white settlers sometimes sought to "adopt" Native American children; often, these offers were initially accepted, but later rejected when the nature of adoption as non-reciprocal and entailing exclusive possession of children was learned by the indigenous groups (Leacock, 1980, p 37). During armed conflicts with white settlers, Native American groups usually spared the lives of young children and adopted them as full members of the group, as numerous narratives testify. The history of white adoptions of Native American children has been largely a melding of imperial expansion and stereo-types of Native Americans as a defeated but noble, dying race (see Strong, in press, 2001) or in the contemporary period as incapable of caring for children due to alcoholism (see e.g., Dorris, 1989).

Intercountry adoption in the US has its modern origins in the reloca-tion of German and other European war orphans to military and other families in the US. This spate of adoptions from the late 1940s through the mid-1950s can be seen as part of the US postwar de-Nazification programme and public relations efforts to paint the US military occupa-tion as a friendly and healing force. In that period, public adoption agencies routinely practised religious as well as racial matching – indeed, matching hair and eye colour – with a clientele that was almost uniquely white and middle income. Under such conditions, placement of "Aryan" children was not difficult, but placement of Japanese war orphans was discouraged. These intercountry adoptions from Europe, many of which involved children who had survived soul-searing conditions during the war and in its aftermath, occurred in an era when post-traumatic stress went unrecognised and psychiatric treatment was viewed as an admission of moral weakness or madness. The results of these adoptions, as we might expect, were highly uneven. Some of the children suffered severe, lifelong emotional and social problems (Dodds, 1997).

A few years later, the first of what would become continuing inter-country adoption began in the wake of the Korean War. This effort, confined primarily to the recruitment of adoptive families within the US military, presented the available Korean children as war orphans, although many were the result of US soldiers' relationships with Korean women. The racial stratification that still marks intercountry adoption today can be seen in the complexities of what constituted permissible and prohibited transracial placement. The children of servicemen and Korean women were rarely welcomed into Korean families, who viewed the children as a taint on family honour, because they were born outside marriage or seen as racially impure. These children usually were abandoned by their mothers under extreme pressure from their families, and also by their fathers. The lucky ones were left at orphanages run by various Christian organisations.

While abandoned children who were Korean, or whose fathers were white and mothers Korean, could be placed for adoption in the US, the colour hierarchy between black and "yellow" was marked. Children of black soldiers were not placed for adoption in the US and, unless they were among the few in that period placed in European families, remained in orphanages until they reached adulthood, facing a lifetime of discrimination in South Korea. Fathers of these children were not permitted to marry Korean women – in contrast to white soldiers, who, in the 1950s, were discouraged but not prohibited from doing so – nor were they permitted to adopt any progeny.

This early intercountry/transracial adoption campaign focused on white military families. To this day there is expedited legal processing and a far shorter wait for US military couples adopting from Korea compared with other US couples. Among couples I have interviewed, the average wait for the non-military couples was a year after the home study was completed; for the military couples it ranged from six weeks to six months. Even today, there is little demand for black Korean children. South Korean policy is consistent with the view that women having children outside of marriage are dishonourable: single women are not permitted to adopt, whether those prospective adoptive mothers are Korean or any other nationality.

Although few of the 1950s Korean-US adoptions involved children who could be construed as black, they nevertheless posed a challenge to a country still marked by miscegenation laws and segregated schools and public institutions. What also made them different from the earlier German adoptions was the prevalence for the first time of infants and toddlers rather than older children. The history of this first wave of Korean adoptions has yet to be written, but the preference for placing the children with US military families is redolent with colonialism.

In addition to the explicit racial hierarchy marking the adoption of Korean-American children, I suggest there is a submerged racial discourse that dates to World War II, when Japanese-American children were portrayed in the media and in US policies that incarcerated them and their families, as not "really" American (see Suzuki, 1980, pp 36–39; Dower, 1997). This compounded the already widespread conflation of disparate Asian peoples in US media as a "yellow horde", although a temporary effort during the war was made to portray the Chinese (at least, Chiang Kai Shek's faction and the Nanking population) as victims of Japanese aggression. With the shift in the late 1940s and early 1950s from anti-Japanese portrayals to those painting the Chinese as communist aggressors, the adoption of Korean infants seemed at least in some way a laboratory for assimilationist beliefs in the redemptive qualities of capitalist culture.

Until the Vietnam War, intercountry adoptions traced the pathway of postwar US military occupation. Korean adoptions were followed by adoptions of Filipino children, again mostly by US military families and again in keeping with a significant US military presence. Latin American adoptions followed the Kennedy administration's "Alliance for Progress" political and economic impetus. Where the US engineered or fostered military juntas or destabilisations of the government, international adoptions followed within five years (Brazil in the 1960s; Chile in the 1970s; Guatemala in the 1980s). The presence of India as a sender of children to the US can be understood in relation to church-based missionary-related activities in that country, and the role India played in US images of the deserving poor and the "population bomb".

Intercountry adoption, however, remained insignificant in US adoptive family formation until the demographic changes of the late 1960s – delayed childbearing among the white population, greater acceptability for keeping children born outside of marriage and the legalisation of abortion – reduced the number of white babies available for adoption.

At the same time, the number of countries permitting international adoption of infants began to expand, particularly in Latin America. Until 1991, the top countries providing children to US families for adoption were South Korea, followed by Colombia, India, the Philippines, and Guatemala (see Table 17.2 in Appendix). In all cases, children were "acceptably coloured" in the US racial hierarchy – even dark-skinned southern Indian children, because of their 19th century categorisation as Aryan or Caucasian.

When the socialist bloc began to crumble in Eastern Europe, the prospect of obtaining definitively white children rose for US adopters. Romanian adoptions of children reared in institutions burgeoned from only 121 adoptions in 1990 to 2,594 in 1991, overtaking South Korean adoptions for the same year (1,818). The point here is that as soon as white children were available, many prospective intercountry adopters opted for same-race or same-colour over other considerations. However, when these adoptions began to show the problems typical of post-institutionalised children and the Romanian government imposed controls, the number plummeted to only 97 in 1993, although they have subsequently increased again – to 895 in 1999. Ironically for the racial situation in the US, the infants in question were predominantly from a despised and racialised minority, the Tigani or Gypsies (Beck, 1992), but were being claimed by white American adopters as white.

When the Romanian free-for-all was stemmed, the floodgates opened in Russia and the number of adoptions rose from 324 in 1992 to 4,491 in 1998. Again, the prevailing explanation for the desirability of Russian infants is that they are white. But this does not explain why South Korea's place should be usurped over the past three years by the People's Republic of China. Explanations centre on the relative ease of adoption in two areas: in China adoptive parents can be older than most other countries permit (into their 50s, depending on the age of the child) and single mother adopters are not treated more stringently than married adopters. Another key factor, not generally acknowledged, is that adoption by Chinese couples is difficult, since it is likely to be seen as a way of evading the one-child policy (see Anagnost, 1999). What makes the Chinese adoption case unique, however, is that the children are almost all girls. This is a direct result of two factors: the one-child birth control policy (see Selman, Chapter 1) and the resurgence of patrilineality and patriarchal practices in the post-economic reform era, resulting in intensified pressure on young wives to bear sons. Until China permitted foreign adoptions, most US intercountry adoptions, like most domestic ones, involved almost equal numbers of boys and girls. Today, the overall sex ratio of US intercountry adoptions favours girls. Looking at the characterisation of these children by their parents, it is impossible to separate racial issues of acceptable exoticism – the position in the US of Chinese as more acceptable than blacks (a so-called "buffer race") – from the stereotype of Asian women as compliant and docile. As one father commented: 'There she was in the airport – our little China doll!' Now that the Chinese adoptions have become so prevalent, new terrain for inquiring into the intersection of gender and racial stereotyping among both married and single white adopters is possible.

The orphan myth

How children come to be available for intercountry adoption is a consequence of laws in sending countries on parental abandonment, whether the support of relinquished children is through foster care or institutionalisation, how physical and mental health are locally defined, local racial and ethnic categorisations, regulations on expatriation of children, and definitions of orphan status.

It is this latter question – how orphans are defined – that concerns me here. Defining children as orphans when one or both parents are living demands explanation. In many countries, the term "orphan" is expanded to include children whose parent or parents have relinquished legal rights by either giving them to the state or having them taken by the state. In either case, the legal fiction of orphan status contributes to an important set of images of intercountry adoptees that has consequences for their later questions regarding origins (see Collard, 1991, 1996).

Statistics on intercountry adoption published on the US State Department's website refer to "Immigrant visas issued to orphans coming to the United States". However, few of the children made available to foreign adopters have dead parents: indeed many adopters are well aware of their children's kinship situation and some may have regular contact with the child's birth parent or other relatives, although such "open adoption" is rare in intercountry adoption. Most intercountry adoptees have been relinquished for reasons of poverty or because social conditions do not permit the mothers to rear the children. In some cases, as during the Romanian pro-natalist nationalist campaigns of the 1970s and 1980s, women have been forced to bear unwanted children because abortions were illegal or inaccessible (see Selman, Chapter 1). In contrast, children born in the US who are legally freed for adoption are no longer termed "orphans" unless both birth parents are dead. To declare potential adoptees in other countries to be orphans disguises the conditions through which they came to be in state care.

In my research, none of the adopters of Chinese girls saw their daughters as orphans, probably because knowledge of the one child policy and desire for sons is so widely known. But in most other cases, the legal fiction of orphan status has a certain appeal to those inter-country adopters in search of clear-cut, exclusive rights to a child, even though most adoption agencies have shifted from earlier practices that urged telling the child about adoption only on a need-to-know basis, to urging parents to tell children in language appropriate to the age level about their adoptive status and origins. I was particularly concerned with how parents adopting Chinese girls would deal with the issue of families not wanting daughters and pressuring mothers to give the girls to the State: an issue rarely considered and never raised in the growing number of newspaper articles on Chinese adoptions. Few had considered how to help their daughters value themselves through an appreciation of the country of origin and its various cultures, or their birth mothers' difficult situation, trapped between government policy and patriarchal practice. Many adopters seemed happy to accept the minimal story regarding the child's origins, the word of the orphanage director or the adoption lawyer, as it reduced anxiety about the possibility of a custody battle. Several mentioned the horror they had of domestic adoptions that had ended in the courts when a birth father or birth mother claimed their legal rights were not terminated. The concern for exclusive possession and the often charged feelings surrounding infertility make it difficult for these parents to discuss their children's histories on other than a very general level. But most children adopted internationally have living birth parents and the curiosity so many adoptive children have about their origins, and especially about why their birth mothers gave them up (Burlingham-Brown, 1994), plants a communications time-bomb for parents uncomfortable with their children's origins (McRoy, Grotevant and Zurcher, 1988). The language of intercountry adoption, thus, creates conditions where the adoptee's birth parents become socially dead. In addition to calming the fears of reclaiming the child, the social death of the birth parents also stems most of the parents' expressed fear of adult adoptees searching for lost relatives.

Although adoption challenges notions of genetic kinship as the basis of attachment, and although these parents felt attached to their children, the fear remains that there really is a "birth bond" stronger than nurturing (Gediman and Brown, 1989). Intercountry adoption acts to reduce the potential for successful searches, ensuring that a possible return journey (as is occurring now through guided post-adoption tours) will be unlikely to create a family crisis. The myth of the orphan, made real through the legal erasure of the birth parents, makes it easier for adopters to commit to their children. The children's interests in this situation are structurally secondary.

"A child of our very own"

Many adopting couples have to face issues of infertility, but the burden of blame seems to fall mainly on the wife. In the couples interviewed, where infertility is associated with the husband, couples spoke of the difficulties "they" had "getting pregnant", but when the wife assumed responsibility for infertility, she spoke of the problems as her own. This concern with infertility may be one factor in the reluctance that the couples who knew their child was not an orphan showed when asked to talk about their child's birth parents. I interviewed one couple who had planned to go to Romania and use some of the husband's business contacts to obtain a child, but when reports started coming in about the psychological problems of post-institutionalised children (see Johnson and Groze, 1993), they decided to adopt from Colombia. 'They've been at it longer and the procedures are more straightforward,' the father explained. 'And the orphanages are clean and well-run. They do so much with so little,' the mother went on, 'Our little girl was well taken care of, you could just tell from her alertness.'

Adoptive parents' concern over their infant's physical and mental condition can be seen in an article in *The Boston Globe* (16 June 1996) which described a couple's sorrow upon the death of a toddler they had adopted as an infant from the Ukraine. When the baby began to show signs of severe developmental delays, requiring much care, the parents, having spent over $30,000 in medical bills and fearing the disruption of family life and the impact that illness might have on their older adopted daughter, decided to return the child to the same orphanage in the Ukraine where they had found him. Later, he died in the orphanage. The article was written in a tone sympathetic to the adoptive parents and made no mention of the impact on their adopted daughter of knowing her brother was given back because he did not perform up to expectations or because he was seriously ill. Nor was there any thought of the likelihood of such an outcome for special needs children in chronically understaffed, overcrowded, and underfunded orphanages. The number of "successful" rejections of intercountry adopted children is not known, nor is the number of children whom parents attempt to return but, being rebuffed by the agencies, decide to keep (Zwimpfer, 1983; Sack and Dale, 1982).

There was an assumption that marriages have stages and that in the long run, married people were incomplete without children: 'We wanted a child of our very own,' one husband explained. 'My parents were getting older and it was time, you know, and then we had trouble getting pregnant.' Adoption was clearly seen as an inferior substitute for child-birth (see Howell, 1999) but if undertaken, was pursued with a clear agenda. The goal these parents expressed, in one way or another, was to minimise the effects of early environment on the child. So, the targeted child was as young an infant as possible, from as stable a background as possible, and being cared for in a setting that was as controlled as possible (agency mediated, well-run and sanitary orphanages, affectionate foster families, etc.). None of the sample would have considered adopting an older child or one considered to have "special needs". They had deep concerns that the child show signs of intelligence and physical health and many had rejected the possibility of public adoption because this was seen as only about "special needs". Fears about unanticipated genetic disorders, diseases, and organic problems were pronounced.

Issues of "race" in intercountry adoption

At a major adoption conference, I spoke with one prospective adopter who told me that she and her husband were going to adopt from Brazil, because of the "shortage of white infants" and the legal intricacies and uncertainties of contracting with a birth mother in this country. 'It turns out to be less expensive, even when you include the bribes for the local officials,' she added. I asked if the colour of the child made a difference to them. 'Well, we want a white child, of course, because we're white, and we've been assured by our agency that Brazil is the right place to go.' She seemed unaware of the racial diversity of Brazilians, particularly in the classes where adoptable children are apt to be born. At the same conference, a headline in the newsletter of one major private agency in the New England region proudly announced: 'Caucasian children from India now available.'

With few exceptions – the single mothers and one of the couples – the notion of family, in the business/professional group of adopters I interviewed, seemed to be associated with essentialist notions of kinship as well as "race". There was more concern expressed in this group about "matching" – looking similar to the parents – than the non-governmental organisation workers/academic group of adopters, none of whom expressed concern about physiological matching. The single women adopters among the business/professional group seemed less concerned with appearances; one of these had adopted transracially with an aware-ness that her lifestyle would have to accommodate the child's need for role models and community (see Ladner, 1977; Gaber and Aldridge, 1994; Pohl and Harris, 1993). Some business/professional couples 'didn't care' about the appearance of the child – 'as long as it isn't black', which at least one wife said she was 'not prepared to handle'.

Kinship as ideology and practice

What ideologies of family are operating here? For many intercountry adopters in my study, children were conceived as virtually kinless prior

307

to placement and as treasured possessions of their parents after. These couples were clear to themselves that they offered a far better life to their child: an ethic of productivity, opportunities for education, a stable home life, and high quality child care by both parents and hired pro-fessionals. (This parallels the tone of Bartholet's (1993) treatise on transracial and international adoption.) Their focus was on the detailed contractual nature of the acquisition of the child, and on the age of the child at the time of acquisition – I believe this was to preserve the image of the child as close to an empty slate as their commitment to genetic causation permitted. Their deep concern with getting as healthy and bright an infant as possible belied their belief that "blood is thicker than water". The love offered by these parents appeared as "caring" and encouraging independence, learning, and negotiating skills. This was demonstrated through the provision of opportunities, quality services, and a generally safe family atmosphere. Several of the couples seemed to have notions of love that were performance-based, subject to evalua-tion and possible rejection, but this did not seem different from the ways they spoke of their marital relationships or their own relationships with parents. Their expectations of adopted children were not qualitatively different than those for birth children in that social class/caste/and gender melange.

The problem remains that what might work in terms of class reproduc-tion – performance-related acceptance – for birth children might have a dramatically different impact upon children whose early lives had been disrupted. The fear of abandonment so often encountered in children experiencing replacements of care-givers – the grief and loss discussed by Jewett (1982) – would be compounded should developmental delays or indifference to schoolwork come to characterise these children of hyper-achieving parents.

Cultural heritage and identity issues were downplayed as issues, although given careful rhetorical attention. The parents talked about providing consumer goods and services – books, dolls, and service personnel – to give the child a sense of his/her heritage. Most of the business/professional adopters I interviewed considered themselves entitled to adopt, because their prosperity and social position guaranteed the child a better life (see also Bartholet, 1993). Almost all chafed at the intrusiveness of home studies and other such processes.

Policy recommendations

Based on the situation of those children adopted from other countries by the families I interviewed in the US, a review of the literature on adoption, and my understanding of the political and economic dynamics underlying international adoption, I would make the following recommendations.

- The US should ratify the Hague Convention and permit agencies to arrange adoptions only from countries that are in compliance with the terms of the Convention.
- Privately arranged intercountry adoptions should be stopped. Given the existence of the private market for infants, kidnapping, pressured relinquishment of parental rights, and even enforced pregnancies have been reported in many countries.
- The term "orphan" should be stricken from international adoption usage, unless both birth parents are no longer living. Children whose parents are still alive should be referred to as "legally available for adoption".
- Adoption agencies arranging intercountry adoptions should be more strictly regulated regarding the content and duration of the home studies and the preadoptive training expected and provided to intercountry adopters. These should be comparable to the training and home studies expected of public agency adopters.
- The training component for international adopters should include awareness of the social and economic conditions of the communities from which the children would be coming. Information and discussion of post-institutionalised children's developmental and attachment issues should be included in the training.
- Wherever possible, open adoptions should be encouraged as in the interests of the child.
- Potential international adopters should be educated by agencies to view the child as the adoption client, not themselves.
- Post-adoption monitoring of child welfare should be conducted

through site visits and other regular contact with the agencies arranging the adoption.

- Post-adoption support groups targeting parents of children of particular age groups or histories should be established through the agencies arranging intercountry adoptions.

Acknowledgements

This chapter is a revised and shortened version of a paper, 'Seeking "Baby Right" ', first presented at the international conference, Mine – Yours – Ours and Theirs held in Oslo in May 1999 (Ryvgold, Dalen and Sætersdal, 1999). A full report of my research can be found in, ' "Blue Ribbon Babies" and "Labors of Love": Race, Class, and Gender in United States Adoption Practice' (University of Texas Press, 2001 forthcoming).

References

Altstein H and Simon R (eds) (1991) *Intercountry Adoption: A Multinational Perspective*, New York, NY: The Free Press.

Anagnost A N.D. (n.d. 1999) *Scenes of Recognition: Maternal citizenship in the age of transnational adoption*, manuscript.

Bagley C and Young L, Scully A (1993) *International and Transracial Adoptions: A mental health perspective*, Brookfield, VT: Avebury Press.

Bartholet E (1993) 'Adoption among nations', in *Family Bonds: Adoption and the Politics of Parenting*, Boston: Houghton Mifflin, pp 118–163.

Beck S (1992) 'Persona non grata: ethnicity and Romanian nationalism', in Gailey C (ed) *The Politics of Culture and Creativity*, Gainesville: University Press of Florida, pp 119–145.

Brooke E H (1994) 'Adoption saga of Rio's streets', *The New York Times*, 144, 29 December, C1.

Burlingham-Brown B (1994) *'Why Didn't She Keep Me?' Answers to the question every adopted child asks*, South Bend, IN: Langford Books.

Collard C (1991) 'Les orphelins propres et les autres', *Culture*, 11:1, 2, pp 135–149.

Collard C (1996) 'Nouer, denouer le cordon ombilical: Illegitimite adoption au Quebec', *Gradhiva*, 19, pp 58–70.

Dodds P F (1997) *Outer Search, Inner Journey: An orphan and adoptee's quest*, Puyallup, WA: Aphrodite Press.

Dorris M (1989) *The Broken Cord*, New York, NY: Harper & Row.

Dower J (1997) *Japan in War and Peace*, New York, NY: New Press.

Flango V and Flango C (1995) 'How many children were adopted in 1992', *Child Welfare*, 74, pp 1018–1031.

Gaber I and Aldridge J (eds) (1994) *In the Best Interests of the Child: Culture, identity, and transracial adoption*, London: Free Association Books.

Gailey C W (1999) 'Seeking "Baby Right": Race, class and gender in US international adoption', in Ryvgold A, Dalen M and Sætersdal B (eds) *Mine – Yours – Ours and Theirs*, Oslo: University of Oslo.

Gailey C W (2001) ' "Blue Ribbon Babies" and "Labors of Love": Race, class and gender in US Adoption Practice', Austin: University of Texas Press, forthcoming.

Gediman J and Brown L (1989) *Birthbond: Reunions between birthparents and adoptees – what happens after...* Far Hills, NJ: New Horizon Press.

Granelli J and Reyes D (1984) 'Court orders girl's return from Mexico: charges "appalling breach" of duty in international adoption case', *Los Angeles Times*, 103:II, 11 February, p 5.

Haberman C (1990) 'Court aborts adoption and tugs at child', *The New York Times*, 139, 1 March, A4.

Howell S (1999) 'Biologizing and De-Biologizing Kinship: Some Paradoxes in Norwegian Transnational Adoption', in *Mine – Yours – Ours and Theirs*, Ryvgold A L, Dalen M and Sætersdal B (eds) Oslo, Norway: University of Oslo, pp 32–51.

Jewett C (1982) *Helping Children Cope with Grief and Loss*, Harvard, MA: Harvard Common Press.

Johnson A and Groze V (1993) 'The orphaned and institutionalised children of Romania', *Journal of Emotional and Behavioral Problems*, 2:4, pp 49–52.

Kirk D H (1985) *Adoptive Kinship: A modern institution in need of reform*, Port Angeles, WA: Ben-Simon Publications.

Ladner J (1977) *Mixed Families: Adopting across racial boundaries*, Garden City, NJ: Anchor/Doubleday.

Leacock E (1980) 'Montagnais women and the Jesuit program for colonisation'. in Etienne M and Leacock E B (eds) *Women and Colonisation*, New York, NY: Praeger, pp 25–42.

McRoy R, Grotevant H and White K (1988) *Openness in Adoption: New practices, new issues*, New York: Praeger.

McRoy R, Grotevant H and Zurcher L (1988) *Emotional Disturbance in Adopted Adolescents: Origins and development*, New York, NY: Praeger.

Modell J S (1994) *Kinship with Strangers: Adoption and interpretations of kinship in American culture*, Berkeley: University of California Press.

Nash M (1992) 'Ordeal in Peru: cuddling a baby, clinging to hope: Americans encounter problems attempting to adopt children in Peru', *The New York Times*, 141, 9 June, A4, A7.

The New York Times (1995) 'Ukraine arrests two in baby-selling case: doctors detained by police officials', *The New York Times*, 144, 3 March, A8.

The New York Times (1990) 'Romania is prohibiting adoption by foreigners, *The New York Times*, 139, February, A8, A11.

National Adoption Information Clearinghouse (NAIC) (1999) National Information on Foster Care and Adoption. Internet Address: http://www.calib.com/naic/index.htm.

Perlez J (1994) 'Britons sentenced in Romania in baby case', *The New York Times*, 144, 19 October, A4, A6.

Pohl C and Harris K (1993) *Transracial Adoption: Children and parents speak out*, New York, NY: Franklin Watts.

Ryvgold A, Dalen M and Sætersdal B (1999) *Mine – Yours – Ours and Theirs*, Oslo: University of Oslo.

Schneider D (1980) *American Kinship: A cultural account*, Chicago, IL: University of Chicago Press.

Sharp C and Punnett S (1982) 'On baby selling: Colombian children', *Christian Science Monitor*, 74, 28 October, p 22.

Stanley A (1997) 'US adoption agencies fear tightening of Russian law', *The New York Times*, 147, 4 December, A5.

Strong P T (2001) 'To forget their tongue, their name, and their whole relation: captivity, extra-tribal adoption, and the American Indian Welfare Act', In *Relative Values: Reconfiguring Kinship Studies*, Franklin S and McKinnon S (eds) Durham, NC: Duke University Press, in press.

Suzuki P T (1980) 'A retrospective analysis of a wartime "national character" study', *Dialectical Anthropology*, 5:1, pp 33–46.

Trimborn H (1983) 'US couple fights for Polish child: Adoption saga', *Los Angeles Times*, 102:I-A, 21 August, p 1.

Zwimpfer D M (1983) 'Indicators of Adoption Breakdown', *Social Casework*, 64, pp 169–177.

US State Department website: http://www.travel.state.gov/orphan

Appendix 1

Table 17.1

Statistics for intercountry adoption in the USA

	Number of ICAs to USA, 1948–1999		
Year	No. of adoptions	Year	No. of adoptions
1948–1962	19,230	1981	4,868
1963	1,481	1982	5,749
1964	1,680	1983	7,127
1965	1,457	1984	8,327
1966	1,686	1985	9,285
1967	1,905	1986	9,945
1968	1,612	1987	10,097
1969	2,080	1988	9,120
1970	2,409	1989	8,102
1971	2,724	1990	7,093
1972	3,023	1991	9,050
1973	4,015	1992	6,472
1974	4,770	1993	7,377
1975	5,663	1994	8,333
1976	6,493	1995	9,679
1977	6,493	1996	11,340
1978	5,315	1997	13,620
1979	4,864	1998	15,774
1980	5,139	1999	16,396

Table 17.2

Major countries of origin of children

1980		1989		1999	
Korea	2,683	Korea	3,544	Russia	4,348
Colombia	653	Colombia	736	China	4,101
India	319	India	648	Korea	2,008
Philippines	253	Philippines	465	Guatemala	1,002
El Salvador	179	Chile	253	Romania	895
Total from *all* countries	5,139	Total	8,102	Total	16,396

Sources: Altstein & Simon (1991); NAIC (1999). US State Department website (2000)

Note: The sum indicates the total number of US international adoptions each year, including a number of children from other sending countries.

18 Pursuing partnerships
Experiences of intercountry adoption in an Australian setting

Jonathan Telfer

Dr Jonathan Telfer is an independent researcher who teaches part time in the Department of Anthropology at Adelaide University, and the School of Social Work and Social Policy at the University of South Australia. His research interests include dimensions of both intercountry and domestic adoption, kinship and identity, the anthropology of emotion, cultural understandings of time and human experience, and the anthropology of the body. His research pursuits have also included field education models for social workers, and the history of correctional practices such as imprisonment and community-based corrections.

Introduction

Australian couples have had a well-established pattern of intercountry adoption, especially since the mid-1970s. Yet the historical, cultural and administrative contexts within which these adoptions have occurred are neither straightforward nor static. More recently, the contours of the Hague Convention have exercised considerable sway in intercountry adoption at all levels, with the Convention coming into full force throughout Australia on 1 December 1998 (Australian Institute of Health and Welfare, 1999).

The federal Attorney General's Department in Canberra is the Commonwealth Central Authority and co-ordination point in Australia for all matters associated with the Hague Convention. The Department provides a focal point for a range of policy, procedural and accountability issues and mechanisms emanating from the Convention. This includes monitoring and responding to developments in each State or Territory. Since relevant legislation exists within the jurisdictions of six States and two Territories (the composite elements of the Commonwealth of Australia), State Central Authorities have been appointed in each of these States and Territories, in order to give effect to local arrangements for intercountry adoption.

Since Australia is constituted by a federation of States, Australian experiences of intercountry adoption involve both federal agencies such as the immigration authorities and state welfare or community services organisations. Yet the intricacies of intercountry adoption in Australia do not merely involve liaison between federal and state bodies. On the contrary, there is considerable variation from State to State in the ways in which intercountry adoptions are processed.

South Australia has been something of an exception in this area, the exceptional status constituting an instance of interest in some contexts and a site for speculation and controversy in others. A single "private"[1] adoption organisation has been licensed to deliver intercountry adoption services since 1992. This organisation is the accredited body through which all prospective adoptive parents must proceed. The organisation is licensed to undertake a variety of functions and negotiations concerning intercountry adoption in South Australia and the Northern Territory, including the provision of Home Study Reports. In 1992, this function was transferred from the then Department for Family and Community Services (a State government body now incorporated into the South Australian Department for Human Services) to a non-government adoption organisation.

The *Australians Aiding Children Adoption Agency Incorporated* (AACAAI), which was established through the sustained efforts of an intercountry adoption parent support group in the 1970s, is based in Adelaide, capital of South Australia. AACAAI is a non-profit organisation that can be taken in this context as a non-government organisation (NGO). The agency is not involved in any intercountry aid or sponsorship. It currently provides a range of services that are central to intercountry adoption in both South Australia and the Northern Territory, including acting as an intermediary between the overseas adoption agency and the client in Australia. For the purposes of this chapter, the Northern Territory can be considered to function akin to a State within

---

[1] In this context, the epithet "private" is used in reference to a variety of organisations that are constituted as independent entities outside the public sector, most commonly on a non-profit basis.

the Australian federal context, having its own parliament and having passed legislation specifically concerning adoption. The Adoptions Services Branch of the South Australian Department for Human Services (DHS) administers the licence and the statutory aspects of effecting the adoption, such as appearing in court when the adoption order is sought and making the final decisions concerning approval of prospective adopters and allocation of a child to a couple. The Adoptions Services Manager of the DHS is the State Central Authority for South Australia, liaising directly with the federal Attorney General's Department in Canberra on matters associated with the Hague Convention. AACAAI's services include assessment of applicants, parent education courses, arranging the placement of children, post-placement support and assessment, as well as direct liaison with agencies in other countries on casework matters, but not on public sector policy matters. AACAAI thus acts as an agency effecting (inter)mediation, similarly to those in Scandinavian countries.

Prior to 1992, social workers in the State government *Department for Family and Community Services* undertook assessments for both domestic and intercountry adoptions. Home studies that are prepared independently of an approved agency are not encouraged in South Australia or other States and Territories and in many instances it is unlawful to do so.

However, partnerships between the public and private sectors in adoption are not confined to South Australia. Aspects of local adoption have been managed by private agencies in New South Wales and Victoria for some time. Services associated with relinquishment of children have also been "outsourced" in those two States. In some Australian States, couples seeking an intercountry adoption have undertaken certain parts of the process themselves, or through parent groups. For example, it is possible for applicants in Queensland to compile their own files and send them directly to an overseas agency. In other States, while it is possible for the couple to contact parties in the other country and negotiate for an adoption directly, such direct contact is not generally permissible. For example, it is unlawful to do so in South Australia. Clearly, in such a system neither the State department nor a private agency acting under licence conditions exerts control over such negotiations.

The fees paid for an intercountry adoption vary considerably from State to State. In New South Wales and Victoria, for example, fees for service amount to some AUD 7,000 (£2,700). In Queensland, fees are approximately AUD 1,000 (£385), but services are apparently minimal. In the Northern Territory, fees of AUD 5,300 (£2,050) are paid to the government, which then pays AACAAI to provide a range of services. In South Australia, AUD 800 (£310) is payable to the Department of Human Services for (compulsory) services provided. A further AUD 4,800 (£1,850) is levied by AACAAI for the provision of a variety of services for the couple.

Eligibility criteria also vary from State to State. For example, couples in a *de facto* relationship are eligible to be considered for intercountry adoption in South Australia, but not in Queensland. Single persons are eligible for intercountry adoption in Queensland, but are only eligible for the placement of a child under special circumstances in South Australia.

The processes involved in intercountry adoption in Australia are characterised by concern at federal level for immigration requirements and health matters, with State legislation and administrative procedures determining much of the machinery that needs to be negotiated by couples pursuing the adoption of a child from another country. Within this demarcation, there is considerable debate within intra-State and inter-State networks concerning intercountry adoption.

While some debate ensues over whether intercountry adoption should be allowed at all, others are committed to pursuing arguments concerning the mode of effecting intercountry adoption. There is no shortage of advocates for various ideological positions, including wholeheartedly privatised services, the abolition of privatised services, less government control or interference, substantially increased government surveillance of all aspects of intercountry adoption and the centrality of disciplines and professions such as psychology and social work versus de-professionalisation of services, with some advocacy for adoptive parent support groups to administer intercountry adoptions. The Australian Intercountry Adoption Network (AICAN) is a network of non-government associations involved in intercountry adoptions. Information concerning the goals of this group, its philosophy, member organisations and other matters are available on the internet (www.topend.com.au/~aican. index.htm).

Couples who seek to adopt children from overseas have often experienced, and continue to experience, a range of emotions and hopes. Various experiences concerning parenthood that precede adoption inquiries and the perception of protracted approval and educational measures often add to senses of frustration and anguish. Some dimensions of current Australian research on the experiences of couples who seek to adopt are noted in the latter part of this chapter. While the experiences of adoptive couples can only ever provide a partial view of the ways in which adoption affects people's lives, detailed familiarisation with the experiences of such couples can contextualise and ground broader policy issues and questions, such as are elaborated below.

It is the variety of issues and dilemmas that congregate around questions of privatisation and concomitant partnerships in intercountry adoption that is the fulcrum for much of this chapter. Such a focus is encouraged by the economic and social climate in Australia (and no doubt elsewhere) that has featured "downsizing", fewer government services and the elliptical appeal of a pervasive "user pays" principle. But more specifically, it is the detailed set of experiences of privatised services in South Australia that generate a series of contentious issues, which offer possibilities for international reflection and debate on a myriad of issues and concerns about exactly how intercountry adoption is implemented in given cultural, social and historical contexts.

The configuration of services in South Australia

AACAAI is the sole licensed private adoption agency in South Australia and the Northern Territory. In South Australia, the couple pursuing intercountry adoption will have some face-to-face dealings with the Adoptions Services Branch of the Department for Human Services. Initial discussions concerning intercountry adoption occur between the couple and the Adoptions Services Branch of DHS. With certain eligibility criteria being satisfied, the couple is formally invited to lodge an application to adopt. Direct contact with Adoptions Services continues until preliminary documents associated with the application are completed by Adoptions Services. After Adoptions Services has forwarded these documents to AACAAI, the couple's interaction will be almost entirely with AACAAI. Overall, the overwhelming amount of the couple's attention will be directed to AACAAI. From the couple's perspective, this organisation is the key to their endeavours to parent a child from overseas and not infrequently the key to parenthood itself. While usually of minor concern to the couple themselves, the structure and profile of the relationship between the government body and the private organi- sation are fundamental to the ethics and efficacy of intercountry adoption.

There are three facets of bureaucratic legitimation for the adoption agency in South Australia: accreditation, approval under South Australian legislation (commonly known as "licence") and funding agreement. The Northern Territory government accredits AACAAI for four years, with a joint review every twelve months, under the terms of the Service Agreement.

During 1999, the South Australian government deliberated over the optimal model of service delivery for South Australia. The government review considered various options, ranging from full "insourcing" to full "outsourcing" of intercountry adoption functions and services. Generally speaking, "insourcing" in Australian contexts refers to the provision of all functions and services within the public body. "Out- sourcing" typically refers to the contracting of services to "private" service providers (either non-government organisations or "for profit" organisations). The desirability of licensing one or more agencies was also considered, together with the option of contracting specific functions to selected agencies, according to very particular kinds of expertise.

A decision was taken to grant a licence for intercountry adoption in South Australia to one private organisation for the next two years. A further review is expected in 2001. While the precise details of this review and its outcomes are obviously matters for the future, at the time of publication there are at least two schools of thought concerning the likely trajectory of the next review.

On the one hand, it is not anticipated that this review will consider whether to transfer the provision of intercountry adoption services back to DHS, but whether there are grounds for issuing a licence to an additional adoption agency. In other words, one school of thought holds that the next anticipated review of intercountry adoption licensing in South Australia is highly unlikely to consider whether to re-locate intercountry adoption services to direct State Government service provision, but to consider whether to extend the existing model of privatisation by licensing an additional private adoption agency. According to this perspective, it is possible to anticipate the likely structural profile of intercountry adoption services in south Australia after the 2001 review if not the number of licensed agencies.

On the other hand, it is also anticipated that the next review will have the opportunity to more fully consider the outcomes of the partially outsourced model of service delivery in intercountry adoption in light of the added accountability imperatives of the Hague Convention on the Protection of Children and Co-operation in Respect of Intercountry Adoption. Similar reviews of the model of service delivery have occurred in other States and Territories. With the exception of the Northern Territory, all other reviews have determined that the full range of services and functions associated with intercountry adoption will remain "insourced". It is this determination of the majority of States and Territories that makes the situation in South Australia both noteworthy and controversial.

In South Australia, a commitment to the government licensing of one or more private adoption organisation(s) appears intact for the foreseeable future. A partnership between government and private sectors seems assured in structure, if not in form.

Intercountry adoption in South Australia has been shaped by a particular mixture of local factors and broader patterns. When coupled with wider national and international economic pressures, the past decade in South Australia has been characterised by a shrinking public sector workforce, the pervasiveness of economic reductionism, the steady waxing of privatisation and the collapse of the State Bank and the ensuing State government debt. While similar trends are no doubt visible in many other locations, the complication of economic stringencies such as the State Bank collapse has tended to intensify and focus the difficulties at a State level. One effect of this has been the encouragement of strategic partnerships between government and the private sector (Encel, 1999; Officer, 1999; Williams, 1997; see also Harding, 1997, for a consideration of public accountability issues and mechanisms in relation to private prisons in Australia and elsewhere).

Within both this general social climate and the specific arrangements of AACAAI's "licensing", a number of issues, dilemmas and options around intercountry adoption can be identified. While having arisen amidst both local and broader circumstances and forces, the issues might constitute catalysts for informed debate in any arena in which the precise details of effecting intercountry adoptions are being considered.

Contemporary issues arising from experiences in South Australia

The most weighty (and contentious) issues that can be gleaned from experiences in South Australia and elsewhere in Australia include:

1. *The extent and nature of government control, surveillance and accountability in intercountry adoption*

Under this ethical and moral umbrella lies a range of questions concerning the extent to which and the ways in which the contemporary nation state can all but guarantee the propriety of mechanisms for intercountry adoptions. Questions of ethical soundness remain irrespective of the degree to which intercountry adoption services are "privatised". The most immediate questions congregate around the means by which the receiving country will be able to demonstrate (within the confines of the Hague Convention and otherwise) that it has acted impeccably, with regard to the best interests of the child. Questions of external auditing, quality control and review inevitably require persistent attention.

The span of time which might be necessary for critical issues to come to light presents challenges of intimidating proportions. In adoption, demands for and the testing of accountability may not occur until the adoptee is well into adulthood. In such circumstances, how might (and ought) public agencies retain overall responsibility? How might public agencies and governments apportion accountability to "private" organisations that are no longer active in adoption or defunct?

2. *What place do (and ought) the "market" and competition have in intercountry adoption?*

This question often arises at the intersection of ideological, moral, economic and political domains. It underpins debates about the desirability of multiple licensed adoption agencies. Exploring these questions often involves confronting fundamental questions of incompatibility between ethical practice in intercountry adoption and configuring human services according to "marketplace" notions and values, with associated assumptions concerning the efficiencies that necessarily ensue from maximising competitiveness. Countries of origin are also likely to hold firm views concerning the propriety and desirability of "competitiveness" in receiving countries.

3. *The issues inherent in privatisation of intercountry adoption services*

The political, ethical and moral dimensions of privatising intercountry adoption services must be seriously debated and clarified prior to service arrangements being settled upon in any given locale. The non-negotiable cast of this point applies as much to the possibility of providing exemplary services to children in need as it does to preventing hasty or ill-advised arrangements for intercountry adoptions to commence.

Ought the processes and debates that centre on "privatisation" to include countries of origin, or only the receiving country? If so, to what extent? Addressing this question involves recognition that intercountry adoption matters, issues and dilemmas in the receiving country may concern countries of origin as well as receiving countries.

4. *The ethics and efficacy of intercountry adoption, and the tensions between them*

Ethics and efficacy constitute primary dimensions of intercountry adoption, but they often appear to be antithetical. While efficacy in intercountry adoption is all too easily equated with the pressing desires

323

and hopes of couples seeking to adopt, ethical practices in intercountry adoption must not be constrained, compromised or denied by the demands of outcome-oriented social pressures. In the final analysis, the ethical fulcrum for intercountry adoption is the child. In other words, the pressures, subtle and otherwise, that are exerted at a variety of levels in the receiving country must not overwhelm or compromise, consciously or otherwise, the care and attention to ethical detail that intercountry adoption requires.

5. *The dreams of couples wishing to adopt from overseas versus the needs of children in other countries and other "stakeholders", such as welfare authorities in the country of origin*

As outlined in later sections of this chapter, the dreams of couples seeking to adopt from another country are highly significant aspects of the intercountry adoption process and the ways in which it might be effected. Yet, the hopes and dreams of couples seeking to adopt must be subordinate to the "best interests of the child". Decisions are sometimes taken in the child's country of origin (and/or the receiving country) that appear to the couple not to be in their interests or favour. The dreams of couples and the needs of the child can appear to be dissociated, even antagonistic forces, emotionally as well as intellectually.

6. *The limits of individual action in intercountry adoption*

There is a myriad of questions concerning the proper limit of action that might be taken by any individual or couple in a "receiving" country. How far ought individuals be able to proceed without approval? How might individually processed intercountry adoption applications fit with an accountable nation state, with the simultaneous tendency to sculpt human services in many areas so that the user of the service performs as much of the task as possible? How are questions of liberty to proceed with an intercountry adoption associated with the need to demonstrate accountability, not only at the local level, but also on the international stage?

7. *Dilemmas concerning the negotiations of agreements with other countries concerning intercountry adoption*

If aspects of the intercountry adoption process are "outsourced" (i.e. contracted from public agencies to non-government agencies or other "private" bodies), which bodies ought to engage in intercountry negotiations over the processes to be followed? Might this involve government representatives from both countries as key players, with representatives from the agencies involved (if any) in both countries as observers and contributors, but not as final arbiters? Can such arrangements not only meet the requirements of accountability, but also foster the kinds of productive, trusting working connections between principals of agencies in different countries that mutual experience and enduring face-to-face relationships can often only provide?

8. *The degree and form of control or influence that parent support groups ought to have on a private adoption agency*

What kinds of relationships are ideal between parent support groups and a private intercountry adoption agency? Ongoing relationships seem to be advisable and parental involvement in education programs for couples considering or pursuing intercountry adoption is valued. Various advantages and disadvantages of certain options need deliberation, such as including representatives of a parent support group on the board of management of the agency.

9. *The degree and form of consultation or influence that adult intercountry adoptees ought to have on a private adoption agency, either through representatives of support groups (where available) or individual inclusion*

What kinds of involvement are ideal between intercountry adoptees who are now adults and a private intercountry adoption agency? Mechanisms that can best utilise the expertise, insights and views of adult adoptees require creativity and sensitivity. While their contribution to policy and operational matters seems desirable, their presence in education programmes for couples considering or pursuing intercountry adoption is equally indicated. Various advantages and disadvantages of certain options need deliberation. How will it be possible to avoid the extremities of inclusion/exclusion, through the complete exclusion of adult adoptees on one hand (as seems to be the case in many instances at present), or the deification of individual experiences on the other hand?

10. *The benefits or otherwise of a single service provider from pre-placement to post-adoption services in any agency, either private or government*

There seem to be distinct advantages in having one agency (either government or private) provide services for couples, from application right through to post-adoption services. Among the benefits are an accumulating knowledge and practice base in agency staff and the length and breadth of commitment by staff in agency to adoptees and the adoptive family.

In South Australia, for couples pursuing an intercountry adoption, AACAAI is experienced as the primary service provider, with DHS appearing to have a less active presence in many stages of approval and pre- and post-placement casework. DHS, however, retains provision of services associated with pursuing a "local" adoption. Such adoptions are sometimes referred to as an "ABC" adoption: an Australian Born Child adoption.

This arrangement means that while continuity of service and ancillary accumulation of practice wisdom is fostered within the single inter-country adoption service provider (AACAAI), continuity of service and ancillary accumulation of practice wisdom concerning "local" (domestic) adoptions ensues in the public agency, DHS. "Local" adoptions have been scarce in South Australia (and other States) in recent years (see Australian Institute of Health and Welfare, 1999).

11. *The rationale for levying fees, together with associating "speed" of placement with fees levied*

While levying fees for services provided for couples is contentious enough in its own right, if combined with pressures on agency staff to effect "quick" placements, the result could be a set of expectations that do not highlight the child as the primary client in intercountry adoption. Excellence of service in intercountry adoption ought not to be, and must not be, confused with promptness. This delineation may pose difficulties in political, social and economic climates that privilege an insistence on the "customer", as well as favouring results over processes.

This factor is complicated in a variety of ways by the kinds of pressures that can be both experienced and generated by prospective adoptive parents, as illustrated in later sections of this chapter.

12. *How to work within the inevitable changes and widespread unpredictability of intercountry adoption*

Given the number and complexity of persons, organisations, cultural expectations and world views that are at work in intercountry adoption, unpredictability is unavoidable. Countries of origin may close down or establish their intercountry adoption programmes, or change criteria or procedures. Numbers sought or available are bound to fluctuate.

Yet, such changes in countries of origin present challenges for receiving countries. While both countries of origin and receiving countries can and do change policies and practices, the question here is how receiving countries might best configure their procedural and auditing mechanisms, so as to not only accommodate changes, but also respond to changes within the parameters of existing policies.

What kinds of configurations of service provision are most likely to be conducive to coping with sudden changes in circumstance? The inevitability of unpredictability must be anticipated when considering other issues, such as outsourcing, privatisation, the place of ideologies that centre on "the market", the responsibilities and accountability of the receiving country and the capacity of any configuration to be seen by all parties to be acting in the best interests of the child.

13. *Which service arrangements enable advocacy for children and/or parents? Which are desirable?*

Is it desirable for an agency in the receiving country to be able to advocate (in countries of origin, receiving countries or both) for a particular child, children in other countries needing adoption generally, and/or couples seeking to adopt? Is the need to be able to advocate a strong argument in favour of "privatised" service provision, such as operates in South Australia? How are various avenues for advocacy associated with the options contained within the spectrum of government-private service configurations, from fully "insourced" intercountry adoption services at one extreme to fully "outsourced" intercountry adoption services at the other extreme?

14. *What value is placed on public funds dedicated to the monitoring of outsourced intercountry adoption services?*

Outsourced or privatised services in intercountry adoption require monitoring and reporting upon, both with respect to the Hague Convention and more generally. How might governments that are hard pressed to meet demands for services value the resources deployed to monitor privatised services?

Allocating public funds for the monitoring of "outsourced" services can appear contradictory. An emphatic need for well-resourced monitoring mechanisms can imply a flaw in the very philosophy that initially celebrates the virtues and benefits of "privatisation" of hitherto public services.

15. *Whether and how to have indicators of success in intercountry adoption*

How might "performance indicators" or other indicators of success be arrived at in intercountry adoption? Ought these to differ for a government agency and a private adoption agency? How might they differ appropriately? How would performance indicators or other measures unambiguously reflect the primacy of the interests of the child?

Further, given that performance indicators are primarily concerned with measurable outcomes in the short term, how might longitudinal research in adoption, over decades rather than months, feed information and results back into milieux where policy and procedures are shaped? In other words, how might longitudinal research be accommodated and exert leverage in climates that favour and require performance indicators, which inevitably address more immediate outcomes?

In various Australian States, considerable lobbying occurs towards individuals or organisations being able to work in the area of intercountry adoption. Governments and public bodies are lobbied by parties that seek freer intercountry adoption on one hand, and by other parties that seek the minimisation or prohibition of intercountry adoption on the other hand. Such lobbying and negotiation makes for a highly politicised area of public life. Yet lobbying and negotiation over intercountry adoption do not occur in a cultural or social vacuum. On the contrary, the cultural, historical and social climate within which these issues are confronted, resolved and reproduced can help us understand the socio-logical dimensions of their form and their importance. The next two sections signal some of the main features affecting the climate surround-ing the perceptions of adoption in contemporary Australian society and patterns arising from recent anthropological research on adoption.

The climate for research in Australia

A number of factors, forces and trends have influenced the ways in which adoption is popularly perceived in Australia in recent years, including through representations in the popular media. Several of these are of particular relevance to the preceding sections of this chapter.

Popular perceptions of the moves to "open" adoptions, combined with the decline in the number of "local" adoptions (sometimes referred to as "domestic" adoptions in other settings), have tended to obscure the (often uncomfortable) conflicts and dilemmas associated with the "rights" and interests of all parties in adoption. Conflicting "rights" are often lifelong issues in adoption, not only for the person concerned, but also their partners, children and other immediate kin as well. To some extent, media reports of contemporary "open" adoptions potentially undermine public understandings of the character of the overall field of adoption, as frequently involving difficult issues that continue to arise sporadically throughout the life of the person(s) concerned.

While "openness" in adoption seems to offer considerable advantages over the secrecy of past practices, it is not without its own difficulties in its current use (Alty et al, 1995; McPhee, 1993). Three factors are especially important. First, the epithet "open" does not always refer to the same concept (Modell, 1999). "Openness" entails a collection of quite heterogeneous notions, practices and values. Such heterogeneity is not always reflected in discourse or the literature.

Secondly, it is sometimes assumed that "open" adoption, by virtue of it constituting the opposite of "closed" adoption, does and indeed must lead to certain (known) outcomes. Research on "open" adoption is required, including longitudinal research, so that all factors can be documented and analysed, including the precise contours of the benefits of "open" practices for various parties whose lives have been affected by adoption (Hughes, 1995).

The third aspect of "open" adoption that is critical is the need to differentiate "open" local adoptions from "open" intercountry adoptions. While both may be possible under certain circumstances, how do the dimensions and dynamics of each differ?

The cultural and political implications of the "stolen generation" have also been influential (see Haebich and Huggins, 1998). The removal of Aboriginal children in previous years has been the subject of much public debate that has been typified by its divisive nature (Fraser, 1998). Paradoxically, media attention to this domain has cast shadows over other realms of adoption in contemporary Australian life. When combined with the conservatism[2] that has characterised much of the Australian political landscape in recent times, this factor has helped to keep the complexities of adoption out of the public spotlight, with the exception of idiosyncratic human interest stories. While powerful in their effects for audiences, such stories do not bring the intricacy or the range of issues around adoption into public arenas for debate or action. On the contrary, such representations work against such a possibility (Hall, 1997; Foucault, 1980).

The preference for permanent care orders rather than adoption orders in some Australian locations, such as Victoria, is framed in certain contexts as constituting evidence "against" adoption. A sustained but subtle trend towards culturally favouring biogenetic connections over social connections in certain articulations of relatedness and kinship, including in popular media portrayals, tends to act in concert with this trend. The

---

[2] The issues sparked by the One Nation party in Australian politics has been one element in this trend.

effect is to minimise the currency, durability, complexity and significance of multiple facets of adoption in contemporary Australian society.

While these features of the Australian social and political landscape generate and constitute forces in their own right, they also need to be assessed within the context of the very specific attributes of the entire field of adoption. As the next section demonstrates, research can provide data to help interrogate the policy-oriented issues cited above in other social and cultural contexts for intercountry adoption.

Anthropology and adoption

Anthropological perspectives, frames of reference and methods bring substantial analytical weight to the constellation of cultural practices and notions under the canopy of "adoption". By seeing adoption as a reflection of, or window on, notions of relatedness, kinship and identity, what are otherwise taken as ordinary patterns or routine matters become sites for cultural inquiry.[3] By using anthropological methods, it is possible to see how similar activities are related to, or refracted by, each other in very significant ways. Following Bourdieu, such constellations of relationships and activities constitute a "field" (Bourdieu, 1986; 1990a; 1990b). The patterns that become visible in the field of adoption are played out across diverse contexts and with diverse "agents" (Bourdieu, 1990b). For anthropologists, when different parts of a field enact various versions of a particular pattern, then it is plain that significant cultural phenomena are at hand.[4]

---

[3] My research explores some of the taken-for-granted elements in the experiences of people whose lives have been affected by adoption – often deeply so. By positioning the taken-for-granted as problematic, it is possible to look for patterns in adoption, not only for adoptees or for adoptive parents, but throughout the arena of adoption. Ethnographic fieldwork over 16 months in South Australia involved compiling data from adoption support groups, networks of individuals and couples, parent education courses, adoptees searching for relatives, adoption privacy lobby groups, and a myriad of other activities that act as a focal point for matters associated with adoption.

[4] Note that while anthropological research methods and ethnographic writing would usually require detailed explanations and examples of instances and examples of the kinds of patterns being referred to, in this chapter I have refrained from so doing, due to space limitation and the broad audience that is anticipated.

One of the most important characteristics of the field of adoption is its politicised cast. This applies to both "local" adoption and intercountry adoption. Those individuals and practices that make up the field tend to stand in relation to each other in particular ways. Often such relational stances are conflictual or ambiguous. This attribute is sometimes visible in the ways in which the "adoption triangle" is discussed, since adoptive parents, relinquishing parents and adoptees are often assumed to have mutually exclusive interests at stake and at heart. For instance, in Australia in recent years, there has been discord over questions of access to information about past adoptions. There have also been reviews of State legislation and public inquiries (see, for example, South Australian Department for Family and Community Services, 1994). That the different agents in the field of adoption have competing or differing interests is a critical factor in the complexity of the issues that have been highlighted in the previous sections.

As a result of reviews of adoption legislation in South Australia in recent years, it is now possible for adopted people aged 18 years or over to obtain access to identifying information about their birth parents, such as their names and dates of birth (if known), as well as any other information in the possession of DHS relating to a birth parent or the circumstances of the adoption. Adult adoptees are also entitled to obtain identifying information about any birth sibling or half-sibling who was also adopted.

Once the adopted person has turned 18 years of age, it is possible for birth parents to obtain the name of the adopted person after the adoption and the names of the adoptive parents. Birth parents may also obtain other general information about the adopted person and the birth parents. Adoptive parents can obtain information about the adopted person's birth parents, provided the adopted person over 18 years of age consents. There is a provision for the Chief Executive of DHS to withhold information which would be an unjustifiable intrusion into the privacy of the person to whom the information relates.

Any party to an adoption can place a veto (restriction) on the release of identifying information about themselves. It should be emphasised that vetoes placed by adoptive parents must not act to prevent contact between the adopted person and the birth parent.

There are also certain provisions which enable the release of information earlier with the consent of all parties, or if it would be in the interests of the adopted person, such as a health crisis of major proportions.

Invariably in the course of public consultation and calls for submissions from interested parties that are inherent in public inquiries and reviews, various parties in adoption have pursued different interests, often based on conflictual relational stances to other parties or groups. Frequently, such enactments of difference have centred on rights to either information or privacy. Often, stasis or changes in people's identity have been threatened or promised by the turns of such political processes. For example, some adult adoptees have pinned their hopes of finding their origins on certain legislative changes allowing access to particular kinds of information. For some relinquishing mothers, on the other hand, such legislative change would have devastating personal consequences as the fact of (and circumstances of) their relinquishment potentially come to public light, thereby threatening the stability of their current domestic circumstances.

Another way of approaching the politicised nature of the field is to note that people strive to bring about, maintain or grapple with senses of various identities and attachments to others within a field that is characterised by conflict as well as by affiliation and harmony.[5] Part of the broader value of anthropological research on adoption is that it highlights the cultural features of our own conceptions of kinship, attachment and identity. In this chapter, it is especially the hopes, dreams and senses of longing by prospective adoptive parents that is central, as they seek to transform their senses of identity, including from "couple" to "parents" in some instances.

The politicised cast of the field of adoption becomes visible with intercountry adoption through the kinds of dilemmas, balances and comparisons of interests that occur between sending and receiving countries, state and private agency, child and parent, and social worker and client.

---

[5] Yet, as Marilyn Strathern notes, Western locations tend to feature a 'cultural bias that encourages Euro-Americans to think of relations as connections rather than divisions, and of connections as cosy, kinship as warm and relating as a nice thing, in general, to do' (1997, p 23).

While various issues around local adoption have been more or less publicly aired at certain times, with intercountry adoption, the profile of the conflictual cast of the field is often less stark. Rather than conflicts of rights and interests being played out in blunt ways (including in persistent media portrayals), in intercountry adoption the parties' interests are not so much taken to be diametrically opposed, as they are construed as delicately counterpoised. Such sensitively configured (but different) interests underpin and fuel the debates and variations in interpretation and priority that earlier sections have signalled.

The experiences of couples pursuing intercountry adoption can help to illuminate and problematise the policy issues outlined earlier in this chapter. Several prominent dimensions of the experiences of couples pursuing intercountry adoption are pertinent to this process. Further, the experiences and aspirations of intercountry adoptive couples can contribute to the problems and senses of partiality that can complicate partnerships over service arrangements, as noted above. While (prospective) adoptive parents constitute only one collection of experiences and views, and while it is critical that the views and insights of all parties help to contextualise and inform the policy-oriented issues that are mentioned above, a glimpse of some of the issues that predominate in their experiences constitutes an example of the imperative to match research findings with difficult policy areas.

The experiences of couples undertaking intercountry adoption

Couples in South Australia come to consider intercountry adoption for a variety of reasons, amidst various circumstances. These include people with children from previous marriages who desire to "complete" their union, as well as couples experiencing different degrees of infertility. Often, couples find themselves under a myriad of pressures in this area: age, social expectations, family pressures and the repeated failure of technological intervention can all add to the imperative to become parents, or to re-experience parenthood with a new partner. Equally, intercountry adoption frequently is perceived to offer the only, or the last, glimmer of hope of ever attaining completeness as a person and as a couple. That parenthood should offer such an avenue to wholeness is of enormous anthropological significance, for this is an entirely cultural set of mechanisms, endeavours and notions (Telfer, 1999; see also Ragone, 1999). It is the amplitude and intensity of the experiences of (prospective) intercountry adoptive parents that simultaneously complicates the policy-oriented issues outlined above, at the same time as they underline the need for precision and attention to detail when negotiating a way through intertwined, contentious policy and practice areas.

Couples do not tend to approach the adoption process with a homogeneous or unranked set of desires or preferences. On the contrary, embedded in the expectations of many couples seeking intercountry adoption are ranked preferences. These ordered options are enormously important in anthropologists' capacity to understand how cultural notions of attachment, kinship and identity are constituted. While not all couples who pursue intercountry adoption are infertile or childless, degrees of infertility and a desire to become parents are potent factors among those who apply to adopt a child from "overseas".[6] The following hierarchy of preferences summarises the culturally ranked alternatives of procreation for many couples, in decreasing order of preference:

- UNASSISTED or minimally assisted procreation.
- ASSISTED procreation
  - using "own" biogenetic material.
  - using donated biogenetic material from a male.
  - using donated biogenetic material from a female.
- ADOPTION
  - Local adoption, very young baby, with no "special needs" characteristics.
  - Intercountry adoption, very young baby, with no "special needs".
  - Intercountry adoption, "toddler", or very young child.

---

[6] Couples pursue adoption for a variety of reasons and amidst a range of domestic circumstances. Some couples seek intercountry adoption for "humanitarian" reasons. Others involve couples who have (biological) children from previous marriages and who wish to "complete" their marriage and their "blended" family by adopting a child *as a couple*.

- Local or intercountry adoption with "special needs".
- Intercountry adoption of older child.
- FOSTERING
  - Longer term fostering or guardianship
  - Shorter term fostering or guardianship

As couples negotiate their way through the alternatives in this hierarchy, they confront possibilities of success (and failure) in their quest to become parents. It would be easy to underestimate exactly what is "at stake" for these people in their pursuit of wholeness (Bourdieu, 1990b). By embarking on the quest for parenthood, individuals and couples place existing and hoped for identities at enormous risk. As couples in this position are acutely aware, there is absolutely no guarantee that embarking on stages of this process will lead to parenthood in any form at all. These dimensions of the "quest" for new identities as intercountry adoptive parents are precisely the kinds of forces that situate the policy-oriented issues elaborated earlier in the chapter in highly emotional, contested and vividly experienced realms for the people concerned.

For anthropologists, it is significant that the preferences embedded in the above hierarchy are "naturalised". This means that the preferences are experienced as entirely straightforward or unremarkable, seeming to be the "natural" order of available options. For anthropologists, such "naturalised" hierarchies signal important attributes of cultural notions of kinship, which are variable across cultural, social and historical setting. As Schneider's (1968) landmark work on American kinship indicated, Western notions of kinship and attachment feature both biological (or "biogenetic") and social foundations as defining cultural characteristics. While this aspect of couples' preferences cannot be pursued in detail here, two points are especially important. First, the above sequence of preferences for parenthood features diminishing concentrations of shared biogenetic substance as the options become less preferable. This characteristic underlines the overwhelming (and increasing) cultural valuing of biogenetic connections in Euro-American cultural contexts. While a biological basis for kinship and relatedness will seem entirely natural to many readers, anthropological studies of a range of cultures have overwhelmingly demonstrated that such a valuing

336

of biogenetic connections is a cultural phenomenon. For example, many cultures measure the degrees and forms of relatedness between persons according to (interconnected) factors such as descent (through the mother, father, or both), or other forms and structures of affiliation, such as lineage or clan (see Parkin, 1997). Secondly, couples pursuing technological assistance with procreation tend to opt for surrendering male biogenetic connections with progeny before female biogenetic connections. Despite technological factors that might seem to explain this at first glance, the persistence of the tendency indicates that this very pervasiveness requires profound cultural notions.

Yet, when couples strive to realise their preferences for parenthood, they also invoke certain cultural dynamics. These dynamics pivot on gender and the quest for a sense of completeness through parenthood.

Quests for completeness and gender

Studying the ways in which couples strive to become parents and the experiences they have in the process also generates information concerning gender, identity and human "agency", the capacity of persons to effect their own destiny in particular ways.[7] Documenting and analysing the needs and experiences of adoptive parents can, with caveats, help contribute to formulating policy frameworks and service delivery configurations that previous sections of this chapter outlined. Similarly, research on adoption can help couples seeking to adopt to understand some of the complex factors and issues that might not be obvious at first glance, especially given the kinds of distressing and frustrating experiences that precede adoption for some couples.

An ethnography of adoption in Australia raises a number of questions about precisely how couples pursue a sense of completeness, both as individuals and as a couple. My research on adoption in Australia suggests that adoption is not only a politicised field, it is also a distinctly feminised one. This is an important aspect anthropologically, since it

---

[7] The benefits of anthropological research on adoption are supported by Terrell and Modell's point that 'adoption can advance theories of . . . creativity, human agency and identity' (1994, p. 160; also Modell, 1994).

involves cultural understandings of gender and the capacity of different persons to move from a state of incompleteness to completeness. In a myriad of ways, various responsibilities, duties, tasks and interests seem to fall primarily (but not exclusively) to women. Whether it is a matter of women acting as the prime movers in strategies to achieve parenthood, women "talking men around", or acting as the "custodians of kinship", women in this field seem to exercise different, often more immediate forms of agency than men (Stivens, 1985). Often this subtle primacy includes feelings of guilt or loss, such that women may be more susceptible to feeling guilty that they could not "give" their husband a child or provide their own parents with grandchildren.

In this cultural setting, relatedness, kinship and efforts to alter fundamental relational senses of identity are first and foremost the province of women (see also Stivens, 1985; Ernst, 1990). While subtle dynamics and expectations also include men, the tendency is for women to assume central positions in a variety of ways. These tendencies are not universal, but cultural. The feminised cast of the field of adoption is linked to the politicised attributes of the field. One of the ways in which this alliance becomes visible is through the cultural construction of emotion, its denigration and subordination in certain contexts and the rendering of women as more prone to "being emotional", especially in relation to matters of kinship and relatedness (Telfer, 2000).

The (often subtle) primacy of women in pursuits of adoption has important implications when considering precisely how the issues and dilemmas outlined in previous sections are likely to affect couples seeking to adopt a child from "overseas". In particular, the intricate but varying forms of both indirect and quite blunt pressures on women and men need to be understood when grappling with the myriad of service delivery options that present themselves in adoption, as noted in previous sections. This is especially so since it is women who often carry unrecognised burdens of responsibility and action in the quest to transform their own identity and that of their partner, through becoming intercountry adoptive parents. The recognition and reflection in broader policies associated with adoption of such gendered patterns of social action constitute a challenge for all practitioners and policy makers.

Time, adoption and kinship

The phenomenon of time in adoption has not been widely researched. Yet certain cultural notions of and practices around the theme of time are absolutely critical to understanding the experiences of the people concerned, the dynamics of the field of adoption and the implications for service delivery. It is people's common experiences of the exigencies of time that tend to fuel and intensify pressures and competing needs and priorities in areas of policy and service delivery, such as have been suggested above. Taking account of the ways in which time is experienced in adoption can help illuminate different people's responses to a variety of predicaments and circumstances associated with (intercountry) adoption (Telfer, 1997).

For example, "time lost" is a phenomenon that is experienced by many persons whose lives have been affected by adoption, including couples adopting from overseas. In relation to intercountry adoption, time lost often encapsulates the experiences of having spent years in striving for parenthood. The pressure of advancing years, the limits of age for adoptive parents and the sheer frustration of running out of time serve to increase the pressures on couples as well as intensifying the personal effects of the pressures.

Similarly, "time waiting" involves experiences that are readily, albeit uncomfortably, identified by intercountry adoptive couples. "Waiting" is an extraordinarily difficult process to entertain, especially when the pressures to "achieve results" are mounting and the horizon of ineligibility looms closer (Crapanzano, 1985). Couples' experiences of "waiting" and pressures on both social workers and couples to "achieve results" combine to exert considerable pressure on adoption services that aim to balance a myriad of needs, priorities and obligations, as previous sections of this chapter illustrate.

Taken together, time waiting and time lost remind us of our limits, of the extent to which humans can actually bring about those ends and longed-for identities that are most deeply desired. As dual temporal phenomena, they underwrite the constraints on couples (and often women most acutely and especially) to effect their own destinies and bring about forms of identity and kinship affiliation that are hoped for and desperately sought. The pressures and time constraints that are involved in quests for identity are examples of themes from research that invite us to appraise the service delivery options and issues that have been noted in previous sections in the light of people's experiences, rather than simply in abstract terms.

Yet, of all the cultural manifestations and understandings of time that infuse and shape experiences in and of adoption, it is the anniversary that permeates the field and exerts powerful influences on experience. Anniversaries constitute very specific expressions of Western notions of chronological time and cyclic time. They enable us to revisit events, occasions and relationships that have powerful anchorage points in and to the past. In the process, they are instrumental in our understandings of the present and the future. Anniversaries both reflect the cultural construction of time and make visible its relational cast. Paradoxically, throughout the field of adoption, anniversaries are occasions for either celebration or dread (Telfer, 1997).

Relinquishment, placement, allocation and "court day" can all constitute enormously important events and anniversaries for various parties whose lives have been affected by adoption. While some anniversaries will be revered by some agents, others are dreaded and mourned every year by others. For example, relinquishing mothers will commonly experience profound, prolonged grief, especially on the anniversary of the relinquishment or birth (Wegar, 1995; 1997). Often, such intense grief is suffered privately, not only on the anniversary itself, but during the inevitable approach of the date on the calendar. Women's private suffering in this context is homologous with Layne's work on women's suffering associated with pregnancy loss (1999).

Anniversaries are equally important for adoptive parents. Couples pursuing local and intercountry adoptions will often celebrate certain milestones in the process. For example, Australian couples undertaking intercountry adoption will typically celebrate any or all of a range of anniversaries: of being allocated their adoptive child, the anniversary of the day they met their child, the anniversary of the child's arrival in Australia and "court day", the day the child and parents are legally transformed from child and "caregivers" to parents and child. Such anniversaries are usually celebrated with particular enthusiasm in the earliest years of the child's presence within the family.

Thus, while intercountry adoptive parents celebrate anniversaries amidst different circumstances from other persons whose lives have been affected by adoption, such as relinquishing mothers, what is significant to anthropologists is that it is the same cultural understandings of "time" and its social mechanisms that enable both celebratory and painful experiences of anniversaries (Telfer, 1997). Social workers and counsellors can work with various parties whose lives have been affected by adoption, to explore the meanings that an anniversary holds for them, and the cultural forces that render such meanings entirely understandable (rather than pathological) for the persons concerned.

Conclusion

Intercountry adoption in Australia takes place within and reflects complex social forces and the interplay of deeply held cultural notions. While the field of intercountry adoption involves distinctive characteristics, current anthropological research indicates that the strategies that are central to its constitution also reflect broader patterns of the pursuit of identities associated with parenthood and kinship. Experiences from South Australia indicate that the configurations of services in intercountry adoption need to be carefully appraised against a backdrop of competing concerns, interests and ideologies. At the same time, the experiences and struggles of couples seeking intercountry adoption need to be consistently given sensitive attention at all levels of intervention and service arrangement, while ensuring that interests of the child come first.

Acknowledgements
I am most grateful to Ms Sue Priest, Executive Officer of the Australians Aiding Children Adoption Agency Incorporated, Ms Cynthia Beare, Manager, Adoptions Services Branch, South Australian Department for Human Services, together with the staff of both organisations, for their willing assistance with my research and the preparation of this chapter.

References

Alty C and Cameron S (1995) 'Open adoption: the way forward?' *International Journal of Sociology and Social Policy*, 15:4/5, pp 40–58.

Australian Institute of Health and Welfare (1999) *Adoptions Australia 1997–98*, Canberra: Australian Institute of Health and Welfare.

Bourdieu P (1986) 'From rules to strategies', *Cultural Anthropology*, 1, pp 110–20.

Bourdieu P (1990a) *The Logic of Practice* (trans. Nice R) Cambridge: Polity Press.

Bourdieu P (1990b) *In Other Words: Essays towards a reflexive sociology* (trans. Adamson M) California: Stanford University Press.

Bourdieu P (1998) *Practical Reason: On the theory of action*, Cambridge: Cambridge University Press.

Crapanzano V (1985) *Waiting: The whites of South Africa,* London: Granada.

Encel S (1999) *Welfare Services and the Private Sector*, Melbourne: Committee for Economic Development, CEDA Information Paper.

Ernst T (1990) 'Mates, wives and children: concepts of relatedness in Australian culture', *Social Analysis*, 27, pp 110–18.

Foucault M (1980) *Power/knowledge: Selected interviews and other writings 1972–1977* (ed & trans. Gordon C), Sussex: Harvester Press.

Fraser R (1998) *Shadow Child: A review of the stolen generation*, Sydney: Hale & Iremonger.

Haebich A and Huggins J (1998) W*ho Will Look After the Children?* St Lucia Queensland: University of Queensland Press.

Hall S (1997) 'The spectacle of the other', in Hall S (ed) *Representation: Cultural representations and signifying practices*, London: Sage.

Harding R W (1997) *Private Prisons and Public Accountability*, Buckingham: Open University Press.

Hughes B (1995) 'Openness and contact in adoption: a child-centred perspective', *British Journal of Social Work*, 25, pp 729–747.

Layne L L (1999) 'True gifts from God: motherhood, sacrifice, and enrichment in the case of pregnancy loss', in Layne L L (ed) *Transformative Motherhood: on giving and getting in a consumer culture*, New York: New York University Press.

McPhee G (1993) 'Exposing adoption myths: access to information about origins in Victoria', *Australian Journal of Social Issues*, 28:2, pp 142–157.

Modell J S (1994) *Kinship with Strangers: Adoption and interpretations of kinship in American culture*, Los Angeles: University California Press.

Modell J S (1999) 'Freely given: open adoption and the rhetoric of the gift', in Layne L L (ed) *Transformative Motherhood: On giving and getting in a consumer culture*, New York: New York University Press.

Officer R R (1999) *Privatisation: efficiency or fallacy? two perspectives*, Melbourne: Committee for Economic Development, CEDA Information Paper.

Parkin R (1997) *Kinship: An introduction to the basic concepts*, Oxford: Blackwell.

Ragone H (1999) 'The gift of life: surrogate motherhood, gamete donation, and constructions of altruism', in Layne L L (ed) *Transformative Motherhood: On giving and getting in a consumer culture*, New York: New York University Press.

Schneider D M (1968) *American Kinship: A cultural account*, New Jersey: Prentice Hall.

South Australian Department for Family and Community Services (1994) *Issues Paper for Review of the Adoption Legislation Act 1988*, Adelaide: Department for Family and Community Services.

Stivens M (1985) 'The private life of the extended family: family, kinship and class in a middle class suburb of Sydney', in Manderson L (ed) *Australian Ways – Anthropological studies of an industrialised society*, Sydney: Allen & Unwin.

Strathern M (1997) 'A return to the native', *Social Analysis*, 41:1, pp 15–27.

Telfer J R (1997) 'Running on time: temporal realms of adoption and Australian kinship', in *Adoption and Healing*, Wellington: New Zealand Adoption Education and Healing Trust.

Telfer J R (1999) 'Individual but incomplete: adoption, identity and the quest for wholeness', in Ryvgold A, Dalen M and Sætersdal B (eds) *Mine – Yours*

– *Ours and Theirs: Adoption And Changing Kinship And Family Patterns*, Oslo: University of Oslo.

Telfer J R (2000) 'Relationships with nobody? "Adoption" photographs, intuition and emotion', *Social Analysis*, 43:3, pp 144–158.

Terrell J and Modell J (1994) 'Anthropology and adoption', *American Anthropologist*, 96:1, pp 155–160.

Wegar K (1995) 'Adoption and mental health: a theoretical critique of the psychopathological model', *American Journal of Orthopsychiatry*, 65:4, pp 540–48.

Wegar K (1997) 'In search of bad mothers: social constructions of birth and adoptive motherhood', *Women's Studies International Forum*, 20:1, pp 77–86.

Williams J L (1997) *Privatisation of Large Publicly Owned Enterprises: A public choice perspective*, Department of Economics, Murdoch University.

Appendix

Table 18.1

Statistics for intercountry adoption in Australia 1988–1998

Year	Number of adoptions
1988–89	394
1989–90	420
1990–91	393
1991–92	338
1992–93	227
1993–94	222
1994–95	224
1995–96	274
1996–97	269
1997–98	245
1988–98	**3,006**

Table 18.2

Number of children and major countries of origin

1990–91		*1992–93*		*1997–8*	
Korea	203	Korea	50	Korea	69
India	41	Sri Lanka	38	Ethiopia	37
Philippines	30	Thailand	26	India	28
Sri Lanka	24	Colombia	26	Thailand	26
Thailand	15	India	20	Philippines	19
Total from *all** countries	393	Total	227	Total	245

Source: Australian Institute of Health & Welfare

*Other countries include Bolivia, Canada, Chile, Guatemala, Honduras, Hong Kong, Poland, Romania and Taiwan.

19 Intercountry adoption in Sweden
The perspective of the Adoption Centre in its 30th year

Gunilla Andersson

Gunilla Andersson was one of the founding members of the Adoption Centre in Stockholm in 1969. The Centre is now Sweden's largest authorised organisation for intercountry adoption. During the past 30 years she has worked with adoption from countries like India, Bangladesh and Sri Lanka. Presently, she works mainly as a pre-adoption and post-adoption counsellor and is also responsible for the Adoption Centre's contacts with researchers on intercountry adoption. She has written widely on intercountry adoption from different perspectives.

Introduction

Sweden today has a population of about 8.9 million, 1.7 million of whom are immigrants of the first or second generation. There are about 40,000 persons adopted from outside the Nordic countries. The majority are from countries in Asia and Latin America, although there are also quite a few from Africa and Eastern Europe (see Tables 19.1 and 19.2 in the Appendix). Other adopted persons, mainly Swedish-born, are estimated at about 60,000, most of them now ranging from 30 to 80 years of age. The adoption of Swedish children by non-relatives is very rare (see Table 19.3 in the Appendix).

The number of internationally adopted children arriving in Sweden has fluctuated over the last 40 years. A peak was reached in 1977 when 1,864 children arrived; there were two additional children from overseas added to the Swedish population by adoption for every 100 that were added by birth (Andersson, 1986). In 1998 there were 928 children adopted from abroad. Adopted children in Sweden have the same legal rights as a child born in wedlock.

In this chapter, I look at the history of intercountry adoption in Sweden and at the development of policies and procedures, with special reference to the role of authorised adoption organisations.

346

The history of intercountry adoption in Sweden

During and after World War II, some Finnish and a few German children were placed in Swedish families and later adopted. But intercountry adoption on a larger scale started in Sweden in the 1960s. It was spurred by the development of transport and mass media. Suddenly we did not merely hear of the plight of children far away, we met them personally when travelling in their countries. We saw them on TV and in the newspapers. Of course this knowledge was available previously and Swedes had travelled abroad but only a few: missionaries, tradespeople and the scientists. Some of them adopted children from countries such as India and Ethiopia.

The adopting Swedes of the 1960s and their children

The first European generation of intercountry adopters has been called the charitable or idealistic generation by many writers and researchers. This is also true of Swedes in that many of these parents did not adopt only out of a desire for a child – they often had one or more biological children already – but also to meet the obvious need of an abandoned child. However, it is necessary to consider the political and ideological context in which these adoptions took place. In Sweden, at that time we had a society where equality was the byword. This sociopolitical view was supported by the scientific trend in the "nature and nurture" debate where the stress was on the latter. Moreover, Swedes were quite a homogeneous population with no colonial past, which resulted in little perceived racism or experience of majority/minority clashes. We also had a fairly open and generous immigration policy, thus making Sweden fertile soil in which the idea of intercountry adoption could grow. The Swedish adopters were convinced that it did not matter that the child came from another country and had another genetic heritage. Once adopted into the new family and society, he or she would become fully Swedish, integrated as a family member as well as a citizen.

At the beginning of this trend, there were more children in need of new families (and legally possible to place) than there were families applying for them. So the social worker or honorary secretary of the orphanage or the juvenile court magistrate selected those they thought

347

had the best potential for survival and adjustment. A certain number of those children were between the ages of four and six, which meant that some families became the parents of children who were considerably older than they themselves had originally thought of adopting. So the first generation of Swedish adopters were the enthusiasts, the pioneers. Their children were the survivors, most of whom had been personally selected either by their carers or by the adopters themselves while residing in or visiting the child's country of origin.

The adopters of the 1970s and their children
In the middle of the 1960s, the government body – the National Board of Health and Welfare – made a procedural agreement with South Korea regarding the placement of Korean children in Swedish families. In 1969, the Adoption Centre was founded by parents who had already adopted and by prospective adopters. So when the involuntarily childless couples discovered the possibility of family building through intercountry adoption, they had one government office and one voluntary organisation to approach. They could also apply on their own directly to children's institutions or to child welfare organisations which were prepared to accept (and sometimes preferred) private/independent applications. In the 1960s and 1970s quite a few adoptions were independent ones.

The parent generation of the 1970s was a durable and patient group. As a group they were among the first truly internationally oriented Swedes. As individuals, many had longed for a child for some years and had perhaps given up hope of ever becoming a family. The organisations abroad were quite sympathetic to these adopters, but the Swedish couples were no longer the only applicants, or even "competing" with just one or two other nationalities. The flow of intercountry adopters increased steadily and this meant that the children's carers saw that these children were wanted by many. They could, therefore, set new conditions for the placement of the children both in respect of the suitability of the parents and of the co-operation between the foreign organisations and the children's representatives. For instance, the adopters of course wanted their children well cared for while the often lengthy adoption process went on. The institutions gladly provided care if the adopters were willing to cover the costs and if the improved child care could also be extended to other children in the same ward or institution. You cannot single out one or two children for medical care and better nutrition; all the children living with the prospective adoptive child needed to benefit from that level of care. The Adoption Centre's response to this need was to collect funds and start special sections for aid and sponsorship work.

These funds were not raised for the adoptions: families covered and still cover their own adoption expenses (including some expenses for the care of other children awaiting adoption). The fundraising was for the children living for longer or shorter periods in the institutions waiting to be reunited with their biological parents or relatives or for other solutions. This improved care resulted in the survival of some more children than previously, which in turn meant that weak or premature babies or children with medical problems also survived and were placed in adoptive families. As a consequence, some children brought their delayed development or medical problems with them into their new families.

By the 1970s, the early adopters who had received children in the 1960s had been taught so much by their adopted children that they realised the importance of preparation for adoptive parents. Special courses were now arranged by the Adoption Centre and parents-to-be discussed their childlessness, their expectations, the child's background, and what they thought it meant to be of a different "race" or ethnicity and grow up in a predominantly white society. These educational activities are still available and today about 90 per cent of all first-time adopters adopting through the Adoption Centre attend one or more of these courses. In this way they also get a chance to create for themselves a support group of adoptive families to add to their existing social network.

So the adopters of the 1970s were a patient lot who took nothing for granted and who were willing to face all odds more than once to become parents. They came from all social strata. They were also a little more knowledgeable and prepared than the pioneers, although the ideology of equality, of sameness, sometimes caused them to stress the similarities between biological and adoptive families too much, thus suppressing the actual differences. Their children were often receiving better care, as the prospective parents could pay for their maintenance and medical care. On the other hand, more children with medical and other problems survived and were adopted.

The adopters of the 1980s

The start of the 1980s brought a new attitude to the concept of inter-country adoption. In the 1970s, couples could wait three or four years for a child; now the waiting time was considerably shorter (which in itself was probably good for the outcome of the placements) and there were nine authorised adoption organisations to choose from. While earlier adopters had considered intercountry adoption a privilege, a gift of grace, the adopters of the 1980s had the chance to call on all the nine agencies, ask what types of children they placed, the length of time it took, and the amount of fees charged. This meant that they got the impression that, once they decided upon an organisation, it was just to "book an order". Of course, each individual family still had their infertility to face, their own anxious wait and hopes and disappointments during the adoption process but, as a general trend, the "shopping around for an adoption" attitude developed.

A positive trend of the 1980s was that now that intercountry adoption was an established way of family building, it was not considered odd or exotic in any way, as almost everybody knew someone who had adopted: a sister, a neighbour, a colleague. This development was, of course, good for the adoptive children; it was also enhanced by the 1989 UN Convention on the Rights of the Child in which the preamble lays down that a child needs a family for his or her full and harmonious development and Article 21 states that an international adoption can be considered if a child cannot be placed in foster care or adoption or be properly cared for otherwise in his or her own country of origin.

The Swedish adopters of the 1980s also had lots of opportunities to become "educated", well-prepared parents. There was now experience and knowledge to draw on, both in the form of articles and books and through support groups of adoptive parents. These support groups were structured as study groups or were informal, spontaneously formed by parents having adopted from the same country, city or institution. Many groups started as preparation groups, initiated and led by a group leader trained by the Adoption Centre, and then took on an existence of its own.

The adopters of the late 1980s also got another bonus: parliament decided to introduce an adoption allowance. This is given to the adoptive family after the finalisation of the Swedish adoption and amounts today to SEK 24,000 (approx £1,800), which is about one-third or one-fourth of the average cost of an overseas adoption. This allowance is regarded as part of Swedish family welfare policy.

To summarise: the adopters of the 1980s, especially the early 1980s, often took too much for granted (an attitude which may be resurfacing at the end of the 1990s). On the other hand, they were a well prepared group who therefore got a better start with their children than many of the adopters of the 1960s and 1970s.

The adopters of the 1990s
The early 1990s brought some drastic changes. From 1987 the number of adopters dropped because the medical profession could help more infertile couples to become parents through donor insemination and in-vitro fertilisation. It had also become increasingly difficult to apply for the adoption of a baby. One of the main reasons for that was that in the late 1980s and early 1990s South Korea, which had been a major "source" of babies, restricted its number of foreign placements. Applicants from Europe, Australia, Canada and the USA sent their applications to the same organisations in Africa, Asia, Latin America and now also Eastern Europe. In 1989, Colombia had 3,000 children (not only babies) for whom the authorities wanted parents abroad – and they had 30,000 foreign applications for adoption. One way for the children's guardians/caretakers to handle this was to set new criteria for an application to be accepted: it could refer to the age of the child applied for – only parents applying for children up to three or four years would be accepted – or a restriction on parents over 30 years of age. And even if you applied for an older child or a child with some medical problems, there would be a long waiting list. Many of the children for whom one had a chance to become a parent, would be labelled "special needs children" in the applicant's own country.

Then the scene changed again. There were "new" countries accepting foreign applicants for their abandoned children: Vietnam and China for instance. (Vietnam is somewhat special. The fact that the Adoption Centre was quite readily accepted as a counterpart for intercountry adoptions is due to the lasting goodwill of our late prime minister Olof

351

Palme and Sweden's long standing political relations with Vietnam.) And in both China and Vietnam, there were many infants given in adoption. As Eastern Europe came into the picture after 1989, adopters who would not have considered a child from India or Thailand or Ecuador, because of racial differences, got the chance to apply for a child from Russia, Poland, Romania or the Baltic countries. Many European children aged between five and seven were easily placed, while the agencies could not find adoptive parents for children of that age from Asia or Latin America.

Gradually, younger children, both toddlers and babies, were being placed from Eastern Europe, as we can see from the Adoption Centre's statistics; in 1993, 56 children from Europe were placed of which 17 (30 per cent) were five years and above: in 1998, 142 European children were placed of which only 25 (17 per cent) were five years and above. You can compare these figures with adoptions from Latin America: 220 children were placed in 1993 out of which only seven (3 per cent) were five years and above, but by 1998, none of the 95 children placed from Latin America were over five years old.

The question arose as to whether the adopters of the five- to seven-year-old children from Eastern Europe were really prepared for the task they had taken on. Did they think that everything would be so much easier because their children's adoptive status was not overtly obvious? Did they believe that the child's traumatic wounds would heal in a better way because he or she was white like themselves? Is it a real fact that if you look like the majority of the population it is such an advantage that it "balances" other difficulties that might exist? We do not know how these adoptions will be experienced by children and parents in the long run; it is too early to tell.

The applicants for a European child are, however, a more hetero-geneous group than suggested above. It was not only their racial origin which mattered; the whole concept of intercountry adoption from countries far away felt for some too unfamiliar, too strange. Some families only considered intercountry adoption when parents were needed in countries which seemed more like their own. Other prospective adopters could not meet the requirements of South Korea or Colombia relating to age and education. Some applicants could as well have applied for an Indian or a Thai child, but found that their application had the best chance of success in Belarus or Romania at the time they decided to adopt. If you compare costs for adoptions from various countries, adopting from Europe was also less costly.

The development of agencies in Sweden

The emergence of today's "authorised organisations" can be traced against the changing context of adoption described in the previous sections. It is a story of evolution and change as parental and societal expectations changed and people learned from their experiences, good and bad. It is also a part of the emergence of a legal and administrative structure designed to ensure that adoption is carried out in the best interests of the child.

When the first intercountry adoptions took place, there was no law governing the intercountry part of them. Only local and central authorities were allowed to mediate in adoptions and proper provisions for intercountry adoptions through organisations were not in place simply because such adoptions were not foreseen as a large-scale phenomenon. The Korean adoptions were, together with a few Greek ones, handled by the National Board of Health and Welfare, which mostly acted as a clearing house and a post office for the applications. When the Adoption Centre started, the organisation kept the authorities informed of its activities and also applied for permission according to the child welfare law to mediate in intercountry adoptions. The application was not granted but the dialogue between the Adoption Centre and the authorities continued. Then the National Council for Intercountry Adoptions was set up within the National Board of Health and Welfare and a structure developed where the formal mediation of applications to adopt a foreign child was conducted through the Council while the Adoption Centre was taking care of the practical handling of the application and the outreach work. In addition to the Adoption Centre, there were other kinds of helplines for prospective adopters and many private/independent adoptions took place.

The Adoption Centre's first years of operation were characterised by much enthusiasm and devotion and less substantial knowledge, and at the same time the organisation benefited immensely from having good administrators amongst the founding members. There were no employed staff, only voluntary workers, and they did their outreach work in many countries, like India, Sri Lanka, Bangladesh, Indonesia, Ethiopia, Colombia and Peru. Some of the workers had personal experience of contacts with these countries, but often they had none and consequently sometimes made mistakes and suffered, or caused, misunderstandings when meeting child welfare workers and the judiciary in the children's countries of origin. However, to the organisation's advantage was the fact that the "other side" knew even less about intercountry adoption and did not have high expectations about the handling of the cases. The Adoption Centre presented its ideas to social workers, doctors, lawyers and officials in the various countries and received co-operation built very much on personal trust. Administrators in the organisation took in these experiences and put them into a structure.

In 1979, a new law came into force, providing for the authorisation of organisations. The Adoption Centre and eight other organisations applied and were licensed. In 1981, the National Council for Intercountry Adoptions was made into an independent authority, the *Swedish National Board for Intercountry Adoptions* (NIA) under the Ministry of Social Affairs, and since then has been responsible for the authorisation of organisations. Many individuals who had helplines of their own inform- ing prospective adopters of adoption opportunities now formalised their existence and applied for authorisation. At the same time, all the Korean cases, earlier handled by the National Board of Health and Welfare, and later by NIA, were then transferred to the Adoption Centre. It was considered more proper that individual cases and outreach work were handled by voluntary organisations in accordance with standards set by NIA.

The new organisations had a difficult time, because entering the intercountry adoption field in 1979 was totally different from the situation of the Adoption Centre in 1969. It was now necessary to be an approved organisation in order to be accepted as a counterpart in the children's countries of origin, and the increased awareness of intercountry adoption as a concept, and its cross-cultural connotations, placed high demands on the professional quality of the work expected, and there was less allowance for mistakes and blunders than in earlier years. Some of the new organisations could not meet the demands and remained in the field for only a couple of years.

Today, there are six authorised organisations with links to agencies in about 25 countries of origin. Four of these have been authorised since 1979; the other two have been established more recently, in 1994 and in 1998. The oldest and largest of these is the Adoption Centre, which was founded in 1969 and currently places about 60 per cent of all children coming to Sweden. There are 23 regional branches with about 600 voluntary workers. The local branches run courses for adoptive parents, both pre- and post-adoption, arrange other activities for adoptive families and act as lobbying groups in adoption matters. The chairpersons of the boards of these local branches convene regularly to discuss policy matters with the central board. Private/independent adoptions are still allowed under certain conditions but these amounted to only 55 (seven per cent) in 1998 and all these arrangements had to be approved by NIA.

The financing of the organisations is mainly done through fees paid by prospective adopters and by parents who have already adopted but remain as member sponsors. Also grandparents and other supporters of intercountry adoption are paying members. There is a government grant administered by NIA but this is small and covers only 1.3 per cent of the Adoption Centre's budget. The smaller organisations receive a proportionately larger sum, as it is seen as being in the interests of the adopters to have organisations of varying size and service to approach.

New areas of work for authorised agencies

At the turn of the century, it is important to mention two additional areas of work on the agenda of the organisations: outreach work in the countries of origin; and post-adoption work with adoptees. Most of the organisations in children's countries of origin have a wider programme for child welfare than intercountry adoption. Adoption is just one part of their work, often a minor part, and increasingly they want their foreign counterparts to also support their other activities. A foreign adoption organisation must then widen its own programme accordingly, meaning that it acquires additional knowledge and financial resources to meet its counterpart's expectations. As you cannot ask the adopting couples or the adoptive families to bear the financial cost of large-scale programmes, you have to find the money elsewhere. We are not talking, as in the early 1970s, about mending a leaking roof or buying some extra clothes for the children or paying for an additional nurse in the baby ward. We are talking about projects like preventing female infanticide, vocational training for children leaving the institution, training of social workers and, in some cases, the promotion of domestic adoptions.

The Adoption Centre's response to these requests has been to collect part of the money needed (about 20 per cent) from adoptive families and then apply for the rest from the Swedish International Development Co-operation Agency. In spring 1999, we hosted, together with two schools of social work and the Swedish committee of the International Council on Social Welfare (ICSW), a conference titled "Children and Residential Care – Alternative Strategies". About 400 participants from 45 countries discussed what could be done to get as many children as possible out of institutions (and what constitutes a "good enough" institution) if no other solution can be found. This conference was mainly sponsored by the Swedish government. So the Adoption Centre is changing its profile, even if adoption is still – in accordance with our authorisation – our core programme. The other Swedish authorised organisations are also finding their own ways to meet the changes and growing demands in the adoption field.

What has also developed with time is a need for a policy and pro-cedure for handling adoptees' wishes for contact with their old institu-tions and for information about their biological background. We are gradually gaining experience in this field, too, as some of the 17,000 adopted persons placed by the Adoption Centre over the past 30 years are now coming back requesting our assistance for this purpose.

Of course, there is also a need for other kinds of post adoption support: for the family with the newly arrived five-year-old having spent his or her entire life in an understaffed orphanage; for the family with the ten-year-old with concept and language deficiencies and severe problems with peer relationships; for the teenager with his or her identity struggle; for the family having difficulties in enabling the adult adoptee to leave the nest. The adoptive family in need of help is supposed to turn to the local community's social welfare or the county councils' child guidance clinics like everybody else. But as the knowledge of what is special in adoption is very unevenly scattered among child experts, counsellors and psychologists, too many families feel they do not receive the assistance they need. And there is unfortunately no centre in Sweden interested in adoption as a special area of social and psychological competence.

Local and central authorities

Local welfare committees

Responsibility for home studies lies with the local authorities all around Sweden. They are responsible for the approval or rejection of applicants (in the Swedish context, the placement of an individual child is always decided by the proper authority in the child's country of origin). The home studies are carried out by trained social workers, sometimes, and preferably, by those also handling foster home placements. These professionals gain a knowledge about children and children's needs, which not all social workers have and which is a great advantage – or actually a must – when you talk to the applicants about adoption. Other-wise it can be difficult to remember that you are the child's representative when you have the childless couple in front of you, desperately longing for a child, and the child is an unknown, unseen individual in another country far away.

Adopters must be over 25 years old and couples may adopt only if married; adoption by single persons is also permitted. After successful completion of a home study, applicants are directed to one of the authorised organisations which have responsibility for linking pro-spective adopters with a child in a sending country – a process we call "intermediation".

NIA (1990) has produced a manual for municipal social welfare committees which gives guidance on how prospective adopters should be counselled and assessed.

The emergence of a central authority

In the 1960s and early 1970s, a central government department handled the applications to South Korea. Then in 1973, the National Council for Intercountry Adoptions was established and took over these Korean cases. The Council also had an advisory role for the local authorities and towards the Adoption Centre. Out of this communication and experience developed a structure outlined in our 1979 law on Intercountry Adoption Assistance. Simultaneously the Council became the Swedish National Board for Intercountry Adoptions (NIA) and its function now is, amongst others, authorisation and supervision of voluntary organisations, distribution of the government grant among the organisations, information to local authorities and to authorities abroad, and approval of adoption orders made abroad. NIA has been designated as the Central Authority for Sweden under the Hague Convention. NIA also produces information leaflets, also available in English, about adoption in Sweden and issues guidelines for assessment and preparation of prospective adoptive parents (NIA, 1990).

NIA handles no individual cases with one exception. Applicants who have a special reason for not applying via an organisation – for example, the adoption of a relative – can apply abroad on their own if NIA considers the procedure in question to be reliable and legal. NIA regularly summons the adoption organisations for discussions and exchange of information. These discussions may concern both the mediation work in Sweden and the outreach work in the children's countries of origin.

How successful has intercountry adoption been?

What does research say about intercountry adoption in Sweden? The most often asked question: Does it work for the adoptees and for the adoptive parents? can be answered. Yes, it does work, if one considers whether the parents and children feel like a family, that there is a sense of belonging on part of the child, that the adoptees succeed in school and in society mostly "like everybody else".

The question of identity is the one most often asked by the opponents of intercountry adoption. They argue that it is not possible for a young

Ethiopian-born, Korean-born or Indian-born adoptee to acquire a "whole", sound identity in a white society without Ethiopian/Indian/Korean parents/close relatives as "objects" of identification. Swedish research does not confirm this fear. Adoptees do achieve a positive identity, sometimes almost totally "Swedish", sometimes more Chilean or Indian, and to a lesser extent Swedish (Irhammar, 1999). But whatever the individual solution to the task of identity building is, it is something they can live with – and live a good life. They have a more difficult job to arrive at this positive solution than most people, i.e. those growing up with their biological parents under "good enough" circumstances, but most manage. How much this is thanks to their innerborn strength, their well-prepared and socially-selected parents, the acceptance of intercountry adoption in society – this we cannot say, but they do succeed.

However, those who have problems tend to have serious problems. For instance, it has been shown that there is an over-representation of internationally adopted teenagers in residential care in Sweden (Statens Institutionsstyrelse, 1999): 39 out of 916 admissions in 1995 were of adoptees (0.23 per cent in comparison with 0.09 per cent in the wider population aged 10–20 years). Staff in these institutions often say that they find it more difficult to help these teenagers and their families than their "ordinary" clientele, which is perhaps not surprising if we think about the additional dimensions adopted persons and their families have to overcome and resolve in areas like belonging, mutual trust and acceptance and the knowledge of this which is required by those trying to help them.

How effective is the Swedish model?

We think we have a system that works well in Sweden. What has contributed to the good outcome? Adoption is a means of rehabilitation for children. It is an individual solution. Children cannot be adopted by collective affiliation or by groups of parents. So the individual need of one child has to be met by the individual need or wish of one set of parents. When these two needs meet across national, ethnic, religious and cultural boundaries, great flexibility and sensitiveness and quick decision-making is a must. We think these goals are best achieved within a voluntary organisation. To survive today, an organisation should also have social work competence and outreach work by people who have cultural competence for the country/countries they work with and relevant language proficiency. And there must always be colleagues with the same or similar competence to discuss with. In many countries of origin, one is accustomed to having non-governmental organisations as agents in child welfare. In Eastern European countries, where the picture is totally different, the fact that there is a government board authorising the organisations and controlling the work delegated to them, in accordance with the 1993 Hague Convention for the Protection of Children and Co-operation in Respect of Intercountry Adoption, guarantees the status of the work. But of course, even before the Hague Convention, the Adoption Centre was careful to choose counterparts subscribing to the subsidiarity principle, seeing intercountry adoption as the fourth alternative for an abandoned child or a child at risk: first must come the biological family, then the extended family, and third adoption in the child's country of origin.

A non-governmental organisation can lobby for issues in a way no public authority can. Child welfare benefits and allowances for the Swedish adoptive family – which are today taken for granted – have been on the Adoption Centre's agenda. Today an increase in the adoption allowances and a qualified post-adoption service are on the domestic priority list and the work for alternative care for children in institutions on the international priority list.

The Adoption Centre has also put in a lot of effort, both in Sweden and abroad, for the 1986 UN Declaration on Social and Legal principles relating to the Protection and Welfare of Children with Special Reference to Foster Placement and Adoption Nationally and Internationally and for the 1989 UN Convention on the Rights of the Child to include an adoption paragraph. The Adoption Centre was also active in forming EurAdopt (see Sterky Chapter 21), an organisation for European organisations for intercountry adoptions where experiences are shared and grounds for common policies are discussed.

We can conclude that the Swedish model, with NIA at the top and the voluntary organisations as the mediating agents, shows that the Swedish government sanctions and promotes family building through intercountry adoption. The highly favourable attitude to adoptive children as future Swedish citizens gives credibility to the work of the organisations.

The social context of intercountry adoption

The developments I have described have of course taken place within a social context. Although fewer children are placed in intercountry adoption today than in the late 1970s and early 1980s, intercountry adoption is an established way of family building and is supported both by the social policy as well as the general public's attitudes. The reason for the decreased number of adoptions is mainly that there are fewer applicants. This is partly due to the success of the new reproduction technologies such as IVF (in vitro fertilisation) and donor insemination, as involuntarily childless couples have always constituted the main applicant group. The economic recession of the 1990s has affected the general birth rate as well as adoption. Unemployment reduces a couple's chances to be accepted as applicants in many countries and, of course, makes it more difficult for them to afford an intercountry adoption. Also, the fact that we have lost our "innocence" when it comes to racism – we must bitterly admit that we are not immune to racist attitudes – might also have some influence.

But 800–900 children are still being welcomed to Sweden each year. I think the main reason is that adoption is seen as quite a normal way of family building. The social welfare policy of the state has taken over many of the family's economic, educational and supportive tasks and religion as a common family bond is often weak. A positive result of this is that the family is not such a closed unit any more, as it was earlier and still is in many countries. This means that the family is more open to take in new members even if they are not related by blood ties, community bonds or religious affinity.

Adult adoptees: what do they say and what role do they want to play in the future?

Despite the wealth of research into ICA in Sweden (see Irhammar and Cederblad, Chapter 8), we still have relatively few studies describing the

361

lives and views of adult adoptees. There are published interviews and individual testimonies showing a variety of both good and bad experiences (von Melen, 1998) and there is one population study in a south-east region of Sweden (Moser, 1997, 1998) showing that adopted persons choose higher education and are rather more successful in gaining employment than Swedish-born young people of today. However, none of this is "conclusive evidence".

There are quite a few groups formed by adoptees from different countries: "Las Esmeraldas" for those adopted from Colombia; "Chile con Carne" for those from Chile; "The Association of Adopted Koreans", "The Association of Adopted Ethiopians" and others. In 1999, when the Adoption Centre celebrated its 30th anniversary, adult adoptees, having for a long time tried to build an umbrella organisation for adoptees, irrespective of country of origin, decided to form a 24th branch of Adoption Centre, a proposal endorsed by the board of Adoption Centre. While the other 23 branches are regional and run by adoptive parents, this 24th branch is not located to any specific area but open to adopted persons from all over Sweden. How should we interpret the adoptees' decision to have their organisation within the Adoption Centre? Have they not cut loose from the parent generation but prefer to remain sheltered by the "mother organisation"? Did the parent generation not push them out of the nest effectively enough and cling to them in an unhealthy way? Do the adoptees support the idea of intercountry adoption and Adoption Centre's way of working so that they feel comfortable to stay within that framework? Or is it only for pragmatic reasons that they remain within Adoption Centre to use its administrative and social network? It is likely that a combination of all these reasons has contributed to its formation.

Today, the 24th branch has existed for a year. Like the other branches, it has its own board. The main activity has been to enable adoptees to meet in small or large groups, where they are the majority, the norm. Thus they can discuss adoption matters without preambles and explanations. They also have a website and a magazine.

One question of common interest is to persuade society to take its responsibility for psychological, practical and economical assistance to adoptees wanting to search for information about their background.

They have also written a letter to the Chairperson of the Adoption Centre stating that they want to nominate a candidate for the Centre's Board for the next two-year period (there are already two adoptees on the Board but they have obviously not been nominated by the 24th branch).

The main advantage of being a 24th branch of Adoption Centre is described as having access to the parent organisation's information channels and professional network.

Concluding thoughts

Will there ever by an answer to the question: Is intercountry adoption right or wrong? Is it successful or a disaster? And for whom is it right or wrong, successful or a disaster?

I have not taken up the perspectives of the biological parents or that of the adopted children's countries of origin, because this is not my task here; I offer only a Swedish perspective. What I think I can confidently say today is this: the Swedish system works well. There is personal commitment and flexibility in the organisations and there is control from the authorities and together they accumulate experience and knowledge.

Intercountry adoption is, as said above, a solution for the abandoned child and for the (mostly) childless couple. It seems that in most cases it has been a beneficial solution for all the members of the adoptive family. The tragic exceptions – which can always be found because nothing in life is ever 100 per cent successful – do not contradict this conclusion. What intercountry adoption will look like tomorrow nobody knows; there are too many political and social factors influencing the future scenario for a reliable prediction. But from the experience we have today, I can only hope the concept will survive as long as there are children in need of a family and adults wanting to build a family with them.

The author may be contacted at: gunilla.andersson@adoptionscentrum.se

The authorised organisations
Adoption Centre
(Authorisation as from 1980, working with Bolivia, Brazil, Bulgaria, Colombia, Ecuador, Estonia, Ethiopia, the Philippines, India, Jamaica, China, South Korea, Latvia, Lithuania, Nepal, Russia, Thailand, Ukraine, Vietnam and Belorussia)
Box 1520, S-172 29 Sundbyberg
Phone: + 46 8 587 499 00
Fax: + 46 8 29 69 28
E-mail: adoption@adoptionscentrum.se

References

Andersson G (1986) – 'The Adopting and Adopted Swedes and their Contemporary Society', in Hoksbergen R (ed) *Adoption in Worldwide Perspective*, Lisse: Swets en Zeitlinger.

Andersson G (1990) 'To feel or not to feel Swedish', *Adoption & Fostering*, 4:91.

Irhammar M (1999) 'Meaning of biological and ethnic origin in adoptees born abroad', in Ryvgold A, Dalen M and Sætersdal B (eds) *Mine – Yours – Ours and Theirs*, Oslo: University of Oslo.

Moser G (1997) *Ett perfekt svenskt uttal lugnar de flesta arbetsgivare*, Unpublished Master's thesis, University of Stockholm.

Moser G (1998) *Jag ar som alla andra fast anda inte . . .* (I am like everybody else, but not quite . . .), Stockholm: Allmanna Barnhuset.

NIA (1990) *Conditions for Associations Authorised under the Intercountry Intermediation Act Intercountry Adoptions – Handbook for Social Welfare Boards*, Stockholm: NIA.

NIA (1990) *Adoption in Sweden, Policy and Procedures concerning Intercountry Adoption Intermediation – Manual for Adoption Organisations.*

Von Melen A (1998) *Samtal med vuxna adopterade (Adult Adoptees Talking)*, Stockholm: NIA.

Von Melen A (1998) *Strength to Survive and Courage to Live: 18 adoptees on adoption*, Stockholm: NIA.

The above NIA publications are regularly updated and the latest version may be obtained on request from NIA. The Swedish National Board for Intercountry Adoptions, Box 22086, 104 22 Stockholm, Sweden, E-mail: adoption@nia.se

Appendix
Statistics for intercountry adoption in Sweden 1969–1998

Table 19.1

Annual number of adoptions of foreign born children

1970	1,150	1987	1,355
1975	1,514	1988	1,075
1976	1,783	1989	833
1977	1,864	1990	965
1978	1,625	1991	1,113
1979	1,400	1992	1,115
1980	1,704	1993	934
1981	1,789	1994	959
1982	1,474	1995	895
1983	1,651	1996	908
1984	1,493	1997	834
1985	1,560	1998	928
1986	1,542		
Total for 1969–1998			39,002

Table 19.2

Major countries of origin of children

	1991		*1995*		*1998*
Colombia	188	Colombia	157	Vietnam	186
Poland	124	Korea	106	China	123
Sri Lanka	109	India	93	Korea	96
India	92	Vietnam	71	Colombia	90
Vietnam	92	China	68	Russia	90
Korea	75	Russia	50	India	78
Total*	1,113	Total	895	Total	928

Source: Swedish National Board for ICA (NIA).

*These totals include adoptions from countries not listed above.

366

Table 19.3

Adoption of Swedish born children 1995–1998

Year	Adoption by non-relatives	Adoption of fostered children	Step-parent adoption
1995	15	19	105
1996	15	12	79
1997	13	20	99
1998	21	26	114

20 Awareness required
The information and preparation course on intercountry adoption in the Netherlands

Albert Duinkerken and Hilda Geerts

Albert Duinkerken trained as a group therapist in the Netherlands and worked for two years on a psychiatric ward in a general hospital. Since 1991 he has worked as an information officer at Bureau VIA and guided almost 200 groups with prospective adoptive parents. Since 1998 he has been chief editor of 'The Adoption Magazine'.

Hilda Geerts trained as a nurse in the Netherlands and worked for 14 years in several psychiatric wards in the United States and in the Netherlands. Since 1992 she has worked as information officer at Bureau VIA and guided about 150 information and preparation groups. She is also responsible for running sessions for English-speaking people in the Netherlands.

Introduction

Intercountry adoption has existed for over 30 years in the Netherlands. Many Dutch couples have adopted children from different countries. In the late 1960s and 1970s many children were adopted from Korea and Indonesia. Soon after that, children came from Sri Lanka, India, Colombia and Brazil. In the last five years an increasing number of children have come from the People's Republic of China. Over 25,000 children have arrived in the Netherlands through adoption and become part of a new family (see Tables 20.1 and 20.2 in the Appendix).

Because there is a long tradition of adopting children from other countries, there is a wealth of information on how these children have developed in Dutch society. These experiences and the results of research carried out at the University of Utrecht were the basis for the legislation on adoption which came into force in 1989. Included in this legislation was the obligation for prospective adoptive parents to be informed by an independent organisation about the legal and educational issues involved in the adoption of a child from a Third World country. In this chapter we would like to tell you about the Dutch adoption procedure and in particular, how the information course in the Netherlands works.

The Dutch adoption procedure

Who can adopt?

On 1 October 1998, a new adoption law (*Act on taking on foreign children for adoption*) came into effect in the Netherlands with the result that not only married couples may register for adoption but so may individuals. The law does not specify that individual applicants have to be single; they could in fact be married or living together. This means that registration is now also open to lesbians and gay men. At the time of registration with the Ministry of Justice, applicants must be under 41 years of age. An exception is made for people who are aged 42–44 on the day that they apply. However, for them the procedure is more difficult than for those aged 41 or under.

Two other rules are important. The age difference between the oldest applicant and the child cannot be more than 40 years at the time the child arrives in the Netherlands. There are possible exceptions to this rule but the Ministry is quite strict. For some of the applicants this means that they can not adopt a young child or a baby. The other rule pertains to the age of the children who are admitted to the Netherlands. They can only come to the Netherlands until the age of six. Children who are older than six years can only be admitted to the Netherlands if they have a younger sibling or if humanitarian reasons make it imperative that the child should come to the Netherlands.

The Central Authority and application

The Netherlands ratified the Hague Convention on 26 June 1998. In accordance with the Convention, the Ministry of Justice (Prevention, Youth and Sanction Policy Department) has been designated as the Central Authority for procedures regarding adoption in the Netherlands. Those wishing to adopt a child from a foreign country must first send their application to the Central Authority. The Ministry of Justice sends the personal data on the applicants to Bureau VIA (Organisation for Information on Intercountry Adoption), which has the task of providing relevant information to the applicants about intercountry adoption.

Information by Bureau VIA

Bureau VIA sends an invitation to the applicants to follow the compulsory information programme. Before coming to the sessions, they will have to pay a fee of about 425 Euro (850 guilders = c £265). The main goal of the programme is to ensure that prospective adoptive parents can make a well-considered choice as to whether they want to adopt a child from abroad. Bureau VIA informs the Ministry (the Central Authority) of applicants' completion of the course.

Home study by the Board of Child Welfare

The Ministry of Justice sends the applicants' data to the Board of Child Welfare to conduct a home study and write a report. The procedure for applicants who were 41 years old or younger on the day they registered with the department is different from the procedure for older applicants. Those applicants who are 41 years or younger are considered to be fit for adoptive parenthood unless the social worker from the Board of Child Welfare finds that they are not. Any finding that applicants are *not* fit must be justified clearly by facts not feelings.

Applicants who are aged 42–44 years are considered unsuitable for adoptive parenthood unless they can prove to the social worker that they are. They have to be suited to raise older children (older than two years at the time of arrival in the Netherlands), and this "suitability" needs to be well defined.

The completed home study report is then sent to the Ministry of Justice with a recommendation to either give or deny consent to adopt. If it is the former, the applicant receives a so-called "permission in principle" from them. The home study report will be sent to one of the intermediary organisations for adoption, which uses it to facilitate the matching between child and parent.

Mediation

Upon receipt of the "permission in principle", the applicant can subscribe to one of the six mediating organisations in the Netherlands which have been licensed by the Central Authority; these are the only organisations allowed to mediate in adoption, and they can only work with parents who have received the "permission in principle". Actual mediation begins when the mediator considers the home study report and has a talk with the prospective adopters. The wishes and limitations (e.g. age and health status, country of preference) of the applicants on the one hand, and those of the mediator on the other, determine the length of time before a child is placed in a family.

Placement

The mediation results in the applicants receiving a proposal for a child: this could take between one and four years. The Dutch mediating organisations are not looking for the right child for the prospective parents but for the right parents for the children who are adoptable. Since the ratification of the Hague Convention in 1998, adoption orders made in other countries are accepted, provided those countries have also ratified the Hague Convention. If this is not the case, an adoption order still has to be made in the Netherlands.

Adoption aftercare

The mediating organisations are required by law to provide aftercare for the adoptive parents and children. In general they do not do this themselves because most of them are small organisations that work with volunteers (mostly adoptive parents). If the adopted child and/or the adoptive parents have problems, the mediating organisation will refer them to institutions where they may receive the care and/or treatment required. The WAN (Adoption Aftercare Centre) takes initiatives to expand aftercare possibilities for adopted children. For example, they try to educate therapists, they establish parent support groups, and they make it possible for several welfare organisations to exchange thoughts and information on adoption.

Bureau VIA (Organisation for Information on Intercountry Adoption)

History of Bureau VIA

In the late 1970s and early 1980s, people started to become aware of the fact that quite a large group of adoptive parents encountered problems in raising their children. For the most part these problems did not originate with the parents, as was thought at first; more often, these difficulties had to do with the background of the children. Some children had been neglected or abused; others had lived in institutions for so long that they had all but lost the ability to trust adults. Starting with a clean slate in a different country with new parents proved to be very difficult for these children.

Books began to tackle the subject (e.g. Grasvelt, 1989, 1999; Egmond, 1987; 1996), and articles in newspapers and magazines as well as television programmemes reported that raising adopted children had its problems. At the same time, research studies were showing that adopted children needed specialised care more often than children who were born and raised in a Dutch family (e.g. Hoksbergen *et al*, 1988; Verhulst and Versluis-den Bieman, 1989; Stams, 1998; Versluis-den Bieman, 1994). This outcome gave cause for concern. It became evident that the trauma inflicted on children in the past had long-term effects despite the resilience children usually possess.

Prospective adoptive parents were not prepared for the difficult task of raising children with behavioural problems resulting from trauma. Social workers and other professionals discovered that adoptive families encountered problems distinctly different from those encountered by families with biological children. When Dutch adoption legislation was modernised in 1989, these findings led to the decision that prospective adoptive parents should be required to follow an information (and preparation) course on all issues regarding adoption, and it was this that led to the formation of Bureau VIA (Van Tuyll, 1994).

Structure of Bureau VIA

Bureau VIA is an independent and unique organisation established by the Ministry of Justice by law to provide information on adoption.

Members of the board of Bureau VIA include representatives of several organisations such as the Ministry of Justice, the Board of Child Welfare, child psychiatrists, and researchers; board members appoint the Director, who is accountable to them.

The Bureau's independence is very important, as it means that it is not under pressure from the mediators or other organisations as to the information it provides. Nor is the information programme designed for the screening of applicants, which takes place later at the Board of Child Welfare. The Bureau's independent status ensures a neutral position with regard to adoption; the Bureau does not promote adoption nor does it try to dissuade people from adoption. The focus is on providing people with information designed to make them aware of what adoption might mean: e.g. that it is not the same as having a biological child, and that adoption is a means of helping children in need by providing them with a family. Bureau VIA does not divulge information about applicants to other parties such as the Board of Child Welfare or the mediators unless consent is obtained. The privacy of the applicants is guaranteed.

The Bureau has its office in Utrecht, where there is a managing director and a secretarial department of three people; 15 information officers in different parts of the country are responsible for running the information courses in various regions. The information officers come from different backgrounds: child therapists, group therapists, social workers and teachers. The most important qualification is that they all have experience in working with groups.

The information programme

The goal of the information programme is to enable prospective adoptive parents to make a well-considered choice whether they want to adopt a child or not. The priority is to give applicants information about what children (may) have been through before they arrive in the Netherlands and the effects this may have on their development and sense of self. Applicants also receive information about legislation, the Board of Child Welfare and mediation.

Information by telephone

The first step taken by people who want to know more about adoption could be to telephone the adoption information line. Other organisations may refer people to the adoption information line if they have not yet applied but want to know more. For many prospective adoptive parents this is their first encounter with the way the procedure works. The information officer tells them about criteria, costs, waiting times, and other matters. This officer may send an application form to prospective parents and an information brochure. He or she often addresses their anxieties, hopes and fears and is able to refer them to others to discuss particular problems.

Information on the internet

Since 1999 anyone interested in intercountry adoption has been able to visit the Bureau's website at www.adoptie.nl. This site provides them with information (in Dutch) regarding all relevant matters, and enquirers can download an application form.

Written information

After registering with the Ministry of Justice, applicants receive a number and their personal data are sent on to Bureau VIA. On payment of the fee, they can follow the information course. They receive a manual on adoption procedures (which is updated annually), and information about the parties in the adoption triangle: the adopted person, the birth parents and the adopters. They also receive four editions of *Adoption Magazine*, a magazine for Dutch birthmothers, adopted persons, both Dutch and those adopted from abroad, and adoptive parents.

Group sessions

After receiving the manual the applicants are invited to the compulsory group sessions. They have to attend six sessions in order to be able to continue the adoption procedure. Each group contains eight applicants, some of whom may be couples, which means that there can be up to 16 people to a group. In the past few years there have been about 140 groups per year. Applicants are placed in groups according to area code. The composition of the groups varies so that in some groups all applicants may be unwillingly childless, while others include people who already have a child or children of their own. The sessions are held in various parts of the country so applicants do not have to travel more than two hours to be able to participate. Applicants can request a written statement declaring that they are required by law to be absent from their work for these sessions and the employer is obliged to make it possible for the employee to attend.

A group session lasts three hours – experience has shown that people are not able to concentrate longer than that for a variety of reasons. Many applicants are not used to attending group meetings, let alone talking about intimate subjects in a group setting, usually with their partner present. The subjects may be new and participants often report feeling fatigued after the sessions. Participants comment that the sessions give them food for thought and conversation as well as an opportunity to think and talk things over; the meetings are usually held at two week intervals.

The sessions are facilitated by two information officers who share the responsibility for the group process and who can split the group if necessary. They can then discuss their observations of interactions between participants and/or themselves. They may also review each of their roles: how interactions were handled; how the information was presented; whether there is cause for change or room for improvement. The pairing of information officers is changed each quarter to prevent the development of set routines. Sessions take place during weekdays; the possibility of weekend and evening sessions was rejected on the basis of cost.

The information officers

A good information officer must be able to present difficult theoretical issues clearly and accessibly, as the level of knowledge on adoption in general and the education level of the applicants may vary a great deal. He or she must be able to initiate group discussions, have the ability to cope with resistance and have some knowledge of child psychology. New information officers receive training before they are allowed to practise.

Information officers participate in supervision groups to discuss their working methods and attend regular team meetings to discuss subjects that are linked to the information programme. Researchers and other professionals are invited to exchange views on adoption, child-raising issues and other subjects. Each year two information officers are able to travel to one of the sending countries to visit foster homes, institutions, and representatives of foreign central authorities.

The focus of the information programme

The information programme is informed throughout by research into the outcome of overseas adoption. Although the starting point is the adoption triangle, in which birth parents, adopters and adoptees are all equally important, the emphasis is on the adopted person. Children are not adoptable because they live in good circumstances; they need adoption because they have been abandoned, abused, or institutionalised. Such experiences are damaging to children and prospective parents need to be well informed about these issues, to enable them to consider their own abilities to help such children overcome their fundamental distrust of adults.

The programme describes the behavioural problems that can result from distressing circumstances and explains the difficulties parents may encounter. Adopted children receive much more special education, are more likely to need institutional care (Verhulst and Versluis-den Bieman, 1989) and need more help from a variety of therapists to overcome emotional problems. Such children are children at risk, not because they are adopted, but because most of them have been living in difficult circumstances before being adopted.

The applicants

About 85 per cent of the applicants have no biological children themselves. Involuntary childlessness is a growing problem in the Netherlands because many men and woman do not start thinking about a family until they are around 30 years old, an age at which fertility problems may increase. However, only a minority of childless couples choose to adopt, as few as one out of twenty according to some studies.[1]

---

[1] So far studies have been limited to couples because single persons were not allowed to adopt until recently.

People who decide to apply for adoption are often strongly motivated to raise a child. On the other hand, they may have had to deal with a lot of frustration on the road that led to this decision. Because of this they may feel angry, hurt or depressed. The requirement to attend the information sessions may add to these feelings, and their frustrations and resistance need to be recognised and addressed.

Apart from this group of childless applicants there are two other much smaller groups: those who have children already, and those who make adoption their first choice. Each group has its own way of resisting the programme: those who have children tend to think of themselves as experienced in raising children, and of therefore being able to raise adopted children. However, surveys (e.g. Hoksbergen *et al*, 1988) show that families with biological children and adoptive children have more problems.

The content of the information programme

The first session

The first session is divided into two halves. In the first part the emphasis is on getting acquainted with each other and with Bureau VIA, and learning about the aims of the course. The fact that the participants are required by law to be present is addressed and people are invited to share their feelings about this.

Participants are asked to share information about their motivation to adopt, levels of awareness and knowledge, what they have told family and friends and their reactions, and how firm their decision to adopt is.

In the second part of the session the first real theme is introduced – the birth parents of adopted children. The purpose is to introduce the notion that every adopted child has or has had birth parents and that this is the case even if a child is an orphan. Participants are asked to think about what this means to them and, if possible, what sort of relationship they feel they may have with the birth parents. This may vary from no relationship at all to wanting to stay in touch. To prompt discussion about this subject and other related themes, a French documentary called *The Fruit of your Loins* is shown. This video film shows women in

Bogota, Colombia who are thinking of giving up their baby for adoption. During the pregnancy they stay in a home called CRAN. Several women are interviewed about why they are considering relinquishing their baby. A few of them have older children as well and part of the video shows these mothers and their children together; viewers can see mothers who care for and love their children. After the video, some issues are raised for discussion. For example:

- What would you like to know about the birth parents of your child and why?
- What would you like to know about the background history of the child that you are going to adopt and why?
- What would you tell your child about the things you know?
- Are there reasons for giving up a child that you would find difficult to accept?
- Would you want to meet the birth parent(s) if it were possible?

In each group a different discussion takes place. It does not matter which discussion takes place as long as the applicants are focused on one of the issues linked to the birth mothers. The discussion concludes this first session. Often people say that the video and the discussion make them confront the "other" side of adoption: it is so difficult to contemplate a mother giving her child up when one is so focused on wanting to have a child.

The second session

The aim of the second session is to introduce the notion that everything that happened to a child in their country of origin may have effects on his or her behaviour once they are adopted. Participants are asked where they stand in the nature versus nurture discussion. There is of course no "right" opinion; scientists cannot resolve this debate. A few examples of the conflicting positions are presented to the participants to consider. For example, a mother who was healthy and took good care of herself or a mother who was ill or drank alcohol during her pregnancy. On the nurture side, it is highly unusual for a child to go straight from them to the adoptive parents. Children have lived in an average of three different situations before they are adopted. For most children, one or more of these was in an institution. That is why a video is shown of life in different institutions in India, Brazil, Colombia, and Romania. The goal is to make people realise that the transition a child makes from living in an institution to living in a family is an enormous one. One big change is that he or she goes from sharing the attention of adults with many other children to suddenly getting the attention of one or two adults 24 hours a day.

Watching the video facilitates imagining the transition. The participants are asked to look at several practical items such as making eye contact, circumstances in which children sleep, cultural habits, ways of comforting children, feeding, environmental influences and language development. A child who was used to holding its own bottle and drinking from it while lying in a crib will probably need some time to get used to being fed by a parent who is holding the child in his or her arms. Also, a child used to always having others around will feel lonely to the point of panic when left to him/herself in a beautiful new room on the quiet side of the house. Hopefully, the future parents will feel inspired to ask questions about these matters once they adopt their child, and possibly even have a look around the institution the child previously lived in.

The second half of this session is devoted to the visit from a parent who has adopted already and who is willing to share his or her experience with prospective adoptive parents. Bureau VIA has a large group of volunteers – adoptive parents who work together with the information officers during this part of the session. About 200 volunteers offer their services. These adoptive parents represent a range of experiences that parents can encounter in bringing up children. Before being involved in the groups, the parents are first interviewed and screened by an information officer. They should be able to speak in a group and must be willing to tell their personal story and answer any questions raised by participants. An attempt is made to invite someone whose story is relevant to each particular group. For example, if many of the participants are around 40 years of age, someone who adopted children older than two is invited. Usually, this is one of the highlights of the programme. It is a story about real live children, not about children who exist only in theory.

The third session

This session is devoted entirely to explaining attachment theory (Bowlby, 1969, 1973, 1980) with the help of a video and through discussion. The theory is described as simply as possible, and its importance in the child's early life is stressed, using the example of a baby's experience of feeding. Different types of attachment – "safe", "ambivalent" and "avoidant" – are also explained and participants are shown how children who experience abandonment or abuse learn not to attach themselves to – or trust – adults (avoidant attachment). These patterns are difficult to change later on in life.

Most children who are adopted (and who have therefore already been abandoned at least once) carry a blueprint inside them which tells them that adults cannot be trusted, and that they should be careful about developing a bond with adults. Some children may even feel that they should not develop a bond with anyone. Most, however, will be able to trust and bond again, provided they come across people who show them that they are worthy of attempting this with. Simply put, this means that the void a child has experienced in early life needs to be filled. This means that an adoptive parent needs to provide safety, reliability, predictability to help an adopted child rebuild attachment and trust. In many groups this theory leaves a deep impression on the applicants. They mostly want to discuss what can be done to create a safe environment for the child in which he or she is able to attach to the adoptive parents.

To illustrate this theory, the video *Do you see me?* is shown. It is about two adopted children in two different families who have both had difficulties with attachment. The boy, Chris, was four, the girl, Minke, was 20 at the time the film was made. They were both one-and-a-half years old when they came to the Netherlands, and they both had negative experiences with the adults in their first year of life. Chris has developed (hyper)active behaviour, which gets a lot of attention; Minke has turned into an extremely well-behaved girl who always seems to be in a good mood. Underlying their behaviour is a fear of intimacy, of being rejected again. In the film they both make some progress on the road to feeling safe with their parents.

Other questions and remarks about both the theory and the movie that are frequently made are:

- Are we better off adopting a baby?
- Are those children going to be OK (those children who lack predict-ability and safety)?
- How long will it take?
- What can we do? Any tips?

The fourth session

At the start of this session an evaluation is done. Participants are asked what they think of the programme thus far. This can be quite useful, especially when there is dissatisfaction, resistance, or even satisfaction among the group members which has not yet been expressed. Having it out in the open may make the next sessions more pleasant.

Next on the programme is a guided fantasy. Participants are asked to imagine that they are approximately five years old again and to listen to a story read by one of the information officers. In this story they are going to be adopted by strangers. The purpose of this is to have people imagine what it feels like when suddenly new parents arrive to take them away from a familiar playroom to the new parents' home in a far away country. Most people are able to imagine this and say they feel scared. When asked they can usually think of several things the new parents might have done, or not done, to make such a child (the five-year-old in the fantasy) feel more comfortable. They become aware that adoption means one thing for the child and another for the adult. They also become aware of the benefits and the limitations in preparing children for adoption. Sometimes group members proceed to do this "exercise" at home with family and friends.

After imagining what it means to leave familiar people and surround-ings it is a fairly logical step to move on to the theory about grieving. As all adopted children have been through separation at least once, but usually more often, they have been through a grieving process as many times. The grieving process for adults is explained (because almost everyone is familiar with that) and then the differences in this process for children are highlighted. Adopted children may experience part of that grief again at different stages of their lives, and they may remain sensitive to loss (real or imagined). To illustrate what grief may look like in the behaviour of a child, a movie called *Johnny* is shown.

It was made in 1989 by two psychiatrists, James and Joyce Robertson, who were interested in children's response to separation. Until then the common belief was that young children especially did not really notice when they were separated. The Robertsons (1989) showed with this movie that this was not true. Johnny is a 17-month-old who has never been away from his mother and is now separated from her for nine days. In those nine days he goes through all the stages of the grieving process: denial, protest, despair, and detachment (acceptance in adults).

In the last part of this session an opportunity is given to the group members to discuss their own thoughts and feelings. Anything goes, but to help the process, cards bearing a variety of statements are passed around. The statements have been made by participants in the past, and deal with:

- unwanted childlessness;
- fertility treatments;
- prospective adopters who have biological children;
- expectations of prospective adopters;
- dividing child care, household tasks, and work outside the home;
- discrimination.

The fifth session
In this session identity formation and conflicts of loyalty are addressed. Of course, all children have to form their own identity, adopted or not. However, for those who are adopted, different emphases may be noticed in that process. A number of facets of identity formation are addressed, such as character, characteristics, place of birth, "race", factual information, and being wanted or unwanted at birth. Participants are asked to look at those aspects of their own identity and to then imagine how things may be different for adoptees.

To explain how adopted children may feel a conflict of loyalty, the theory of Nagy is used (Onderwaater, 1989). Nagy is a well-known family-oriented psychotherapist who has written extensively about issues pertaining to adoptive families. The starting point of his theory is that every individual becomes part of a generation line when he or she is born, and that simply being part of that line means that one feels a sense of primary loyalty to the others in that line. This sense of loyalty does not imply anything about the quality of the relationship; it just means that the bond, the blood-tie, exists. It is a bond that cannot be severed. Even when a mother gives up a child to be adopted that bond between mother and child remains. Nagy argues that being relinquished creates an 'existential rift', which cannot be healed by adoption. It is something that should be acknowledged, so that a child is given the opportunity to incorporate it in its sense of self. Adoption, Nagy says, usually means that a child becomes part of another generation line, that of its adoptive family. This is what may give rise to conflict of loyalties. A child may think: do I feel more loyal to the family I was born into, the family that gave me life, or do I feel more loyal to the family I was adopted into, the family that takes care of me now? Of course this conflict may be exacerbated by a real or perceived wish on the adoptive parents' part for the child to actually make that choice.

Both themes, identity formation and feelings of loyalty, are illustrated in the film, *Birthplace Unknown*, that is shown in this session. It is a film about two girls who were adopted from Korea and who now, at the ages of 19 and 20, travel back to Korea. They were not adopted together, nor were they biological sisters, but they were adopted into the same family, so they became sisters by adoption. They are very different, and therefore deal very differently with the fact that they are adopted, although some of the basic questions they have are very much the same, for example: 'Why was I given up for adoption?' In this session the prospective parents discuss the possibility that their future child may be curious about his or her roots. How would they feel if that were the case? How will the parents help their child, or will the possibility that the adoptee wants to search be threatening to the adoptive parents?

The sixth session
This session is devoted entirely to the procedure after the information programme: the home study by the Board of Child Welfare, registration with one of the mediating organisations, the actual mediation and the follow-up care after the placement of the child. To illustrate why a home study is done, group members might be asked to imagine that a niece or nephew is orphaned. Unfortunately, they cannot take this child in themselves, but they are responsible for finding a family that will take

care of it. The participants usually come up with many of the same criteria that such a family would have to meet as the Board of Child Welfare requires, and more.

Applicants who receive "permission in principle" can register with one of six mediating organisations. The information officers explain what goes into making that choice: demands made by the sending countries, demands made by the mediating organisations, and the circumstances and wishes of the applicants. The combination of these factors eventually leads to the choice of one organisation.

At the start of the contact between applicants and mediator, applicants are encouraged to say what they have in mind with regards to the child they hope to adopt, and what they think they are capable of – often in more detail than will be explored in the home study. This is also the point where it may become evident that the starting point of the future parents may be different from that of the mediating organisation. As outlined before, applicants want to become parents; the organisations want to place children in a family. Those seem to be aims that match perfectly, and often they do, but this is not necessarily the case. A good part of the sixth session is used to make that difference clear, and to stress the importance of applicants knowing what they want.

The future parents are asked to state what they have in mind: the numbers of children, the age(s) of the child(ren), what country of origin they are thinking of and what has this to do with "race", and whether they are willing to consider adopting a child with a disability and why. Hopefully, it helps people to make a well-founded choice when they verbalise what they have been thinking and then get reactions from the other group members. Stating a preference is difficult for many participants as they think each child in need should be welcome in their family. For most people, however, this is not the case. Discussions between group members are often about age and "race". What is a good age for a child to be adopted? Is it all right to state a preference as to "race"?

Conclusions

The adoption information and preparation programme is an effective method to make prospective adoptive parents aware of the issues involved in adopting a child. However, one should not expect miracles from such a programme. It achieves its goal: most future adoptive parents are well aware after attending the programme that a child becoming available for adoption may have been hurt in many ways and that he or she may need special care and attention.

For the most part the information programme is now an accepted part of the total procedure. It is not known how many people withdraw their application because of what they learn in the programme; what is known is that about 33 per cent of all applicants withdraw their application at some point in the procedure. The main reason is pregnancy; another is divorce. Most withdrawals occur before attending any of the sessions – and so before paying.

The social workers of the Board of Child Welfare say that they encounter a different kind of applicant since the information course came into existence. The applicants are more aware of the risks involved in adoption. The mediators also report this difference, which does not always please them, because it makes their job harder. The prospective parents now have a tendency to act as a negotiating party in the adoption procedure instead of acting as a partner of the mediators. In a way, this makes sense because mediators and prospective parents are not necessarily interested in the same thing. The mediator wants to place children who live in difficult circumstances in a family – it is a way of helping a child at risk. What the applicants want most of all is to become a family. In addition, they may like the idea of helping a child. It is essential that future parents are aware of this difference and act accordingly.

A survey carried out for VIA shows that most of the people (about 80 per cent) who have attended the course say that they are satisfied with the way the information was given, although many also say that the information depressed them or made them have doubts.

The past ten years have shown that the programme needs constant updating and development. The information officers do this regularly. The risk of over-encouraging adoption is small because the programme development is carried out by an independent organisation which, along with its "chain-partners" (Central Authority, Board of Child Welfare, mediators and aftercare organisations) work towards the same goal: the wellbeing of children.

The authors may be contacted at Bureau VIA Postbus 290, 3500 AG Utrecht, NL, The Netherlands, Tel + 31 30 232 1550, Fax + 31 30 232 1777 or by e-mail heeren.state@wxs.nl

References

Bowlby J (1969) *Attachment and Loss Vol. 1: Attachment*, New York: Basic Books.

Bowlby J (1973) *Attachment and Loss Vol. 2: Separation*, New York: Basic Books.

Bowlby J (1980) *Attachment and Loss Vol. 3: Loss, Sadness and Depression*, New York: Basic Books.

Grasvelt C (1989) *Justo een gekwetst kind* (*Justo, a hurt child*), Haarlem: De Toorts.

Grasvelt C (1999) *Adoptie, Ouderschap of Hulpverlening* (*Adoption, Parenthood or Welfare work*), Haarlem: De Toorts.

Egmond van G (1987) *Bodemloos Bestaan: Problemen met adoptiekinderen* (*Bottomless Existence: Problems with adoptive children*), Baarn: Ambo.

Egmond van G (1996) *Adoptie in de Adolescentie* (*Adoption in the Stage of Adolescence*), Baarn: Ambo.

Hoksbergen (1986) *Adoption in Worldwide Perspective*, Lisse: Swets & Zeitlinger.

Hoksbergen R, Spaan J and Waardenburg B (1988) *Bittere Ervaringen* (*Bitter Experiences*), Lisse: Swets & Zeitlinger.

Onderwaater A (1989) *De Onverbrekelijke Band Tussen Ouders en Kind: Over de denkbeelden van Ivan Boszormenyi-Nagy en Helm Stierlin* (*The Unbreakable Bond between a parent and his child: The thoughts and ideas of Ivan Boszormenyi-Nagy and Helm Stierlin*), Lisse: Swets & Zeitlinger.

Robertson J and Robertson J (1989) *Separation and the Very Young*, London: Free Association Books.

Stams G J J M (1998) *Give Me a Child until He is Seven: Longitudinal study of adopted children followed from infancy to middle childhood*, Utrecht: University of Utrecht.

Van Tuyll L (1994) 'Intercountry adoption in the Netherlands – compulsory preparation classes for new adoptive parents', *Adoption & Fostering*, 18:2, pp 14–19.

Verhulst F C and Versluis-den Bieman H J M (1989) *Buitenlandse Adoptiekinderen: Vaardigheden en probleemgedrag (Foreign Adopted Children: Skills and behavioural disorders)*, Assen: Van Gorcum.

Versluis-den Bieman H J M (1994) *Interlandelijk Geadopteerden in de Adolescentie: Vervolgonderzoek naar gedragsproblemen en vaardigheden (Intercountry Adoptees in the Adolescent Stage: New research on skills and behavioural disorders)*, Rotterdam: Erasmus Universiteit Rotterdam.

Appendix

Statistics for intercountry adoption in the Netherlands

Table 20.1

Annual number of adoptions of foreign-born children: 1970–1998

Year	Total	Year	Total
1970	192	1990	830
1972	263	1991	819
1974	619	1992	618
1976	1125	1993	574
1978	1211	1994	594
1980	1594	1995	661
1982	1045	1996	704
1984	1099	1997	666
1986	1122	1998	825
1988	577		
		1990–98	6,291
		1970–98	15,138**

Source: Ministry of Justice; **Adoption Centre, University of Utrecht
NB In addition to the figures cited, many children were adopted from Greece and Austria between 1950 and 1970.

Table 20.2

Major countries of origin of children

1970–91*		1992**		1998**	
Korea	3,751	Colombia	181	China	210
Indonesia	3,071	Sri Lanka	97	Colombia	178
Sri Lanka	3,031	India	71	Taiwan	50
Colombia	2,943	Brazil	57	Brazil	50
India	2,365	Ethiopia	49	Korea	42
Brazil	580	Poland	29	Ethiopia	40
Total from *all* countries	19,567	Total from *all* countries	618	Total from *all* countries	825

Sources: *Adoptie Centrum, University of Utrecht; **Ministry of Justice.
The above totals include adoptions from countries not listed in the table.

21 Maintaining standards
The role of EurAdopt

Kerstin Sterky

Kerstin Sterky is a licensed psychologist who worked for the Swedish Adoption Centre from 1974 until her retirement in 1996. During this time she was Senior Programme Officer responsible for adoption co-operation with Thailand, Indonesia, the Philippines and Romania, and had special responsibility for co-operation with Nordic, European and international organisations. She was Chair of EurAdopt in 1996 and 1997 and Swedish representative on the EurAdopt Council from 1998 to 1999.

Introduction

EurAdopt is an umbrella organisation of non-profit accredited European adoption organisations actively working with adoption placements in their own countries of children from other countries. Based on the belief in every child's right to grow up in a family and with respect for the subsidiarity principle,[1] the overall objectives of EurAdopt are:

- to advocate intercountry adoption as an option in child welfare when pursued in the best interests of the child, with respect for his or her fundamental rights, and according to the principle of subsidiarity;
- to establish common ethical rules and promote their application in intercountry adoption;
- to promote co-operation between governments and authorised non-governmental organisations;

---

[1] The subsidiarity principle is clearly expressed in Article 21 of the UN Convention on the Rights of the Child which states that: 'The primary aim of adoption is to provide the child who cannot be cared for by his or her own parents, with a permanent family. If that child cannot be placed in a foster or adoptive home and cannot in any suitable manner be cared for in the country of origin, intercountry adoption may be considered as an alternative means of child care.' The Hague Convention endorses this principle in its Preamble (see Duncan, Chapter 2) where it states that intercountry adoption 'may offer the advantage of a permanent family to a child for whom a suitable family cannot be found in his or her State of origin.'

- to share knowledge in matters of intercountry adoption between participating organisations;
- to work for improved legislation and other measures for the protection of children;
- to promote the ratification or accession of the 1993 Hague Convention by all States involved in intercountry adoption.

History of EurAdopt

Starting in 1980, at the initiative of the Dutch organisation NICWO/ Wereldkinderen (Worldchildren), European meetings were held regularly. Organisations met informally to exchange information and discuss issues of common interest. Apart from topics like parent preparation and support, follow-up studies, etc., questions on ethics always arose in the discussions. The acceptance of intercountry adoption as a means to form a family had led to a "demand" for babies, which in turn had led inevitably to a disturbing growth of malpractice. On several occasions these meetings made statements on ethical issues, sometimes making an appeal to their own authorities, e.g. to control private/independent adoptions.

In the Milano Statement of 1983, fundamental principles for the organisations were laid down, including adherence to and promotion of the then draft UN Declaration and the ICSW *Guidelines on Procedures for Intercountry Adoption* (see Appendix 2). Regular meetings were to be held, at which participants could include any European placement agency officially recognised for work in intercountry adoption. Participation in these meetings was later made conditional on signing the Milano Statement.

A desire for closer and more formalised co-operation was expressed at the meeting in Liege in 1986, especially by the Belgian and Italian organisations. A proposal to establish a European Council of Adoption Organisations (ECAO), with a rather ambitious brief, and to include a secretariat and part-time clerical officer, was discussed at the following meeting in Padua in 1988. While supporting the principle of co-operation, the Nordic organisations in particular did not feel ready to join ECAO (see Appendix 3), but organisations from Belgium, Italy, Switzerland and West Germany signed a charter as a modest beginning for ECAO, while the others confirmed their intention to continue co-operation.

ECAO did not develop any further, but the process of formalising European co-operation was speeded up by the fact that being a proper international organisation was a necessary requirement to obtain observer status at the Hague Conference on Private International Law, which had commenced its deliberations on intercountry adoption in June 1990. So, in 1991 it was decided to formalise this co-operation, and in 1993 EurAdopt was established.

Developing a code of ethics for intercountry adoption

In the beginning of the 1980s, the Swedish organisations had agreed on common ethical rules, inspired by the *Guidelines on Procedures for Intercountry Adoption* (1982), drafted in connection with the meeting of the ICSW (International Council on Social Welfare) in Bombay in 1981 at which several of today's EurAdopt members were present. The Swedish ethical rules later developed into ethical rules for the Nordic organisations and, in March 1993, EurAdopt members agreed a similar set of ethical rules based on the ICSW guidelines and other key international documents:

- The 1986 UN Declaration on Social and Legal Principles Relating to the Protection and Welfare of children, with Special Reference to Foster Placement and Adoption Nationally and Internationally;
- The 1989 UN Convention on the Rights of the Child;
- The 1993 Hague Convention on International Co-operation and Protection of Children in Respect of Intercountry Adoption.

EurAdopt today

At the time of writing (September 2000) EurAdopt has 26 member organisations from 13 different countries (Belgium, Cyprus, Denmark, Finland, France, Germany, Iceland, Italy, Luxembourg, Netherlands, Norway, Spain and Sweden). The organisations vary in structure and size, placing between ten to over 600 children a year. In 1998 the total number of adoptions through EurAdopt members was over 3,400, the children coming from 39 different countries (see Appendix 1).

EurAdopt members vary considerably from each other, not only in size but also in structure and functions. Some are democratically organised with an elected governing board, while in others the board is self appointed. Some are parents' organisations; others are not. Some carry out home studies for applicants, while others do not as this is a duty of local authorities in their country. But, as mentioned above, to be eligible for membership of EurAdopt, an organisation must be currently involved with intercountry adoption placements to their own countries, in direct co-operation with authorities or accredited bodies in the children's countries of origin. Member organisations must also be recognised as adoption intermediaries by their own authorities if such a system of recognition/accreditation exists in their country.

Every other year EurAdopt holds a general meeting with an open session where non-members are also invited. The last three meetings have been held in Antwerp (1996), Florence (1998) and Vasa (April 2000) and the next is planned for Spain in 2002. A council with one representative from each country meets annually and an executive board of three people is elected by and from the members of the council. A new chair from a different country is elected every other year to ensure the post is alternating between member countries. EurAdopt is registered in The Netherlands, and has its secretariat in The Hague.

Apart from an ongoing exchange between EurAdopt or individual member organisations and other parties involved in adoption and related areas, the open sessions at the general meetings create a forum for fruitful discussions and sharing of information and experience as well as an input of new knowledge. Representatives of central authorities will be found here, together with international organisations, experts in the field, adopted persons and adoptive parents.

The role of non-governmental organisations in intercountry adoption

All members of EurAdopt are non-profit voluntary organisations, "accredited bodies" in those countries that have ratified the Hague Convention. EurAdopt believes that such organisations are best placed to provide mediation in intercountry adoption and to safeguard the best interests of the child. Most have greater opportunities than public authorities to visit countries of origin on a regular basis and so ensure that prospective adopters can be given detailed up-to-date information on conditions in those countries.

They are also in a position to monitor the financial side of adoptions. It is extremely important to check the expenses, fees, etc. charged, to make sure they are correct and reasonable. The prospective adoptive parents must not be left to handle this on their own, when they are in an emotionally vulnerable situation where they can hardly be expected to refuse to pay what is demanded of them. To ensure good control over such costs, all financial matters should be handled by a body with a thorough knowledge of the whole area,

In some sending countries, there are hardly any costs, but here the problem is rather the burden on the administration. Applicants naturally have a number of questions and worries while they are waiting for a child. An organisation in the receiving country functions as a buffer between the applicants and the sending country, and can get information about several couples in one letter and take on the task of informing (and calming) individual families. The quality of this service depends very much on the degree of familiarity with conditions in the country, the institution and the adoption offices.

If applicants are free to directly contact the adoption authorities in the country of origin, social workers in that country will have to spend a lot of time answering questions and instructing individual families, instead of proceeding with the necessary work to prepare adoption cases. And the costs for this service to the applicants is forced on an administration that is weaker and poorer than in the receiving country.

Common ground

Thus, long before the adoption in 1993 of the Hague Convention on International Co-operation and Protection of Children in Respect of Intercountry Adoption, many European adoption organisations, both in theory and practice, adopted fundamental ethical rules. Respect for laws, no pressure on mothers to give up their children, no "payment" for children, domestic adoptions to be given priority, and no contact between birth parents and prospective foreign adoptive parents before an inter-country adoption had all been decided to be in the best interests of the child. Should any of these rules turn out to have been violated, the organisation would be quick to react. In their own countries, the organisations had long realised the need for parent preparation, support for adoptive families, and recognised the adoptees' right to know about their background and search for their roots. Exchange of views and experience between the organisations on these matters, as well as in respect of research findings, have been functioning smoothly for many years.

The fact that there is an ongoing discussion on improvement of practice and a search for deeper insights into related problems only illustrates the awareness in EurAdopt members of the importance of high standards in adoption work. As the mutual trust and respect among members, with understanding of constitutional differences among them, continues to grow, EurAdopt now has the strength to tackle emerging issues.

Present concerns

There are at present three areas in particular where the practical adherence to the ethical rules and the principles in the Hague Convention is more difficult. Inter-related in a complicated way are the topics of:

- "reasonable" fees or salaries to lawyers and co-workers;
- avoidance of unnecessary delays in the adoption process;
- financial assistance to other child welfare or development schemes.

The risk of commercialisation of intercountry adoptions is evident and presents a challenge for EurAdopt.

Reasonable fees and salaries

"Reasonable" means concomitant with the service given and the level of remuneration that can be regarded as normal in the community (Article 32.1 and 32.2 in the Hague Convention) (see Duncan, Chapter 2). Introduction of higher levels of payment draws people from their ordinary posts within the legal system, administration, health, social welfare, teaching, etc. This adds to shortage of suitable staff on the domestic level and has negative effects on the national budget. The responsibility for creating this problem is shared between foreign business enterprises, the international organisations, independent adopters and also adoption organisations.

Intercountry adoption can often be seen as a good source of income for individuals involved in the adoption process. However understandable this may be, the risk of a negative development is evident. To avoid being caught in an upward spiral of costs, great care must be applied by the organisations in choosing co-workers, legal aids, etc. Ongoing discussions within EurAdopt seek to reach some sort of "common feeling" where the dangerous upper limits for remunerations are located. EurAdopt has already decided on ways to avoid undue internal competition for co-workers.

Acting expeditiously in the interests of the child

Article 35 of the Hague Convention states that the Contracting States 'shall act expeditiously in the process of adoption'. The responsibility for establishing that a child is free for adoption, and that an intercountry adoption is the best available solution for the child, lies with the sending country, and the organisations in the receiving country shall not play a part in this. However, once it has been established that an individual child should be placed in intercountry adoption, there is a long series of actions that need to be taken, each involving the risk of delays. The question is: who is interested enough in a speedy process for the benefit of the waiting child? Social workers may have other pressing priorities, e.g. tending to victims of floods or rescuing children from prostitution and feel that a child in an institution at least has food and shelter. The underpaid clerk in the court sees no reason to regard the typing of an adoption protocol as an urgency, and so on.

The organisations in the States of origin, with their perspective of the individual case, who are pressed by the waiting adopting parents and their own conviction that the child ought to come as soon as possible to his or her family, also have the financial resources. Thus the handling of these situations with observance of the ethical standards is again dependent on the quality of the co-operation between the organisation and their counterparts. What support is it acceptable for an organisation to give in order to facilitate the process? And how can a feeling be instilled in everyone involved that they are helping one of their own children to a better future, instead of focusing on foreigners as made of money?

Support to other welfare programmes in States of Origin

Here there are two specific pitfalls: the source of the money and the quality of the adoption placements. The children's countries of origin are often poor or have an uneven distribution of wealth, with society often turning a blind eye to the problems of single mothers, abandoned children and poverty in general. Thus, those responsible for the inter-country adoption placements may see them also as a way of getting much needed financial assistance to their other welfare programmes. Similarly, Article 17 of EurAdopt's ethical rules lays down the member organisations' duty to promote domestic adoptions and to help prevention of abandonment in the countries of origin. But following Article 32.2 of the Hague Convention, adoptive parents must only be charged for adoption costs and expenses.

For small-scale projects the organisations can normally raise funds among the families who have already adopted and from the general public. Large-scale projects are of course more demanding, with different possibilities depending on the country. In the Nordic countries, organisations can have joint projects with the government development assistance authority (see Andersson, Chapter 19); in other countries fund-raising is the sole means. In any case, this situation poses a problem for EurAdopt members. It also requires insight into true adoption costs, which is not easy when an authority or accredited institution in the sending country fixes a lump sum per adoption. Here, a joint approach by EurAdopt members working in a specific country, or by EurAdopt itself, might be helpful in clarifying cost issues with the sending country. Another practice established in some countries is to ask for a fixed donation for every adoption case, which again poses particular problems in relation to the principles laid down in the Hague Convention.

Generally, there is a particular risk involved: namely, that priority is not given to the quality of the individual adoption placement, but rather to the overall financial support given. Promises of support for other projects may also be introduced as a factor of competition between organisations for attractive co-operation partners, i.e. those organisations placing children for whom there are many applicants. This is a most delicate issue. Some organisations deal with it by having a policy of giving support only to bodies with whom they do not have an adoption co-operation. Others rely on the integrity of their co-operation partners and trust there is no undue influence in the specific case. What is important is to act in such a way as to minimise the risk of support being conditional on the number of children placed.

Longlasting co-operation between the organisation in the receiving country and its counterparts and co-workers in the sending countries, founded on mutual trust, understanding and shared values, seems to be the best guarantee of intercountry adoptions based on the best interests of the child. The role of EurAdopt is to keep the ethical discussion between its members alive, to stress the importance of prudence in choice of co-operation partners and co-workers, and to maintain an open exchange of experiences and ideas between themselves and other parties in the adoption process.

A broader view

With a shared genuine concern for children and a commitment to high ethical standards, the common base of co-operation is being consolidated in EurAdopt. From a focus on children in need of an adoptive family, EurAdopt has widened its perspective to include other children who, temporarily or permanently, lack the protection of their own families. An example of this is an effort to draw attention to the uncontrolled conditions under which thousands of children from residential homes in Eastern Europe are taken to families in the West for their holidays.

The EurAdopt General Meeting in Vasa addressed this problem in letters to the Council of Europe, Committee on Migration, Refugees and Demography as well as to the Swedish Prime Minister in view of Sweden's Presidency of the European Union from 1 January 2001. In their letter to the Prime Minister the delegates to the General Meeting also pronounced their strong support of the proposal by Euronet, the European Children's Network, for a EU children's policy and the establishment of a special Children's Unit within the EU. The delegates also expressed their hopes that all member and applicant countries of the EU should be strongly recommended to ratify the Hague Convention of 1993 on protection of children.

Appendix 1

Member organisations of EurAdopt at December 1999

Country	Name of Organisation (and number of adoptions in 1998)
Belgium	Amarna (105); Enfants du Monde (40); Enfants de l'Espoir (50); Hogar para Todos Interadoptie (11); Sourires d'Enfants (48)
Cyprus	Cyprus Adoption Organisation (12)
Denmark	Adoption Centre (305); Danadopt (246); Terre des Hommes (73)
Finland	Interpedia (75)
France	Rayon de Soleil de l'Enfant Etranger (170)
Germany	Protestant Adoption Centre (new member in 1999)
Iceland	Icelandic Adoption Society (15)
Italy	Ai Bi (74); CIAI (58)
Luxembourg	AIAE (35)
Netherlands	Wereldkinderen/NICWO (472); Kind en Toekomst (130);
Norway	Adopsjonsforum (332); Children of the World (286) Inoradopt (25)
Spain	Fundacion ADDIA (61)
Sweden	Adoption Centre (546); Children above All (64); FFIA (130); Friends of Children (46)

EurAdopt agencies accounted for all the adoptions in Denmark and Norway; the great majority of adoptions in Sweden and Netherlands; but only 5 per cent of intercountry adoptions in Italy and France.

Appendix 2

Ethical rules of EurAdopt, agreed in 1993

In 1993 members of EurAdopt agreed to supplement existing rules and legislation in respective countries with the common ethical rules as stated in the ICSW Guidelines and other documents cited earlier in this chapter. These follow the order of the ICSW Guidelines and are divided into four parts:

- The biological parents (Articles 1–3);
- The child (Articles 4–11);
- The adoptive parents (Articles 12–15);
- The adoption organisations and their co-operation with other bodies (Articles 16–28).

The full text can be obtained from the EurAdopt website at: http:// www.euradopt.org/ethical-rules.htm

**The *Guidelines on Procedures for Intercountry Adoption*, generally called the ICSW Guidelines, have been reviewed, updated and extended. The booklet, *The Child's Right to Grow Up in a Family – Guidelines for practice in national and intercountry adoption and foster family care* was published in 1997 jointly by the Swedish National Committee of ICSW, International Social Service (ISS), Geneva and the Adoption Centre. The full text can be found on Adoption Centre's home page: http://www.adoptionscentrum.se/guidelines/. Copies can also be ordered from The Adoption Centre, Box 1520, S-172 29 Sundbyberg, Sweden.

Appendix 3

The Nordic Adoption Council in the year 2000

The member agencies of EurAdopt, which are based in the five Nordic Countries, are also members of the Nordic Adoption Council (NAC). In this appendix, Lars von der Leith, who was Chair of NAC from 1997 to 1999, gives a brief account of the Council's current work and philosophy.

Introduction

In 1979 the First Nordic Conference on International Adoption was held and the Nordic Committee on International Adoption was created. It was an informal organisation bringing together most of the adoption agencies and parents' groups in the Nordic countries. As such it played an active part in the work of the Hague Convention and worked closely with the Nordic national authorities responsible for intercountry adoptions and researchers working in the field. Over the years it became clear that a more formal organisation was needed, and on 1 January 1996 The Nordic Adoption Council (NAC) was formed. A loose co-operation between the Nordic organisations with an informal steering body had evolved into a formal association of organisations in five countries, placing more than 2,000 children each year.

Today NAC has 12 member organisations, of which one (*Adoption & Samfund* in Denmark) is an organisation entirely of adoptive families with 3,000 members; two (the Danish *Adoption Centre* and *DanAdopt*) are agencies without members; and the rest contain a parent organisation as well as an adoption agency. Together these organisations have more than 20,000 members. Only a few smaller agencies and parent organisations in the Nordic countries are not members of NAC. All the member agencies are also members of EurAdopt.

All the agencies have paid staff, varying from part-time positions to 30 full-time employees. The agencies between them have more than 3,500 families in progress with 2,600 actually going through a home study.

The start of the new millennium is a moment for reflection and new planning. Intercountry adoption has come a long way since the start of the Nordic co-operation 20 years ago. The national organisations have achieved legal recognition and respect from society for their work and intercountry adoption has become a respected and legally regulated way of forming a family. All five Nordic countries have ratified or acceded to the Hague Convention and this has helped to give intercountry adoptions a stamp of respectability.

Current activities of the Nordic adoption agencies
Preplacement activities
On an annual basis, more than 400 preparation courses and information meetings are offered by the member organisations of NAC, with over 6,000 participants.

Placement activities
Each year more than 2,000 applicants in the Nordic countries are accepted by the sending countries and offered a child, which most of them accept. After this the adoption procedure continues in both sending and receiving country. Between 70 and 80 per cent of the children are under one; 9 per cent are under three; and the remaining 10 per cent more than three years at the time when the matching in the sending countries takes place.

Postplacement activities
These can be seen as meaning all adoption specific activities which facilitate the development of the adoptee during his/her life after the placement, or as an expression which covers all the special needs of a child being brought from one country to live as adopted in a family in another country:

i) *Health*
In the Nordic countries all citizens are equal and adoptees and their family have access to all social and educational services, but we still have to work to ensure that special help is offered when adopted children have particular problems arising from their adoption, such as:
• physical problems connected with changes in living conditions;

- developmental problems – cognitive as well as behavioural;
- psycho-emotional – in both pre-school and school-age children;
- existential and mental health problems during adolescence.

ii) *Post-adoption counselling*
Although the organisations are all devoting resources to this area, there is still much to do before we can talk about a "Nordic model" as in other aspects of adoption. Nevertheless, the area is of great interest to the organisations which feel very responsible for the establishment of good post-placement services. One way of moving forward could be to encourage telephone counselling services, using volunteers who them-selves are adoptees under the supervision of trained counsellors.

Culture and roots
One of the areas where adopted persons differ from others is in awareness of their origins. While they mostly feel like Nordic citizens, they also have the knowledge of having links to another culture. This can influence their lives, especially during the adolescent years, when many think about their roots. The Nordic organisations try to provide services which can help adopted persons come to terms with their culture and origins:

- *Get-together facilities such as children's camps, courses*
Each year the Nordic organisations arrange over a hundred social and/ or cultural events and workshops, involving more than 4,000 partici-pants.

- *Establishment of special interest groups*
There is a growing interest in establishing smaller groups among adoptive families as well as among adoptees themselves. Such groups are often bound together by connection to a country of origin or even to a particular orphanage or agency within that country. The Nordic organisations have a role to play in establishing such groups which may be independent or part of the organisation.

- *Homeland tours*
Between seven and ten "homeland tours" are arranged each year, with

approximately 200 participants. The countries involved so far have been Colombia, Guatemala, India, Korea, the Philippines and Sri Lanka.

• *Summer camps in the country of origin*
Some young adoptees are offered the possibility of participating in a longer stay (4–6 weeks) in their country of origin together with other adopted persons from Europe and the USA. Such camps are established by the agencies in the State of origin.

• *Exploring roots*
In co-operation with the Central Authority and agencies in the country of origin, the Nordic organisations are active in trying to get information for adopted persons about their roots and eventually facilitate meetings between birth relatives and adoptees. This is done on an individual basis or in connection with homeland tours, in accordance with the laws in the country where the child is now living.

• *Reports to States of Origin*
Some 15 of the sending countries require regular reports on their children for either 5 or 18 years. This means that over 1,000 families have an obligation to report to the country for up to 18 years after the adoption has taken place, and a further 2,000 families have to send reports for five years. For most agencies it is an important part of their work to co-ordinate such reports.

Conclusion
There is still is a need to keep up to date in the above fields, which will entail joint work in the future with the authorities, the agencies, the adoptive families and the adoptees. To facilitate this co-operation, it is necessary to work towards acknowledgement of differences amongst both sending and receiving countries in family dynamics, cultural base, health and education systems, and in recognition of adoption as a lifelong process.

All this points to the need for research and information gathering in the area of intercountry adoption and for the distribution of information both to professional groups in contact with adoptees and their families and to the general public (e.g. to counter the influence of racism). One of the goals for NAC will be to help its member organisations to establish such research/information units in each member state.

Acknowledgements

My thanks are due to the organisations for their co-operation in collecting the material for this paper through the NAC inquiries in 1996–98; a special thanks to the board of the Nordic Adoption Council for their valuable comments, and last but not least a thank you to the secretary of the Board, Maria von der Lieth, who translated and printed this report.

22 Child adoption in India
An overview

Andal Damodaran and Nilima Mehta

Andal Damodaran is the Chairperson of the Central Adoption Resource Agency (CARA), which is the Central Authority for adoptions in India. She is also the President of the International Forum for Child Welfare (IFCW) and Vice President of the Indian Council for Child Welfare (ICCW). Mrs Damodaran has helped to organise three International Conferences on Adoption under the auspices of ICCW, Delhi. She has participated as a resource person at several conferences on adoption in India and abroad.

Dr Nilima Mehta is an adoption consultant from India. She has been in the field of adoption and child welfare for 25 years. Dr Mehta is on the Visiting Faculty of the College of Social Work, Bombay University and is a consultant to several NGOs. She is the author of a book, 'Ours by Choice, Parenting through Adoption', published with UNICEF support. Dr Mehta has published and presented papers at national and international conferences. She has recently completed her Doctoral Research on Child Adoption Law in India.

Introduction

Somewhere a child awaits a home
Somewhere a home awaits a child
Adoption brings them together...

Adoption creates a parent–child relationship through a legal process between persons who are not related to each other by birth. Adoption meets reciprocal needs – the child's need to be brought up in a nurturing family environment and a childless couple's need to have a family. It is the most suitable form of rehabilitation for the orphaned child since it involves permanency planning in a substitute family. Adoption is seen as a triad formed by the child, the adoptive parents, and the birth parents, the three corners of which are connected by adoption agencies or children's homes, to form a complete circle.

Adoption is, in a sense, a "beginning" and an "ending": the start of a life long relationship for two individuals who have chosen to be adoptive parents and a termination of parental rights and relinquishment of responsibilities by the biological parents. One might think of adoption as synonymous to grafting: when one grafts, one unites parts from two plants to form a single plant. One cuts a part from the original plant, binds this to the second one and eventually, a completely new and enriched plant grows out of the process. Similarly, adoption involves a wound, a separation from the original relationship of birth and subsequent bonding, assimilation and integration in a new relationship. Through the process of healing, a permanent bond is created between the parents and the child.

Historical perspective

Child adoption in India has been a prevalent social practice from ancient times but with a different perspective. Earlier the practice was to adopt a child from one's own family and a childless couple took it upon themselves to "adopt" and bring up a relative's child. The primary consideration was the interests of the childless adoptive parents, namely, the perpetuation of family name and lineage, protection in old age, performance of death rites and salvation of the adoptive parents. Adoption in this case was influenced by patriarchal values and meant the adoption of only a male child, thereby providing a "son for the sonless". The practice of adoption did not take into consideration the needs of the orphaned, abandoned or destitute child. Adoption was not so much for the child and his/her welfare or to give shelter to the child in need, but a social practice that met the needs of the prospective adoptive parents.

The adoption of an unrelated child into the family had its beginnings in the 1960s and the intervention of child welfare agencies in the process of adoption began only in the early 1970s. This professional intervention led to a systematisation of the process so that the best interests of the child, adoptive parents and the birth parents could be protected. The adoption programme saw significant changes in the 1980s at the legal, social and practice levels. The practice of adoption is also witnessing an evolution in which the "best interests of the child" is becoming the focus of adoption. With the awareness brought about by the UN Convention on the Rights of the Child the attention of child welfare agencies is shifting from "a child for a family" to "a family for a child".

The evolving scenario and changing trends

The attitude towards adoption in urban India has changed significantly in the last decade. The adoption of an unrelated child is now receiving acceptance in Indian society. The sensitisation and awareness of society to this issue has also helped to create a more positive climate for adoption. Today more childless couples and single parents are considering the adoption option. Some years ago it was only the adoption of a male child that was common, but now, more couples are coming forward to adopt girls. The positive experiences of adoptive parents are also encouraging other couples to adopt. Promotional programmes on adoption undertaken by committed social welfare agencies have brought about openness in adoption. However, the stigma attached to "infertility" on the one hand, and "unwed motherhood" on the other, still presents a paradox in society, namely, motherhood being glorified in a married woman and totally stigmatised in a single unwed mother.

Prospective adoptive parents have now begun to understand the legal and social process of adoption and recognise the need to go through child welfare agencies since it ensures legal security, both for the adopted child and the parents. Private adoptions that were done earlier directly through hospitals are discouraged because there is a risk involved in the process and there is no future legal security for the child and the parents.

On the legal front, a Supreme Court judgement pronounced in 1984 gave the desired legal frame of reference to the adoption programme. The judgement provided norms and guidelines for placement of children in intercountry adoption and also introduced the intervention of the government in regulating and monitoring adoption work. The judgement also clearly defined the functions of placement agencies, scrutinising agencies and the voluntary co-ordinating agencies, thus bringing in the necessary checks and balances to ensure that there were no malpractices.

Child welfare agencies began to prepare home study reports, child study reports and other relevant documents for legalisation of adoption through courts. Scrutiny agencies were appointed by the Court to peruse all the relevant documents related to the child and to ensure that the adoption was in the best interests of the child. The voluntary co-ordinating agencies that were established facilitated collaboration between adoption agencies to ensure that every child received an opportunity to be rehabilitated within an Indian family. Whenever this was not possible the child would be placed in intercountry adoption.

The earliest intercountry adoption placements from India were mainly to Sweden, Norway, Denmark, Switzerland and Holland. Adoptions by families in the USA were also a significant number but many of these were not considered intercountry adoptions since they were to families of Indian origin who had migrated to the USA. The adoptions done through child welfare agencies were of unrelated children who were orphans or abandoned, and not of relatives. Even today, as statistics show (Appendix 2), the largest number of intercountry adoptions is to the USA. Again, most of these are not transracial adoptions because in many of them at least one parent is of Indian origin.

As mentioned earlier, the trend towards domestic adoption has definitely improved in the last decade, as evident from the statistics (Appendix 1) from 398 domestic adoptions in 1988 to 1,746 in 1998. However, considering the magnitude of the problem of destitute children in India, this is an insignificant number and more concentrated efforts still need to be made to promote domestic adoptions.

As for research related to adoption in India, it is very limited and does not give any significant data related to the trends and outcome of adoptions. Some of the findings reflect that, except in larger cities, families in India are still in favour of relative or family based adoptions. In urban areas this attitude is changing and more families are willing to adopt an unrelated child; the family and community at large also have a positive attitude towards adoption. Research related to the Indian children's adjustment in transracial adoption is not available. Generally, domestic adoption placements have been successful, according to the experience of most adoption agencies in India.

The legal situation

In India, there is no uniform law of adoption that is applicable to all Indians, irrespective of their religious affiliation. Adoptions in India are at present governed by personal laws of various religious communities and only the Hindus have an adoption law (Hindu Adoption and Maintenance Act 1956) under which they can adopt a child. Personal laws for Muslims, Christians, Parsis and Jews do not recognise complete adoption and hence persons belonging to these communities desirous of adopting a child can do so only through guardianship under the provisions of the Guardians and Wards Act 1890. This does not accord the child the same status as that of a child born to the family. The act confers only a guardian–ward relationship. All intercountry adoptions are also processed under this guardianship law. Hence the legislation related to adoption can be seen as falling into two broad categories: the Hindu Adoption and Maintenance Act 1956 (HAMA, 1956) and the Guardians and Wards Act 1890 (GWA, 1890).

Intercountry adoption of Indian children

The UN Convention on the Rights of the Child clearly declares that every country must first make exhaustive efforts to ensure that the orphaned child grows up in a family within his/her own social-cultural milieu and with parents of the same ethnic origin because this is in the best interests of the child. However, when there are compelling circumstances and it is not possible to locate suitable adoptive parents within their own country, then the next best option is an adoptive family in another country, and the last resort should be residential/institutional care.

Intercountry adoptions involve the universal issue of developing ethical practices that ensure the best interests of the child in the receiving country. Intercountry adoption is the adoption of children from countries that are unable to rehabilitate orphaned, abandoned and destitute children within their own country. In India, intercountry adoptions began in the 1960s and saw a considerable rise in the next two decades. Adoption agencies in the receiving countries established links with child welfare agencies in India and a large number of children were placed for intercountry adoption. Several malpractices were brought to light by the media. There were instances of very small, underweight, malnourished infants being sent abroad, and since there were no checks and safeguards in those days to regulate intercountry adoptions, large sums of money were involved in the process. All this was a cause of serious concern to professionals in the field of adoption and child welfare. Many private individuals were involved in adoption, and children were sent abroad without proper paperwork, health check-ups or supervision. There were no rules or regulations that applied to intercountry adoptions and hence they far outweighed the number of domestic adoptions. In response to some of these problems, a writ petition was filed in the Supreme Court of India. This eventually led to the historical Supreme Court judgement of 1984, which attempted to regulate intercountry adoption.

The purpose of this judgement was to provide certain guidelines and lay down principles, norms and procedures for adoptions in order to ensure the welfare of the child. This was a fairly comprehensive judgement and, in the absence of a uniform adoption law, it provided directives and guidelines in processing adoptions, under the Guardians and Wards Act 1890. This judgement regulated several aspects of adoption in terms of the destitute child, the birth parents, adoptive parents and social welfare agencies, with a view to promoting adoption among Indians. It laid down firm procedures for processing guardianship petitions in the case of intercountry adoptions. The judgement directed that no destitute child could be presumed to be abandoned and free for adoptive placement unless certified as such. The placement agencies were now required to make an application to the Juvenile Welfare Board for declaring a child destitute and thereby legally free for adoption. This procedure was not required if the child had been relinquished by the biological mother or parents in which case a Deed of Surrender was signed by the surrendering party. The relinquishing parent was given a reconsideration period of two months, during which time the child could be claimed and after which the child could be considered legally free for adoption. As per the guidelines, every destitute child who is free for adoption should be first offered for adoption to Indian parents and only then considered for intercountry adoption.

Subsequent to the judgement, the Indian Government formulated a new set of guidelines called the Revised Guidelines to Regulate Matters Relating to Adoption of Indian Children. The aims and objectives of these guidelines were to provide a sound basis for adoption within the framework of the norms and principles laid down by the Supreme Court judgement. The guidelines incorporate within them adoption procedures, rules, regulations, the process to be followed and the role of various agencies in the field of adoption as follows.

The Central Adoption Resource Agency (CARA)
The Central Adoption Resource Agency was set up in 1990 within the Ministry of Welfare, Government of India. The main aim of CARA was to facilitate and promote domestic adoption and regulate intercountry adoption of Indian children. The agency acts as a Central Authority with regard to information about adoption and every intercountry adoption placement is routed through this organisation. CARA issues a recognition certificate for intercountry adoption to Indian adoption agencies and also enlists foreign agencies that wish to sponsor applications of foreign adoptive parents for adopting Indian children. A foreigner can apply for intercountry adoption only through those organisations recognised by CARA. Those countries that do not have a child welfare agency recognised by CARA have to route their applications through an agency that is part of its own government. Currently there are 290 foreign agencies and government departments that are enlisted by the Indian Government for intercountry adoption and 80 Indian agencies that are recognised by CARA for intercountry adoption.

The other functions of CARA include monitoring and regulating the work of recognised child welfare agencies, receiving periodical follow-ups from agencies abroad about Indian adopted children, and organising meetings and training workshops on adoption. CARA also issues a No Objection Certificate (NOC) for every child who is proposed for intercountry adoption. No placement for intercountry adoption can be made without an NOC from CARA. A "quota" system has also been introduced by CARA, whereby a minimum of 50 per cent of children in the care of a child welfare agency must be placed in domestic adoption, and this has helped to promote these. Special needs children are

411

exempted from the quota and they can be placed directly with families adopting from abroad.

Voluntary co-ordinating agencies (VCA)
Voluntary co-ordinating agencies have been set up in several Indian states. VCA is a consortium of all the adoption agencies in a particular area. The role of the VCA is to network among adoption agencies, maintain a central list of prospective adoptive parents and children available for adoption, and actively make efforts to promote domestic adoption. Usually a 60-day period is available to locate a family in India, and if this is not possible, then a "clearance certificate" is issued by the VCA to release the child for intercountry adoption.

Scrutiny agencies (SA)
Scrutiny agencies are appointed in different States by the courts to peruse all the relevant documents of the child, adoptive parents and birth parents to ensure that the child is legally free for adoption and that the adoption is in the best interests of the child. Only when the SA recommends an adoption does the court issue a final court order appointing the pro-spective adoptive parents as legal guardians of the child.

Today all intercountry adoptions are regulated by the judgement of 1984 and the stipulated guidelines of the Government of India. No private adoptions are permitted between individuals, as per these guidelines. All adoptions have to be carried out by child welfare agencies that are recognised by CARA in both the referring country and in India.

Procedures for intercountry adoption in India

The following is the procedure typically involved in an intercountry adoption from India:
- A prospective adoptive couple/individual contacts a child welfare agency or a government agency in their own country that is licensed in their own country and recognised/enlisted by CARA, Government of India.
- An adoption application dossier is prepared as per the requirements. All documents are notarised and then attested by the Indian Embassy/

High Commissioner in the receiving country. If the documents are in any language other than English then the originals must be accompanied by attested translations.

- The referring agency that is sponsoring the application for intercountry adoption contacts a placement agency in India that is recognised by CARA, and sends all the relevant documents. No direct application from prospective adopters is accepted. A complete set of these application documents is also sent to CARA.
- When a suitable child is identified by the placement agency, a referral is sent to the adoptive parents through the referring agency. At this stage, the placement agency has to ensure that only a child who has received a VCA "clearance certificate" for intercountry adoption is referred to a foreign family.
- Once the prospective adoptive parents accept the referral of the child, the application is returned by the referring agency to the placement agency with the necessary authentication. The placement agency then sends this to CARA for approval. A No Objection Certificate (NOC) is issued by CARA if the application is found suitable.
- The placement agency then files an adoption/guardianship petition in the relevant court in their city.
- After the necessary court procedures, a court decree is issued appointing the foreign adoptive parents as guardians of the child. This is only a Guardianship Order and not a final Adoption Decree (except for Hindus). The parents have to complete the adoption in their own country as per the laws of that country.
- Subsequent to the court decree, a passport is prepared for the child and the child can leave the country to be with his or her new parents.
- All costs involved in the process of intercountry adoptions have to be monitored by the court and the Intercountry Adoption Guidelines in India.

ICSW guidelines for intercountry adoption

ICSW has produced a set of international guidelines, which form the basis for intercountry adoption practice (see Sterky, Chapter 21). The following are some of the guiding principles:

1 Any measure taken for the protection of a child must be guided by the

best interests of the child and for upholding the rights of the child.

2   Every child has a right to grow up in a family.

3   When biological parent/s and the extended family of origin do not meet conditions that guarantee the full and healthy development of a child, competent bodies responsible for child welfare and protection must seek alternative solutions. Offering a permanent substitute family to a child through adoption or long-term foster family care when necessitated by circumstances shall prevail over care in an institution.

4   As a priority, the child shall be adopted within his/her own state. Intercountry adoption can be considered as an alternative only after having ensured that a satisfactory solution for the child cannot be found within his/her State of origin.

5   The adoption of children shall not be a source of improper financial or other gain. Abuse, sale and trafficking in children shall lead to severe prosecution.

6   Governments are encouraged to accede to or ratify the Hague Convention on Protection of Children and Co-operation in Respect of Intercountry Adoption. These guidelines are in accordance with its provisions.

Current issues facing adoption professionals in India

The current issues facing the adoption professionals are related to both the practice of adoption and the law of adoption in India. The following are some of the issues that need attention:

- The first and the most important lacuna in adoption that needs attention is the enactment of a special adoption law that is "child-centred, genderjust, secular and enabling" and which is applicable to all adoptions of Indian children.
- Adoption must put the child at the centre of all work, and the best interests of the child should be the guiding factor. The adoption focus must move from "parent-centred" to "child-centred" adoption and from the concept of "child for a family" to a "family for a child". It is necessary that the process of adoption is facilitated and streamlined so that there is no undue delay and so that it does not deter prospective

parents from coming forward to adopt. There should be uniformity in the documentation and procedures all over India, so that there is one set of practice in all States.

- It is essential that the juvenile justice system in India, keeping in mind the best interests of the child, expedites the procedures related to investigating the child's background and declaring the child destitute and thus legally free for adoption.

- It must be ensured that in all child adoption placements there is intervention of a licensed/recognised child welfare organisation. This is necessary in order to prevent any malpractices and prevent direct, private adoptions that do not give any legal protection to the child and the adoptive parents.

- India also needs to evolve a practice and policy on the adoptee's search for "roots" and the right to information about his/her background. More and more grown-up adoptees are returning to India and, as of now, agencies can give only non-identifying information to the child due to a sealed record system. The birth mother's right to confidentiality and the adoptees' right to information are conflicting rights and, considering the socio-cultural realities in India, this issue needs to be looked at from the perspective of all persons involved.

Conclusion

In all matters related to intercountry adoption of Indian children, efforts must be made to follow the provisions of the UN Convention on the Rights of the Child, the ICSW Guidelines on Adoption and the Hague Convention. Once all the clauses of the Hague Convention are adhered to, India can consider ratifying it. The National Policy for Children in India considers children as a supremely important asset of the country; hence all efforts must be made to rehabilitate the child in his/her own socio-cultural milieu through the promotion of domestic adoptions. However, there are some children for whom it may not be easy to find homes within India, in which case intercountry adoption would definitely be the preferred option over institutional care.

Child adoption in India clearly needs a paradigm shift, from "parent-centred" adoption to "child-centred" adoption. Intervention strategies at the level of lobbying for a special law on child adoption must focus on the need for a "child just" adoption law. Activists involved in children's rights need to draw attention to the marginalised and neglected group of homeless children. A new construct of "child rights and child protection" must be the central theme for reforms in the sphere of child welfare.

The authors may be contacted at:

Mrs Andal Damodaran
Indian Council for Child Welfare, T.N.
5, III Main Road West
Shenoy Nagar
Chennai – 600 030
India

Dr Nilima Mehta
Family Service Centre
Eucharistic Congress Building III
5 Convent Street
Mumbai – 400 001
India

Appendix 1

Table 22.1

A statistical profile of Indian children placed in intercountry adoption and domestic adoption

Year	Intercountry adoption	Domestic adoption
1988	1,661	398
1989	1,213	757
1990	1,272	1,075
1991	1,190	936
1992	1,007	1,293
1993	1,134	1,382
1994	1,128	1,409
1995	1,236	1,424
1996	990	1,623
1997	1,026	1,330
1998	1,406	1,746

Source: Central Adoption Resource Agency (CARA), Government of India.

Appendix 2

Table 22.2
Distribution by country of Indian children adopted in 1999

Country	No.
USA	265
Denmark	119
Italy	96
Spain	93
Netherlands	55
France	45
Germany	38
Norway	36
Sweden	30
Belgium	26
Australia	25
Austria	25
Gulf countries	23
Switzerland	18
United Kingdom	18
Canada	11
New Zealand	5
Singapore	5
Mauritius	2
Thailand	2
Africa	1
Indonesia	1
Ireland	1
Kuwait	1

Source: Central Adoption Resource Agency (CARA), Government of India.

23 A home away from home
The experience of an Indian child welfare programme

Neena Macedo

Neena Macedo is Treasurer of the Delhi Council for Child Welfare.

In the aftermath of the Partition of India in 1947,[1] when one of the largest known migrations of people took place, the bloodshed and violence left in its wake thousands of families either destroyed or broken; children were lost in the melée, and would have been largely overlooked had it not been for Prime Minister Nehru's legendary devotion to children. He asked a group of women to form a non-governmental organisation (NGO) that would undertake to feed these children and provide crèche facilities to as many as possible. There was then no question of building institutions for them. The need was immediate: the "homes" would come up in due course, after the government had settled down to governance.

This was the founding of Delhi Council for Child Welfare (DCCW), a voluntary non-profit organisation managed by an honorary Executive Committee. I joined the Executive Committee of DCCW in 1982. At the time, it was also running a village workers training programme on behalf of the government. DCCW has since expanded its activities to cover:

- *Crèche services for children from 0–5 years of age in 18 centres*
  Crèche workers in the city provide services for working parents, giving the children a very basic non-formal education and also helping them to get admission into government-run primary schools in the vicinity. Once the children are in school they are helped to keep up with their school work by a teacher, for a small fee, as most of these children came from uneducated families.

---

[1] In the wake of the independence of India from British rule, the country was divided into India and Pakistan. Millions of people crossed the new borders to migrate from one to the other country.

- *A training programme for anganwadi workers*
  (The word "angan" means courtyard and quite literally it means to be spread in the courtyards of the villages.) This programme, known as the Anganwadi Training Programme, was meant to train women village workers who would go into the rural areas, which were shunned by the educated and highly qualified persons as being bereft of opportunity (largely economic). With over 80 per cent of the population living in the rural areas, this was a much-needed service provided by the Central Government. The workers were trained in the rudiments of nutrition, health (especially women's health), birth control, immunisation and basic education for children. Since the workers themselves were from rural areas they could identify with the villagers' cultural background and had little difficulty in being accepted by the community.

- *The programme for street and working children*
  The service first counsels the runaways to return home, and more often than not we have succeeded in escorting them back. Those who are adamant about not returning home are persuaded to return to school and stay in a "drop-in" shelter run by the police. These children are sponsored by individuals.

- *An orthopaedic programme for polio-affected children*
  Recently a new programme has been introduced to also cover children with cerebral palsy from middle class homes. This is run by the parents of the children. DCCW gives them the basic infrastructure such as a room, physiotherapy facilities and equipment.

- *Vocational training for both disabled and non-disabled children*

- *Sponsorship programmes* where individual sponsors can participate in either the rehabilitation of a disabled child, or the education of either disabled or non-disabled children.

- *PALNA[2]* – a home for abandoned children where suitable adoptive parents are selected.

All of DCCW's programmes are aimed at giving underprivileged children a chance in life. A chance to have a childhood, belong to a family, and be equipped to face life as an educated trained adult. Every effort is made to

---

[2] "Palna" means cradle.

keep families together. If a family is under stress and feels constrained to give up the children in adoption, the children are kept in PALNA for as long as three months, the parents are counseled and pointed in the direction of NGOs which can help them, and the children are then returned to their parents. During their short stay they undergo full medical tests, receive immunisation if necessary, and are given suitable nutrition.

The children at PALNA

Since its inception 21 years ago, PALNA has received 2,981 children, of whom 537 have been restored to their families, 816 have been placed for adoption with Indian families, and 886 children have been placed for adoption with families abroad. By law, all adoption agencies are required to try and place the children with Indian families, but PALNA receives an inordinate number of older children and siblings. So far the oldest child we have been able to place with an Indian family is 3½ years old. We do not break up sibling groups, and have had to place them in families abroad. The older children who are abandoned are particularly vulnerable and traumatised. They are counseled and introduced to the idea of adoption, and given time to accept the concept before they are introduced to a family. The children have the right to choose whether or not they wish to be adopted, failing which they would be transferred to a suitable institution or "home". DCCW does not believe in placing children in institutions, but if that is the child's choice, it is respected. Fortunately, we have had only one older, abandoned child so far who has refused to be adopted. He is being educated by a sponsor in a boarding school on the outskirts of Delhi, under the supervision of /DCCW.

Why are children abandoned? Most of the time it is due to poverty, sometimes the child is unwanted because she is a girl, and sometimes one of the child's parents has died and the surviving parent wants to marry again. According to Indian law, if the baby is left in the cradle outside our gate, it is an act of abandonment and we are not obliged to try and track down the biological parents. However, as a matter of policy, PALNA does not offer very young children for adoption. The child has to be at least three months old, and medically stable before his or her papers are filed in the Court clearing him or her for adoption.

If the mother should turn up in that period (or even later) and can identify the child, we restore the child to the mother. If the child has an extended family that can obtain a Court order then the child is restored to the family. It is only when we are reasonably sure that there are no claimants to the child, that we feel able to have the child adopted.

Adoption procedures

The adoption programme is very closely monitored by the Government of India. The adoption procedures were set down by the Supreme Court in 1984 (see Damodaran and Mehta, Chapter 22). Subsequently, in some states, the NGOs themselves have set up co-ordinating agencies in order that children are placed in families as early as possible. The Government has set up CARA – which monitors the work of the adoption agencies, ensuring that the adoption is carried out with due care. The Supreme Court has established the adoption fee, and no agency may charge more. This is meant to cover the cost of the care given to the child while awaiting adoption. At a recent seminar, I was challenged on the validity of this charge. Apparently countries such as South Africa and Nigeria do not charge for adoption work; the adoption homes, however, are run by the Government, not by NGOs, thereby making it feasible for the Government to absorb the cost. By restricting the amount that can be charged, and preventing children being transferred from one State to another, the Indian Government has effectively stopped any trafficking in children.

Adoption procedures require that the child first must be cleared for adoption, that is to say, all efforts must be made to locate his/her parents or family. If the child does not have any claimants, then he or she is cleared by a magistrate for adoption. All adoptions must be done through Government-recognised adoption agencies. The Government holds the agency accountable not only for following the procedures, but also for ensuring that the family has been selected with due consideration for the child's needs. The accredited agency is required to ensure first that there is no suitable Indian family for the child. (A child adopted by Indians living abroad has to fit in within an "alien" environment, even though the parents may be Indian.) If the child is an infant, there is no problem, but an older child, even of two or three, may show signs of bewilderment.

But love is a wonderful bonding agent, love tempered with patience and compassion. Parents must accept the children for what they are. The children have to take their parents at face-value, and that must be reciprocated. Children have amazing resilience given love and a sense of security; they not only survive but blossom. They need to belong to a family, sometimes they need siblings to interact with. What they do not need is to be left to languish in an impersonal institution, just one of many children whom no-one in particular wants or cares for.

The need for a family

Ever since the glare of publicity has intensified on children all over the world – their welfare, their needs, their rights, their development or non-development – the aspect that has perhaps attracted most attention is whether or not abandoned or destitute children should be placed for intercountry adoption. Central to this is the fact that every child deserves a family, a home. A child is born to a mother and father, not to an institution. His/her best interests will only be served in a family that loves and cares for him or her. This conviction has its roots in our experience not only with abandoned or destitute children, but even children who have strayed too far from their homes, or run away in the heat of the moment.

PALNA has now become a household word for the care it gives to any child that enters it. We have children found by the police or even concerned citizens, being brought to us. DCCW makes every effort to locate the child's family, and when they come to pick up the child, there are many angry recriminations from the child: How could you let me get lost? That is the maxim we work with: every child must be placed with a family that has the child's best interests at heart. Ideally, it would be best if the child could be placed within his/her own country, but when those efforts fail, he/she may be placed with any family that will commit itself to the child's well-being. Political, religious or cultural barriers are adult imposed. No-one asked the children if they were important.

A look at the history of the human race shows that migrations have been an intrinsic part of society. The weather turns too cold to be comfortable? Move to a warmer climate. Not enough grass for the cattle?

Move to fresher pastures. Not enough work opportunities for the young? Move to a more economically dynamic society. These migrations may range from the nest country to the nest continent or just a vast, long journey across troubled waters. These were family or even community movements, where children had to fit in and endure the hardships of their parents and community. How did they succeed? They succeeded because the children had a sense of security in knowing that they were not the only ones. They were part of a group and the children's security lay in the fact that their parents, and the group they were travelling with, were looking out for them. If there were travails and hardships to be faced, they were not alone in having to face them. So, in essence, what a child is looking for is a sense of belonging and identity.

The children adopted from PALNA

How would a child placed for adoption with a foreign couple manage? Is adoption good for a child? It has been our experience that counselling plays an important part in helping the child as well as the parents to make the adoption "work". The parents are counseled on what to expect from the child, and once helped to understand his/her background and culture, they will be better equipped to care for the child. The child is encouraged to voice fears and doubts, questions are answered, and only when the child is ready to go into a family selected by the Council is he or she offered to a family. A child who is given a lot of loving care and patience will do very well indeed.

A child who enters PALNA is exposed to the concept of adoption from day one. The nursery children are quite used to having visitors (*not* potential parents) smiling and playing with them. The toddlers watch children whose adoption formalities have been completed, going away with their new parents. There may be a few tears at having to leave behind friends or "family", but those who go have been prepared for this day with photos of their adoptive family, and gifts from the parents at festival times. Children going to Italy receive Italian lessons, so that the language is not entirely alien. While staying in PALNA, the children are taught some music and dancing, they watch selected TV programmes, they are treated to picnics by Indian adoptive parents, or the local hotel invites them to special festival parties. We try to make PALNA a happy place. Since we try to minimise their stay at PALNA (and away from a family), the children cannot be sent to school, but volunteers come and fill in the gaps in their education. This interaction with people outside PALNA helps them to join the mainstream of society with ease.

By law we are expected to try and find an Indian family for each child. However, there are situations when an Indian family is difficult to find. Age is a deterrent; Indians prefer to adopt a child as young as their age will allow. We do not break up sibling groups on principle. As it is very difficult to find families who will accept sibling groups, we turn to Italy, where siblings adopted from India have been very happily settled. Indian families are also superstitious about adopting children with a small birthmark. These are the children for whom we have to look further afield. It is gratifying to find that there are parents who just want to care for a child – nothing matters to them, the child's size, shape, colour and disabilities are accepted, not as a problem they have to cope with, but as a child who has to be loved and cared for.

PALNA'S relationship with foreign agencies

DCCW works with only a few agencies in a few countries for a number of reasons.

- We need to streamline our operations so that the children find a "home" as quickly as possible. Several countries were consequently eliminated from our list, because they took too long to process a visa for the child. England, Ireland and Australia were amongst the first to go.

- We work with only those adoption agencies that have a similar philosophy as ours, that is to say, we suggest that parents who are adopting a child through us should also join our sponsorship programme, thereby benefiting other children who need assistance. This idea has worked so well that today all the children who leave PALNA still feel bound to their roots. One of our boys became a football star in his Italian village. He sent PALNA the first $100 he won as a prize. The families go to the extent of discussing with their children if they want birthday presents from the family or whether they would like to collect the money and send it to PALNA. All this love is wonderful, and we don't know where we would be without it. When we had the floods in Gujerat, we were inundated with phone calls of concern: and what could they do to help? The bonds are strong indeed.

- By placing children in fewer countries we hope for closer interaction between the children. It is necessary to work with like-minded people who share our aims and objectives for the children. Interacting with these agencies has given us a larger perspective on the needs of children and the importance of counselling.

- We are aware of the children's need to know their roots. We have recently started a Record Room, where children may go through our records to find out whatever they can about their background. We warn the adoptive parents that if the child has been abandoned in the cradle we will have no information about the biological parents.

DCCW interacts with adoption agencies in only six countries – Italy, Denmark, Sweden, Finland, Belgium and the USA. Children are allotted to a particular country based on the particular needs of the child. Older children and sibling groups fit into Italy best, because we already have children placed there, and the Parents Association is a strong one. They meet frequently, share their experiences or problems, talk of PALNA and India. The children meet and chatter in Italian, but they have a strong sense of roots and belonging. They go through the normal growing pains, fall in and out of love, get married, have babies. They belong to their adoptive parents in every sense of the word. All this has been very successful in motivating the Italian Parents Association to visit India, see the needs of the country, and do fundraising, not just for PALNA but for other projects in India. Every adoption agency, be it Indian or foreign, needs to go beyond adoption and care for the well being of children.

Children with special needs

"Special needs" children are generally given to carefully selected families in Belgium or the USA. Families in both countries have been especially sensitive in caring for these children. Take the case of Gopi –

in every way a healthy baby, but blind in one eye and with marginal vision in the other. We had him examined by specialists in India but they could not do anything to help him. He has been in Belgium for the last six years and the last time someone from the agency visited him, he was well and happy. He has a charming smile and endearing ways. Who could walk away from a child like that? The family cannot love him more and he has blossomed. Leena was left in our cradle when she was tiny. She appeared to have every card stacked against her. Complete physical disability, her knee joints were bent in the wrong direction thus preventing her from standing. She appeared to be mildly developmentally delayed and her speech was garbled for all the years she spent with us while we searched for a suitable family. She had a squint and an eye examination revealed myopia. So what was it that set her apart? An indomitable spirit, a very loving heart, and a smile that could melt the hardest heart.We found her a family in the USA. They had five other children with special needs. We received a video of Leena's arrival in the US. Not only had her family come to receive her, but so had half the town. She leapt unerringly into her mother's arms and smiled at every one with the grace of a queen coming home!

Prithi and Mamta were left with us by a widow who had five children, and wanted to marry again. She could not expect her new husband to take all five, so she left two with PALNA. What was the basis of her selection? We will never know, but the girls were traumatised. The burning question was, 'Why us?' It took several years of counselling and loving, a bit of spoiling with a few "girlie" things like bright new clothes and bangles. They loved Indian pickles so these were added to supplement the bland food we give the other children. Gradually, they saw other children going off happily with their adoptive parents. With some counselling and chatting, they agreed that adoption was the best option for them. We found an Italian family willing to take the two sisters, and as a bonus they would be accompanied by our Honorary Secretary to Italy – the parting with Aruna Kumar was fraught with emotion on both sides but they are happily settled and write frequently.

One cold winter night, just before Christmas, we found a two-and-a-half-year-old left in our cradle. She had third degree burns. Our staff took her in, cleaned her and rushed her to hospital. It took several months for her to recover. She never smiled! We applied to our Italian partners. Would they find us a family who would adopt her? It was heartwarming when within days the response came back with a resounding fanfare: We would love to have her. It took several years and a great deal of plastic surgery to remove the burn marks, but the love in her eyes and the smile on her lips show that the past is behind her.

Not all the children who go abroad are disabled or older children. We have sent twin girls aged six months. They could not be adopted in India as the law only permits Indians to adopt one of each sex. CARA and the adoption agencies are working towards removing these anomalies in our legal system. We hope to overcome!

What makes it work?

Time and again we have been told that PALNA children show an amazing ability to adapt to their families. This is not a chance happening. A great deal of work goes into giving them a sense of security; they know that we would never push them into an unwanted situation. They have been exposed all along to children who are adopted by both Indian and foreign families. Sometimes, if their turn takes a bit longer in coming, they ask, 'Is there no one who wants us?' and our answer has always been: 'Trust us, we must find someone who would be best for you!' They understand.

Meanwhile, the rehabilitation work goes on. If they need physiotherapy, counselling, a bit of book learning, someone to talk to, some table manners, outings into the big world outside, music, picnics, parties, and festival celebrations – PALNA children get it all. Every February we have an Adoption Day celebration, to which all our adopted children are invited, along with Friends of PALNA. It's party time. There is music, balloons, snacks of the kind children love. Last year's big attraction was a horse and buggy ride, the year before it was an elephant. PALNA children dance for the occasion and every PALNA child is in party clothes and will be second to none. It is a big family reunion which gives our children a sense of pride and belonging.

What is it that makes adoption work for children? Children need to know they are going into a family that has been selected for them. They need to be secure in PALNA, to receive as much love and care as they would in a family. When an infant or a child enters PALNA, he/she is tested for TB, hepatitis, HIV/AIDS, or any other obviously manifested diseases. If anything is detected, the child is put on the road to recovery straightaway. If the child has a low birth-weight, he/she is admitted to our intensive care unit. Every child is treated with the same loving care as if he/she had entered a family. PALNA is a transitory home for the child, but it must be as near the eventual one as possible. Sometimes the older children profess boredom, especially during the long hot summers. It is not easy to devise entertainment for 75 or so children of varying ages. However, our adoptive parents who are fortunate enough to have large homes, invite our children to spend the day, sometimes sending air-conditioned buses to transport them. It is important to *listen* to the children and, if possible, accede to their demands for an outing or a party on our own grounds. We have a counsellor who talks to the older children, trying to get them to express their fears and worries. If any staff member is harsh with the children, they know they can speak to either the adoption officer or the secretary, who will handle the matter with tact and understanding. Indian children are comfortable with the knowledge that adults make certain decisions on their behalf, and since they trust the adults who make these decisions, there are fewer fears.

It is true that children going abroad are removed from their familiar surroundings, but that is true even of adoptions within the country. India has so many diverse cultures that a child from the South may feel a bit lost in a school in the North. But that does not mean that the child cannot adapt to an adoption. It is far more difficult for a biological child who belongs to a broken home to adjust to its circumstances, than for an adoptive child to adjust within a loving family. Too much emphasis on "culture" and too little emphasis on the child's security may lead to erroneous decisions. By restricting our adoption work to six countries only, we hope that PALNA children will get together at least once a year and keep some of their old camaraderie.

The last word
Finally, the children adopted from PALNA should have the last word. Here are translated extracts from just three of the many letters we have received from the children and their adoptive parents.

Pradamano, 8 July 1998

Dear Kumar Madam,

I'm in good health and how are you? Here it's very hot and now, since the school finished, I go to the swimming-pool and I run with my bycicle.

During the month of July I attend a parish summer centre where I enjoy myself and I learn some new things. The last week, along with Sarwan, Babloo and my cousin Claire, I went to 'Gardaland'. Gardaland is a big fun park. I enjoyed myself very much especially on the Big Dipper.

Since one year I have a little dog named Cleo. It's a female dog. It's white with some brown spots. Cleo is a very scamp dog but it's also nice and beautiful. My parents are fine. We enjoy us all together and I'm very happy to live here. I'm learning to play the Mandolino (a type of guitar) and I'm playing with my father.

I hope you will come soon to Italy because I would be very happy to meet you.

At school I passed the 3rd class of the primary school so next year I'll attend the 4th class. My school report was good and my parents take me to Gardaland as reward.

I hope you are in good health and I hug you with love.

Nayeem

Dear Mrs Kumar,

Nayeem was so happy to write to you directly by himself! Here we are all of us well and so we hope it is for you and for your family.

We hope to see you again soon and in the meantime we send to you, such as to miss Loraine and all your collaborators, our best wishes and regards.

Most fondly yours

[Nayeem's family]

Pradamano, 4 July 1999

Dear Kumar Madam,

I write to you this letter in order to tell you that I'm living happily in Italy. I would like to know how the Palna's children are.

My father, my mother and my brother are sending you their best regards. In Italy I have a lot of friends and I'm lucky because I'm living near Nayeem.

I'm a clever child at school. My teacher is happy and satisfied with me.

On the occasion of my 'First Communion' we had a party with many friends: Tara, Babloo, Dinesh, Kunno, Nathu, Nayeem and Italian relatives. Now I'm sending you my regards and I hope you are fine. A Big kiss for you.

Sarwan

Dear Kumar Madam,

We seize the oppurtunity of enclosing for you the picture taken on the occasion of Sarwan and Nayeem's Holy Communion partly to send to you our best regards.

Many thanks again for what you have done for Sarwan.

[Sarvan's family]

31 March 2000

Dear Mrs Kumar

We arrived safely in Italy and we have settled into Italian life. We go to school every day except Saturday and Sunday.

A girl called Cristina is teaching us Italian three times a week. She is very nice and patient. We have fond memories of Palna and hope to see you again sometime in the future.

This summer mommy and daddy are taking us to the seaside. We are looking forward to it.

We hope all continues well for you. Please say hello to everyone at Palna for us.

Lots of love,

Shabnam

Aslam

Reshma

Udine, 7 September 1999

Dear Mrs Kumar,

We are sending you a few pictures of Suneeta taken six months after her arrival in Italy.

Suneeta is a very happy child and has become an avid swimmer (she was the best in her summer course) and enjoys going to kindergarten.

After six months with us she speaks fluent Italian and understands and speaks some English since she is attending an English-language school.

We would like to thank you again for your kindness with Suneeta who speaks to us with fondness of the year spent at PALNA.

Sincerely yours

[Suneeta's family]

Section V
Personal perspectives on intercountry adoption

The research on adoptive parents and adopted persons which was reported in earlier sections provides much insight into the process and outcome of intercountry adoption, but cannot substitute for the direct voice of members of the adoption triangle and those who work closest with them. In this section we hear directly from an adoptive parent and adoptees from the UK and Sweden read an account of the plight of birth mothers in Argentina, and are offered some insights into the problems of adoptees who have experienced sexual abuse prior to placement from the perspective of a therapist working with children placed from her own continent of birth.

Amalia Carli offers the view of a practitioner, born in Argentina, who has worked in Norway with children subjected to sexual abuse before being adopted from Latin America. She argues that such children – and their adoptive parents – are likely to need much support after adoption. Carli demonstrates the potential for work with adoptive families and the need for specialist help, an area sadly lacking in the UK, where parents have increasingly turned for help to the USA, e.g. in linking to the *Parental Network for the Post Institutionalised Child* (PNPIC). But Carli does more than describe a therapeutic process. Her case studies of children traumatised by abuse provide an insight into the problems which lie behind many intercountry adoptions and the challenges these provide for adoptive parents and those who support them.

Eva Giberti provides an insight into the much neglected plight of the birth mothers. Hughes and Logan (1993) have referred to these as the "hidden dimension" in British domestic adoption, but this is even truer of ICA, where children are typically presented as abandoned. Giberti's concern is for birth mothers in Argentina whose plight has seldom been explored and many of whom have had their children "stolen" whether for domestic or intercountry adoption. The needs – and rights – of birth parents in domestic adoption are slowly being recognised in the UK, but in overseas adoption they are either "excluded" (Giberti *et al*, 1997) or are hidden as a result of the shame, stigma or threat that surrounds unmarried mothers or those who might offend against the expectations of their country.

Roger Shead provides an account of intercountry adoption from the viewpoint of the adoptive parents. This shows clearly the problems of the lack of support for British citizens wanting to adopt from abroad at a time when most social services departments lacked any expertise in intercountry adoption. In particular, the value of the guidance provided in the later stages by an American agency shows the urgent need to develop "mediating" agencies. He readily acknowledges the moves forward in the UK in recent years and the more positive attitudes emerging in many local authorities, but his chapter reminds us that the success of intercountry adoption is dependent on the love and commitment of adopters and that services must respect their needs and use their experience. The chapter also demonstrates clearly that prospective adopters are aware of many of the wider issues discussed in this volume, but reminds us of the need for parents for children deprived of a normal home life, whatever their country of origin. In his final paragraph, Shead reminds us that while the adopted child may have a better future than if he or she remained in an institution, it is wrong to call them "lucky" children as 'it is we, their parents, who are really the lucky ones'.

Sue Jardine and Katherine Samwell Smith look at overseas adoption from the adopted person's perspective speaking from their own experience and that of other young people adopted from abroad including those they have met through their involvement with the Catholic Children's Society Project 16–18. Both chapters explore the themes of openness, cultural roots, loss and isolation and reflect on the authors' experiences of visiting their birth countries. Sue Jardine talks about her feelings of loss arising from a lack of information about her origins and the importance of visiting her country of origin, but also about the difficulties in meeting Chinese people when she could not speak 'their' language. Katherine Samwell Smith argues the need for adoptive parents to learn about their children's heritage and share this with them as they grow up and ends her chapter by suggesting the need for a national centre for adoption, which could store information about internationally adopted children and their birth families and offer support to both adopted persons and adoptive parents. These accounts bring out clearly the importance of adoptive parents understanding the inevitable dilemmas faced by children in intercountry adoption.

Finally, I am privileged to be able to include extracts from a book published in Sweden and edited by someone herself adopted from overseas (von Melen, 1998). **Anna von Melen** has talked to 18 young adults adopted from a wide range of countries. The extracts included record her conversations with three young people adopted by Swedish families and reflect her own experience as a Korean adoptee. As with the two British accounts, these case studies show clearly the importance of listening to those most affected by intercountry adoption and learning from the mistakes they feel have been made by those most concerned with their interests, as well as underlining the inevitable personal costs of overseas adoption, whatever the benefits.

References

Giberti E, Chavanneau de Gore S and Taborda B (1997) *Madres Excluidas* (*Excluded Mothers*), Buenos Aires: Grupo Editorial Norma.

Hughes B and Logan J (1993) *Birth Parents; The Hidden Dimension*, University of Manchester: Department of Social Policy and Social Work.

von Melen A (1998) *Strength to Survive and Courage to Live: 18 adoptees on adoption*, Stockholm: NIA.

24 Latin American children adopted in Norway: A therapist's account

Amalia Carli

Amalia Carli is a Clinical Psychologist at the Psychological Centre for Refugees, University of Oslo, Norway.

Introduction

In this chapter I talk about my clinical experience with Latin American children who have been adopted by Norwegians and treated in infant and juvenile psychiatric clinics where I have worked. Norway has a free national health service, which includes educational psychologists and child psychiatrists. There are nine infant-juvenile psychiatric polyclinics (BUPs) in Oslo, serving less than half a million inhabitants; the ratio of similar services to the resident population in other towns is also relatively good. The BUPs are run by multidisciplinary clinical psychologists, infant psychologists, educational psychologists and social workers. Between 1991 and 1997, I worked clinically with around 20 Latin American children in various BUPs. I have also been consulted by parents and led orientation groups for parents. Consultations with social workers and conference proceedings involving multidisciplinary groups have given me further indirect access to the problems affecting some of these children and their families.

Child adoption in Norway

Most of the six hundred children adopted each year from abroad are less than three years old when they arrive in Norway, but those in my consultations have been the older ones, ranging in age from three to nine years. Many of them have had very traumatic experiences: emotional loss, living in the streets, humiliation, and abuse of all types.

A view from the clinic

Investigations carried out across Scandinavia show that 70 to 80 per cent of adopted children adapt well in school, social life and work settings (Dalen and Sætersdal, 1992; Botvar, 1994). However, investigations based in the clinical population show that although adopted children under 12 are not found registered in BUPs as often as other Norwegian children, after that age the situation appears to reverse and it is two or three times more probable to find them in psychiatric institutions. One interpretation of these figures is that the parents try to help the children themselves when they are young but that the problems become worse in adolescence, often requiring in-patient treatment.

Below, I report on my clinical experience with 20 Latin American children and young people. All the names have been changed and I have chosen not to identify their countries of origin. I have worked in Norway since 1977, first as a mother-tongue teacher to Spanish-speaking children, mostly Chilean refugees, and since 1986 as a psychologist specialising in infant and juvenile clinical psychology, mostly with refugee families and children. My previous experience with refugee children and families has been very useful as I have found significant parallels between the life experiences of adopted children and the victims of repression in various countries of Europe, Asia, Africa and America (Carli, 1999).

Marta, a young girl raped by the police

One of my first encounters was with an adopted Latin American girl I will call "Marta". The adoptive parents, a young couple, believed that they were to adopt an infant of one-and-a-half to two, but when they collected Marta in her country of origin she was about three-and-a-half, although she looked younger, and was seriously malnourished. The documentation stated that she was two but her true age was ascertained later in Norway in a medical examination. A number of factors led the adoptive mother to suspect early on that Marta had been sexually abused; in the first few nights Marta had nightmares, screaming "No, no" and covering her genitals. She also rejected all contact with her father and when the parents took her to say goodbye to the orphanage personnel she reacted with desperation as they approached the building.

In Oslo the parents' suspicions were confirmed by a team of specialists in the diagnosis of sexual abuse in children. Marta spoke few and unconnected words when she arrived in Norway. It is not known how long she had lived in the orphanage where, we are told, she spent most of her time sitting on a bed with the light switched off. There were no games or songs and the combination of limited food and exercise had caused malnutrition and muscular weakness that were quickly overcome once she had left the orphanage.

The love and dedication of her adoptive mother, a young woman of great spirit and intuition, helped Marta develop in such an astonishing way that my colleagues noticed the difference just from seeing her in the waiting room from session to session. Marta learned Norwegian quickly and was able to tell her parents, at barely four years old, that she had been raped by police who came regularly to the orphanage and who also took photographs. Later, during therapy, Marta said the police had raped and killed her biological mother whom I call the "first mum" to differentiate her from the "mum" (adoptive mother).

I believed that this could be true. Maybe her parents were members of the Opposition, young people connected with a left-wing organisation. Marta's fantasies about her first mum as a loving person concerned for her daughter made us think that she had had a "good" mother. Having little information concerning her arrival at the orphanage, her adoptive father thought it possible that the police had stolen Marta from "good" people, as she had such good behaviour, folding her clothes carefully and eating carefully; above all she was so loving with them. He also believed that the orphanage was responsible for her malnutrition. These speculations, real or not, demonstrate their very good relationship with the girl and maybe also a consolation that she was not so damaged after all; she had had a good base in the past and that fixed everything.

In Argentina, my country of origin, hundreds of children disappeared after their parents were killed by the police and military. The children were sold, given for adoption, abandoned in orphanages or killed. It is not known how many children have had the same fate as Marta. The idea that this was real, that Marta had been robbed of the opportunity of growing up with her biological parents, affected me greatly. Everything suddenly came closer, as if one of the many children whose photographs hang on the walls of the office of *Abuelas de Plaza de Mayo* (Grand-mothers of the Plaza de Mayo who meet there regularly to protest against "the Disappeared") were here with me.

Traumatic pasts of adopted and refugee children – some parallels

By focusing on the situation of refugee children in situations of war and persecution many parallels can be seen between adopted and refugee children. The literature concerning child victims of political repression and clinical work with them and their parents shows that they have often suffered serious trauma, both directly and indirectly (Carli, 1987, 1991, 1994, 1996, 1999; Carli and Dalen, 1997, 1999; Cohn, 1983; Gustaffson, 1989). The experiences of these children, as with adopted children, are characterised by massive emotional and material losses.

As much as a result of political persecution as of adoption or abandon-ment by their parents, children suffer social shame that comes from the rejection, humiliation and abuse of which they are often the victim. Naturally other traumas arise from witnessing destruction and war but above all from personal experience and the witnessing of physical, mental and sexual abuse. This type of experience causes deep pain in the children, filling them with confusion.

In the case of sexual abuse, sexualised behaviour is another possible consequence of trauma. This is seen most often in children who have been the victims of abuse and who have become accustomed to relating to adults according to the latter's sexual demands. In taking an active role the children may be trying to regain control through the mechanism of identification with the aggressor.

Sexual abuse

Children left to their own devices, or those experiencing frequent change of guardians, run the risk of various forms of abuse, including sexual abuse. We know that children have been abused after the arrest of their parents (Sanhueza, 1990), or tortured in other ways (Cohn, 1983). Children displaced by war also find themselves more exposed to this type of abuse (Kadjar-Hamouda, 1996). At times, those who are violated, and thus facing rejection from their families, leave their parents in early adolescence (Jareg, 1997) thus adding to the approximately two million children and youths separated from their parents.

Discussions with a large group of adoptive parents in Norway show that children above the ages of three or four coming from Latin America have frequently been the victim of severe abuse. Girls of seven years old have told that they had been sexually abused in exchange for food to survive and to feed their younger siblings.

The Swedish infant psychiatrist Marianne Cederblad (1991) investigated the clinical histories of children adopted from abroad and living in the south of Sweden, and found that a number of them had been sexually abused. This is one of the few studies documenting the traumatic past of the children, which is lamentable as the traumas often cause problems in adapting to the new families.

Examples of sexualised behaviour in adopted children
Sexually abused children often show sexualised behaviour, as they are already socialised in, and accustomed to, relating to adults in this way to obtain attention, or food, or to avoid punishment.

- A girl who came to Norway at the age of six had been punished for her compulsive masturbation, which caused great feelings of guilt. A psychologist interpreted this as a way of searching for consolation for the loss of her parents and excluded the possibility of sexual abuse, which was later confirmed on her arrival in Norway, where her adoptive mother supported her by explaining that it was acceptable to masturbate.
- A girl of four years pinched her adoptive father's penis on some occasions when she felt particularly insecure; firmly but caringly he explained to her that he did not like her to touch him there.

The behaviour of these girls can be interpreted as a way of gaining control of an abuse situation; they take the initiative with their own body or that of their parent. However, if they find themselves with an adult who misinterprets this as a sexual initiative from the child there exists the possibility that the abuse is repeated. Other children show such aggressive behaviour that their parents, school or kindergarten have serious difficulties. Parents often need help to express the pain caused by the fact that their beloved children have been mistreated, and often have the physical marks of punishment or abuse.

Clinical material

Case Study 1: "Marta"

When Marta was adopted at the age of three she did not know how to play. The care and empathy of her adoptive mother, and her pleasure at playing with her daughter, along with Marta's intellectual ability and capacity for fantasy soon made it possible for Marta to express herself through play, words, and drawings that were simple but full of meaning. Marta presented a repetitive play that filled her with anxiety, and which she played a number of times a day in different circumstances. Briefly, the theme was that the police arrived at the orphanage searching for children. Marta told her parents to attack the imaginary police and she enjoyed it when her mother or father 'hit or kicked them', and she wanted the game to be repeated again and again. In this way Marta was shown many times that her parents loved her and defended her; they gave her physical contact and consolation. But her parents became exhausted and anxious and presented with this game as a problem, asking for help so that Marta could play other games.

Brief psychodynamic therapy

Marta's parents wanted her to finish her therapy a couple of months later, hoping to start a "new life" as soon as possible. They were somewhat ambivalent to the idea that Marta should re-live her traumatic past in therapy. Marta was given a short therapy of 17 hours during two-and-a-half months. Together with my supervisor, Svein Mossige, we considered that Marta had overcome the worst of her experiences when she began to play games other than the repetition of abuse both in therapy and at home.

The mother tongue as an element of therapy

In the first telephone conversation, Marta's adoptive mother made it clear that I should not speak in Spanish as Marta did not want to hear her mother tongue which was associated only with negative experiences. This changed little by little until Marta asked me at times during the sessions to speak or sing in Spanish. It was a small victory and I hoped that positive experiences were returning or being created for Marta, like those she had had with her first mum.

In the first hour of therapy I asked Marta to draw the country she came from. She drew a big circle with many "windows"; it was the orphanage. I asked her to draw herself in one of the windows and I asked her what she could see from her window: 'a car, with mum and dad coming to find me'. I asked her to draw them. In another picture Marta drew me in one of the windows. In another she asked me to draw the police coming to the orphanage, entering and 'the children telling them to go away, but them not going'. The fact that Marta drew windows was seen as something positive; it reaffirmed our hypothesis that Marta had had positive experiences outside the windows. The good lay outside the windows that were the first thing she remembered when asked about her country. It also seemed positive to us that she drew me in one of the windows, at her side, as if to say, 'It's okay, you can come into my sad and ugly experience'.

From the drawings Marta moved quickly to play in the sandpit and the doll's house, showing a rich fantasy and a notable creativity and ability to play that I have rarely seen in other children. From the microsphere of games with dolls, Marta moved to the macrosphere of dramatic representation in role play where she instructed me to represent her mum, herself as her older sister (that she would have had before) and a doll as 'Martita', herself as a baby. The theme of the various games was more or less the same; the police came and raped and killed her mother. The mother put Ana, the older sister, in charge of Martita, but the police managed to trap her and rape her. Marta directed me in the game, giving me roles and telling me what to do.

Case Study 2: "Gustav" and "Johan"

Gustav and Johan were adopted at the age of six and three respectively. Their mother had abandoned them a year and a half before and they had been in the care of various people who did not look after them well, so that they spent most of the day doing nothing. They lived for a few months in the streets with a group of children stealing food and getting on trains to 'go for a ride'. Gustav looked after his brother all this time, and, unlike the younger child, remembered his birth parents.

The children were adopted by a Christian professional couple who had an excellent relationship but who were somewhat confused about their role as parents. In the two-and-a-half years that the children lived with them they had tried, as recommended, to impose clear limits. The result was a mix of the parent role and that of "teacher of street kids", which was detrimental to the parent–child relationship which they wanted to build. They came to the consultation very worried because the younger child, Johan, at the age of five-and-a-half, was showing extremely controlling behaviour. The parents felt helpless and feared that Johan would develop a psychotic personality.

The fear of being "returned" and Maradona the Champion

Johan and his parents, but not Gustav, came to the first interview. The child was withdrawn and did not want to talk, but stayed, listening to the conversation, at his mother's side. His parents assured him that they wanted to help him and, seeing his anxious look at the sight of the long corridors and the games room with a bed, I felt it vital to tell him that this was an institute where families came to talk or play with us when they had problems and that everyone went home to sleep. I told him that no children stayed to live here, reassuring him that these were the mother and father he would have for the rest of his life. Johan was uncertain, but calmed himself a little when I told him that I came from Argentina and spoke the same language as he had before he came to Norway. Straight away he asked me if I knew Maradona (the national football "hero") and the contact, although guarded, was made.

Before deciding the type of therapy to offer them, I asked the parents to come to the consultation with both children, even though they did not have problems with Gustav who was a good student and was responsible and obedient. On seeing Gustav I felt a sensation of anxiety and pity. He had a very sad face and appeared bewitched. He was also very guarded, and his mother told me later that, before his first visit he had said, resignedly, 'I'm certain these ladies are going to say that we can't keep on living with you', making reference to the numerous experiences of changes of home in his country. With a social worker, and myself as psychologist, we jumped into the unknown, and offered the whole family an hour of therapy each week with the basic intention that they get to know each other better. Taking as a starting point the moment of the first meeting, with stories from the parents and spontaneous drawings from the children, we were putting together part of the puzzle which now made up a part of the common history of the whole family.

At the start of the therapy Gustav continued to appear reserved and rather uncomfortable at Johan's unashamed and infantile outbursts, shooting incessantly with a toy gun, joking with myself and my colleague, and above all talking a lot about 'shit', 'piss', and later 'copulation' and 'penis'. Slowly Gustav began engaging with the therapy. At first he was nervous with the pistol and the noise it made, but his mother helped him to take courage. He also answered questions and drew in a spontaneous way, at times drawing scenes from before the adoption. The most important part was the conversations that the whole family had between sessions and to which the parents made reference.

Meanwhile, at home, the situation was turned on its head. Johan became more peaceful and caring and no longer presented a problem to his parents who saw his behaviour as 'normal for his age'. Gustav, on the other hand, started to react against his parents, exploding in tantrums when they went against his will. The parents were conscious that this was an advance for him, and reassured him that they loved him. It showed that now they could love him more because he was showing them parts of himself that they had not known. Previously Gustav had not been able to show his feelings for fear of being punished by the grown-ups who had mistreated him. Moreover, Gustav had had to cover up his anger and fear, without crying, because, as he told us, 'Johan cried a lot, and two can't cry at the same time'. Now, finally, he could show us all the emotions that he had carried within himself.

At times Gustav and Johan were annoyed by the over-protection shown them by their parents, amongst other things, in not being allowed to see violent films like the Teenage Mutant Ninja Turtles, nor go too far from the house, nor go to bed late. This was all in sharp contrast to the life they had experienced in their country: crossing enormous roads of heavy traffic at two and four years old, living with violence, walking the streets at all hours, going for walks in the cemetery, eating and sleeping wherever they could.

The older brother told his parents at home before sleeping the story of how their mother had abandoned them and the pain they had felt. Little by little this withdrawn child started to share with his parents parts of his life of which they had known nothing at all.

In parallel with the changes in the children, their parents were seeing how difficult it must have been for Gustav and Johan suddenly to have such coddling and protective parents after living alone and with little care. Above all they thought it must have been difficult for Gustav, who had previously looked after his brother, to now have parents who decided everything. But in front of the children, I supported the parents in being who they were and maintaining their way of bringing them up. 'What can they do? Maybe they are a little stricter and more old-fashioned than others, but these are the parents you will have for always, and they will be the grandparents to your children'. Furthermore, I emphasised that it was precisely the parents who had been so alone before, who should be helped to find lost parts of their childhood through love and care, although at times they – the parents – did get out of hand. This gave cause for much laughter.

In one session the father told us that his mother had been adopted too, and had suffered a great deal, and thus a dialogue began in which the parents shared aspects of their own pasts, including their inability to have children. The puzzle was being completed and the family enabled us to put together the information that was being revealed and give it meaning.

Case Study 3: "Stefanie" and "Elizabeth": Entering therapy through a half-lie

Stefanie and Elizabeth were eight and five at the time of the consultation and had been adopted from a Latin American country six months previously. The girls had been taken from their birth parents for lack of care and before being adopted had lived in a Catholic children's home. Stefanie looked after Elizabeth a great deal and it was evident she had had a maternal role for her sister and other younger siblings left in her charge by their birth mother. The girls were referred by a social worker because Stefanie had told her adoptive mother that a man in whose care their birth father had left them in their country had sexually abused Elizabeth. Stefanie explained in detail how Elizabeth bled and cried and how later their birth father had come to look for them and had got angry with the man in question. Elizabeth confirmed the story told by her sister.

It was decided that the girls should be seen together a couple of times before deciding on the therapy. With the suspicion that the older girl might also have been abused, I suggested that both girls be examined. The medical review showed genital and anal scars indicative of penetration in the older girl but not in the younger. Very embarrassed Stefanie told her mother that her birth father, and not another man, was the one who had repeatedly abused her, but not her younger sister. Stefanie felt ashamed about what had happened and guilty for having lied to us. Her mother, on the other hand, was pleased to know the truth and be able to help her and support Stefanie. Considering the situation, it was decided that Stefanie be given a short therapy of 12 hours. She reacted against coming alone and wanted her mother to be present so that she would not have to talk about what had happened. In the sessions Stefanie's behaviour was quite aggressive towards her sister and towards me and she was very dominant, wanting to take toys home with her and over-ruling me. She defied me to see if I could cope with all the anger that she carried inside and that made her feel evil and dirty.

Repairing elements: Jesus, the Guardian Angel, and our mother tongue

Marta, like Gustav and Johan, was adopted by practising Christian parents, a very common factor in Norwegian adopters (Botvar, 1994), who are different in a number of ways from the other Norwegian parents with whom I have contact. They are active in the area where they live, and have specific values that they want to transmit to their children. They are also critical of the television programmes that many children watch and give very great importance to the role of the family.

Marta's mother, although very affected by Marta's experiences, told me, 'I believe that Jesus wanted Marta to come to us'. With her eyes still fixed on me, I found myself perplexed for a moment then responded sincerely and spontaneously that she was right; that if Jesus was going to choose he would choose them. This answer has become more secure for me over time, and sometimes I say it directly to the parents: 'God wanted you to be the true parents'. The case is that, faced with the horror of Marta's experiences, it is difficult to imagine a mother who could support and understand her better – later it was understood that the mother too had been sexually abused by a member of her family.

Gustav and Johan struggled to win themselves a place in a warm, almost perfect home. After all, they had been dirty, they had robbed and considered themselves thieves, they had lived in the street, and their adoptive father, who was very formal, could not bring himself to repeat in sessions the insults levelled at him by Gustav. The therapists viewed Gustav's verbal attacks as a way of showing how adults had treated him in the past. After all, his birth father had abandoned him, leaving him very sad. The parents quickly understood and saw also that the children worried at times when the parents argued, since some of their school-mates spoke of divorce.

In one of the sessions, Gustav said that when they had been alone Johan smelt bad, and that the toilet they had to use was outside and made of earth. He went on to explain that one night an angel appeared to him. The children joked about the situation, drawing a caricature, and saying that it was a bat and not an angel. The mother, however, recognised the importance of the event, reminding them that it had been important for them. The therapist then said that it appeared that a guardian angel had looked after them, giving them strength to continue for the joy of their present parents. The co-therapist then read to them from a book in which an angel appears to prisoners of the Nazis in the Second World War: it was an extremely emotional moment.

Gustav and Johan told me that they used to say a prayer before going to bed, and so I wrote for them, in Spanish and Norwegian, one that I learned as a child:

Angelito de la guarda	Guardian Angel
Dulce compañía	Sweet companion
No me desapares	Do not leave me
Ni de noche ni de día.	Not by night, nor by day.

Just as when I said caring words to the doll which represented 'Martita' in the games that she directed, as a therapist and a Latin American with a more fortunate history than the children, I wanted perhaps to give them a positive experience in their mother tongue.

Stefanie, despite being very lively and having taken the role of mother to her younger sister, showed regressive conduct which disorientated her parents. Among other things she was afraid to sleep alone. Without the transitional objects that they might have had from an early age I felt impotent faced with what I saw as a desolate infancy. At the end of the therapy I gave each of them a musical box.

Presents from therapist to patient are a taboo subject, but I have had the privilege of the supervision of Monica Gydal, a Swedish psychologist who gives children presents full of symbolism. The musical boxes gave great peace to the children. The parents were surprised, considering the children too old for such a gift. Internally, I hoped that I had returned them some small part of their first years of life, and maybe placed myself within it.

The name as a symbol of identity

Faced with the pain that is caused to me by the things that the children do not know, by the very important pieces of their lives that they have lost, their families, their brothers and sisters, the vestiges of their innocence broken so young, I am helped by searching in the tunnel of their dark eyes, always absorbed, always demanding an answer. Then I fill spaces, talking of their names, of their surnames, of the places they come from.

Silvina is a young girl who arrived in Norway at the age of seven, charged with responsibility for her three younger siblings, and having been violated several times. Convinced that she was of low value, and of the worthlessness of her deepest self, she cut and maltreated herself, and the others, in various ways. After the social report her father called her, let's say, 'Silvio'; it is quite common in our countries to give the name of the father to the first-born child, and she was just that. I told her that clearly her father had a great image of her, and had decided to give her something of great importance: his own name. This defiant youth listened to me with humility. Later she asked me about the meaning of her second name, and also spoke of the deeper meaning of this name, of the myths of its creation, of the countries and religions through which the name had travelled before being given to her and that all of these qualities were encompassed in the name.

I remember the emotion of one couple when I explained that the place of birth was to the child a precious object, just as the child was to the parents. It is fascinating how parents, so correct and formal at times, such Norwegian realists, allow themselves to be carried away by the tropical scents of mango and guava so that they go home to read Garcia Marquez.

Self-destructive behaviour

In some young people the chaos resulting from the loss of their birth parents, especially the mother, together with the psychological and physical traumas at birth, later abuse, malnutrition and illness, can create a situation that is difficult to overcome. Often the result is negation, the alienation and the aggression move inwards in a self-destructive way – like Silvina, who cut herself with glass and a razor blade.

Jorge is another example. At the age of 15 he continually threatened to kill himself as a result of his feelings of wretchedness and uselessness, of not deserving to live how he did when others in his country were hungry, of being a coward for not helping them. In other cases the young people become violent, breaking things, or threatening their parents with knives, giving themselves a sadistic power that terrifies them and at the same time leaves them vulnerable. They can also become promiscuous, searching for the closeness that they cannot obtain without eroticising a relationship, or for the apparent control which a sexual relationship gives as a result of the seduction and sexual abuse to which they have been subjected without being able to defend themselves.

We know that abandoned and abused children face a high probability of the abuse being repeated. Among other things, this is the result of sexualised or provocative behaviour and, for some, because they appear to search for dangerous situations. The fact that these children feel betrayed by adults often makes it difficult for them to create new bonds with other adults, making the work of adoptive parents very hard. These children can never be compared with biological children in terms of the practical and emotional resources that will be needed from the parents, the school and others who have contact with them. Starting kindergarten, the arrival of a new sibling, coming into the care of other people, as is common in Norway, being left alone in the house when older than ten or eleven, must be considered in relation to the specific history of the child. Some authors suggest that creating emotional bonds requires at least those number of years that the child had lived on arrival in the new family – a child adopted at the age of six will not feel secure in the adoptive family until the age of 12. Obviously this is debatable but it can help us to see how vulnerable the emotional state of the children can be. Often the feelings of loss and of low self-esteem and the internal chaos of the child are reflected in a confusion that results naturally in poor school results and undesirable behaviour.

High-risk adoptions

The children and youths referred to in this chapter constitute a small group formed from a selection of my clients over a number of years. Taking into account that children above the age of five make up a small minority of those adopted internationally, and that in themselves only a small percentage of children present problems, we find ourselves dealing with a sample of high-risk adoptions.

Dutch and Australian studies (Hoksbergen, 1991; Harper, 1994) show that factors such as the older age of the adoptee, a negative meeting with the adoptive parents, children with special emotional or psychological needs, those with traumatic past experiences, and those with emotional difficulties and long periods of uncertainty before being placed in adoption cause problems in adoptions. These authors also indicate that other experiences have negative effects, for example, experiences of other adoptions that did not work; the impact on a child when forced to break from everything they know, such as family, friends, school, siblings; adoptions involving groups of more than three children; when the adopted child is older or of a similar age to the biological children; and when the expectations of the parents do not correspond to the qualities or resources of the child.

The fact that most adoptive parents are academically qualified is an important resource at the stage of primary education if the parents dedicate sufficient time to the child. However, it can be difficult for professionally successful parents to accept that their adopted child has a lower intellectual capacity or interests that are less sophisticated. In some cases this can be a new loss for the parents to cope with.

US child psychologist and therapist Vera Fahlberg (1994) emphasises the importance of focusing on the bonds between parents and adopted children to promote a better development in these cases. This is often very difficult to carry out. In many cases it may appear that the therapists want to take over the adopted child, even to the point of competing with the new parents and disqualifying them. The adoptive parents are very sensitive to this, and we should not use it to analyse them; instead, to prevent their feelings of insecurity, we should reaffirm the importance of their role and encourage them in it.

In some cases the children transfer to their new parents the role of perpetrators of abuse that their biological parents or other abusers had in the country of origin. This can cause difficult situations if, for example, the father is accused unjustly of sexually abusing the child.

'Gloria', a girl adopted at the age of nine after living from the age of five in a religious home with a prison-like system of punishment, was convinced that the man who adopted her was the one who had killed her mother and tried to rape her in her country of origin. Unfortunately, Gloria never managed to form a positive relation with her adoptive mother, who rejected her. Paradoxically, it was her adoptive father who supported her and maintained relations with her as she reached 18, having himself given up a son for adoption and experienced a very hard life.

Transference of traumas from children to parents

Within psychoanalysis it has been seen that the patient's destructive feelings can be transferred to the therapist, causing what is known as secondary trauma. Taking as a starting point the traumas of survivors of concentration camps, the negative effect that parents can have on their children has also been studied. This transposition occurs when children place themselves in the experiences that their parents have lived in an attempt to magically cure and rescue them. A visual example of this process is illustrated in the film, *Mendel* (Røssler, 1997), which tells the story of a seven-year-old boy whose parents want to protect him from their past experiences in a concentration camp. Mendel becomes obsessed with discovering the secrets that his parents are guarding and by searching through books and boxes he comes to identify deeply with their traumas.

I believe that adoptive parents may become traumatised by their children. Sometimes it even appears that the child is externalising everything, depositing all their past abuses on the parents, at the same time wearing themselves out painfully. One reaction of parents is to protect themselves and deny the pain experienced in children's homes, the hunger, the separation from their mothers, and instead attempt to "educate" the "uncivilised" child. Focusing on the child's experiences can cause great pain to the parents. In other cases, in individual consultations or those with both parents, they tell me that the trauma of the children causes them pain and of how, at times, the children superimpose their experiences on the parents. This can have immense therapeutic value and, by working with the therapist, parents can prepare themselves well for dealing with the situation.

Final words

The Brazilian child psychiatrist, Silva Alvaro Seligmann (1992), indicates the importance of the role of the therapist to these adoptive parents, 'helping them to be able to confront the reality of the violence that the children have suffered and carry within them, so that the children can begin to trust and feel secure and protected, with the knowledge that the family they now have can support the heavy charge of experience that they have brought without disintegrating or seeing the child's experiences as a destructive threat'.

For Seligmann (1992) these symptoms are often the only way for children to 'defend themselves from their internal and external worlds'. Clinical work with these children allows us to see more closely the reality of millions of children in Latin America and in the world. It is of vital importance that the parents and children are able to deal together with these experiences of abandonment and distress and that we help the parents to understand and the children to control their emotions. Without this possibility, the adaptation to a new family is made more difficult, and the behaviour of the children can form a vicious circle, which can lead to a repetition of physical and psychological maltreatment. In individual work with parents they have told me that the defiant behaviour of the children has led them to reactions of which they did not believe themselves capable, such as physical punishments (in Norway, even the smallest smack has been illegal since 1962), anger and shouting, and generally a great frustration at not being the good parents they imagined they could be. With a few hours of therapeutic work, both parents and children can reverse difficult situations, with a significant change in the family situation and the development and opening up of each of its members.

Acknowledgements

This chapter is adapted from a paper first presented in Spanish at the Symposium on Adoption organised by the Association of Psychologists of Buenos Aires, 22–23 August 1997. It has been translated by Alexander Selman and Monica Bousquet.

References

Botvar P K (1994) *Ny sjanse I Norge*. Oslo: Diaconia College.

Carli A (1987) 'Psychological consequences of political persecution: The effects on children of the imprisonment or disappearance of their parents', *Tidskrift for Norsk Psykolog Forening*, Nr. 24.

Carli A (1991) 'Psykologiske følger av politisk undertrykkelse på barn og familier, pskososiale konsekvenser og utfordringer for skole og hjelpeapparatet', *Tidskrift for Norsk Psykolog Forening*, Nr. 11.

Carli A (1994) 'Den skjulte historien: klinisk arbeid med utelandsk adopterte barn og deres foreldre', *Fokus på familien*, Nr. 4.

Carli A (1996) 'Flygtningebørn og deres familier', en Arenas J (comp.) *Inter-kulturelpsykologi*, Copenhagen: Hans Reitzel Forlag.

Carli A (1999) 'Refugee children re-united with their biological parents, unaccompanied refugee children and children with a traumatic background adopted overseas: Some risk factors in their new placements', in Ryvgold A L, Dalen M and Sætersdal B (1999) *Mine – Yours – Ours and Theirs: Adoption, changing kinship and family patterns*, Oslo: University of Oslo.

Carli A and Dalen M (1997) *Adopsjonsfamilien*, Oslo: Pedagogisk Forum.

Cederblad M (1991) 'Sverige adopsjonnsland', *Innvandrere och Miniriteter* 4–5, Stockholm.

Cohn J (1983) 'Barn og Tortur', en *Umenneskelighetens ansikter*, Copenhagen: Amnesti International Dansk Forlag.

Dalen M and Saetersdal B (1992) *Foreign-adopted children in Norway: adaptation – training – identity development*, Doctoral thesis, University of Oslo.

Fahlberg V (1994) *A Child's Journey through Placement*, London: BAAF.

Gustafsson L et al (1989) *Krigens Barn*, Oslo: Kommunneforlaget.

Harper J (1994) 'Counselling issues in intercountry adoption', *Adoption & Fostering*, 18:2, pp 20–26.

Hoksbergen R A C and Walenkamp H (1991) *Kind Van Andere Onders*, Houten: Bohn, Stafleu, van loghum.

Jareg E (1997) Ponencia en la conferencia, *Children and War*, Oslo: Redd Barna.

Kadjar–Hamouda E (1996) *An End to Silence: A preliminary study on sexual violence, abuse and exploitation of children affected by armed conflict*, UNICEF.

Røssler A (1997) *Mendel*, Oslo: Largometraje.

Sanhueza C (1990) 'Effekter på barn av ufrivllig, traumatiske adskillelser fra foreldre under et militærdiktatur', Valgfrittoppgave I Medisin, Univ. i Tromsø.

Seligmann Silva A (1992) personal communication.

25 Excluded mothers
Birth mothers relinquishing their children

Eva Giberti

Eva Giberti is a psychologist and psychotherapist and Director of the Master's degree course in Family Studies at the National University of San Martin in Argentina. She is well-known throughout Latin America as an expert in adoption and an advocate for the rights of birth mothers. She has written many books and articles on adoption and related matters. This chapter is based on her book, 'Madres Excluidas', written with Silvia Chavanneau de Gore, a lawyer, and Beatriz Taborda, a social worker, which was published in Argentina in 1997.

Introduction

In our country, Argentina, who are the women who give their children for adoption? What are their motives? What is the story of their lives? It was these questions that prompted this project on excluded mothers, i.e. mothers who have given their children up for adoption and whose experiences have not previously been studied in Latin America.

The years of having been in professional practice – academic, legal and social work – allowed those of us in the project group to maintain permanent contact with the women, the civil servants, the professionals involved in adoption, and with the adoptive parents. We were also well informed about judgements in adoption cases. However, at the same time we found a great lack of statistically processed data about the histories and identities of the women who gave up their children for adoption, nor could we find this information in any literature by Latin American authors.

Our hypothesis in the investigation was that the institutions (the universities, the Ministries of Justice and of Public Health) are not interested in these women as people, but rather as productive wombs to provide children for couples unable to conceive. Once the children had been given to the adoptive families the institutions distanced themselves from the mothers. Before starting our study about these birth mothers, we saw that we had focused on an important and uncomfortable theme: we were unable to obtain financial backing from the Argentine institution responsible for funding investigations of national importance. In the end, thanks to the intervention of CENEP (Centro de Estudios de Población: Centre of Population Studies), we received some support from a Swedish non-governmental organisation, SAREC (Swedish Agency for Research Co-operation with Developing Countries).

The aims of the study, carried out between 1991 and 1994, in addition to our basic conjectures about the professionals involved in these adoptions, were:

• to gain an understanding of the basic socio-demographic circumstances of the mothers who give their children up for adoption, and
• to understand the circumstances that led them to the decision to give up their children for adoption.

The study

We decided to review the files recording interviews with birth mothers conducted by psychologists and social workers between 1980 and 1989. We first used 123 files, 53 from the Department of Minors and the Family (Ministry of Health and Social Action), 49 from the Minors Tribunal of the province of Buenos Aires (locality; San Isidro), and 20 clinical histories from the maternity ward of the Piñeiro hospital (Buenos Aires). Methodological requirements forced us to reduce the sample after having conducted the first analysis, but the same trends were found in the 123 cases and the reduced sample of 53.

Reviewing the files we found significant gaps in the women's answers; the interviewers repeatedly wrote "Doesn't know" or "No answer" leaving the information incomplete. This was one of the reasons that we reduced our original sample. The professional lack of interest in the women's silence concerned us. We recognise that over-worked psychologists and social workers may not have sufficient time for each case but each of these women had a story that deserved more attention. We found a cover-up that showed a serious social problem and also an important problem in university politics. In our view, the institutions involved in adoption do not pay sufficient attention to the stories of the mothers who were close to and responsible for the children. This calls into question the way these women are perceived by the professionals who deal with their cases and initiate the process of adoption. This also applies to academic study, which does not recognise the psychological situation of these women and does not attempt to change the prejudices and dogmas of the property owning social classes. A large number of academics also follow the thinking that recommends the transference of the children to families "better" than the original. Included in these "better" families are those from other countries, despite the fact that Argentina does not adhere to international treaties on intercountry adoption.

As our study progressed, we found verification for our theory that these women were considered only as productive wombs for "better families".

Who are the mothers?

The ages of the mothers ranged from 12 to 42 years. More than half were under 21 and three-quarters under 25. That is to say, the women were predominantly very young, which leads us to question whether all of them wanted to give up their child or whether they gave in to family pressures – when dealing with a minor an adult (the mother or father) must be present.

More than a third had not completed primary education, and four were illiterate. Of the rest, the majority had not completed secondary schooling. Those under 17 had attained lower levels of education.

Most of the women had moved from their place of birth to look for work, although some had moved because of their pregnancy. Having a baby makes finding work very difficult, primarily because the women usually look for jobs in domestic service and will not get employment if they have children with them. Two-thirds of the mothers were employed in domestic service; the rest in the industrial sector, and in sewing and dress-making.

When we consider the migration of these women from their home area alongside their low education levels and the type of employment they had, the relinquishment of their children is predictable. In order to stay with the baby, these mothers would have needed day care as well as family support and housing.

Relations with family

Most of the mothers in our study were brought up by only one of their parents – their mothers. It is not known if they had other close relatives. It would have been very useful to learn if any of their siblings had given children up for adoption. The marital status of their mothers was not known. It was also not known if the women maintained contact with their parents. A third of the sample (the under-17s) lived with their parent(s); another third lived with either their husband or partner; and the final third with others not from their family.

The fact that some of the women lived with their family might lead one to suppose, erroneously, that they have family support: in fact, 50 per cent said that they had given up their child because their families did not support them. Eleven per cent had a husband or stable partner (all were over 25) but the existence of a partner did not mean that there was a wish to or a possibility of keeping the child. The rest of the women in the sample were single.

Who are the children given for adoption?

Fifty-seven per cent of the women had one or more other children and only gave up the last one. This is significant, not only because the adopted child will not know that he/she has siblings, but also because the siblings who remain with the mother will see their little brother or sister disappear[1] one day from the family and will not know what happened, so that they are then faced with a suspended mourning. For 90 per cent of the women, it was the first time that they had given up a child for adoption, and for half of these it was their first child. The relinquished children comprised equal numbers of boys and girls.

---

[1] The category "disappeared" is deeply significant for Argentinians. During the military dictatorship (1976–1984) our country saw the disappearance of 30,000 people. As a result, the disappearance of a baby from the family circle, even though the mother knows what has happened, constitutes a traumatic situation for the other children.

Age at adoption

Seventeen per cent of the children were new born and a further 47 per cent were under one month at the time of the adoption. This is important in respect to the imprinting that occurs during the first month of life; a new born baby differs significantly from a one-month-old in the attachment levels achieved from the effects of breast-feeding and psychological and sensorial experiences. In the majority of cases the baby studied stayed in an institution rather than with the mother before adoption.[2] Fourteen of the women (24 per cent) maintained contact with their baby for a number of months (up to 18 months), which had an impact on the situation and the baby's reaction on separation. We can only guess that in these cases the mothers did everything they could to keep the child.

Who is the father of the child?

In the majority of cases the women said that the father was a friend or acquaintance, either casual or sustained. Other responses in order of frequency were a partner, a husband, an unknown man (including a rapist), and finally a boyfriend or a member of the family. The answer "unknown" may well be an attempt to protect the father in the fear that institutions might intervene to legitimise the child; if living with the father, the woman may fear he would leave.

Among the adolescents, "unknown" may cover up sexual abuse by the father or step-father. The occurrence of incest is a significant factor in campesino (peasant) and conurban cultures and in urban areas (Giberti and Lamberti, 1998). The description of the father as "transitory" may also be a way of retaining the authority to give up the child. In any case, this leads to an important question because, by responding in this way, the women present themselves as maintaining planned and accidental sexual relations without any pretence of stability. In other words, it would seem that there was a high percentage who established sexual relations

---

[2] Babies adopted in Buenos Aires are placed in a family, paid for by the Department of Youth, where they live with up to three or four other babies in the charge of an employed woman. This system does not exist in the provinces, with the exception of some private organisations, and the babies are thus institutionalised until they are given to the adoptive family. If the family changes its mind about adoption, the babies thus risk continued institutionalisation.

with friends and acquaintances. This is not credible and appears to be a strategy to protect the father. Further, the type of response given seemed designed to strengthen the justification for giving up the child. Anomalies were found in the responses to the questions about motives for giving up the child. Half of the women responded "abandonment by partner" when previously they had identified the father as a friend or member of the family.

Reasons for relinquishing the child

The reason most commonly cited was a "lack of family support" but without making clear as to what exactly this meant. This response, like the previous "abandonment by partner", suggests that had the women received the support of a partner or their family, they would not have given up the child. Responsibility thus falls on a third party. Another reason cited quite frequently was "incapable of bringing up the child" and – very rarely – "rejection of the baby". This final answer was given by women with a husband or partner and it is possible that the child was conceived following marital rape.

The decision to give up a baby exposes the myth of the maternal instinct. The stereotype which associates the womb with maternal function, understood as a necessary value in women, is a product of the confusion of biology and axiology (Giberti, 1980, 1996). That is not to say that maternal love does not exist, but rather that its universalisation[3] as an instinct is false. The history of civilisation shows the falsity of the concept, considered so commonly as some unavoidable genetic factor. In situations where the survival of the mother is impossible with the child, the instinct is for self-preservation. This should be distinguished from what I have elsewhere (Giberti, 1987) described as "enforced

---

[3] 'At the end of the 18th century, for prosaic economic reasons, the myth of motherly love was given a prime place' (Badinter, 1981). Effectively, in 1870 Chancellor Brochard turned his eyes towards Prussia and, conscious of the reduced birth rate, begged mothers to fulfil their duty to France by reproducing and ensuring the survival of their children. The proposal proved successful for the bourgeoisie and the patriarchy from this century onwards; theologians, priests, doctors and other specialists insisted on the necessity of this form of love, and that, as a natural form, it should be instinctive in all women.

abandonment", i.e. where the economic position of the mother makes it impossible for her to raise a child. Such cases are distinct from many that we have discussed above, where the mothers found themselves obliged to give up their children for various reasons, often imposed by third parties.

Some final considerations

Although the sample with which we worked is not representative, it shows a tendency that can be seen in other areas of Argentina and other countries in Latin America. The findings of our study revealed the "invisible violence" found in the processes involved in the adoption of children. Fundamentally, the professional sectors and the adoptive parents take as their starting point their supposed cultural superiority compared to those of the child and his/her origins. This is a form of "invisible violence" (Bordieu, 1983). However, the women who give up their children do not regard it as such, having accepted the treatment they received. The father of the child showed no concern at the point of conception and later left the burdened woman; the family did not have the means to support another child; there are no national policies to protect a woman's reproductive rights and permit an expression of sexuality without the risk of unwanted pregnancy; and there are no policies to protect single mothers who wish to keep their child.

It is vital to make these facts known to illustrate the position of the victim and the effects of social and psychological abandonment. Those in favour of adoption as necessary and effective to provide protection for children who need it, insist on prioritising the "best interests of the child" whom the authorities consider as the only victim of the separation, without seeing that the mother is also a victim. It is true that generally these women earn very low wages or lack the basic necessities to bring up a child, but that cuts across other factors such as their being extremely young, being migrants, and fundamentally, being women.

These factors cannot be considered as only obvious; they are a clear reflection of the living conditions in Latin America and form part of a history characterised by the social exclusion of vast sectors of the population, in particular women and children. Among the younger mothers the reason most commonly stated for giving up a child was the lack of support from the family: as we indicated earlier, we had doubts about how to interpret "lack of support", and at the same time it appeared that the decision to give up a child represents a break in the family model that keeps the children within the birth family framework.

Mothers who already had one or more children made up the largest group in the sample: most of these had just given up the last child that they could not maintain; but there were also those who repeatedly relinquished children. Some of the mothers had separated from the baby just after birth, while others had lived for a considerable period with the child. Some had been violated, others wanted the pregnancy, and yet others did not understand what was happening to them. It would seem that the decision to give a child up for adoption signals a break from the cultural model which sustains children in the family group.

Our study shows a culture in the depths of poverty, of people whose social values or norms are different from those considered normal and correct. It has not been studied but one supposes that the mothers may feel grateful to those who free them of an unwanted baby; certainly many perceive it as such but we do not believe it applies to all. These women who give their children up for adoption, ignored by the statistics, ignored by public institutions, morally denigrated, misunderstood by so many professionals, and taken advantage of by certain "charitable" souls, have made their appearance on the scene.

This chapter has been translated from the original Spanish by Alexander Selman and Monica Bousquet.

Acknowledgements

I would not have been able to make this study without Catalina Wainermans' intervention and Alejandra Pantelides's generous advice, both members of CENEP as investigators. The results of this research have been edited at the request of Daniel Filmus. He is the director of FLACSO (Latin America University for Social Science).

Readers can learn more about Eva Giberti's work at her website: http://www.tasknet.net/giberti.

References

Badinter E (1981) ¿Existe el amor materno? (*Does Maternal Love Exist?*) Buenos Aires: Paidos.

Bordieu P (1983) *Campo del Poder* (*The Field of Power*), Buenos Aires.

Giberti E (1980) *Maternidad e Ideología Obstétrica* (*Maternity and Obstetric Ideology*), Ficha ofset No 71 del Centro de Estudios de la Mujer, Buenos Aires: editada en Temario Psicopatológico Año VII, No 8, 1982.

Giberti E (1987) *Abandono y Maternidad* (*Motherhood and Abandonment*), Buenos Aires: Conferencia dictada en el servicio de Neonatología de la Maternidad Sardá, Inéedito.

Giberti E (1996a) 'El lado oscuro de la maternidad' ('The dark side of maternity') in *Actualidad Psicológica*: Diciembre.

Giberti E (1996b) 'Niñas-madres, una expresión perversa' (Child-mothers: a perverse expression) in *Sociedades y Políticas*: Fundación Pibes Unidos.

Giberti E (1996c) 'Desvalimiento y exclusión: la adopción y el tráfico con niños como paradigma' (Devaluing and exclusion: the adoption and traffic of children as a paradigm), Texto de la participación en panel sobre Exclusión Social y Desvalimiento: Universidad de Bar Ilan, Octubre.

Giberti E, Chavanneau de Gore S and Taborda B (1997) *Madres Excluidas* (*Excluded Mothers*), Buenos Aires: Grupo Editorial Norma.

Giberti E and Lamberti S (1998) *Incesto Paterno-filial* (*Parent-child Incest*), Buenos Aires: Ed Universidad.

26 Experiences of adopting from China

Roger Shead

Roger Shead works as an engineer in the electrical supply industry; he is married to Marion who is Head of Music in a large secondary school. They have two daughters; both were adopted in the People's Republic of China.

Introduction

This chapter describes the experience of intercountry adoption (ICA) from the viewpoint of the adopters. It is based on the experiences that my wife and I have had from 1992, when we decided to adopt a child from China, through to the present. In that time we adopted our two daughters now aged five and four. Although in many ways our experiences have been typical of those adopting from China, I have also tried to include others in order to give a broader picture.

In the past eight years we have met many other adopters through our participation in the national support group Children Adopted From China (CACH), for which I acted as membership secretary for the first two years after its formation in 1995. Through CACH, our local ICA support group and membership of UK and overseas adoption groups we try to keep informed of developments in ICA. While circumstances have changed considerably – and often for the better – over that period, when we talk to those considering ICA or applying to adopt we recognise many aspects that have not altered.

The decision to adopt

We decided to investigate adoption when we realised that we were very unlikely to have birth children. Like many other adopters, we had tried fertility treatment without success and concluded that the success rate was not so high as to convince us to continue. In addition, we did not regard having our own birth children as of overriding importance. We knew there were many children in the world who, for a variety of reasons, either had no living parents or whose parents were unable to care for them.

We started to research adoption, learning whatever we could from any source we could find including the published experiences of adopters and adoptees, organisations concerned with adoption, and press and other reports. We also approached our local social services department and it very soon became clear that we would not, because of our ages – then 39 and 43 – be considered as suitable adoptive parents for a baby or young child. Like many childless would-be adopters, we had hoped that our first experience of parenthood would be as similar as possible to that of birth parents. In any case, neither of us then had any experience of parenting and the prospect of adopting an older child who might in addition have behaviour difficulties was one that we found very daunting.

At this time, in the early 1990s, there seemed to be many articles about older mothers and this, coupled with the trend towards later parenthood, made the arbitrary rule of domestic adoption that those aged over 35 were ineligible to adopt a baby or young child seem particularly callous and illogical. In addition, the availability of fertility treatment had made matters worse for those for whom it was unsuccessful by delaying the consideration of adoption.

All these factors led us to consider intercountry adoption where at least some countries required prospective adopters to be over a certain age to be eligible – suggesting to us that maturity and stability of relationship were valued. However, choosing the country to apply to was difficult and took us months to decide. There was a bewildering variety of requirements for the many different countries and in some cases doubts about the integrity of those involved in administering the process of adoption in the children's country of origin. In the end our choice was China because there were many genuinely abandoned children and a clear system of regulated administration.

Although domestic adoption did not seem to be the path for us, other adopters had come to intercountry adoption through applying and being approved to adopt in the UK. We met one couple who had been approved as prospective adopters, but their routine telephone enquiry to their local social services department to keep up to date elicited the reply, 'We've taken you off the list – you're too old'. Perhaps unsurprisingly, they were taken aback both by the information and the way it was conveyed.

Approaching social services

Our initial approach to our local social services was not encouraging. We arranged an interview with the adoption advisor to talk about intercountry adoption. One of the first things she made clear to us was that they treated ICA in exactly the same way as domestic adoption – making no distinction whatsoever in the standards that were applied. While it is quite proper that a child should not be treated in a way that is inferior to agreed best practice on the basis of his or her country of origin, it raised a problem for us. As already mentioned, some countries have rules that adopters have to be over a certain age – at that time, 35 years old in the case of China. As far as our ages were concerned, we were eligible to adopt under Chinese law, whose adoptions, as a "designated country", are recognised under UK law. The adviser offered no resolution or guidance on this point.

The matter of the age of adopters raises the general question about the compatibility of different nations' adoption laws and regulations. If the requirements of "sending" and "receiving" States (to use the Hague Convention's terms) differ, the Convention, which contains minimum standards agreed by ratifying countries, recognises the variations in national laws but leaves the reconciling to the particular sending and receiving countries.

In all, this and the rest of the discussion seemed to us almost wholly negative and left us feeling that an application via our local social services had nothing to offer us. In retrospect, I wish I had formally challenged the content of that interview.

In general, the reception that ICA adopters received at that time varied considerably from the welcoming and informed, though this was a rarity, through the impartial to the actively hostile. In addition, we soon realised that a great deal of control rests with others, in this instance with the local authority. The control may be expressed as statute, regulations, rules laying down procedure or simply in accepted practice itself. However expressed, the path to parenthood for adopters is, once a decision to adopt has been made, in very large measure controlled by others. The contrast with the experience of birth parents – especially with regard to their age – is stark.

The need for regulation and oversight is usually clearly recognised by adopters and, among the adopters from China we have encountered, compliance with the administrative requirements has been very thorough. However, the way in which that regulation was exercised was sometimes hard to bear.

Preparation classes

Although we had concluded that an application through our local authority was pointless, we nonetheless decided to attend the forthcoming preparation classes. We were sure that the classes would be useful in improving our knowledge and understanding of adoption.

While we were waiting for the first of the four one-day sessions of the preparation classes, we contacted an independent social worker with a view to commissioning a private home study, as some countries, including China at that time, permitted adoption applications on this basis. We were fortunate in contacting someone who was both very well qualified and had long experience as a senior social worker in a social services department and who specialised in intercountry adoption and worked under contract to local authorities. That she was the mother of birth children and an adopted child from overseas as well as being an adoptee gave us considerable confidence that a home study by her would be both thorough and to a high standard.

We also talked to our families about our hopes. For us, ICA seemed complex and difficult to grasp although we had been researching it as thoroughly as we could. Our families did not know what to think, having no direct experience of ICA. We told few people at that stage because of the uncertainty that we would be able to adopt. Being asked repeatedly what progress you are making when you often have no idea of the answer simply serves as a reminder of the uncertainty. In any case, the emotions evoked by involuntary childlessness are complex, and sometimes unpredictable and well-meaning comments can touch a raw nerve. One friend with children, when learning of our plans said jokingly, 'Oh! You can have my children'. That simply illustrated the gulf between someone who was confident and relaxed about her experience of parenthood and we who stood outside that experience wondering if we would ever share it. The remark was not malicious or meant in any way unkindly nor were remarks like it uncommon.

Our experience of the preparation classes was a mixed one. The classes were intended for prospective domestic adopters and covered a wide range of adoption issues including reasons for and perceptions of adoption, the adoption process, separation of a child from his/her birth family, case studies, the needs of adoptive children and helping children understand their adoption. Although the classes were well planned they tended to be rather stilted, with the prospective adopters being – as we were to a degree – guarded in their participation and one of the two staff running the classes making the sessions rather formal.

At the outset, it was made very clear that adoption is a service for children, that it must not be regarded as a last resort for the childless and that one of the aims of the classes was to get adopters to see the process from the social services' standpoint. While all these have merit, our perspective was somewhat different. We understood very clearly that adoption is not another form of fertility treatment or a service for parents and wholeheartedly agree with that but throughout the classes there was no acknowledgement that adoptive parents were of any value. There seemed to be no recognition that for a child to find a loving, caring family, that family has to be there for the child.

The idea that adoption was not a last resort is largely fanciful. For many of the adopters we have spoken to it is the last resort. Indeed this may be desirable if it means that a clear decision has been reached that infertility treatment has been put aside. Many adopters come to adoption in this way. They would like to have birth children – just as the majority of readers of this chapter will have chosen for themselves – and most will have tried to do this. To have acknowledged that they will not have birth children and to make a clear-minded decision that they still want children, leaves adoption as the "last resort" for many adopters. This does not mean that they regard adoption as trivial or inferior – indeed quite the opposite is true – but it is nonetheless their last resort and to suggest otherwise is unrealistic.

There also seemed to be an element of control conveyed in that it was made clear that decisions were made about adopters and that information was tightly controlled. This came out during questions in the last session of the preparation classes when an adoptive mother came to talk to the group. Her account of her experience of the adoption process indicated how little the prospective adopters knew of what was happening once they had been approved to adopt. At this session, the discussion was both more animated and relaxed and, after all the talk and study of the previous classes, it was encouraging to know that adoptions did actually take place. Indeed, this last session was the only one that actually showed that adoption had any positive aspects.

Meeting adoptive families

As well as listening to an adoptive mother at preparation classes, we were very glad to have the chance to visit two families who had already adopted from China. It was delightful for us to meet them and see how well the two girls were settling in to their new families, and to learn from the parents about their experiences. For what seemed to us like a very long time, the adoption process had seemed rather theoretical and at times also like a paper chase. In adoption, and particularly intercountry adoption, it seemed at times that everyone connected with us had to be consulted and give their formal approval. While it was all quite properly directed to determining whether we were fit to be adoptive parents, we had actually met only one nine-year-old intercountry adoptee, although we knew a number of adult (UK) adoptees, indeed more than we at first realised. So meeting adoptive families suddenly made the process real for us. Though we had met and spoken to adopters, actually meeting adoptive families with their children from China was a marvellous experience. It also enabled us to tell our families more about what we hoped to do and to reassure them that we really did have some idea of what we were doing.

At that time also, adopters were one of the main sources of information about the adoption process and even now, with important sources such the Overseas Adoption and Information Service (OASIS), the Department of Health (DoH) and the Overseas Adoption Helpline available, meeting adopters and adoptees is still very valuable for prospective adopters.

The home study

When we had completed the preparation classes, we started our home study with our independent social worker, a process which spread over the following two and a half months. This covered all the areas a domestic home study would normally include and also dealt with issues such as cultural identity and racism and how we planned to deal with them. Our social worker also helped us to broaden and deepen our understanding of adoption and encouraged us to expand our network of contacts, both of which we were happy to do.

Her completed report, covering all the elements of the commonly used Form F but without using the form itself, ran to 25 A4 pages. To this were added her reports on her interviews with our referees and all our supporting documents.

At about this time we attended a meeting organised by an American adoption agency. Although they were very experienced in assisting American adopters and had staff in China with good working relations with the Chinese authorities, they had no experience of UK adoption processes. However, their approach was that if we could manage the UK application process, they could assist us in China. We were quite clear in our minds that we would definitely need help if we ever got to China. Subsequently we contacted UK adopters who vouched for the agency and we decided to ask them to help us in China.

All this was in marked contrast to the situation in other European countries where so-called "full service" agencies are permitted in law and can assist prospective adopters throughout the whole adoption process. This enables them to build up considerable expertise and knowledge and leads to a more consistent and integrated system. Such agencies may also be involved in supporting the work of particular orphanages and childcare institutions and helping to improve standards of child care. This in turn informs their ICA work.

In due course, having completed our dossier of documents, we had them notarised and legalised and took them to the Chinese Embassy in

London to be consularised before sending them to Beijing. While we were waiting for this, we had a telephone call from another couple who were at the same stage to say that China would no longer accept home studies without a DoH certificate – and that the DoH would not issue certificates for independent home study reports.

We then contacted our local social services again, told them what had happened and asked them if they would consider our application. After some correspondence they agreed to a joint presentation to the adoption panel by our independent social worker and a local authority social worker, with whom we would do additional work for a composite home study. However, this was followed by a period when the promise to arrange the first visit went unfulfilled and we started on more correspondence to restart the process. At the time we were not sure why this delay of several months occurred but in the last year my wife has had two separate and quite independent conversations with social services staff who both gave the same explanation. At that time our local social services did not feel adequately prepared for ICA work and simply hoped that we would go away. In fact we were, in one respect, very fortunate, although at the time this was not obvious. Although they were not prepared for ICA at least they were not hostile to intercountry adoption.

At that time there were social services departments that were adamantly opposed to ICA. The policy statement of one of them gave its reasons for opposition by equating ICA with baby trafficking and grouping all sending countries together in having at least inadequate and at worst corrupt practices. In their opposition, such authorities, while seeming to put the interests of children in their culture first, block the actions of those who would give at least some children arguably the most important thing that any child can have – a loving, caring family.

When our home study resumed with our local authority social worker, it took several sessions before formality gave way to a more relaxed working relationship. There was I think initial wariness on both sides. We were not sure about the attitude of our local social services to intercountry adoption and our new social worker was probably not sure what to make of us.

We are fortunate that circumstances have changed greatly in the last few years. Our local social services department is now well placed to carry out intercountry adoption work and has encouraged links with the local ICA support group.

In general, like many prospective adopters, we found the home study and, to some extent, the preparation classes stressful events and weighed up every reply and comment made in the presence of any social worker. This is partly because we perceived social workers as "gatekeepers", having the power to exclude or admit adopters from a vital stage in the adoption process, without knowing what the social worker or the adoption panel were looking for or what their attitude to ICA might be.

While we were honest and conscientious, we were also circumspect in our comments, although there were the occasional moments of humour. When we were asked to write about the experience of being childless, my wife compiled a list of observations, many of them, to her, unfavourable, including having to talk to social workers. In general, adopters often accept as best they can whatever treatment is meted out to them in order to make the process work. They are often extremely reluctant to complain for fear, as they see it – and as we saw it – of putting the outcome in jeopardy.

Moving on

In due course our extended home study was completed and presented to the local adoption panel jointly by our social workers and a couple of weeks afterwards we received formal approval and our papers were passed to the DoH for further legal and medical scrutiny.

At that time the DoH was not in general regarded favourably by prospective adopters. Calls to the Department seemed at times to be unwelcome, the information obtainable was very limited and not always accurate, there was no monitoring of documents sent to China and the Department appeared to us as simply another gatekeeper. Undoubtedly there were constraints placed on the staff of which adopters were not aware and which were never explained. This situation, however, has changed greatly to the point where the staff are approachable and well-informed and the section concerned provides useful guidance to adopters about the administrative process and keeps track of the progress of applications to China.

After legalisation and consularisation at the Chinese Embassy, the dossier was sent at our request to the Ministry of Civil Affairs in Beijing, which at that time was jointly administering the process of intercountry adoption in China with the Ministry of Justice.

The American agency we had contacted earlier confirmed that our papers had arrived and were being processed. While this was very reassuring another matter was causing us concern. Six months before our papers were sent to China, my wife Marion, who is a teacher, had informed her head teacher that we hoped to adopt from China and asked for a period of adoption leave of about three months duration, preferably paid. As we hoped to travel to China at Easter, when combined with the normal school Easter and summer holidays, this would allow her about five months with our daughter to help her to settle in her new home.

In the event things did not work out like that. Neither the school, at that time grant maintained, nor the school's local education authority, had an adoption leave policy. The tone was set in a meeting with the school's bursar when Marion made a formal request for adoption leave. The bursar's response was, 'I don't think the governors are going to pay you to sit at home and do nothing'. At that time there were two members of staff planning to take paid maternity leave and return to work afterwards. The contrast was stark.

The request for adoption leave was rejected by the school and shortly afterwards Marion found out by chance that her part-time job was being advertised as a full-time post. After seeking legal advice, Marion complained that the school had not acted legally; thereafter, the school did not offer the post to any of the candidates they had interviewed but instead offered it to her providing she started full-time work the following term. By this time, however, we had received an adoption referral from China. The referral included a passport-sized photograph of a baby tightly wrapped in a yellow jacket and looking impassively at the camera, the corners of her mouth turned down. There was some brief information about her giving her date of birth, saying that she was healthy and giving the name of the welfare institution caring for her. It was then two-and-a-half years since we had first approached our local social services department to ask about adoption and looking at the photograph, it seemed extraordinary that we had at last been matched with a baby on the other side of the world.

We faxed back our acceptance and started to make plans to travel, arranging, with the agreement of the school, to fly to China on the last day of the spring term. Accepting the school's offer of the post would have meant putting our daughter into child care within a week of returning to the UK, something that we would not even consider.

In general, the provision of adoption leave is still very uneven. Many employers have no adoption leave policy at all while others treat adoptive mothers on an equal basis to birth mothers. In the case of adoptive fathers, however, there is usually complete parity with birth fathers. That is to say, fathers are expected to take at most three days off work and any other leave of absence is expected to be taken as annual leave. Obviously fathers are not considered to have any significant role in parenthood.

The 1999 announcement that the UK will implement the European Union Parental Leave Directive is a welcome improvement. This will mean that for the first time in the UK there will be a statutory entitlement to adoption leave that will apply to both parents and that can be spread over an extended period. However, the leave will be unpaid and will apply until the child concerned reaches the age of five years. Unpaid leave will restrict its usefulness for families on low incomes; limiting it to children under five is anomalous as it will discriminate against families adopting older children, whether domestically or from overseas. Despite these reservations, we would certainly have welcomed the proposed statutory entitlement to adoption leave.

Meanwhile, the American agency had put us in touch with another couple and a single woman, both in the UK, who were adopting children from the same institution and we arranged to travel as a group. Although we were prepared to travel on our own, the thought of having the support of others who would understand exactly how we felt was very welcome. Practical suggestions from a family who had recently adopted from China were also very helpful as we prepared to travel.

At last all our arrangements were made and we drove to Heathrow to meet our fellow adopters for the overnight flight to Beijing. Neither Marion nor I slept and instead passed the time trying to reconcile our completely incompatible lists of girls' names and talking to a Chinese passenger. He was surprised to learn that we were going to China to adopt but nonetheless very positive about it. This set the scene in a small way for the general response that Chinese people have expressed to us about the adoption by westerners of abandoned children. Although a few other adopters have told us of Chinese people who have disapproved, in the main the Chinese seem to take a very practical view of the fact that many children, especially girls, are abandoned and often regard those who are adopted as "the lucky ones".

On our arrival at Beijing Airport we were met by a local representative of the American agency who asked us to call him Robert. We stayed overnight in Beijing before travelling the next day to Nanjing in Jiangsu Province. There we were met by the director of the welfare institution and travelled by minibus to the city of Wuxi.

About an hour before we were due to arrive in Wuxi we stopped for petrol and the Director made a phone call. When we were back on the minibus, Robert explained that we were going first to the welfare institution to collect the children before going on to our hotel. We were all stunned by this – too surprised to question a change in our planned schedule of staying at the hotel overnight and going fully prepared to the institution the next day. In part this acquiescence was the result of anxiety about this final phase of the adoption process. As a childless couple, our first adoption was an all-or-nothing event; when we became an established family with one child our outlook certainly altered. In fact, many UK adopters have reported being presented with their adoptive children for the first time unexpectedly, for example, in their hotel lobby as they are checking in. The only explanation we have ever heard for this is that the adoptive child has the evening and following morning to get used to his or her adoptive parents and vice versa before the formal adoption process starts. At least we had a little time to prepare ourselves.

When we arrived at the institution we were shown to a meeting room where three nurses were standing, each holding a baby tightly wrapped in clothes and a shawl. Looking from child to child we suddenly recognised our daughter from the tiny photograph that had arrived just two months before. Marion took Dongmei from her nurse and held her in arms all the while gazing at her. Dongmei gazed back impassively and silently, undoubtedly confused and having no idea that this was an event that was going to change all our lives so profoundly. I took a couple of photographs and within fifteen minutes we were back in the minibus on the way to our hotel. It was at this time that we first realised that both Dongmei and one other baby, who was also six months old, had chest infections and we could feel the congestion in their lungs as they breathed even through the layers of clothing. Also neither of them could hold their own heads up and instead had to be supported like much younger babies. At this stage, although we were concerned about their breathing, we were preoccupied for a while with getting to the hotel and trying to settle the children in as it was now early evening and getting dark.

In our hotel room we changed Dongmei out of her five layers of clothes into clothes we had brought and changed her nappy. We prepared a bottle for her using the formula we had been advised to bring with us, fed her and settled her down for the night on the makeshift cot we improvised from two arm chairs and some blankets. We unpacked and took it in turns to get something to eat in the hotel restaurant before going to bed early. By then we had had enough excitement for one day.

The next morning it was clear the children were no better and we asked Robert to call a doctor. She arrived shortly afterwards and examined both children. She reported that while Dongmei possibly had a mild case of bronchitis the other baby had pneumonia and should go straight to hospital. The baby and her mother together with Marion and Robert went to the hospital while I looked after Dongmei.

Over the next three days, the baby with pneumonia was treated on a day-patient basis; Dongmei was examined twice more and also diagnosed with pneumonia and treated at the hospital. New cots arrived for the children and Dongmei started to develop a rash, which was later diagnosed as eczema caused by the cow's milk based formula we had brought with us. In the welfare institution the children were probably fed a soya-based formula.

We also completed the administration for the adoption. The interviews at the Civil Affairs office for the finalisation of the adoption, the notary public for the issue of notarised birth, adoption and medical certificates and the Bureau of Public Security for the issue of the children's passports, all went well. At the notary public's office, after hasty discussion, we agreed that Dongmei should become Rosalyn Dongmei, immediately shortened to Rosie. These visits were a blend of formal administration and the informality that a group of adults and young children engaged on a happy and at times anxious life-changing process created. I got the impression that for the officials these particular tasks were ones that they enjoyed and indeed many of the Chinese people we met showed great interest in and affection towards the children. However, this is not always the case and some adopters have encountered Chinese people who have made clear their objection to ICA.

Before leaving for Beijing we returned once again to the welfare institution. We were welcomed by the Director and the children's nurses into the same room we had seen a few days before. We paid the institution treasurer the statutory orphanage donation and the mother of the baby who was in hospital asked if she could see where her daughter had been living. At first this was refused but when repeated the request was granted. She was able to see the very plain room with cots pushed together in rows and children peering from beneath covers and took some photographs before the staff insisted she should leave.

Even at this time, before the television programme "The Dying Rooms" had been broadcast, the access adopters had to welfare institutions and orphanages was very variable. Although in our case very limited, other adopters found institutions much more open. It was also clear from Norwegian adopters we met in China that established links between institutions and adoption/charitable agencies could lead both to very good access for adopters and improvements in child care in the institutions through support from agencies for the work of the institutions.

The next day we were relieved that the children were well enough to travel and we returned to Beijing. After visiting the British Embassy to apply for the children's visas we took the two younger children to a hospital for a check-up. This confirmed they were recovering well but that they should be kept indoors. We collected the visas later that day and a few days later we were ready to fly home. As we walked along the aisle of the plane, I was surprised to be warmly greeted by another passenger, an acquaintance I had not seen for several years. He and his wife were in a party of about forty people from the UK who had been touring China. We got talking and within a little while Rosie, who was by this time able to hold her head up largely unsupported, had acquired forty new uncles and aunts who seemed both surprised and delighted by her story. In many regards their response has been typical of the many people we have encountered over the last five years. So far, we have experienced no overt racism towards our children although we know families who have. As the children grow older this will almost certainly change and we are not complacent about this.

We returned home, relieved that we had at last succeeded in our hopes of becoming parents and arranged to visit our GP for Rosie to be examined. The doctor reassured us about Rosie's health, in particular that the pneumonia had responded well to treatment, although his examination was brief. Later we arranged for a blood test because of our concern, amongst other things, of the chance of Rosie having been exposed to hepatitis.

One of our earliest visitors was our health visitor who started the standard health record book and at our request noted Rosie's areas of "blue spot" on her back and wrist to avoid confusion with bruising – and a suspicion of child abuse as happened to another adopter. At that time we had not seen growth curves for Chinese children, later published by OASIS, and had to rely on the ones for Western children in the health record book; on these Rosie was on the lowest curve. We also informed social services that we had adopted Rosie and later received a letter from them sending their good wishes.

The pneumonia that the two children suffered was serious and potentially life-threatening had it not been treated quickly and effectively. In general, the majority of children adopted seem to be in reasonable health. However, a few have been very seriously ill indeed; a larger minority have had respiratory and other infections; a significant minority have cleft lips, palates or both, later corrected with surgery but with implications for speech development and the need for future surgery. Some of the children have suffered significantly from lack of care and have difficulty, for example, forming attachments or with sensory integration.

Among the letters waiting for us when we returned home was one for Marion from her school saying that, as she had not accepted the offer they had made, her post would be re-advertised. Marion took the school to an Industrial Tribunal, supported by her union and the Equal Opportunities Commission. After two years this resulted in an out-of-court settlement and a binding agreement on the school to introduce an adoption leave policy.

Marion stayed at home with Rosie for five months before returning to work, at first covering for a teacher on maternity leave. It was about this time that the first meeting of the support group Children Adopted From China (CACH) took place with a weekend gathering of 25 families. Together with OASIS and AFAA, the Association for Families who have Adopted from Abroad, CACH, which now has over 300 members, is a valuable point of contact for adopters and prospective adopters. In our experience, although there are now many sources of information, there is no substitute for the support of those who experienced the process at first hand.

As well as supporting those in the process of adopting, the support groups are increasingly turning their attentions to the children already adopted and growing up in the UK. Both nationally and locally, adopters' groups are looking to the future for their families with a combination of meetings about adoption, identity and racism, celebrations of Chinese festivals and forming links with Chinese community associations and families. The children who will remain in institutions in China are not forgotten; a group of adoptive families have founded the charity The One World Orphanage Trust to raise money for direct and practical support for them.

The absence, at present, of any UK ICA agency means that UK adopters get their most up-to-date information by piecing together reports from a variety of sources. It is also still the case that what you experience, the way you are treated, including how much you are charged, depends on where you live as regards the policy, resources, experience and attitude of the local social services. The UK's ratification of the Hague Convention may bring changes to this situation.

Final thoughts

Finally, to return to the personal, Rosie has grown into a very articulate and able girl, achieving well at school and with a more active social life than her parents. We went on to adopt again, this time a girl two years old, now called Jessica, who had two periods in an institution and two period of foster care. She is a happy, outgoing girl and has adapted well to the enormous changes in her life. Both children have weekly Chinese lessons and I continue to go to Chinese evening classes.

At the time of Jessica's adoption, Marion was eligible for two weeks unpaid leave of absence but at least did not lose her job. I was fortunate to have, by UK standards, a very enlightened employer and was granted four weeks paid leave and combined this with three weeks time off in lieu of payment for overtime I had already worked plus three weeks of my annual holiday entitlement. We have been fortunate until very recently to have an excellent local authority-run nursery nearby that has helped both children greatly, although this has now been closed by the same local authority.

When people learn about what has happened to Rosie and Jessica we often get the same comment – that they are lucky children. While we understand what they mean, our view is different: to be abandoned, institutionalised and then adopted to a place where everything is different is better than some of the options but it is we, their parents, who are really the lucky ones.

27 **In whose interests?** Reflections on openness, cultural roots and loss

Sue Jardine

Sue Jardine is an Information Officer at the National Institute for Social Work (NISW). She is a member of the Association for Transracially Adopted People (ATRAP) and on the Management Committee of the Chinese Information Advice Centre London. She has participated in conferences and led workshops exploring issues relating to transracial adoption and intercountry adoption. Her involvement in Project 16–18[1] was to work in collaboration with the Catholic Children's Society (Nottingham) to set up a website to encourage siblings separated by adoption to share their experiences on the web.

I was born in Hong Kong during the 1960s. From a young age I knew that I was adopted. What I had been told about my background was that I had been found on the steps of a Buddhist Temple, after which I was taken in by an orphanage run by a Baptist church located in the New Territories, mainland China.

Openness

When I was about one-and-a-half years old I came over to the UK, initially fostered, then adopted into my family. I have older brothers and sisters who are my adoptive parent's birth children. When I was a child my adoption was not something I felt had a great impact on me. On occasions I remember comments being passed about me e.g. 'Where

---

[1] In 1999, Overseas Adoption Helpline, in partnership with Catholic Children's Society, Nottingham, produced a training resource on the post-adoption implications of inter-country adoption. Comprising extracts from audio taped interviews and a set of practice notes, the resource provides a unique insight into the experiences of 7 young people adopted from overseas. This initiative forms a small part of Project 16–18, which sought the views of young people from the UK placed for adoption by Catholic Children's Society, Nottingham. Chapters 27 and 28 are contributions which formed part of this project and were written up by Gill Haworth.

was I from?' and that I was adopted, but they were infrequent, so I was not forced into a situation where I had to really think about it.

My adoption was not talked about because to be adopted was to be integrated into a new family in a new country. This meant taking on values, attitudes, etc. of that country; after all, that is where we would be living and growing up. My adoptive status was, therefore, something which was not dwelt upon.

The fact that I grew up in an area where there were very few Chinese people, in fact very few people from ethnic minorities, meant that I was not placed into an environment which reminded me of how different, and visibly different, I am to my family. I grew up with a colour-blind approach to myself. It was very easy for me to distance myself from my origins and my physical appearance and because I was so isolated as I grew older, it became increasingly unsettling for me to think of myself as being different to my family and the people I was growing up with. One of the consequences of this is that comments about me, in particular racist comments, have been very hard for me to deal with. It was difficult for me to seek support and understanding of these situations as at the time I was not able to articulate my feelings about them.

As I got older, another reason why my adoption was not talked about in the family was because I did not want to be associated with it. I lacked confidence in talking about my origins because there was so little information. e.g. a simple question like do your parents live in this country, can elicit numerous answers and raise many more questions. I was in a position of having to explain my circumstances, much of which was painful for me to speak of. The difficulty I had in speaking of my background is also due to the criticism I got for not being able to speak Chinese, e.g. as an adult I have been approached by non Chinese people asking me questions in Chinese, who have then reproached me for not being able to respond in the way they wanted. In a Chinese restaurant, when I was in the company of Chinese people, I have been ridiculed by a waiter because I could not understand what he was saying. I have therefore experienced negative comments from both sides.

I have also been reluctant to talk about adoption because of the mixed messages I absorbed about it – mostly negative. I did not regard being adopted as meaning I was "special". After all, hadn't I been abandoned? My perception of adoption has been formed through external factors such as the media and remarks made by people who, for example, have (unthinkingly) told me that a way of hurting their brothers or sisters was to tell them they were adopted. In my experience, telling a child they are adopted is a way of threatening them.

Recent examples where this has been done is in comedy television programmes such as *The Simpsons, The Royle Family* and *Men Behaving Badly*. The notion that adoptees are special because they have been "chosen" does put pressure on us to perform well and fulfill the wishes of our adoptive parents. There is also a greater risk if we fail because in the back of our minds there can be a feeling that, if we do not live up to expectations, we can be "sent back". Because of the circumstances in which I was found (abandoned) I feel there are expectations that I should be "special". But the way I wanted to be special was to have special powers, like Superman or Harry Potter. Myths and fairy tales such as these romanticise what it is to be an abandoned baby.

Cultural roots

At the time of my adoption, cultural origins were not seen as being important for the development of an intercountry adoptee. Living in a predominately White area perpetuated these beliefs. Having little inform-ation about my origins, having no memory of my first few years, and being told that I had been "rescued" from my country of origin made it very easy to relinquish any connection I had with Hong Kong.

Today attitudes towards cultural identity are different. I believe this is partly because black and minority ethnic people living in the UK have succeeded in gaining a stronger voice for themselves (though this tends to be confined to urban areas where a greater number of black and minority ethnic people live) and because adoption agencies have taken on board the cultural needs expressed by transracially adopted adults.

Adoptive parents are now expected to encourage and support this aspect of their child's identity. My adoptive family did in fact have strong connections with Chinese people while I was growing up. Before I joined the family they lived in Singapore. Also, when I was growing up, my Godparents lived in Hong Kong and we had a Chinese student living with us for a number of years.

I was therefore in a situation where my family knew Chinese people. During my teens there was a great opportunity for me to learn Chinese from the student, and in fact her mother wanted to take me to live in Hong Kong. These, however, were the last thing I wanted to do. I distanced myself from the student because her likeness to myself made me feel uncomfortable. I did not want to go to Hong Kong.

Whilst language and cultural origins are increasingly being recognised as important factors in enabling a child to gain a sense of self, I believe that the following are important considerations:

- Language and culture need to be acquired within the relevant "community" – in my case with Chinese people.
- Learning needs to be age appropriate, preferably from a young age, when it is easier, but also in the context of the relevant "community".
- Living and breathing one's cultural roots with other children/young people from the same country of origin is more appropriate than learning from books and adoptive parents. For adult adoptees who have not had such contact, a "buddy" or "family twining" (as is done with towns) would be useful. A resource centre would also be of great value to support adoptees in finding about themselves.
- It is not enough for adoptive parents to learn the language in the belief that language is an adequate substitute for lack of cultural roots. Language is one aspect of identity formation; e.g. when I was in a group of Chinese people, I was told by one person that when she was young she chose not to learn Chinese. She therefore felt that she could not speak the language. However, she did understand what was being said in Chinese and Chinese rituals were part of her upbringing.
- When children learn about their country of origin, it is done within a context which is continuously reinforced by positive images, role models and respect for one's country of origin. This means that responsibility lies not only with the family but also within schools and society as a whole. I have a vivid memory from my teens of how my parents responded when I told them I had been called names. They said that I needed to ignore what had happened and that I should be

proud of my origins. But I really didn't know what to be proud of. I had no inclination to find out because what use could it be to me? This incident also resulted in my not wishing to tell them of other occasions when I received racism. What saddens me is that when I have spoken with other adoptees about racism, although they describe situations they have been in which are racist in nature, they do not recognise that that is what has happened, and do not wish to acknowledge that they are being targeted in that way.

Loss

In addition to the loss I feel, which is inevitable when a baby is abandoned and has missed out on the crucial bonding process with the mother and has no information about blood relatives, there is also the loss of connection with Chinese people.

This loss I feel is encapsulated for me at times of Chinese New Year; for example, I have been to Soho in London on a number of occasions for the Chinese New Year celebrations. It is a time when Chinese people are most visible in the UK and it is a time of celebration for them. I say for "them" because for me it is a painful reminder of my losses. Going to Soho, is for me, going to observe what Chinese people do at this time. I feel I am like any other tourist, but I am vulnerable because I look Chinese. I do not want to be questioned by tourists about what is going on, for fear of showing my ignorance and I do not want to be spoken to by Chinese people because I cannot speak Chinese. I am fearful that I will be exposed as an impostor and this is hard to bear. I want to be part of the celebrations, I want to feel that it is my birthright, that being Chinese is something to be proud of, and something that I am comfortable with.

Isolation

There are a number of factors which have contributed to my feelings of isolation:

- Lack of information about my origins and the lack of trust I have in the information I have been given. Over the years I have been told different stories about how I was abandoned. I grew up in the belief that I had been left on the steps of a Buddhist temple, but when I looked at my records they said that I was found on a street, and with further investigation I have now been told that I was found on the stairwell in a block of flats, which is a great distance from the New Territories. Rather than being in one orphanage, I have also been told that I was in two orphanages.

- Being physically different to my brothers and sisters, who are birth children of my adoptive parents, drew attention to my difference. I attracted attention, invariably racist comments or stereotyped images of what people think Chinese people are like, e.g. hard working.
- I knew very few Chinese people when I was growing up, so had nobody I could identify with.
- I found it difficult to tell anyone about racism I have experienced.
- I am always being challenged if I question transracial adoption. I am seen as being ungrateful and 'surely I would have died if I hadn't been adopted'.
- Being told I am OK but Chinese people are . . . (whatever stereotype they wish to refer to).
- Learning very little about Chinese history or achievements at school.

Visiting the country of origin

I have been to Hong Kong and China. At the time of planning my trip to Hong Kong, it was really important to me to visit China as I had been told that my birth parents had probably come from the mainland. I also wanted to be among Chinese people who have not lived under British rule. It had taken me a long time to consider even the possibility of going to Hong Kong. My parents had already visited one of the orphanages where I had lived, and other members of my family had been to Hong Kong.

I held back for a number of reasons:

- I didn't want to go with my family. I wanted my own experience of Hong Kong, which was not influenced by them. I knew that if I went with them the response to me would be very different to the one I would get without them. I didn't want to be visible. I wanted to gain a sense of culture for myself that was independent of their views.

- For a long time I believed there was no point in me going to Hong Kong because I would not find my birth parents. The assumption being that I would want to trace. I did not question the fact that there may be more information about my background (not necessarily about my birth parents) than that which I had been given. I held the belief that it was only possible to approach adoption agencies if you wanted to trace. This view was confirmed when I contacted a couple of agencies which then sent me membership forms asking me who I wanted to find. This put me off contacting them again.
- I needed emotional support, but did not know whom to go to because at the time I was unclear about what I wanted and I felt guilty about wanting to find out more about my origins.
- I did not feel comfortable being among Chinese people and not knowing the language increased this.

My visit to Hong Kong and China turned out to be very successful. At the start of the trip I visited one of the orphanages in Hong Kong. I came away with very mixed feelings. I felt great sadness that I could not remember the time I had been there, I felt glad that I was not still there, but guilty that I was not feeling more grateful for having been "rescued" because I was angry at having been removed from my country of origin. I found Hong Kong difficult to be in because there were many English people living there, and I had more in common with them than the Chinese people.

When I was in China I felt in some ways it was easier for me to find a connection. I was more able to get a sense of what it must be like to be among "my own people". I was not visible. I was pleased when people talked to me in Chinese because it meant I did not look like a "foreigner". The other side of that though, was that my looks are only surface deep, and I could not reply to them. It was also painful for me to see Chinese families, see billboards and advertisements and television programmes featuring Chinese people because they are images which are uncommon in the UK.

It was very important for me to have made the journey and during the planning process I found more information about my background. If children show no interest in visiting their birth country, adoptive parents must not assume that they are not interested. Adoptive parents need to also bear in mind that their eagerness to give their children cultural identity can put the children off completely.

Conclusion

While we know how successful adoption can be – and in many respects I would say that of mine – I think we need to constantly remind ourselves in whose interests intercountry adoption is, and not neglect the motivation to keep children in their own country of origin and work in partnership to encourage this. Partnership and joint working with communities, for example, the Chinese community in this country is essential too. These communities do exist and they are a valuable resource for adoptive parents and adoptees.

If babies are involved in adoption there is a need to acknowledge that, although it is easier for the adoptive parents to integrate them into the family, as adults, adoptees do have needs. The fact that intercountry adoptees are "good" or "well behaved" or "work hard" doesn't mean that they do not have issues about their adoptive status. They are often unaware of themselves until they meet other intercountry adoptees with whom they are able to validate their experiences. I feel this has been the case for me. I believe there is a need to explore in greater depth the experiences of adult intercountry adoptees and I welcome more research that would inform intercountry adoption policy and practice. I also recommend more resources for pre- and post-adoption services.

Further information about 'Adoption in My Life – The intercountry experience' can be obtained from Project 16-18, Catholic Children's Society, 7 Colwick Road, West Bridgford, Nottingham NG2 5FR, UK Telephone 0115 955 8811 Fax 0115 955 8822 e-mail enquiries@ccsnotts.co.uk.

28 Meeting our needs
Some proposals for change

Katherine Samwell-Smith

Katherine Samwell-Smith is currently reading for an MA in Medical Anthropology at the University of London, School of Oriental and African Studies. For her first degree she wrote a dissertation entitled "Is Blood Thicker than Water? An anthropological perspective on transracial adoption." She contributed to Project 16-18 and participated in the dissemination of the Project at two national conferences entitled "Adoption in my Life".

She is currently working at UNICEF in New York on a worldwide polio eradication campaign.

I shall discuss some ideas which I feel would make adoption services and post-adoption services better suited to the needs of adoptees and prospective adopters. In particular, I shall consider how a person adopted internationally has different needs from those of someone adopted nationally.

Background

I was adopted in 1977 from Santiago, Chile. The reason my parents adopted from Chile was due to chance. My mother's best friend, now my godmother, was Chilean and her father, whom I call "Tata" (grandpa) Lucco, lived in Santiago. He visited the only orphanage in Santiago and chose me. "Tata" Lucco was in constant close touch with my parents and he and his wife looked after me until the adoption had been finalised. They then flew to England with me, where my adoptive mother, father and brother were waiting to pick me up. I have visited Chile twice since then: once when I was 16, when I went to the orphanage where I was born and travelled extensively in the country, and once in my "gap" year when I spent six months teaching at a school.

Cultural roots

Recently, adoption policies and practice in the UK have recognised that cultural identity and the "roots" of the adoptee are very important for constructing the role of the "self". "Race", ethnicity and culture are all features that prospective parents should take into consideration before, during and after they adopt a child, if they want to help create a positive identity for them. I feel that prospective adoptive parents need to try to come to terms with their own cultural identity and roots before they can even consider learning about their adopted child's heritage. By doing so, they should become aware of the importance that this holds for them and, therefore, understand to a greater extent the need for a similar under-standing in their adopted child's life.

One way in which they could do this effectively is by learning about their child's country of origin: the religion, the language and the main festivals. I have always regretted that I did not learn Spanish when I was young. I wish that my parents had organised lessons for me or had employed a Spanish speaking nanny. It would have given me some confidence when first returning to Chile. However, when I visited Chile for the second time, I had had a few lessons beforehand and therefore learnt the language relatively fast. The most important thing that occurred, due to my new acquisition of Spanish, was that for the first time I was able to thank and talk with Tata Lucco. Up until that moment I was only able to talk through my godmother, which made our conversations quite impersonal. It made a huge difference to me and to Tata Lucco.

There are other matters that one may consider to be of little import-ance, but which can be important to an adoptee later on in their life: how to do their hair and makeup. An example that I can refer to from my own research work concerns a girl who was adopted transracially, who wanted and needed someone to style her frizzy hair. Her parents did not have any experience in hairdressing. However, the family had always lived in a very close-knit community which was multicultural. They had made friends and therefore a simple solution to the girl's need to have her hair done was by involving friends of her ethnic background. A service which could be provided for adoptive parents, which might make parents feel less alienated from another country, would be to provide them with a "buddy". The "buddy" would usually be from their child's country of origin and could help answer any questions they may have about the country and questions that the child might have.

Openness

An issue that is central to an adopted person's life is when, how and from whom they learn that they were adopted. It has been shown that in the majority of cases looked at in Project 16–18, and from my own personal experience, that being told the truth about one's adoption, from the earliest age possible, is needed by the child in order to be able to help to create one's own identity. I have always known that I was adopted and therefore it has never been an issue that has worried or concerned me. I have always considered myself to be just like anyone else. This does not diminish from the fact that, although contradictorily, I also feel special having been adopted.

Leading on from this is the aspect of identity. An adopted child is often called "special", because he or she has been chosen. The title of being "special" can be hard for a child to bear because they believe that if they fail in anything, or do not meet the required standard, they have let their parents down and no longer live up to the title placed upon them. I do not mean to suggest that everyone feels this way, but the connotations of having being chosen and living up to certain expectations are ever present, I feel, in any adopted person's life. My advice for adoption services is simple: they just need to make prospective parents aware of the difficulties that could occur if they keep referring to their child as "special". Awareness is crucial in the role of parents because they can prevent, so far as it is possible, anxieties and problems that might occur in the future.

Isolation

Adoptees can feel isolated because of their concern about being "special" and by being different from their peers. This is especially apparent in intercountry adoptions because they are usually of a transracial nature. I cannot comment upon feeling isolated, as a result of my adoption, but once again shall draw upon my research. A transracially adopted black girl felt isolated whenever she left London. Her father recalls an incident which occurred when they went to Cornwall: 'Twice as we walked along, people, complete strangers patted her head . . . and one of them said "I've seen one like that at Saltash", and another said "It's just like a sheep".' This is just one example of a way in which an adopted person can be made to feel isolated. Isolation can come in a great number of forms, but often occurs as a result of racism. Post-adoption services should be prepared for an adoptee to feel this way, and therefore have appropriate support services ready in anticipation of any problems.

Loss

The sense of loss is often a central concern of adopted children. The relinquishment of a child by a mother is the first time that a child is separated from a loved one, and therefore the first time that they are subjected to feeling a loss. This feeling of having lost someone so important is not necessarily apparent when the child is young, but may only come to the fore when they are older. It is an issue which every adopted child has to deal with in their own way. Adoption is often represented as a good solution to an unfortunate problem. The perception that many people have of adoption is that once the child has been adopted everything is going to be "plain sailing". This is often not the case and I believe that post-adoption services are most needed. Such a service is really needed before the adoption has taken place in order to remind families of the realities that can occur: bereavements, divorce and other forms of loss. Adoption services should be there for the family and the adopted child, if they actually experience any of these losses. It is crucial to recognise that the child may react badly to losing another person, that they may blame themselves because it happened to them before, and that counselling may be required. In certain ways adopted children have special needs which should be recognised, but on the whole they should be treated just like anyone else.

Children who are adopted intercountry are likely to be curious about the country they were born in and may be interested in finding out about their birth parents. Children can become curious at any age and therefore the adoptive parents have to be prepared for this eventuality. They may only be curious as to what the country looks like, want to see where they were born and get to know their "roots". If this is the case, then I would like to suggest that the whole family goes with them on the trip. Adopted children need a great deal of love and support to be able to enjoy the time there. Once again, this is an ideal opportunity for adoption agencies to make their services available. The kinds of services which could prove particularly useful would be some form of counselling for the parents and the child before the journey is taken, so that all the family are able to discuss their worries and concerns. Once they are back from the trip, it may be useful for the child to have more counselling sessions because they may have found that it evoked memories and raised further questions.

One of the most important ways in which prospective adopters could be made more aware of events that might occur in the future, is by trying to ensure that adopters and adoptees openly discuss the many potentially sensitive issues surrounding adoption. This method of discussion is a good way in which prospective adopters can find out what they really want to know, and in an informal setting. An example of what may be considered a delicate subject is adopted children looking for their birth parents. By talking this over with adopted young adults the prospective adopters could dispel their worries and be more prepared for when their own child wants to discover his or her roots.

Visiting the country of origin

Adolescence is one time in which adopted children are most likely to want to go back to their place of birth and find their birth parents. Unfortunately for children adopted from overseas, the probability of finding their birth parents is low because of the lack of information that is available to them and therefore a lack of support. Looking for birth parents could be considered a "do it yourself job": if you do not do it, then no-one else will. In my opinion there should be some centralised institution which contains information about intercountry adopted children and their birth parents. Obviously, the birth parents must have given their consent for the information to be given out and likewise the adopted child, but at least then there would be a starting point for the search. Once the information that is needed for the search is found, counselling could take place before the trip, with the whole family being present. I do not believe that everyone needs counselling, but the services must be available to them. My advice for the adoptive parents is to be as supportive as possible. The child needs to know that whatever happens they will be there for them.

I know that when I visited Santiago, it was both an exciting and terrifying experience. The different emotions that I felt were very confusing. I was thrilled to feel a sense of belonging. That is not to say that I did not have a sense of it before the trip, but rather I was worried that I may not have felt at home there. In contrast, when I visited the orphanage where I was born, the situation provoked me to feel guilty. I had been chosen and the children who were there had not been so lucky. These are only a couple of my feelings which I can really put into words; and I can hardly begin to imagine what it must feel like to look for one's birth parents. I did not look for my birth parents because I did not feel the need to. For these reasons, I can only suggest that anyone who searches for their birth parents should have a choice of agencies which will support them. Returning to one's place of birth is a life-changing experience, for better or for worse, which people may not fully understand and this could be a reason why there are so few supportive, specialised agencies.

Conclusion

These are my thoughts and feelings about the adoption process and I trust that I have not misrepresented adopted people. I think that adoption can be a wonderful and successful process. One has to take into account, though, that not all adoptions are successful and there are many factors which can contribute to a family member's unhappiness. I propose that the government should set up a national centre for adoption in which they consider up-to-date statistics, hold information about domestic and intercountry adoptions, and deal with adoptees and prospective adopters sensitively. I hope that in the future the kinds of services which are available to adoptees and adopters will be useful, practical, up to date and supportive. Availability and access are most important although not everyone will use the services; however, the potential support it could offer would be invaluable to the adoptive community as a whole.

Further information about 'Adoption in My Life – The intercountry experience' can be obtained from Project 16-18, Catholic Children's Society, 7 Colwick Road, West Bridgford, Nottingham NG2 5FR, UK Telephone 0115 955 8811 Fax 0115 955 8822
e-mail enquiries@ccsnotts.co.uk.

29 Strength to survive and courage to live

Anna von Melen

Anna von Melen was born in Korea in 1987 and adopted in Sweden in 1969. In May 1996 she wrote to the Swedish National Board for Inter-country Adoption (NIA) pointing out that adult adoptees should play a central role in collecting and spreading information about intercountry adoption and suggesting the idea of a book based on interviews and conversations with other adult adoptees. NIA welcomed this idea, which led to a book published in 1998 entitled 'Strength to Survive and Courage to Live: 18 adoptees on adoption'.

This chapter contains some brief extracts from Anna von Melen's book, including three portaits, based on conversations with three adoptees – Susanna, Theresa and Anders – with some introductory words from Anna about the themes emerging from their conversations.

The inner journey

Adoptees travel more than others, often by different routes, and with different priorities. International adoptees also usually travel too: from their country of origin to their country of reception; from biological parents to adoptive parents; between inheritance and environment; between different cultures and ethnic groups; and quite often from poverty to wealth.

When I came to Sweden all I had with me, apart from the clothes I was wearing, was a pink handbag and a plastic Santa Claus. For a few childhood years I was also very much occupied by the thought that I, unlike friends of the same age, had flown an uneven number of times. I'd come from South Korea but hadn't made the return journey. I was also at that age when aeroplanes are fantastic, and when having flown confers status: the more times you've flown and the further the distance, the higher the status. However, I couldn't work out if you got extra status if you'd flown an uneven number of times.

Everyone shares life's journey. It's a journey with time as the only companion and no one can escape it. The past is all that unites us on our journey regardless of fuel, packing and means of transport. Beyond that, the individual variations take over.

As far as intercountry adoptees are concerned, the main journey they embark upon is the so called return journey. It is the journey that transports the adoptee back to their country of origin and the journey so many refer to: 'Have you been back?'; 'Wouldn't you like to go back?'; 'How many times have you been back?'

It's true that many adoptees both want to return and often actually do return to their country of origin. They do this for different reasons and with different expectations. However, few adoptees embark upon a return journey.

The journey that an adoption involves can be described in many ways. One of those ways is as an inner journey; a counterbalance to the external return journey to the country of origin. Many articles are written about the latter, but rarely is the inner journey addressed. This is probably due to the fact that return journeys are more tangible, and easier to put into words. Generally speaking, it's easier to describe work-related and holiday trips, for example, than an inner journey, for what is an inner journey really? A journey inwards, to the core of who you are? It can be many things: a journey in feelings; a journey of imagination; for Susannna it was a journey of memory.

Strength to survive and courage to live – *Susanna*
Susanna is a survivor and an optimist who enjoys life to the full. She knows that she'll survive and because of that she can treat herself to life. She lives without fear and without demands. Her courage to live stems from the strength born in her after surviving one of the worst fates possible: abandonment.

Susanna looks upon the fact that she was separated from her biological family as something that has led to a lot of positive things. It has formed her into the person she is today, with an enormous will to live and the ability to let go of difficult situations.

Susanna was very small when she was abandoned, but she was big enough to carry her small siblings on her back. The family situation in her native country had changed in such a way that it was impossible to remain there. She was put into a children's home, and left there with her little sister, a few possessions and a lot of responsibility. It was a crucial moment that at one blow ended her childhood. Susanna then made an instinctive decision to search for and find the strength within her to make her an adult, which gave her the strength to survive. When her sister died Susanna was made available for adoption. As she travelled to her new country all she carried with her was a small handbag, a few fragments of memory and a strong will to live.

I have to travel far to meet Susanna, but when we meet I feel that the distance between us melts away. We are both in the midst of life and I soon discover that we have an instinctive affinity with each other. It isn't long before we realise that our experiences and attitudes to life are in many ways similar, for example, we both think that you should never give up, or stop developing. We also feel though that one sometimes should pause to think about where your life is going.

Susanna's outlook on life could be summed up as an inner emotional journey that has carried her far beyond her adoption.

Susanna: I see the idea of an inner journey as being the most essential thing in my life; and it involves continually keeping in touch with your feelings and to be aware on an inner level in order to develop as a person. It's an ongoing process that never ends. You get new impressions all the time, and the people who constitute the pieces of your life come and go. Many of those pieces have nothing to do with adoption, and in that sense the inner journey is something universal, which involves everyone. I've seen so many people who have chosen to stop developing and thereby stopped living, because, as I see it, having an inner journey is the same thing as being alive.

On the surface Susanna is very successful. Enterprising and full of initiative, she got a top business job with good prospects immediately after graduating from university, whereupon student life was replaced by business trips, working overtime and a bulging diary. The future will be shaped by people like Susanna who's at the cutting edge of 21st century development.

Yet Susanna doesn't make a big deal of her success and the fact that she doesn't need to display her professional achievements demonstrates that she's secure about what she does. Susanna states matter-of-factly that she likes her work, but prefers to talk about her inner success. This inner success has been an important part of her life for a long period, and she devotes much of her time to cultivating it.

Susanna: I try to set aside a few weeks every year when I can just be by myself. For example, it can be a weekend when you refrain from answering the phone and just isolate yourself. On the whole I don't do anything, yet at the same time I'm very busy on an inner level. I let the world around come to a halt and concentrate all my energy on what's happening inside. At times like that my motto is to always try to reach the essence of your being. If you can't feel that essence then in some way you've lost contact with yourself. My goal is to feel that I have both the strength and the courage to go within myself as far as I possibly can.

The question of whether or not Susanna had the courage to reach her emotional core was tested in earnest when she was a teenager. Emotionally it was a dark period, and one in which she did a lot of soul-searching. Susanna says that she didn't really realise how bad she in fact felt: 'I thought it was a natural state.'

Ultimately her teenage years were about emancipation, independence and the choice between adapting yourself to others or being your own person. Susanna had a large circle of friends at that time, but had no one who understood her. 'I've always felt that I have another depth compared to people of my own age. I understand things that others sometimes don't even understand about themselves,' she says.

Susanna's always been the strong one, the one who listened to others and took responsibility. It was she who took care of the others and encouraged them. In the long run, however, it couldn't last and so once again it was time for Susanna to test her courage and challenge herself outwardly in the form of a return journey and inwardly in the form of another inner journey.

Susanna: The return journey to my native country was, in many ways, a journey in time. It involved throwing myself into something unknown, which was still to do with myself. The physical return journey was the outward symptom of the inner journey I was taking. On the outside I was travelling to a foreign country, a new culture and all of that, but on an inner level it meant that I was transported back to the person I was when I was abandoned. In this sense it was very much a journey in feelings, back to the desertion and vulnerability I once felt. During the first few days I experienced an enormous sense of alienation and a terrible sense of loneliness, which I, at the same time, felt at home with. I had thrown myself into the deep end to see if I could swim.

The physical return journey can often be the key to an inner journey on a conscious or subconscious level. Susanna's return journey is the bridge between the person she is today and the person she was then. She believes that this development was made possible when she gained contact with people in her native country who could tell her things about the little girl she once was, and the responsibility that was put on her, and about her sister, who died.

Colours, smells and everyday circumstances also helped to physically reconstitute her fragments of memory. During the six months that Susanna spent in her native country she, in the midst of feeling vulnerable and lonely, now and then experienced enormous joy. This joy came from recognising things from her past, and one moment of recognition in particular left a strong impression on her. It was when she caught sight of a woman squatting in a courtyard preparing vegetables. Susanna recalls: 'She was wearing typical clothes, you know, flowery trousers and a colourful top. And when I saw that woman I knew at once that I'd seen that situation before.'

The return journey in many ways made Susanna a more complete person. As Susanna sees it, adoptees have a stronger reason than others to start an inner journey. Indeed, perhaps New Age (which grows evermore popular) is an indication that most people have a need for an inner journey. Maybe people need to feel that there is a point not just to life but to their life in particular.

Susanna: In a sense things are easier for adoptees as adoption creates a situation for the adoptee that provides them with both a tangible goal and an inner motive. The goal is to achieve contact with the child who was once abandoned, whilst the motive stems from the strength that has grown out of the moment of abandonment and the fact of survival.

In many children's homes around the world, conditions are very poor and children die as a result of malnutrition, illness and a lack of emotional stimulation. Many perhaps even lack the strength that is required to survive a separation and living in a children's home.

The strongest impression I gained when I visited a children's home was the silence that prevailed. In a room with over fifty small children no-one either whimpered or yelled. It was as strange as it was frightening, and to my mind it was a clear sign that something wasn't right. The children I saw weren't children who lived; they were children who were fully occupied with surviving.

Susanna believes that adoptees often possess a reflex survival instinct, which has directly resulted from the separation before they were adopted. Being in contact with this survival ability on a conscious level is another thing altogether however, you need strength to survive, and also courage to gain certainty about that strength. The critical difference between surviving and living lies in gaining insight into your own inner strength.

Susanna: I believe that the trauma that a separation involves activates an instinct to survive. It is an enormous process that's set into motion at the very moment that you're abandoned, regardless of how young you are. I think it's instinctive because you can't think logically when you're so young. After all, you can't carry out a logical discussion with yourself, saying sensible things like: 'You understand of course that your parents have to leave you, but it's not because of you.' I also think that that instinct, strength and the will to survive are things you always have with you, because they were once activated so strongly.

I feel very clearly how power is activated in me as soon as anything difficult happens, almost like a reflex. I might have been completely confused at first, had difficulty sleeping, or a stomach-ache, or that sort of thing, but it doesn't take long before I have a comfortable conviction that everything will work out for the best. The external problems haven't been solved, but I've found calm inside. This ability of mine is something that I very much like and that I believe that all adoptees have, more or less. It's an ability that we gained when we were abandoned and I believe that many adoptees would feel far better if they didn't make their adoption a problem but rather a strength.

Appearance

Many people claim that skin colour doesn't matter, but they can't deny that appearance does. Whichever way you look at it, appearance is the first thing you see when you meet another person.

A friend of mine has tried to describe the significance of appearance: 'First you have to get your fill of the outside before you can fully concentrate on the inside.'

My friend has explained that this adage can of course apply to another skin colour, but it could equally refer to a strikingly large nose, a pair of unusually beautiful eyes or an amazingly thick head of hair.

Many times we restrain ourselves from staring at our fellow humans, even though we would dearly like to, because it's considered rude. If our eyes could do as they wished we'd probably stare much more often, for far longer and much more penetratingly. In particular we would stare at the strange, the uncommon and the different, for longing glances are seldom drawn to the uninteresting and indifferent. We look because we quite simply can't help it.

The two young people you'll meet in the following portraits have in common the fact that they, in varying degrees, have had to get used to people who can't stop looking at them – or asking them questions. The people around them have been fascinated by them, but have also despised them merely for the sake of their appearance.

The conversations I had with Theresa, Anders and other adoptees have covered everything from misunderstandings, prejudice and xeno-phobia, to discrimination and pure racism. We talked about how those around us view us and how we as adoptees, immigrants and Swedes experience our situation in Sweden.

An Indian looks in the mirror – *Therese*

'One day there was an Indian who suddenly looked back at me from the mirror,' says Therese, who was adopted from India when she was just over six months old.

The Indian had been there for the whole of her upbringing, not least of all through Therese's two sisters, who also come from India. The family had even lived for a year in an Asian country not far from India. But despite all the Indian influences, Therese has felt herself to be very Swedish. Or rather something in between.

> *Therese*: For a while I avoided everything that was to do with India, without realising it myself. Many people asked me if I was interested in India, but I just said: 'No, not especially.' Afterwards I've realised that it was perhaps because I couldn't deal with it for some reason. There was a time when I didn't really know where to turn with my questions about identity, as there was no-one who could deal with them.
>
> Nowadays, however, I find India exciting. It's a new and unknown place for me, yet even though I'm more interested now, I still don't feel that I'm Indian.

For Therese it's been a process which has been helped along by the question: 'Where do you come from?' This is possibly the most common question in Swedish society in the 1990s, though some get asked it more often than others. Therese says she's gradually learnt the answer people want, which is usually the one that fits in with their conception of the world. She used to answer 'Staffanstorp' however, which lies a few miles outside of Malmö, because that's the place she considered her home.

> *Therese*: At that time I didn't think about India, as Staffanstorp was my home, and people there didn't look at me as something different. Everyone there was used to me and my sisters, and another family

who had adoptive children from Africa lived in Staffanstorp as well. I was 13 years old the first time I went to Malmö with my friends, and that's when I suddenly discovered that I looked different. I hadn't really thought about it earlier. I remember being very surprised when I realised that I in fact looked different.

Therese left home when she was 18. She believes that leaving home had significance for her gradual acceptance of things Indian. When the protection of her adoptive parents disappeared, it wasn't as obvious that she was only Swedish. It was also at this time that she first started to travel overseas by herself, and saying that she came from Sweden didn't work.

Therese: Saying "Sweden," just didn't stand up when you were abroad, and people didn't believe you. Once you've explained things a number of times you feel as though you've become more Indian. I also think that the side of you that comes from your genes, your genetic inheritance I suppose you'd call it, has previously been inhibited. Admittedly, I've mostly been influenced by my adoptive father, but my genetic inheritance has probably emerged more and more since I left home. I feel it's important that I let that side of me express itself.

When Therese was 25 she made a return journey to India. It was a powerful experience, and she relates how the trip brought the Indian in her to life. Everything affected her: the way that people moved, their clothes, the food, the animals, the smells – things she'd previously only seen on TV or in pictures.

Therese: I'd prepared myself to go for so long that it was a relief when I finally left. Then there were just so many impressions at the same time, and I don't think that I've worked through everything yet. I want to go there again, but it'll probably have to wait awhile. India affected me so strongly that after the trip it hasn't felt as easy just to be completely Swedish. The Indian side of me has become much stronger since I came home from India, and that feels a little strange.

Therese regularly meets other adoptees because she feels it's important to meet people who have the same background, in other words, people who can understand the feelings that other friends really can't, such as the feeling of living halfway between two cultures.

> *Therese*: I am somewhere in between. Mentally I feel Swedish, because Swedish culture has very much left its mark on me, but at the same time I'm not really Swedish, as it's a little difficult to be completely Swedish when you look Indian. It feels so obvious when I first think about it but then it feels difficult, even though it's obvious.
>
> There are Swedish-born adoptees, or invisible adoptees, who think it's easier to be internationally adopted because people can see you're an adoptee just by looking at you. As a result those adoptees can't avoid talking about their adoption. Yet you can still hide a lot of things, even when you're visibly adopted. Things aren't necessarily easier just because they're visible on the outside.
>
> When I was in India I was just as surprised every time I looked around and saw Indians, even though it was nice to walk around amongst people who looked exactly like yourself – and yet I wasn't fully accepted there either. I guess I'd realised that I wouldn't blend in there, but when they too asked me where I came from, I found myself wondering: "Why can't I come from here?" It was the same sort of thing there as in Sweden, where you are forced to explain who you are. At passport control, for example, it took a very long time before they realised why I had a Swedish passport. They're not in much of a hurry in India either. I met some Africans there as well, and we could sit and joke about Indians, exactly as I can do in Sweden about immigrants. It was the same kind of feeling, and a bit confusing.
>
> People still ask the same questions as they used to, like 'Where do you come from?' and all that, but these days my answers have changed.

Adoptee VIP – *Anders*

'Many adoptees start their life in Sweden with a silver spoon in their mouth,' says Anders, an adoptee from Ethiopia.

Anders was just over a year old when he came to his Swedish family who live in a town in southern Sweden. Both parents are well-educated, live in a detached house, and have both a car and a house in the country. They also have plenty of economic and cultural capital to give their three children a good start in life. Thank to his parents Anders has learnt all the right codes.

Anders: Many adoptees are born, as you say, into the upper middle classes. We have a significantly more favourable starting point than many immigrants and refugees who come here as adults. We land in a social context where we have status and gain acceptance from the white majority right from the beginning. Above all, we have knowledge of Swedish society: we speak perfect Swedish, dress in the style of the west, and behave as Swedes in every conceivable way. How one then uses that knowledge is of course up to each individual.

I have talked with a lot of adult adoptees about racism in society. Some think that it's not our problem, and that as long as we stay with our Swedish families and white friends, it won't affect us, and so we don't need to worry ourselves. I don't think that attitude is due to their being racist; in fact it's probably got as much to do with the fact that they've enough difficulties of their own to deal with.

In my opinion Sweden is a democratic country, and is both just and equal. I don't feel that I've been treated any differently by the authorities than native Swedes have. However, that's not enough. Swedish society has to embrace many more people. There shouldn't just be a VIP-lane for adoptees, whilst all the others who look different are left to live a life on the margins in immigrant areas like Rinkeby and Rosengård.

Anders has worked and studied in both Stockholm and Malmö. He has a degree in sociology, and in his work he meets many different types of people. This suits Anders, who is socially skilled and likes to have a good time. Amongst other things, he's a considerable expert on Stockholm and Malmö nightlife.

Anders: There is quite a difference between nightlife in Stockholm and Malmö. There are places in Stockholm that are tremendously multicultural and mixed, where you can find everything from twenty-year-old Ninja warriors from the immigrant suburb of Norsborg to slick snobs from the affluent suburb of Lidingö. In all those places there's no trouble at all because there's a great deal of tolerance in Stockholm. It's a matter of having the right style to get into these places, rather than the right skin colour. However, in Malmö, where there isn't any style at all, it's simpler to categorise people by "race", at least in my experience. In some ways it's simpler because then you know it's a matter of pure racism.

In the middle of the 1990s many of Malmö's most popular nightspots didn't let blacks in. There was a lot of discussion about this in the media and one of the club owners openly said: 'We don't want any negroes in our clubs!' I used to go out quite a lot then but could never be sure whether I'd get into certain places. When I didn't I knew it was because of my skin colour, because I was the right age, had the right clothes, and avoided any place that had a queue. There were no other objective reasons for why I couldn't get in and yet still you heard that the place was full, and it was only for members – even though friends of mine, who weren't members, had already gone in.

It was so enormously paradoxical because this was at its worst in 1994, the same year that apartheid was abolished in South Africa, and here I was in Sweden unable to get in to a night club just because I'm black! It's a feeling that can't be described; you just get a sort of knot in your stomach, and feel totally powerless.

But Anders refuses to give up. Maybe it's because he's had such a privileged upbringing as an adoptee. After all he's got a stable background, a good education, as well as considerable personal resources and knowledge.

Anders: When things were at their most difficult I talked a lot with friends who gave me support. It's important to feel that it's me who's right and them who are in the wrong, otherwise it's easy to start doubting yourself.

Firstly I talked directly with some of those bouncers and owners because I think that's the best way. And of course they promised that it wouldn't happen again. But then I remembered that racial discrimination is in fact against the law. So, after the next incident, when I was completely convinced that it was a case of pure discrimination, I contacted the police. Then I got to the next unpleasantness. I expected to get support and that they'd believe me, but instead I was met with suspicion and doubt. The first policeman said: 'Did it say that negroes weren't allowed in? Had they put up a sign saying "No Negroes"?'

There's a great deal of ignorance about what the law does or doesn't permit. Many people are unaware that it's illegal to discriminate against people because of their skin colour and that it's a crime punishable by two years imprisonment – in other words it's quite a serious crime. The problem, however, is one of evidence because it's difficult to prove that discrimination has occurred. It's also a matter of which policeman you meet when you report the crime. There are all sorts of police officers with varying competence, and also with different personal opinions and attitudes.

Our conversation moves onto the question of what it is that makes certain people get involved, while others choose to bury their heads in the sand. Perhaps it's ultimately a matter of belief in the possibility of changing things. Perhaps it starts with an emotional reaction, which leads to thought and action. Those who get involved are often both interested in people and society – and usually feel passionately about what they do.

Anders: I don't know if it's a question of passion. Mostly I feel ashamed, ashamed for Sweden. I take personal offence because after all I'm a Swede too. Sure, I have a double identity: I'm Swedish, but I'm also adopted from Ethiopia. However, it doesn't have to be schizophrenic if you give both aspects room to breathe. Some people think that you have to decide between one thing or the other, but you can in fact be both. I have contact with several Ethiopians in Sweden, for example, and I see things in them that I think are missing in

Swedish cultural life. For example, the whole social thing: there's none of that 'You mind your business and I'll mind mine' – instead you help each other. Ethiopians are never alone in the same way that Swedes are.

I've also been brought up to believe in values like striving to make society as fair as possible, for example, through wealth redistribution. I remember the debate between party leaders Olof Palme and Thorbjörn Fälldin in the run-up to the 1976 general election. I was about ten and sat up until late in the evening watching with great interest, without really understanding everything of course. I think it was then that my commitment was first aroused. I don't remember anything specific about what they said, but I felt that it was important.

In the Sweden that I know and want to live in it's unacceptable that people aren't let into certain night clubs because they look different. That's not the way Sweden really is. We're far from being that harsh if the truth be known, but there evidently is a problem and something must be done about it.

Anna von Melen's book, *Strength to Survive and Courage to Live*, can be obtained from the NIA, the Swedish National Board for Intercountry Adoption, Norr Malarstrand 6, Stockholm, Sweden. The cost is £10 (including post and packing) if ordering from the UK.

30 **Conclusion**
The way ahead for the UK

Peter Selman

In this final chapter of the book, I shall attempt to link the various contributions together, within the framework of ethical concerns outlined by Chantal Saclier, Derek Kirton and Kerstin Sterky, to consider a way forward for the United Kingdom as it moves to ratifying the Hague Convention.

The growth of intercountry adoption

In Chapter 1 I discussed the rapid growth of intercountry adoption in the last decade – following a period of stabilisation and decline in the 1980s. This has been the result of a number of factors, including the opening up of new "markets", initially Romania in 1992 and subsequently China, Russia and other parts of the former Soviet Union. Other factors include a growing demand from receiving States and a greater awareness of the availability of children for international adoption (e.g. through media publicity and access to the internet). While the number of children received from some countries, e.g. Colombia and South Korea, has fallen and adoption from Sri Lanka, Chile and El Salvador has virtually ended, this has been more than compensated for by the large numbers coming from Romania, China and Russia. There have also been increases in number of adoptions from other countries such as Vietnam, Cambodia and Guatemala, where concern has been expressed over irregularities as these countries have responded to the growing demand, accompanied by an increase in potential payments from childless couples seeking young babies.

Amongst receiving States, the increase has been most marked in the United States, where the number of visas issued for "orphans" from overseas doubled from 8,102 in 1989 to 16,396 in 1999 – and in France where the number of ICAs rose by over 50 per cent in ten years from

2,441 in 1988 to 3,777 in 1998 (Tables 1.1 and 14.1). In the Netherlands and Sweden, the number of adoptions today is much lower than in the early 1980s (see Table 1.2), although numbers have been rising again in recent years. Sweden, Denmark and Norway now have the highest "rates" (per 1,000 population) of adoption from abroad, in relation to population size (Table 1.5).

Accurate data for the UK are not available until 1993 and even today figures are based on the number of applications (homestudy reports) received by the DoH, rather than actual adoptions. The most recent (1999) official figure of 272 is the highest since the Romanian influx in 1992, but still leaves the UK with one of the lowest rates of all receiving States.

The regulation of intercountry adoption

Alongside this increase, there have been major attempts by the international community to find agreed guidelines for intercountry adoption and to introduce controls which would help to ensure that ICA is practised only in the best interests of the child. Ethical guidelines were first introduced in the 1989 UN Convention on the Rights of the Child, but detailed implementation of these was left to the Hague Convention on the Protection of Children and Co-operation in Respect of Intercountry Adoption of 29 May 1993, which was agreed in the aftermath of the Romanian crisis. By autumn 2000, the Convention had been ratified or acceded to by 41 states (most recently Albania on 12 September 2000 – see Appendix I) and signed by a further 12, including the Russian Federation (on 7 September 2000), the USA and the UK, both of which countries are now moving towards ratification. Other receiving States which have signed but not yet ratified the Convention include Belgium, Germany, Ireland and Switzerland. The situation is more problematic for States of origin, where only 4 of the 15 countries sending the most children to the USA, France, Sweden, Norway and the Netherlands in the late 1990s (see Table 1.3) had ratified or acceded by the end of September 2000 and those not yet formally endorsing the Convention include Russia, China, Korea, Vietnam and Guatemala which were the five main sources of children: of these only Russia has signed the Convention.

Nevertheless, there is now, in principle, international agreement about the need for co-operation to eliminate abuse, and the review of the Convention held in November/December 2000, as this book is in press, will be attended by most of the major sending and receiving countries. The idea of reconvening the Hague Conference was written into the Convention and there is now a wide recognition of the need to examine its implementation in general and by particular countries to see whether the aims are being met.

It is, of course, impossible for me to record the outcome of this meeting, but already a number of areas have been identified as in need of examination (see Duncan, Chapter 2) and International Social Service (ISS) (2000b) have submitted a detailed document listing some of these which is available on their website [http://www.iss-ssi.org]. Amongst the areas identified by the ISS – and by authors of chapters in this book – as in need of attention are:

- A lack of clarity about the responsibilities of competent authorities in the State and in particular the role of the Central Authority;
- Inadequate resourcing and/or staffing of the Central Authority;
- Implementation of Article 9 of the Convention by some countries in a way that has removed previous requirements to proceed through accredited organisations;
- The creation of too many "accredited" bodies in some States and inadequacies in the standards of many of these;
- Organisations in one receiving State seeking to intervene in another by placing children from various States of origin;
- Poor procedures in determining the adoptability of a child, resulting in placement of children able to remain in their families or communities and the neglect of others left in institutions for life;
- Lack of information about children and their birth families – needed both at placement but also for the adopted person as he/she grows up;
- The absence from the Convention of any guidance on matching;
- Ethical problems over financial support to "orphanages" by bodies accredited to handle adoptions;
- Payments/contributions required from individual adopters by governments of States of origin to finance projects for the protection of children;

- The absence of potential sanctions against States Party to the Hague Convention and/or the UNCRC which are clearly violating the rights of the child.

Many of these points are relevant for the UK as we move to ratification and implementation of the Hague Convention and I shall discuss some of them in more detail later. The chapter by Kirton suggests a framework for developing an ethical policy for intercountry adoption which respects both the international obligations stressed by Saclier and the rights of foreign-born children in a multiracial society. Not everyone will agree with his particular conclusions, but the need for ethical issues to be debated alongside practical details about improved regulation must surely be accepted by all concerned. In the next section I shall discuss what is needed if we are to implement the Convention with honour and avoid some of the pitfalls identified by the ISS.

Improving services for intercountry adoption in the UK

By the time this book is published, the process of consultation on the implementation of the Adoption (Intercountry Aspects) Act 1999 will have commenced, but it is evident from William Duncan's observations about the implementation of the Hague Convention that this must be an ongoing process – just as we are continuing to review our rules, regulations and practice in respect of domestic adoption, e.g. the Prime Minister's *Review of Adoption* (PIU, 2000).

Michael Brennan (Chapter 10) is right to say that we now have a framework for making the Convention work in the UK and the rest of the contributions in Section III show clearly that there is no shortage of examples of good practice, but provision remains patchy and there is much to do in training practitioners who will be involved in intercountry adoption, as well as in preparing prospective adoptive parents. Jan Way and Julia Fleming argue convincingly that parents who have already adopted from abroad have a crucial role in such training.

A meaningful policy for intercountry adoption must work within the framework of the Hague Convention and our other international obligations. The role of the Central Authority(ies) will be crucial and it is good that all parts of the UK will be fully incorporated with new legislation impending in Northern Ireland. In England, the Department of Health will be the Central Authority and it is to be hoped that the extra resources promised to the newly formed Adoption and Permanency Section in the Department of Health will be extended to those responsible for intercountry adoption, as the ratification and implementation of the Convention is likely to stretch existing resources, especially if one consequence is an increase in the number of applications to adopt from abroad. The requirement for all local authorities to provide a service for intercountry adopters will require consideration of the format for home studies and training for those without experience of overseas adoption, an area explored by Simmonds and Haworth in Chapter 15. More delega-tion of tasks to accredited bodies will be needed and some radical thinking about the role of these in post-adoption support (a development also needed for domestic adoption). Finally, in all of this we need to consider our responsibilities in respect of relative adoptions, an issue identified in the chapters by Brennan and Haworth as much neglected to date (see also Jenkins, 1990).

Information and preparation

In their chapters, Haworth and Fleming both stress the need for reliable, easy-to-access information for those contemplating overseas adoption. The original decision to set up the OAH seemed to indicate official support for this view and recognition that it was the responsibility of government to provide such information. Today both OAH and OASIS are registered charities and together provide the bulk of information for prospective adopters, although the DoH does have its own helpline. The value of information rooted in experience is noted by both authors and is central to the philosophy of OASIS. However, there is still nothing to compare with the information on countries offered by the US State Department on its website.

The importance of preparation for those embarking on intercountry adoption is widely recognised and the OAH has been involved in developing courses with Childlink. In the UK preparation groups are usually seen as part of the assessment process, whereas in the Netherlands the compulsory preparation course (Duinkerken and Geerts, Chapter 20) precedes the homestudy and in Sweden preparation is shared by local welfare committees and the authorised organisations, which offer additional preparation and advice *after* assessment

Assessment – the provision of home studies in intercountry adoption

The new adoption legislation finally clarifies the position in respect of private home studies in the UK by making it clear that assessment in intercountry adoption – as in domestic adoption – should only be provided by an approved adoption agency. Section 13 of the Adoption (Intercountry Aspects) Act 1999, which implements this proposal, came into force on 31 January 2000. This seems to me a desirable move in the light of previous confusion, added to by varying court decisions as to the legality of payments for private home studies. It would, however, be a serious mistake to think that in itself this clause will do anything to improve assessment procedures. Many "private" home studies were carried out with skill and empathy by well qualified social workers who had the interests of the child at heart and in the past all too many LA assessments were marred by hostility and/or ignorance on the part of those undertaking the home study (Mason, 2000). I would hope that at least some of the "independent" social workers involved in ICA can be incorporated into the statutory services so that their skill and experience will not be wasted.

The chapter by Simmonds and Haworth, based on material originally prepared for the Irish government, covers many aspects of the assessment process and points to the key elements of good practice. Their recommendations see assessment as closely linked to preparation and information-giving.

Although home study reports are required by all States of origin and assessment is central to the responsibilities of receiving States as laid down by the Hague Convention, there is still much variation amongst the latter in the manner in which they are provided. In the Scandinavian countries and the Netherlands they are the responsibility of local authorities and are provided free of charge. In the USA they are typically provided by private agencies and charges are determined by those agencies. In Australia there is variation from state to state and an apparent movement from assessment by public authorities to home studies provided by NGOs as a part of a wider intercountry adoption service. In the UK assessment is now only possible through Local Authority Social Services Departments (LASSDs) or a voluntary agency approved for ICA work, but there are major variations in the level of charges imposed and the level of service provided: the cost of a home study by the two agencies described in this book (see chapters by Harnott and Hesslegrave) was £3,600 (excluding VAT) at the time of writing.

My own view is that this aspect of the intercountry adoption process should ideally be free of charge – as is assessment in domestic adoption – but I am realistic enough to see that this is unlikely when the government is talking about cost-neutral reforms and NGOs can only provide a service if funded by applicants or statutory bodies. The only acceptable alternative is that there should be some consistency – at least a strict maximum – and that prospective adopters should be told clearly why the fees are fixed at the prescribed level.

The existence of fees, added to the cost of travel and papers or payments to States of origin – amounting to £10–15,000 overall – clearly restricts the potential pool of adopters, but also seems to place ICA in the category of a luxury – or, as with most of the new reproductive technologies, something the State cannot or should not support. In contrast, the Dutch preparation course costs less than £300, while in Sweden and Norway successful adopters receive a subsidy from the government of up to £1,800 (about a quarter of the total costs in those countries). Free home studies and a state subsidy to adopters are sadly outside the remit of realistic proposals for the UK.

The need for authorised agencies which can link to similar bodies in States of origin

The issue of (inter)mediation remains central to the future of intercountry adoption in the UK but has still not been tackled (Selman and White, 1994). The new legislation has nothing to say about this, although Brennan (Chapter 10) makes it clear that there is no objection by the

DoH to local authorities or accredited bodies developing direct links with any State of origin processing an application prepared by them. There are powers to approve non-governmental organisations for inter-country adoption work – and four had been accredited by the end of 2000 – but it is unclear whether this will mean any encouragement to extend this work into direct co-operation with agencies or public author-ities in States of origin, taking over some of the work currently under-taken by the DoH (Brennan, Chapter 10). Yet the experience of the Northern European countries described in Section IV shows clearly how important approved mediating agencies are – it is not enough to equate the prohibition of private home studies with the achievement of agency-to-agency adoptions.

We need to start a debate now about what sort of agency(ies) would best serve the needs of the UK; about the balance of responsibility between public authorities and accredited agencies; and also about the need for proper post-adoption work in the area of overseas adoption. It is clear from the chapters on India that most sending countries would prefer to work with agencies rather than government departments and that they would prefer to work with a few rather than many agencies, provided these are authorised and well staffed. A similar view was expressed to me by the China Centre for Adoption Affairs (Chu, 1997).

The ISS recommendations (ISS, 2000b) are particularly clear on this point, stating that they are '. . . in favour of involvement of accredited bodies, particularly in receiving States, since they provide a concrete personalised link, case by case, between the State of origin and the receiving State, between the child and the adopting family, between the local level and the governmental level'.

The responsibility for exchanging information about the child and the prospective adoptive parents and taking appropriate measures 'to facilitate, follow and expedite proceedings' (Article 9b of the Hague Convention) would of course remain with the Central Authority, but would be delegated to accredited bodies, just as home studies are delegated to local authorities and other approved adoption agencies.

Agency to agency adoptions offer the best prospect of avoiding irregularities (van Loon, 1990) – e.g. by having representatives in States of origin and direct contact with accredited bodies there – and the role of Central Authorities in receiving States should be to ensure that such organisations are regulated and maintain the highest standards. Article 9 of the Convention needs clarification here to avoid a situation where prospective adopters can opt to negotiate directly with the sending country. The Convention [Article 22 (2)] allows for individuals (e.g. lawyers) to mediate in ICA, provided they have been approved by the Central Authority, and this practice is widespread – without the safeguards of approval – in the USA and many States of origin. The UK has made it clear that it does not wish to follow this pattern – and already many States of origin have indicated that they do not wish to allow adoptions other than through public authorities or accredited bodies. What we have not done is to take the next step and say that it is not satisfactory that prospective adoptive parents, however well prepared and however carefully assessed, should continue indefinitely to be able to go to a State of origin and negotiate an adoption themselves.

The development of mediating agencies is as much in the interests of prospective adopters as of the child. British adopters are currently barred from adopting from some countries that have ratified the Hague convention and also from other countries such as Korea, which will work only with those coming through agencies. Many adopters are seeking help from American agencies in making travel and other arrangements (see Shead, Chapter 26).

There are a number of possible models for a UK agency involved in mediation:

- A new agency dedicated to ICA alone but doing all stages from home studies and preparation groups through linking activities with authorities and agencies in States of origin and travel arrangements to post-adoption follow-up – as in Australia or for many US agencies.
- A dedicated ICA agency, which does linking activities but *not* the home studies (which would remain with LASSDs or other approved agencies) – the pattern in the Netherlands and Scandinavia.
- An established *domestic* voluntary adoption agency, which extends its remit to ICA, initially through home studies, but then in "intermediation" and post-adoption activities: – e.g. Childlink or PACT.
- A "big" voluntary with regional offices – and ideally some existing

international links – e.g. Barnado's or one of the religious organisations – taking on ICA as an additional activity.

- A series of smaller country-specific organisations arising directly from parents' groups. This facilitates the expertise in respect of particular countries, but can make it hard to create and maintain standards and makes such agencies very vulnerable to changes in the availability of children.
- A consortium of LASSDs offering home studies and linking activities on a regional basis – or indeed one LASSD (e.g. Hampshire) with a well-established ICA service and specialised panel, offering a service to a wider geographical area – or at least an extended service, incorporating mediation, for its own applicants.

The choice of type of agency is less important than the opening up of a debate about the process of mediation, although Sterky (Chapter 21) argues that NGOs are more suited to mediation than public authorities. Likewise the establishment of an agency or agencies will not provide a panacea for the problems of ICA in the UK. Such a process will take time and could initially provide links with only a limited number of countries. The creation of an agency will create new ethical dilemmas about its need for children to satisfy the demands of adopters and about financial arrangements with organisations in sending countries. What we have to acknowledge is that the current process of adopting from abroad would not be acceptable in domestic adoption and that the current treatment of and support for prospective intercountry adopters is at best inadequate and at worst insulting.

Supporting intercountry adoptive parents in the UK

It is clear from the chapters written by parents who have adopted from abroad (Way, Chapter 11; Fleming, Chapter 13; Shead, Chapter 26) that they are fully aware of the importance of ensuring that ICA is in the best interests of the child, and that they endorse the plans to ratify the Hague Convention and would be supportive of any proposals to encourage accreditation of NGO mediating agencies. However, they also clearly point to another central problem of intercountry adoption in the UK –

the hostility that has so often been shown in the past to those contemplating such adoption and the unacceptable delays faced by many prospective parents, even when a child has been identified as in need of adoption.

The aims of any changes in the provision of intercountry adoption services must be to remedy both the issue of unregulated adoptions where the interests of the child are lost and the issue of unsupported overseas adoption where prospective parents are left to find their way through the 'maze of intercountry adoption' (see Haworth, Chapter 12) and condemned for so doing! These issues are of course not unrelated. Regulation is more readily accepted when implemented in a spirit of shared responsibility and positive support for parents throughout the adoption process, including an acknowledgement that their actions are legitimate and can provide a home for children otherwise facing a future without a family, maximises the chances of a successful placement.

What can we learn from other countries?

Section IV of the book contains chapters describing aspects of intercountry adoption in five individual countries and two wider groupings within Europe. Each chapter deals with different facets of such experience from the author's chosen perspective. As such it cannot provide a comprehensive picture of the complexity of arrangements for ICA around the world – or even within the countries described. What it does do is suggest the need for the UK to be aware of the patterns in other countries – and especially those with a longer and more extensive experience of intercountry adoption than Britain.

The receiving State with most experience is of course the USA. Gailey's perspective is highly critical but it is useful to review her recommendations and see how many are relevant to this country. It seems to me that the US today should not be seen as a model for the UK for a number of reasons:
- The widespread variations in policy and practice reflecting its federal structure;
- The slow progress towards ratification of the Hague Convention;
- Its commitment to private adoption – both domestic and intercountry;

- The unwieldy number of intercountry adoption agencies of variable standards;
- Involvement of some agencies or individual attorneys in suspected irregularities;
- Evidence of the demand for healthy babies at any cost.

But as with health care, where few would wish to emulate the American system with its high costs and manifest inequalities (see Ham, 1997; White, 1997), there is much to learn from American practice at a micro-level. The best agencies have very high standards and a quality of provision much appreciated by States of origin. Support for adoptive families is widely available, whether through parents groups such as the AFA (Adopted Families of America) with its excellent newsletters and website or in dedicated health provision such as the International Adoption Clinic at the University of Minnesota (Johnson, 1999). Official statistics are rigorously recorded by government and clearly presented and information on procedures and on individual sending countries is easily accessed on official websites. The National Adoption Information Clearinghouse (NAIC), funded by the US government, provides another source of data about all aspects of adoption, while the Evan B. Donaldson Foundation provides an equally informed NGO alternative.

Many of the above bodies now see the internet as their main means of communication and I have listed several key sites at the end of this chapter. The internet is the starting point for an increasing number of Americans (and others) wishing to explore ICA, but here the impact, and implications, of an "advertising" approach becomes evident. While several sites list "recommended" agencies, there is also a plethora of individual agencies publicising their services, often with disturbing selling points such as links to package holidays in China or Thailand, promises of beautiful young children or a guarantee of "no birth mothers to worry about".

In contrast the Scandinavian/Dutch models of ICA, which I have commended elsewhere (Selman, 1991, 1992, 1998), have a common structure of assessment by public authorities and mediation by NGOs, while varying in the number and size of such organisations and in their toleration of "independent" adoptions. What they share is strong leadership by a Central Authority, which demands high standards of accredited bodies, but also clearly endorses the legitimacy of inter-country adoption, and agencies which utilise both professional social workers and the voluntary effort of adoptive parents to offer a mediation service which links prospective adopters to responsible organisations in States of origin.

It would be wrong – and impracticable – to suggest that the UK should adopt any one of these countries as a model, but there are many aspects of their provision which we might usefully consider and the commitment of public authorities and accredited bodies to high standards provides a model we should emulate. The Dutch preparation course has been criticised for deterring potentially good adopters, but no-one interested in preparation could read Duinkerken's chapter without picking up some ideas for their own courses. Similarly, the work of the Swedish Adoption Centre shows how an agency develops and matures over time, but depends for its success on other parts of the overall system. The Swedish agencies acknowledge and accept the work of the local welfare com-mittees in assessment and the role of the National Board (NIA) in regulating them. NIA is of particular interest as having been designated as the Central Authority rather than a government department. As Andersson shows, its origins in the past were as a body deeply involved in arranging placements, which subsequently shed all activities with individuals to concentrate on its role in regulation and advice. NIA's publications (many free and available in English) range from general information and advice on ICA to an excellent manual for social workers carrying out home studies.

One important consequence of the development of mediating agencies in the UK would be the potential for their joining EurAdopt and sharing in the much longer experience of properly regulated ICA in our Northern European neighbours. But even before that is possible, all concerned are welcomed at the open days in the biennial meetings and there could be much to be gained by talking to key people in member agencies about the problems of establishing effective mediation. There has been growing interest in intercountry adoption in both the European Union and the Council of Europe, whose membership includes several States of origin. The European Parliament debated the issue in 1997 (Selman, 1998) and

Sterky (Chapter 21) describes proposals from the European Children's Network (Euronet) for an EU children's policy and calls for the EU to press for ratification of the Hague Convention by all current and prospective member countries.

Learning from States of origin

It is of course not only from other receiving States that we are able to learn. The chapters from India are an effective answer to those who see ICA as only about the exploitation of poor countries by rich childless couples seeking perfect babies. Indian adoption professionals and the Indian Government still see a role for intercountry adoption alongside them determination to develop domestic adoption and are grateful for the opportunity to find homes for children, many with special needs, who would otherwise spend their lives in institutional care. But they are clear as to the criteria informing choices about the most suitable receiving States and the importance of working through agencies, wherever possible. A similar story would be found in Korea, where the number of countries accepted to receive children has diminished over time and the quality of the agency is seen as crucial. One indicator of our success in developing mediating agencies would be the acceptability of these to countries such as India, Korea, Philippines and Thailand (taken as examples of countries wanting to develop agencies). There are also negative lessons to be learned from the situation which has developed in Cambodia and other countries where both children and adopters have been exploited by intermediaries concerned primarily with profit, a theme I develop in the following section.

Abuses and profiteering in intercountry adoption

During summer 2000 there were several reports from IRC/ISS (Lerche, 2000) of continuing problems in Guatemala, Cambodia and Vietnam.

Guatemala

Guatemala (population 10.8 million in 1998) is one of the poorer countries of Latin America (Bellamy, 2000 – see Table 1.8). It now sends more children for intercountry adoption to the USA than any other country from that continent and in 1999 was the fourth most important source – after Russia, China and Korea – with over 1,000 "orphan" visas granted. In the period 1993–1999, it was also the fourth most significant country for the UK in terms of intercountry adoption (Table 10–1).

In Chapter 1 I showed, using data from five receiving States, that in 1998 Guatemala was one of the States of origin with the highest rates of intercountry adoption and that the number of adoptions had doubled since 1995. Goldsmith (2000) confirms this latter pattern with data from within the country where there were 731 adoptions in 1996 and expectations are that in the current year (2000) there could be over two thousand.

There are an estimated 25,000 children in orphanages in Guatemala, so that the need for family placement is great, but reports suggest that many adoptions involve young children, for whom there is a greater demand, and that some of these involve irregularities. Lerche (2000a) cites a report to the UN Human Rights Commission in Geneva claiming that a majority of international adoptions in Guatemala 'involve a variety of criminal offences including the buying and selling of children, the falsifying of documents . . .'. In July 2000, a detailed report by the *Instituto Latinoamericano para la Educacion* was published detailing many irregularities in a virtual trade in young babies in which lawyers make lucrative profits from American couples willing to pay $15,000 or more for a young child (ISS, 2000b). If the reputation of ethical and legitimate intercountry adoption is to be preserved, the receiving States most involved – the US, France, Canada and Spain – must respond to such allegations and act to prevent such abuses if they are found proven. The US State Department's website notes 'problems . . . including pressure on birth mothers to relinquish against their will' and asks prospective adopters to report 'unethical and illegal behaviour on the part of your Guatemalan attorney', but at the time of writing had not advised against adoption from Guatemala, as in the case of Cambodia, which is discussed below. The UK and Ireland now require a DNA test report to vouch for a biological parental link between child and relinquishing mothers (ISS, 2000c).

Cambodia and Vietnam

Cambodia, with a similar size population but much lower GNP per capita ($300 in 1998), had only a third of the number of adoptions from Guatemala in 1997, but recent articles in the *Phnom Penh Post* (O'Connell and Saroeun, 2000) describe orphanages buying babies from a local village to meet the overseas demand for young babies. The cost of payments to government officials and the orphanage were over $10,000 (compared to $3,000 in China), but adopters were prepared to pay the higher sum, as the process of adoption is much faster than in China. In recent years the number of ICAs has exploded – those to France alone rising from 34 in 1995 to 154 in 1999. On 15 June 2000, the Cambodian Government suspended all adoptions by foreigners so that they could 'appropriately re-organise the adoption procedures and . . . examine the situation of baby or child orphans'. There were reports of many prospective adopters, most of them French, being trapped in Phnom Penh (Eaton and Agret, 2000) and US citizens were advised not to pursue adoptions until further notice (US State Department, 2000).

Similar reports were found a year earlier in neighbouring Vietnam (population 77.6 million; per capita GNP $310)), which led the French Government to suspend intercountry adoptions from that country (Henley, 1999). In 1998 there were 1,328 adoptions from Vietnam to France, four times the 1994 figure; similar increases were found in other countries such as the USA where ICAs from Vietnam rose from 110 in 1993 to 712 in 1999. The US State Department notes that 'document fraud is widespread in Vietnam' and that the extreme poverty means families may be tempted to release children 'inappropriately' for adoption.

What can we learn from research?

Choices about policies and practices to follow are often based on the apparent relevance to the structures of law and provision in a country – or to its values and history. Ideally such choices should also be informed by objective evaluations of the effectiveness of such services or their impact on the quality of life of adopted persons and their family. Sadly such research is largely lacking and the evidence on outcomes presented in Section II has little to say about the impact of different types of provision. The "success" of the Romanian adoptions clearly owes little to well organised mediation, but equally cannot show that agencies are irrelevant in today's world. What is clear is that, in the last resort, any system is only as good as the families it enables to adopt and that such families demand our respect and help as is demonstrated so vividly by Carli.

Optimists will read the research literature on outcomes for children as an endorsement of intercountry adoption, pointing out the "miraculous" recovery, both physically and mentally, of very damaged children when placed in loving families. Pessimists point to evidence of much higher continuing rates of problem behaviour and disruption in comparison with native born children. One consistent finding is that more persistent difficulties are experienced with children placed at older ages and especially those with longer experience of institutional care (Rutter, Chapter 6). Some studies find that problem behaviour increases in adolescence (Verhulst, Chapter 7). Such findings create new dilemmas as they seem to indicate that – as in domestic adoption – those children in most need of a family are also the most likely to present difficulties. However, children are seldom rejected and fewer adoptions break down than in domestic "special needs" adoption of older children – a testimony to the courage and determination of the parents. But new prospective adopters aware of the findings may hesitate to take on such children.

Another area of importance in the studies of older adoptees is that of ethnic and personal identity. This can involve both an "inner" and "outer" search or journey (Irhammar and Cederblad, Chapter 8; von Melen, Chapter 29). Studies show that most of those adopted from abroad develop good self-esteem and a sound sense of personal identity, but that this may depend on identification with the host country as well as their country of birth. Thus Irhammar and Cederblad found that adoptees with a "Swedish" self-identity showed better development and higher self-esteem, while those with an "ethnic" self-identity had problems arising from a sense of being different. Saetersdal and Dalen (1999 – see Chapter 9) found two patterns of "successful" adjustment: one characterised by an active exploration of ethnic identity and biological background; the other by a denial of the significance of the adopted person's own genetic and cultural background. In adolescence this latter reponse led to many young adoptees distancing themselves from immigrant groups of the same background and countries of origin as themselves (Dalen and Sætersdal, 1987).

For many adoptees the importance of ethnic identity seems to be strengthened in adulthood, as can be seen in Anna von Melen's conversation with Anders (Chapter 29), which highlights issues of racism in receiving countries. Likewise, research into adults adopted from Korea (Evan B. Donaldson Institute, 1999) found a significant shift in adoptees' views of themselves, with a clear majority (64 per cent) seeing themselves as Korean-American or Korean-European, a position taken by only 28 per cent as they were growing up. Such findings reflect the adopted person's 'struggle to arrive at a harmonious understanding of their identity as regards who they are and how they want society to define them' (Sætersdal and Dalen, Chapter 9).

In summary, two key themes emerge clearly from the knowledge that we have acquired from research on overseas adoptees, which suggest the need for action by governments.

• Early childhood deprivation can no longer be seen as irretrievable. Most children subsequently placed in stable loving families show a great capacity for catch-up in physical and emotional development. But for a minority of the most deprived, this can still leave major problems which do not go away with time and may worsen in adolescence, imposing considerable strain on the parents who care for them.

• Adoption is a lifetime experience for all concerned and involves a constant exploration of identity which is made more difficult by many adoptees' lack of knowledge of their past. This is particularly true for those adopted from abroad who have lost both their birth family and their birth country. In adulthood most will want to find out more about their background and many will wish to return to their country of origin or seek out their birth families.

Problems of the post-institutionalised child

One theme emerging from research is the recognition of the problems many adoptive parents face where their children have a background of institutionalisation or other problems (e.g. foetal alcohol syndrome in children adopted from Russia) which are largely outside the experience of the helping professions in this country. The chapters by Rutter and Verhulst show that many adopted children and their families will require support after placement. This is one area where the support in the UK falls far short of that available in other countries such as the USA, where there are examples of clinics being set up devoted entirely to the "health" problems of internationally adopted children (Johnson, 2000). British parents adopting from Romania have turned for help to PNPIC (Parent Network for the Post-institutionalised Child) and organised a successful conference addressed by leading American specialists such as Johnson and Federici, both of whom are contributors to an important collection of papers sponsored by PNPIC and available on their website (Tepper *et al*, 1999).

Identity and the adopted person's need for information

The theme of "identity" runs throughout many of the chapters in this book. The need and right of adopted persons to know about their origins is now firmly established in the UK, but there has been little exploration of how such rights could be extended to those adopted from abroad. In England and Wales, the adopted person's right of access to birth records from age 18 was established by the 1975 Children Act (now section 51 of the 1976 Adoption Act) and it is recognised that many adopted persons will want to go beyond this to find out more information from those involved in their placement and in many cases to trace and meet their birth relatives (Selman, 1998; Howe and Feast, 2000).

It is impossible to extend such rights to foreign-born adopted persons, as their birth – and often their adoption – will have taken place far away. However, it is imperative that we find a way to enable overseas adoptees to be able to obtain information about their origins when they reach adulthood. Storbergen's study of Greek adoptees in the Netherlands cited by Hoksbergen (Chapter 5) shows that a majority have sought information about their birth families and that many have tried to trace their birth parents. The experience of Korean adoption in the USA has also demonstrated this (Evan B. Donaldson Institute, 2000; Meier, 1999; Sarri *et al*, 1998) and the growth of homeland visits and development of a search registry in Korea itself (Park, 1998) is an indication of the extent of interest. Some sending countries such as India and Korea, are moving towards an exploration of more "open" adoption, which is increasingly recognised as a part of domestic adoption (Grotevant and McRoy, 1998).

Gailey (Chapter 17) exposes the myth that a majority of foreign-born adoptees are "orphans" and even when this is true, there is a birth country and often other birth relatives. The storing of information about origins is required by the Hague Convention (Article 30(i)) and is in itself a strong argument for ending independent or non-agency adoptions, as agencies in receiving States are more likely to have been able to obtain and store the background information needed to enable an adopted adult to explore his or her origins. However, Duncan (Chapter 2) notes that in some cases dilemmas arise where access to such information is permitted in the receiving State, but prohibited under the domestic law of the adoptee's State of origin.

Facilitating access to any available information should be a priority for the UK in building on the foundations laid by our new legislation. For many of those adopted over the past thirty years, this will be too late, but good practice surely demands that this be rectified as far as possible for new adoptions. Many adoptive parents report meeting birth parents and obtaining information which they can give to their child as (s)he grows up, but there is also a need for adoptees to be able to access such information in their own right. A first step would be to establish a central point to which overseas adoptees could turn for help (Samwell-Smith, Chapter 28).

Developing aftercare services for intercountry adoption

Both of the above examples indicate the need for post-adoption services for overseas adoptees and their families. The development of such services is one of the responsibilities placed on Central Authorities by the Hague Convention (Article 9c) and existing NGO services like the

Post Adoption Centre in London *or After Adoption* in Manchester report an increasing number of approaches from those adopting or adopted from abroad. Yet there is sadly still a reluctance in some adopters to seek early help with difficulties, fearing a negative reception comparable to that experienced during their assessment (Selman and Wells, 1996).

In the Netherlands, adoption "aftercare" is the responsibility of a small organisation called WAN (*Stichting Werkverband Adoptie Nazorg* – Foundation Adoption Aftercare), which was established in 1981 and is subsidised by the Ministry of Justice. WAN deals directly with adoptive parents and adoptees, but also advises professionals such as teachers, lawyers and doctors. Courses are offered to adoptive parents, including one dealing specifically with problems arising in adolescence. In addition, the Dutch mediating agencies are required to offer post-adoption support for at least one year and many now see this as a responsibility that extends throughout the life of any child they have placed. More recently, the *Information Centre Roots* was set up to help those adopted from abroad to explore their background and meet other adoptees.

The achievements, failings and limitations of intercountry adoption

No-one reading the two chapters on India can doubt that agencies in that country have the best interests of the children at heart in pursuing intercountry adoption for some of them. In particular, the point is made about the difficulty of placing some children domestically and the success of intercountry placements for children with special needs, who would otherwise spend their childhood in institutions. The letters to PALNA from children placed in Italy show their positive reaction to their placements. Similar commitment can be found in many other States of origin. Likewise, a majority of adoptive parents devote their lives to providing a home for children who would otherwise have faced a life of poverty and have demonstrated the power of family life to counter the damage of early deprivation.

Throughout this book a message comes through about what inter-country adoption can achieve for individual children, when it is practised with integrity by countries which have a firm control over proceedings. But important as the development of a more satisfactory framework for intercountry adoption in the UK may be and positive as the findings of much research, these can not resolve the ongoing concerns which face all countries involved in the movement of children across national boundaries.

We saw earlier that adoptions are still too often carried out without regulation and with the focus on the needs of adopters, exploited by unscrupulous agents. None of the sending countries discussed had ratified the Hague Convention, but most of the receiving States involved either had ratified or were in the process of legislating for ratification. There have also been reports of continuing abuses of intercountry adoption in Romania, including private arrangements in Italy and excessive fees. This should remind us that there is no guarantee that adoptions between ratifying countries will be unproblematic and points to the need for a mechanism to handle those States which fail to live up to the standards expected.

Duncan (1993) has argued that the Hague Convention provides only a minimum set of requirements – good practice demands that individual countries build on these commitments and work at an international level to ensure that intercountry adoption can indeed be in the best interests of the child. The next few years will be a crucial test of the UK's ability to build on its new legislation to ensure that our practice follows the spirit of the Convention and develops working relationships only with States of origin which share a similar commitment.

Very little attention has been paid to the situation of the birth parents in intercountry adoption. Reading Giberti's account of birth mothers in Argentina, one is inevitably reminded of how long it took us to recognise the pain experienced by birth parents in the UK and to acknowledge how little choice many have in their "decision" to relinquish a child (Howe, 1992; Hughes and Logan, 1993). This should be a reminder of the importance of ensuring that children placed for intercountry adoption could not have remained in their birth families.

Finally, there is a growing awareness of how little ICA contributes – or can contribute – to the wider problems faced by many of the States of origin. In this context we can at least hope that more receiving countries will seek to link ICA to wider support for child welfare in the sending countries, whether through international aid or by encouraging and supporting the development of domestic adoption and fostering, following the pattern in Sweden (Andersson, Chapter 19).

Better regulation can eliminate many of the abuses described earlier, but even well-regulated intercountry adoption, leaves us with ethical issues about the social implications in the long run. Whatever the achievements of intercountry adoption we are left with the fundamental questions raised by commentators over the years, as when Rene Hoksbergen (1991) expressed the hope that *"culture and economic circumstances in all Third-World countries change to the extent that it will be the exception when a child's only chance for a satisfactory upbringing exists with a family thousands of miles from its birthplace"*: a view echoied by Hans van Loon in his Foreword. The challenge of developing domestic family placement services in States of origin and attacking the circumstances which lead to so many children being placed in institutions must be taken up alongside any policy to ensure that intercountry adoption is properly regulated and only practised in the best interests of the child.

References

Altstein H (1984) 'Transracial and intercountry adoptions: a comparison', in Sachdev P (ed) *Adoption: Current issues and trends*, London: Butterworth.

Altstein H and Simon R (1991) *Intercountry Adoption: a multinational perspective*, New York: Praeger.

Bellamy C (1999) *State of the World's Children 2000*, New York: UNICEF.

Chu Xiaoying (1997) Personal communication from the Deputy Director of Document Review Department 1, China Centre for Adoption Affairs, 16 October 1997.

Duncan W (1993) 'The Hague Convention on the Protection of Children and Co-operation in Respect of Intercountry Adoption', *Adoption & Fostering*, 17:3, pp 7–13.

Eaton D and Agret P (2000) 'Le Cambodge suspend les adoptions, mais laisse des parents sur le carreau', *IRC/ISS Information flash*, 4 July 2000.

Evan B Donaldson Institute (1999) *Survey of Adult Korean Adoptees* [available on website listed below].

Goldsmith R (2000) 'Guatemala's baby business', *Crossing Continents*, 31 August 2000, London: BBC.

Grotevant H D and McRoy R G (1998) *Openness in Adoption: Exploring family connections*, London: Sage Publications.

Ham C (ed) (1997) *Health Care Reform: Learning from international experience*, Buckingham: Open University Press.

Henley J (1999) 'France moves against Vietnam's baby trade', *The Guardian*, 5 May 1999.

Hoksbergen R (1991) 'Intercountry adoption coming of age in the Netherlands', in Altstein H and Simon R (eds) *Intercountry Adoption: A multinational perspective*, New York: Praeger.

Holt Children's Services (1999) *Love in Action*, Seoul: Holt Children's Services Inc.

Howe D, Sawbridge P and Hinings D (1992) *Half a Million Women*, London: Penguin.

Howe D and Feast J (2000) *Adoption, Search and Reunion: The long term experience of adopted adults,* London: The Children's Society.

Hughes B and Logan J (1993) *Birth Parents: The hidden dimension*, University of Manchester: Department of Social Policy and Social Work.

International Social Service (2000a) *IRC/ISS News Bulletin* No 29, August 2000.

International Social Service (2000b) *Draft Submission to the First Evaluation Meeting of the Hague Convention of 1993*, The Hague, November–December 2000, Geneva: ISS, 18 August 2000.

International Social Service (2000c) *IRC/ISS News Bulletin*, no 30, September 2000.

Jenkins J (1989) *Intercountry Adoption*, LLM Thesis, University of Leicester.

Johnson D (1999) 'Adopting an institutionalised child: What are the risks?', in Tepper T, Hannon L and Sandstrom D (eds) *International Adoption: Challenges and opportunities*, Meadowlands, PA: PNPIC.

Lerche C (2000a) 'UN Expert: majority of international adoptions in Guatemala Illegal', *Worldwide Circular from IRC/ISS*, 31 March 2000.

Lerche C (2000b) 'Baby selling is a major business in Guatemala', *IRC/ISS, Information Flash*, 7 June 2000.

Mason K (1999) 'Intercountry Adoption in the UK: Families' experiences of the adoption process', in Ryvgold A, Dalen M and Sætersdal B (eds) *Mine – Yours – Ours and Theirs?*, Oslo: University of Oslo.

Meier D (1999) 'Cultural identity and place in adult Korean-American intercountry adoptees', *Adoption Quarterly*, 3–1, pp 15–48.

O'Connell S and Saroeun B (2000) 'Cambodia – Babies bought for sale to foreigners', *IRC/ISS Information Flash*, 6 June 2000.

Park In Sun (1998) *People Who Search*, Seoul: Hana Medical Publishing.

Performance and Innovation Unit (2000) *Prime Minister's Review of Adoption*, London: PIU, July 2000.

Sarri R, Bail Y and Bombyk M (1998) 'Goal Displacement and Dependency in South Korean–United States Intercountry Adoption', *Children & Youth Services Review*, Vol 20 nos 1 and 2, pp 87–114.

Selman P (1993) 'Services for intercountry adoption in the UK: some lessons from Europe', *Adoption & Fostering*, 17:3, pp 14–19, 1993.

Selman P (1998) 'Intercountry adoption in Europe after the Hague Convention', in Sykes R and Alcock P (eds) *Developments in European Social Policy: Convergence and diversity*, London: Policy Press.

Selman P (1999a) 'The demography of intercountry adoption', in Ryvgold A, Dalen M and Sætersdal B (eds) *Mine – Yours – Ours and Theirs?*, Oslo: University of Oslo.

Selman P (1999b) *In Search of Origins: Twenty two years of access to birth records in England & Wales*, poster presentation at International Conference on Adoption Research, Minneapolis, August 1999.

Selman P and White J (1994) 'The role of "accredited bodies" in intercountry adoption', *Adoption & Fostering*, 18:2, pp 7–13, [Reprinted in Hill M and Shaw M (eds) *Signposts in Adoption*, London: BAAF, 1998].

Tepper T, Hannon L and Sandstrom D (eds) (1999) *International Adoption: Challenges and opportunities*, Meadowlands, PA: PNPIC [website listed below].

Triseliotis J, Shireman J and Hundleby M (1997) *Adoption: Theory, policy and practice*, pp 187–195, London: Cassell.

van Loon J H A (1990) *Report on Intercountry Adoption*, The Hague: Permanent Bureau of the Hague Conference.

White J (1997) *Competing Solutions: American health proposals and international experience,* Washington: Broadhurst.

Websites

Adopted Families of America
http://www.adoptivefam.org

Evan B. Donaldson Institute:
http://www.adoptioninstitute.org/index.shtml

Hague Conference on Private International Law
   Countries ratifying 1993 Hague Convention: http://www.hcch. net/e/status/adoshte.html

International Social Service (ISS)
http://www.iss-ssi.org

National Adoption Information Clearinghouse:
http://www.calib.com/naic/

Parent Network for the Post-Institutionalised Child (PNPIC)
http://www.pnpic.org

US State Department
   Adoption Statistics from http://travel.state.gov/orphan_numbers.html

   Country profiles
   http://travel.state.gov/adoption.html

Appendix I

HAGUE CONVENTION OF 29 MAY 1993 ON PROTECTION OF CHILDREN AND CO-OPERATION IN RESPECT OF INTERCOUNTRY ADOPTION

THE CONVENTION ENTERED INTO FORCE ON 1 MAY 1995

CURRENT STATUS OF RATIFICATION AND ACCESSION (SEPTEMBER 2000)

Last updates: 12 September 2000 (signature & ratification Albania)
7 September 2000 (signature Russian Federation)
28 April 2000 (accession Mongolia)

The following States have signed, but not yet ratified the Convention:

Uruguay	1 September 1993
United Kingdom	12 January 1994
United States	31 March 1994
Switzerland	16 January 1995
Luxembourg	6 June 1995
Ireland	19 June 1996
Germany	7 November 1997
Belarus	10 December 1997
Belgium	7 January 1999
Slovakia	1 June 1999
Portugal	26 August 1999
Russian Federation	7 September 2000

Total number of states having signed but not yet ratified: 12

The following States have ratified the Convention:

	Date of ratification	*Entry into force*
Mexico	14 September 1994	1 May 1995
Romania	28 December 1994	1 May 1995
Sri Lanka	23 January 1995	1 May 1995
Cyprus	20 February 1995	1 June 1995
Poland	12 June 1995	1 October 1995
Spain	11 July 1995	1 November 1995
Ecuador	7 September 1995	1 January 1996
Peru	14 September 1995	1 January 1996
Costa Rica	30 October 1995	1 February 1996
Burkina Faso	11 January 1996	1 May 1996
Philippines	2 July 1996	1 November 1996
Canada	19 December 1996	1 April 1997
Venezuela	10 January 1997	1 May 1997
Finland	27 March 1997	1 July 1997
Sweden	28 May 1997	1 September 1997
Denmark	2 July 1997	1 November 1997
Norway	25 September 1997	1 January 1998
Netherlands	26 June 1998	1 October 1998
France	30 June 1998	1 October 1998
Colombia	13 July 1998	1 November 1998
Australia	25 August 1998	1 December 1998
El Salvador	17 November 1998	1 March 1999
Israel	3 February 1999	1 June 1999
Brazil	10 March 1999	1 July 1999
Austria	19 May 1999	1 September 1999
Chile	13 July 1999	1 November 1999
Panama	29 September 1999	1 January 2000
Italy	18 January 2000	1 May 2000
Czech Republic	11 February 2000	1 June 2000
Albania	12 September 2000	1 January 2001

Total number of ratifications: 30

The following States have acceded to the Convention:

	Accession: Article 44(3)*	Entry into force	Expiry date under
Andorra	3 January 1997	1 May 1997	1 August 1997
Moldova	10 April 1998	1 August 1998	1 November 1998
Lithuania	29 April 1998	1 August 1998	1 December 1998
Paraguay	13 May 1998	1 September 1998	1 December 1998
New Zealand	18 September 1998	1 January 1999	15 April 1999
Mauritius	28 September 1998	1 January 1999	15 May 1999
Burundi	15 October 1998	1 February 1999	15 May 1999
Georgia	9 April 1999	1 August 1999	1 November 1999
Monaco	29 June 1999	1 October 1999	15 January 2000
Iceland	17 January 2000	1 May 2000	15 August 2000
Mongolia	25 April 2000	1 August 2000	

Total number of ascessions: 11

* *In accordance with Article 44(3) of the Convention, the accession has effect only as regards the relations between the acceding State and those Contracting States which have not raised an objection to its accession in the six months following the date on which the depositary gave notice of the accession. The date specified here is the expiry date of that six-month period.*

Appendix II
Useful contact points for ICA

Many organisations involved with adoption have been mentioned in the various chapters of this book. In this appendix to the whole book we have listed as many of these as possible with their postal address, telephone and fax numbers, and e-mail address and websites where these are available. Websites for the USA are listed at the end of Chapter 30.

There are two sections; one for the UK and one for the rest of the world. Within these sections, organisations are listed alphabetically and I have placed acronyms first where these are the normal and recognised way of referring to the body (e.g. BAAF, OASIS), while in all cases giving the full title as well.

UK telephone numbers are given as for domestic use: overseas callers should add their own international code + **44** and omit the first **0** of the area code. For overseas countries telephone numbers give the international version e.g. + **31** for Netherlands – and omit the **0** in the area code. Readers should then add their own internal connection e.g. **00** for the UK.

UK organisations involved in intercountry adoption

Adoption UK (formerly PPIAS)
Lower Boddington
Daventry
Northamptonshire
NN11 6YB

Tel: 01327 260295
Fax: 01327 263565

AFAA (Association of Families Adopting from Abroad)
Membership and subscription enquiries
Maurice Thomas
Carlton Lodge
Woodhead Road
Wortley
Sheffied S35 7DA

Tel: 01142 885845
Advice Line: 01622 755065 (Phone & Fax)
e-mail: information.afaa@cwcom.net
website: www.afaa.mcmail.com

ARC (Adopted Romanian Children Society)
Pam Day (Membership Secretary)
Woodlands
Hanoverian Way
Whitleley
Sareham
Hampshire PO17 7JP

Tel: 01489 557 353
e-mail: woodlands4@supernet.com

BAAF (British Agencies for Adoption & Fostering)
Skyline House
200 Union Street
London SE1 0LX

Tel: 020 7593 2000
Fax: 020 7593 2001
e-mail: mail@baaf.org.uk
website: www.baaf.org.uk

Born in Romania (BIR)
31 Court Lane
Wolstanton
Newcastle
Staffordshire ST5 8DE

Tel/Fax: 01782 858915
e-mail: bir@cwcom.net

Childlink
10 Lion Yard
Tremadoc Road
London SW4 7NQ

Tel: 020 7501 1700
Fax: 020 7498 1791

Children Adopted from China
10 Woodcote
St Catherine's Drive
Guildford
Surrey GU2 5HQ

Tel: 01483 440370
e-mail: Davidanne.Brice@btinternet.com

CICA (Campaign for Intercountry Adoption)
85 Regent's Park Road
London NW1 8UY

Tel 020 7722 9621
Fax: 020 7722 1913
e-mail: kbpmc@barclays.net

Department of Health
Adoption & Permanency Section
Wellington House
133–135 Waterloo Road
London SE1 8UG

Tel: 020 7972 4545

Family Thais
website: www.adoptionthailand.com

Guatemala Support Group
Catriona Aldridge
P.O. Box 16911
London SE3 9WB

Tel/Fax: 020 8318 0836
e-mail: CAALD@AOL.com

Home Office Immigration & Nationality Directorate
Block C Whitgift Centre
Croydon
Surrey CR9 1AT

Tel: 0870 606 7766
Fax: 020 8760 3017

OASIS
P.O. Box 2702
Lewes BN7 3DW

Helpline: 01792 844329
Helpline: 01273 382601
website: www.oasis.ndirect.co.uk

Overseas Adoption Helpline
PO Box 13899
London N6 4WB

Tel: 020 8342 8599
Fax: 020 8348 1522
e-mail: info@oah.org.uk
website: www.oah.org.uk

PACT (Parents and Children Together)
48 Bath Road
Reading RG1 6PG

Tel: 0118 958 1861
e-mail: pactcharity@compuserve.com

PNPIC (Parent Network for the Post Institutionalised Child)
31 Court Lane
Wolstanton
Newcastle
Staffordshire ST5 8DE

Tel: 01782 858915
Fax: 01782 61909
e-mail: pnpic@cwcom.net
website: www.pnpic.org

Organisations involved in intercountry adoption in other parts of the world

Adoption Centre (Sweden)
Box 1520
S-172 29 Sundbyberg
Sweden

Tel: + 46 8 587 499 00
Fax: + 46 8 29 69 28
e-mail: adoption@adoptionscentrum.se
website: www.adoptionscentrum.se

Australians Aiding Children Adoption
Agency Incorporated (AACAAI)
72 Fullarton Road
Norwood 5067
Australia

Tel: + 61 8 8362 0588
Fax: + 61 8 8362 0530
e-mail: adoptos@senet.com.au

Bureau VIA (Organisation for Information on ICA)
Postbus 290
3500 AG Utrecht
The Netherlands

Tel: +31 30 232 1550
Fax: +31 30 232 1777
e-mail: heeren@state@wxs.nl

CARA (Central Adoption Resource Agency)
Ministry of Social Justice and
Empowerment
West Block 8, Wing 2, 2nd Floor
R. K. Puram
New Delhi 110066
India

Tel: +91 11 618 0194
Fax: +91 11 618 0198
e-mail: cara@bol.net.in
website: www.cara.nic.in

China Centre of Adoption Affairs
7 Baiguang Rd
Zhongmin Building
Xuanwu District
Beijing
P.R. China 100053

Tel: +86 10 635 75785
Fax: +86 10 635 75786
website: www.china-ccaa.org

Defence for Children International
1 Rue de Varembe
PO Box 88
1211 Geneva 20
Switzerland

Tel: +41 22 734 05 50
Fax: +41 22 740 11 45
e-mail: dci-hq@pingnet.ch
website: www.defence-for-children.org

EurAdopt
Riouwstraat 191
NL – 2585 HT
The Hague
The Netherlands

Tel: +31 70 350 66 99
Fax: +31 70 354 78 67
e-mail: mail@euradopt.org
website: http://www.euradopt.org

Hague Conference on Private International Law
Permanent Bureau
Scheveningseweg 6
2517 KT The Hague
The Netherlands

Tel: +31 70 363 33 03
Fax: +31 70 360 48 67
e-mail: secretariat@hcch.net
website: http://www.hcch.net

International Resource Centre for the Protection of Children in Adoption (ISS/IRC)
c/o International Social Service
32 Quai du Seujet
1201 Geneva
Switzerland

Tel: +41 22 906 7000
Fax: +41 22 906 7701
e-mail: irc.iss@span.ch
website: www.iss-ssi.org

NIA (Swedish National Board for Intercountry Adoption)
Box 22086
104 22 Stockholm
Sweden

Tel: +46 8 651 92 92
Fax: +46 8 650 41 10
e-mail: adoption@nia.se
website www.nia.se

Thai Department of Public Welfare
Child Adoption Centre
Krung Kasem Road
Bangkok 10100
Thailand

Tel: +66 22 81 3330
Fax: + 66 22 80 0284

Wereldkinderen/NICWO (Worldchildren)
Riouwstraat 191
2585 HT
The Hague
The Netherlands

Tel: +31 70 3506699
Fax: +31 70 3547867
e-mail: info@wereldkinderen.nl
website: www.wereldkinderen.nl